SECONDARY CLASSROOMS

Teaching Students with DiVERsE Needs

Edited by
JAC ANDREWS
University of Calgary

Nelson Canada
I(T)P An International Thomson Publishing Company

Toronto • Albany • Bonn • Boston • Cincinnati • Detroit • London • Madrid • Melbourne
Mexico City • New York • Pacific Grove • Paris • San Francisco • Singapore • Tokyo • Washington

I(T)P
International Thomson Publishing
The ITP logo is a trademark under licence

Published in 1996 by
Nelson Canada
A division of Thomson Canada Limited
1120 Birchmount Road
Scarborough, Ontario M1K 5G4

Canadian Cataloguing in Publication Data

Main entry under title:
Teaching students with diverse needs : secondary classrooms

Includes bibliographical references.
ISBN 0-17-605546-0

1. Special education. I. Andrews, Jac, 1952–

LC3965.T42 1995 371.9 C95-931779-1

Team Leader	Michael Young
Acquisitions Editor	Charlotte Forbes
Developmental Editor	Heather Martin
Production Editor	Jill Young
Senior Production Coordinator	Carol Tong
Art Director	Liz Harasymczuk
Cover Design/Interior	Sharon Foster
Cover Illustration	Daphne McCormack
Composition	New Concept
Input Operator	Elaine Andrews

Printed and bound in Canada

1 2 3 4 (BBM) 98 97 96 95

Table of Contents

Preface

Teachers are well aware of the student diversity in their classrooms. They are also aware of the challenges arising from teaching students who have exceptional learning conditions (i.e., learning disabilities, developmental delays, advanced cognitive abilities, behavioural disturbances, and physical and health impairments) as well as different racial, ethnic, and religious backgrounds. No longer is exceptionality equated with separate classrooms and programs, rather, a dramatic increase of students with special learning needs are being taught in regular classrooms. Hence, many teachers are being tremendously impacted by the changes in their roles and responsibilities as they are facing the reality of contemporary education in Canada.

This book is about teaching students with a wide range of needs in Canadian schools and classrooms. The major aim of this book is to provide practical information that teachers can apply in their schools and classrooms to meet the increasing student diversity. However, it is *not* a recipe book because teaching students with varied backgrounds, identities, frames of reference, abilities, interests, and belief systems is too complex for simple solutions. It is a book that presents theoretically grounded and empirically based procedures for addressing the operational issues related to teaching and managing a heterogeneous population of students in the educational mainstream. Beyond the provision of practical techniques, this book attempts to provide an accountable foundation for the recommended educational practices and promote a deeper understanding with respect to their usage.

The idea for this book grew out of my numerous conversations with colleagues within the field of education and teachers at conferences and workshops, as well as my students in pre-service and in-service courses. All of these people expressed the need for additional educational resources to assist them in addressing the challenges of accommodating the growing crowd of diverse students within Canadian schools and classrooms. To this end, Canadian educators were asked to contribute chapters in relation to the central focus and critical components of the book and in accordance with their areas of expertise.

Central Focus and Critical Components of the Book

The underlying position throughout this book is that schools throughout Canada are including more students who have special needs within regular classrooms and segregating fewer students into special classrooms. Moreover, an increasing number of schools across the country are adopting a philosophy of *inclusive* education that reflects the view that schools are communities in which everyone should feel that they belong, are accepted, and are respected and valued for their individuality. Accordingly, the emerging mission for these schools is on how to operate classrooms so that student diversity is valued, potentials of all students are maximized, and teachers have the necessary support and assistance to provide appropriate educational experiences for all of the students in their classrooms. Hence, the central focus of this book is on ways schools can deliver educational services in accordance with their philosophy of inclusive education; classrooms can accommodate student variance; students can achieve appropriate educational goals; and teachers can be empowered to deal with the changes in their roles and responsibilities. This is accomplished by presenting and discussing what are considered to be critical components of teaching students with diverse needs:

1. Understanding the nature of student diversity and inclusive education,
2. Knowing how to prepare oneself for educational reform and student diversity,
3. Knowing how teachers, administrators, parents, and other professionals can collaborate with one another and collectively meet the diverse needs of students,
4. Knowing how to identify the learning needs of students,
5. Knowing how to plan for accommodating the wide range of students' needs,
6. Knowing some instructional strategies that can meet the learning needs of all students in the classroom,
7. Knowing how to manage students within inclusive classrooms,
8. Knowing how to enhance social competence and acceptance among students in the classroom,
9. Knowing how to promote sociocultural development and awareness,
10. Knowing how to build mutually beneficial family-school partnerships,
11. Knowing how to use computer technologies to better serve the needs of all students,
12. Knowing how to promote post-school opportunities for students with diverse needs, and
13. Understanding the major factors and enabling conditions conducive to inclusive education.

Audience

Teaching Students with Diverse Needs: Secondary Classrooms is written primarily for all pre-service teachers in colleges and universities across Canada who will be faced with the reality of student diversity in their future classrooms as well as for in-service teachers who are presently facing this reality. However, this book is also considered to be useful for parents and professionals (i.e., teachers' aides, psychologists, social workers, physical and occupational therapists, and counsellors) who work with special-needs students and collaborate with teachers in preparing and delivering educational services.

This book can stand on its own as a primary text for any course that is aimed at preparing teachers to manage diversity or as a supplementary text for course work related to collaboration and consultation, assessment, instructional methods, individualized program planning, classroom management, social skill development, second-language and second-culture learning, family-school partnerships, computer instruction, and transitional counselling in education.

Features of the Book

This book provides interesting and useful information relative to inclusive education in Canadian schools. At the beginning of the book, a conceptual overview is provided to highlight some of the important ideas covered in each of the chapters. Throughout the text case studies and realistic vignettes that are drawn from the authors' experiences in teaching students with diverse needs are presented. In addition, tables and figures are included that expand the text discussion and illustrate how some of the information can be used by teachers and their students. Moreover, a resource section concludes each chapter so readers can pursue further information and materials for assistance and support.

Acknowledgements

Many people contributed to the preparation and completion of this book. I would like to thank all of the authors of this book who demonstrated a great deal of commitment to this project and who submitted very readable and creditable chapters. I would also like to thank all of the people who are cited in this book for providing us with a body of work that positively impacts the lives of many.

Thanks also to all the editors at Nelson Canada. Thank you Charlotte Forbes for accepting the proposal of this book and for providing continual support, guidance, and encouragement. Most importantly, thank you for having faith in me and in this project. Thank you Heather Martin for always being there and for always being positive, helpful, and responsive to the issues and challenges that emerged throughout the process of finishing this book. Thank you Jill Young for all your efforts in transforming the manuscript into a polished product in a timely fashion.

I would like to thank Rick Freeze, University of Manitoba; Nancy Hutchinson, Queen's University; Gladene Robertson, University of Saskatchewan; Liz Stenson, Toronto Board of Education; John Walsh, University of Victoria; and Jack Wendt, Acadia University, for their reviews of the original manuscript and for their constructive feedback and support for the project. I also owe a large debt of gratitude to Anne Waddell who helped prepare my work so it was presentable for further reviewing and editing. As well, I would like to thank all of my students over the years who have taught me how to be a better teacher.

Finally, at the top of the list of all the people who made this book possible are my wife Debbie and my children Jenna and Chad who make all things possible for me.

An Introductory Overview

Teaching students who have a wide range of needs within regular classrooms is one of the biggest challenges of Canadian educators in the 1990s. This book addresses the issues related to student diversity in today's schools and classrooms. The authors in this book recognize that contemporary efforts to educate students with diverse needs differ from earlier attempts in at least two significant ways. First, current approaches are characterized by a more collaborative system of educational service delivery because teaching has become an increasingly complex task. Teachers need to network with each other and develop partnerships within the community in order to address the unique learning needs of all students and deal with the issues created by sociocultural, political, and economic changes. Second, while the education of students with diverse needs has been the responsibility of schools for many years, they have tended to provide segregated educational programming and instruction rather than inclusionary educational practices. The current trend in Canadian education is the inclusion of students with diverse needs within regular education settings. This book provides a description and discussion of some practical approaches that can be used by secondary teachers to provide high-quality education for the diverse population of students in their schools and classrooms.

The first two chapters of this book provide some introductory thoughts about teaching students with diverse needs and some ideas about how to cope with student diversity and educational reform. In **Chapter 1**, Jac Andrews draws upon his academic and applied experience to discuss the past and current trends with respect to the education of students with diverse needs. He maintains that all students have needs that require various levels of support to maximize their potential, and that all teachers have to assume a shared responsibility to ensure quality instruction for all students. He acknowledges that the nature of teaching in today's schools has become very complicated due to increasing student diversity and highlights collaborative, dynamic, proactive, and empathic approaches as ways of teaching and managing students with different needs.

In **Chapter 2**, Donna Patterson reminds us that many teachers might find educational reform and student diversity to be overwhelming. She asserts that schools exist as much for teachers as for students and that they need to become effective change managers and agents to cope with their new roles, responsibilities, and functions. She believes that teachers need to take care of themselves in times of change and recommends that they build a network of support to help each other adapt to the changes. She argues that teachers should prepare for transitions in education by creating personal goals and determining the processes for achieving these goals. According to Patterson, having goals and steps for reaching them strengthens one's resolve and mobilizes energies for change. She points out that many teachers might experience occasions of discouragement with the change process and recommends that they take one step at a time, have patience and confidence in their efforts, and consider how the innovations can make things better for themselves as well as their students.

Growing diversity within our schools and classrooms coupled with increased fiscal constraint has resulted in more attention to educational alternatives that make more efficient use of limited resources. One innovative response to this situation has been the utilization of collaborative approaches to educational service delivery. Many benefits can come from a collaborative work environment. Benefits will accrue from the varied perspectives, skills, and knowledge available from the different disciplines represented in the collaborative team. Benefits will also come from the group interaction that can broaden as well as focus upon ideas relative to serving children with a wide range of needs. Collaborative approaches provide opportunities for teachers to access information from one another, share materials and instructional techniques, and to have more responsibility in school-based problem solving and decision making.

In **Chapter 3**, Henry Janzen discusses a practical problem-solving collaboration process within a teacher assistance team framework that secondary teachers can use to address the diverse learning needs of their students. First, Janzen briefly describes the nature and composition of teacher assistance teams as well as some of the componential skills considered to be important in the teacher assistance team collaborative process. Next, he delineates eight critical steps in the problem-solving process and overviews important aspects and issues of the step-by-step model. He concludes the chapter by providing a case study that practically illustrates the use of the eight-step problem-solving collaboration framework for a particular high school student. The underlying message throughout the entire chapter is that collaborative approaches provide a way for teachers, administrators, parents, and professionals across a variety of disciplines to learn from one another and collectively meet the diverse needs of students. Moreover, collaborative approaches provide a resource for supportive problem solving and can empower participants by involving them in the decision-making process.

Effective teaching of students with diverse needs requires an evolving process of student assessment, program planning, instruction, and classroom management. The next four chapters in this book focus on ways to identify students' learning needs, plan and make accommodations for student diversity, provide learning experiences that help students reach appropriate educational goals, and arrange classroom environments that promote successful learning. Assessment, program planning, instruction, and classroom management are ongoing and interactive aspects of teaching. Although each of these components is presented separately in this book, all of the authors of these four chapters point to their interconnections.

In **Chapter 4**, Claudio Violato and Anthony Marini discuss classroom-based assessment for instructional planning within secondary classrooms. These authors stress that the evaluation of pupil performance will be enhanced if teachers develop high-quality assessment procedures and undertake careful interpretations of their findings. In accordance with this view, Violato and Marini begin their chapter by distinguishing between assessment, testing, and evaluation, summarizing the role of assessment in teaching and learning, and discussing the critical importance of validity and reliability in classroom assessment. From these areas they move onto an examination of grading and reporting procedures as ways for providing feedback to students, directing, rewarding, and motivating pupil effort, and providing information for instructional planning. Although the use of performance assessments as a way to observe and judge students' work and development is recommended by Violato and Marini in the last part of their paper, they conclude by stressing the need for teachers to consider the use of a combination of assessment activities for instructional decision making and planning.

Classroom assessment of students and the identification of their learning needs is the foundation from which teachers can prepare lessons, specify learning goals and objectives, gather materials, monitor their lessons and evaluate their interventions. Holistic and comprehensive program planning is essential for effectively responding to student diversity. In **Chapter 5**, Vianne Timmons provides a program planning framework that can be used by teachers to more effectively address the diverse learning needs of adolescents in secondary classrooms. She begins by presenting some important considerations for secondary teachers with respect to instructional planning. She points out that secondary teachers have been traditionally guided by the curriculum in their planning efforts; however, increasing diversity in the classroom has caused a necessary shift in focus from the curriculum to the learner. Teaching in today's secondary classrooms requires flexible planning, curriculum adaptations, differentiated instruction, and greater collaboration among teachers to develop and implement strategies to accommodate the wide range of students' needs. Timmons goes on to describe the major steps involved in comprehensive planning that include gathering and organizing student information, consulting with other teachers, parents, and support personnel, specifying desired outcomes and evaluation procedures, determining instructional techniques, and modifying lessons in response to student performance. In the second half of the chapter, she highlights multilevel instruction, cooperative learning, peer support and peer tutoring, partial participation, and reciprocal teaching as effective strategies for teachers to incorporate in their teaching regime. Throughout her discussion of these strategies Timmons stresses that all students should be included in the lessons and be actively involved in their learning.

In **Chapter 6**, Margaret Brown and James Fasano present some instructional strategies for meeting the learning needs of all students in the classroom. They maintain that the key for successful teaching in secondary classrooms is instructional flexibility and the use of effective teaching practices. Their chapter is organized in relation to four categories of instructional strategies that they believe accommodate student diversity. First, effective instructional preparation and delivery is partially driven by valuing student participation, expecting different learning outcomes, and favouring meaningful learning experiences for students. Second, teaching students with diverse needs requires a well-organized environment, well-established routines and support personnel, and well-structured learning activities. Third, one's values, attitudes, and beliefs are revealed to others through actions and words. Hence, teachers can demonstrate to students, by what they say and do, their values in teaching, attitudes regarding individual differences, and beliefs about student learning. Fourth, a review of some curriculum material strategies that can facilitate the inclusion of all students in the process of classroom learning is provided. In this section of their paper, they present activities and strategies such as crossword puzzles, word searches, matching activities, cryptograms, board games, and card games as ways to introduce students to lessons, review content, practise skills, extend the curriculum content, and evaluate learning.

In **Chapter** 7, Cheryll Duquette discusses behaviour management skills within the context of teaching in secondary classrooms. According to Duquette, secondary teachers who successfully teach students with diverse needs possess personal qualities (e.g., they are friendly, supportive, reliable, and responsible), model excellent teaching practices (e.g., they show commitment to individual students and demonstrate a willingness to spend time making program adjustments), and use effective management skills (e.g., they select appropriate content and activities, design objectives for lessons that are meaningful and relevant to students, use differentiated assignments, and monitor their students' progress). Most of Duquette's chapter focuses on the results of her study that investigated the attitudes, characteristics, and behaviours of secondary teachers who were considered to be successful in teaching students with diverse needs. She found that although the teachers varied in terms of the courses they taught and their style of teaching, they displayed many common teaching behaviours. For example, they all used a variety of learning activities, varied their rate of presentation to accommodate to students' ability to receive information, presented concepts through explanation, made adjustments in their lessons to better meet the needs of their students, mediated students learning, responded to disruptive behaviours swiftly, and effectively followed well-planned lessons. Moreover, she notes that all of the teachers shared a respectful and positive attitude towards their students and were calm and confident in the classroom. Duquette concludes her chapter by discussing the supports that teachers need to enable them to adequately address the student diversity in their classrooms.

Success in school is a function of both academic achievement and social development. Teachers have always wanted their students to be cooperative and respectful to one another and have generally guided their students toward appropriate social behaviour. However, it should be recognized that for a variety of reasons contemporary efforts to interface academic and social development are distinguishable from earlier attempts in a few important ways. In essence, many students within contemporary regular classrooms do not have the prerequisite social skills that are required for them to work, share, and learn together.

In response to this situation, teachers are currently finding it necessary to provide systematic instructional procedures that effectively promote personally satisfying and beneficial interpersonal experiences for their students and concurrently enhance their academic mastery. Current approaches to social skill development are designed to benefit all students within the context of the regular classroom.

The next chapter in this book presents some ways for promoting social development within the secondary classroom. In **Chapter 8**, Nancy Hutchinson focuses on approaches that foster collaborative learning and interdependence among the students in the classroom. Central to her discussion is the view that students enhance their learning and thinking capabilities through social interaction with each other. Hence, she stresses the importance of constructing learning environments in which students can communicate with one another and actively participate in meaningful tasks related to their real life experiences. Most of her chapter focuses on student grouping methods that allow teachers to capitalize on the social nature of learning, accentuate students' cognitive development, and enhance their social competence and acceptance. Hutchinson presents information relative to the use of collaborative learning methods such as cooperative learning, problem solving in pairs and groups, and peer tutoring. She then discusses some of the issues related to collaborative learning and offers some suggestions for overcoming these problems. Throughout the chapter, Hutchinson exemplifies the covert thinking of a secondary teacher who considers the actions she will take to ensure that her student will experience a sense of community and peer support in her classroom.

One of the most compelling concerns of Canadian educators is the dramatic increase of second-culture and second-language students in their schools and classrooms. Students in today's classrooms are members of different racial, ethnic, and religious groups who have different identities, frames of reference, and belief systems. These students should be provided with learning environments that promote acceptance and respect for individual differences and that foster understanding and appreciation of others.

In **Chapter 9**, Terry Piper and David Piper present their views on how to maintain and foster sociocultural awareness in a community of secondary school learners. They discuss the culture of secondary school and highlight its significant features (i.e., content is organized around independent subject areas and instructional emphasis is on content rather than process), the importance of group membership and identity to adolescents, and the responsibility of schools to educate students with respect to these dynamics. According to these authors, people have to get in touch with their feelings before they are able to develop and change their attitudes towards members of other cultures. To facilitate the process of inspecting one's own attitudes and beliefs, Piper and Piper present a set of 10 questions and answers regarding cultural identity. They emphasize that cultural identities change in relation to social context; people promote the cultural identity that best suits the particular situation; the complexity of social roles makes it difficult to be sure of the cultural identities of others; discrimination can deprive people from securing their own self-esteem and cultural identity; cultures are dynamic and therefore groups of individuals have the power to change norms and values; and there is a fundamental need for a secure self-image. Throughout the chapter, the authors stress the importance of understanding how cultural membership relates to the development of self-identity and the need for more sensitive understanding of the cultural adjustments of second language learners.

Over the last decade, a widespread trend toward inclusive education and growing support for collaborative exchanges within the field of education has resulted in a greater movement towards school-family partnerships. In **Chapter 10**, Evelyn Lusthaus and Charles Lusthaus discuss parent and teacher partnerships throughout students' high school years. In the first part of their paper, the authors examine the context for family-school partnerships. They describe the parallel trends in society and school with respect to the values, attitudes, and beliefs about student diversity and maintain that the current disposition in society and within many school systems supports inclusive education.

Lusthaus and Lusthaus report that an increasing number of school boards, schools and classrooms have made policy and operational changes to support inclusive education, however, they emphasize the importance of building strong family-school partnerships to ensure the attainment of desired goals. They maintain that it is critically important that educators more fully understand the dynamics and challenges of families of students with disabilities.

There would probably be little disagreement with the idea that as educational goals, teachers should try to establish a foundation for students from which they can better control and direct their own learning, make independent decisions, solve problems, and adapt to changes in their life. Dramatic changes in the business world concurrent with rapid changes in technology have placed greater demands on the educational system to prepare students to effectively learn and adapt to the post-industrial information age.

In **Chapter 11**, Maurice Hollingsworth discusses computing technologies in secondary education with special attention given to serving the needs of students with disabilities. Hollingsworth reviews the employment status of people with disabilities and reports that by and large people with a disability are much less likely to be employed than people without a disability. However, it appears that higher levels of education can positively impact the chances of being employed and that there seems to be an increasing demand for people with advanced computer skills in the job market. Hence, Hollingsworth stresses the need for educators to prepare all students for the utilization of modern computing technologies. To this end, he describes a number of primary software tools (i.e., word processing, databases, spreadsheets, and telecommunications) that can be used across a variety of subject areas and simultaneously enhance students' academic development, computer skills, and critical thinking abilities. To clearly depict how computer technology can be integrated within the curriculum, Hollingsworth presents two sample lessons. For each lesson, he presents the purpose and objectives along with a brief description of the materials and procedures to be used. Central to each lesson is the idea that the computer serves as a key component to achieving the goals and objectives. Underlying the description and discussion of computing applications in secondary education is his view that technology may serve not only to help students resolve specific problems at hand, but it might also change the ways they resolve other problems in the absence of the technology.

Students experience many transitions in their life without many adjustment problems. However, many students with disabilities seem to have difficulty with these transitions. The transition from school to work is particularly difficult for many adolescents with disabilities. Hence, one of the goals of secondary education should be to better prepare these students for independence and employment.

In **Chapter 12**, Jennifer Leigh Hill discusses a variety of options available to students with disabilities after completing their secondary education and presents a number of ways to promote post-school opportunities for students with diverse needs. She believes that schooling may be even more important for persons with diverse learning needs and examines how schools can become more responsive to these students in order to encourage them to remain in school until graduation and help them make the transition from school to work or continued education.

Hill discusses the issue of dropping out of school and then presents some strategies for preventing students from dropping out (e.g., using adult mentors to support and guide students to complete school and plan for the future). She then addresses how schools can help students, especially those with diverse learning needs, make the transition from school to work or from secondary school to post-secondary education settings. She delineates 12 variables that can help facilitate the transition from secondary school to work (e.g., job training, job search skills, counselling for post-secondary options, and mobility and transportation skills). Hill suggests that if schools would strive to emphasize these areas within the educational curriculum they would provide the type of transition services conducive to the needs of many students. She concludes her chapter by discussing how individualized transition planning for students throughout their secondary school experience can help students move from one educational program to another.

In **Chapter 13**, Jac Andrews provides a thematic review of the entire book and presents a few more ideas relative to future educational efforts for improving the teaching of students with diverse needs. According to Andrews, group effort, proactive and adaptive teaching, and classroom climate is emphasized throughout the book. In the first part of the chapter, specific dimensions related to these themes are presented and expanded. In the second part of the chapter he discusses three conditions that can enable teachers to better accommodate student diversity in their classrooms (i.e., administrative leadership and support, professional training and development, and educational research). Andrews concludes his chapter and the book with the view that our current challenge is to prepare ourselves with the knowledge and skills that can empower us to deal with the changes in our schools and the changes in our students.

CHAPTER 1

Some Thoughts about Teaching Students with Diverse Needs

Jac J.W. Andrews

University of Calgary

All students are different from one another. They vary with respect to their academic abilities, social competence, interests, motivation, behavioural tendencies, cultural backgrounds, and approaches to learning. Moreover, they differ in terms of their family and general life experiences. Although some students have greater challenges in responding and adjusting to their environmental conditions compared to their peers, all students have needs that require various levels of support in order to maximize their potential.

The dramatic changes in the nature of families in our country (e.g., immigrant families, single-parent and two-wage-earner families), along with the rapid technological developments in many fields and inflated requirements for students to meet their potential as adults (e.g., higher educational attainment), have significantly increased the demand for schools to provide expanded educational services for students. According to Murray (1993, p. 173), "there are simply too many students with too many needs. Fewer and fewer students fit neatly into the traditional teacher-centred classrooms of the past. Teachers who overemphasize large-group activities and teach to the middle are reaching fewer and fewer students."

The social and economic developments occurring contemporaneously over the past number of years, along with the growing discontent about educational service delivery and student outcomes, have culminated in an intensification of reform movements within the field of education. Although there are disagreements about how the educational system should change to accommodate greater diversity within our schools, many agreements can be found among parents and educators. Most reformers want our schools to change in ways that minimize the possibility of children falling between the cracks of the system and maximize the availability of higher quality education for all students. Most reformers want more effective schools without segregation. Most reformers want educational environments in which people are tolerant and respectful of student diversity. Most reformers want students to receive fair, equitable, and excellent instruction in ways that meet their needs without social stigma. Most reformers want to encourage increased parent participation in student programming and instruction. Most reformers want greater collaboration among all educational stakeholders and service providers. Finally, most reformers want changes to be made through a bottom-up rather than top-down process where educators and parents can team together in open-ended ways to develop and practise innovative educational service delivery approaches.

Educators have debated for decades about how to best meet the diverse needs of students. Typically, the focus of the debate has been on *where* students with special learning needs should be taught. During the 1950s and early 1960s, special class placements were favoured by educators for children who were unsuccessful with the age appropriate curriculum. In the mid- and late 1960s, children typically qualified for special education services on the basis of intellectual functioning. For example, by the late 1960s, special education programs for students with educable mental retardation had the greatest number of children receiving special education services (Reschly, 1988). During this time, reformists opposed the narrowness of this criterion, and various parental and professional groups lobbied governments to broaden the qualifications for special education services. This activity, along with increasing discontent over the placement policies, led to a burgeoning of operational definitions of students by category of special need and became the basis of educational funding support. This resulted in the establishment and proliferation of special education classes and schools. It also dramatically increased the number and type of students serviced in special education programs (e.g., students with gifts and talents, behavioural disturbances, and learning disabilities). At the same time, it also increased labelling practices for placement determinations and the segregation of students with special learning needs from their peers in the mainstream.

In the early 1970s, many teachers and parents in the general public were becoming concerned with the viability of special education classes, particularly for mildly handicapped children (Dunn, 1968; Deno, 1970). A philosophical and attitudinal move away from categorical approaches in special education and toward the integration of children with particularly mild disabilities emerged. Along with a growing social consciousness of desegregation and legislative initiatives such as the U.S. federal legislation of Public Law 94-142 and similar provincial and territorial policies within Canada (see Csapo & Goguen, 1989) to facilitate integrated placements and ensure the least restrictive educational environment for exceptional children, school boards during the 1970s and 1980s were being pressured to mainstream students with special learning needs into the regular classroom. Today, the concept of mainstreaming has been replaced by the concept of inclusive education whereby school boards are attempting to more fully integrate handicapped students within their schools and classrooms by restructuring their schools (Reynolds, Wang & Walberg, 1987; Villa, Thousand, Stainback & Stainback, 1992), melding special education and regular education services (Stainback, Stainback & Bunch, 1989; Mesinger, 1985), and instituting innovative instructional strategies and professional teaming approaches (Glomb & Morgan, 1991; Nevin, Thousand, Paolucci-Whitcomb & Villa, 1990; Porter, 1991).

These trends represent a paradigm shift for meeting the diverse educational needs of students. The traditional paradigm that has been widely adopted and practised in schools throughout the country is represented by a dual system of educational service delivery (regular education and special education) for meeting the diverse educational needs of students. This dual system has been characterized by static and standardized assessment, student labelling, classification and categorization, segregated learning environments, fragmented programming and instruction, and top-down decision making. The "new" paradigm represents the merging of the regular and special education systems into one unified system of service delivery to address the individual needs of all students. This "inclusive" model has been adopted and implemented in an increasing number of schools and school systems across Canada *because it is becoming increasingly evident that student diversity is no longer just a special education issue.* This paradigm is characterized by the application of cognitive, developmental, and sociocultural perspectives of teaching and learning, dynamic-, ecological-, and instructionally- based assessment procedures, integrated learning environments, holistic programming and instruction, home-school partnerships, collaborative-based decision making, and greater partnership between regular and special educators.

We can no longer depend on special education to be responsible for students who do not fit the middle of regular education classrooms. Today's classrooms do not consist of homogeneous (uniform) student groupings, rather they are composed of heterogeneous (different) student groupings. As our classrooms take on a new look, our teachers' approaches to teaching must change to accommodate student diversity. Teachers should be provided opportunities to work together in teams to make the task of teaching manageable and to ensure quality instruction for everyone. Teaching students with diverse learning needs requires the adoption of more flexible and creative instructional approaches. Traditional teacher-centred approaches where teachers stand in front of the classroom and only provide large-group instruction and direction will not be effective within today's multidimensional classrooms. Instead, multifaceted instructional plans need to be orchestrated in ways that incorporate large-group instruction less often and utilize individualized and small-group instructional formats more often. Successful teaching techniques in today's classrooms include the utilization of team-teaching procedures, cooperative learning groups, peer and cross-age tutoring, formative assessment strategies, self-regulatory management approaches, cognitive strategy instruction, differentiated lesson plans, and other procedures that maximize students' involvement with one another and in their own learning.

The current trend toward greater inclusion of special-needs students in today's regular classrooms has significantly complicated the nature of teaching. The greatest challenge for teachers is to create educational environments that provide structure as well as flexibility for students and that enhance the learning of all students. In other words, inclusive education has to maximize the potential of students who have significant learning and behavioural difficulties, promote the achievement of those students without exceptional conditions, and enrich the development of those students who have advanced talents and abilities.

Inclusive education means that everyone is welcomed and valued in their neighbourhood school. To be included in your community school means that you have the same opportunities as every other child in the school, you have a variety of choices available to you, and you can be in the same classes as your peers. As with communities, schools are places where diversity should be expected and appreciated. In some cases, this philosophy might result in multi-age and/or multi-grade classrooms where peer uniqueness, student assistance, and child-centred perspectives can be fostered. In any case, student diversity within classrooms can promote learning communities that expose students to differences within and across their peers, sensitize them to the needs of others, and offer opportunities for them to learn how to help one another construct knowledge, solve problems, complete projects, and live and work together collaboratively inside and outside their school. *Essentially, all students benefit from an atmosphere created by student diversity.*

Whereas some people have suggested that inclusion means getting rid of special educators, special education, and its continuum of services (e.g., individualized instruction and tutoring) (see Stainback & Stainback, 1992), others have suggested that inclusion means that special personnel, instructional methods, and a continuum of services get brought into the regular classroom. *Inclusion reflects an important societal value* (Lusthaus & Lusthaus, 1992) *and emerges from a sociology of acceptance, in contrast to a sociology of exclusion* (Flynn & Kowalczyk-McPhee, 1989). As noted by Little (1992, p. 12),

> ...it may help to think of inclusive education as that educational response in which each individual student is included in the thinking and planning process, is included in instruction, included in activities, included as a fully participating bona fide member of the class or group. Inclusion precludes being segregated, or isolated in the ordinary class. Of paramount importance is its opportunity for helping children who have been separated from one another to begin to see each other as real people. It is simply not assigning children with special problems to the ordinary classroom. It is the conscious decision to create a sense of community out of accepted differences.

Inclusion requires variable and flexible educational processes in order to provide opportunities for children to have meaningful and enjoyable school experiences and for them to reach their maximum potential.

Inclusive education embraces the concepts of normalization, integration, and mainstreaming. The concept of **normalization** reflects the idea that all individuals, regardless of their abilities, have a right to the opportunities of everyone else in everyday life (Wolfensberger, 1972). **Integration** refers to the education of handicapped children with their nonhandicapped peers. **Mainstreaming** is a process of integrating students that includes a continuum of services (e.g., professional teaming approaches, resource rooms, teacher aides) that aims to provide students with educational experiences that are the least restrictive and the most ordinary. Inclusion is not a cohesive plan to eliminate special services and place every student, regardless of condition, within the regular classroom. As noted by York, Doyle, and Kronberg (1992, p. 2) *"Inclusion does not mean that students must spend every minute of the school day in general education classes (no student should), that students never receive small-group or individualized instruction, or that students are in general education classes to learn the core curriculum only"* [italics added].

Inclusion should mean that there is more than one acceptable way to organize and structure education; more than one way to provide a differentiated curriculum to children; more than one way for teachers as well as students to share and work together in the teaching and learning transaction; more than one way for teachers to achieve desired educational outcomes for their students;

more than one way for teachers to assess and evaluate student progress; and more than one way for teachers to prepare our children for the future. Essentially, inclusion means that everyone has a contribution to make and that the educational career of a child should be one that is maximized and *not* restricted.

We know that over the past few years there has been a growing institutionalization of successful collaboration-based and consultation-based service delivery systems in schools to help address student diversity. For example, a consultative-collaborative model for serving students with diverse needs in regular classrooms has been developed and practised in the province of Manitoba for many years (Freeze, Bravi & Rampaul, 1989). This model incorporates the use of different support service teams that comprise various personnel (e.g., classroom teachers, resource teachers, clinical specialists, program specialists) to assist classroom teachers in assessing their students, developing and implementing instructional programs, and evaluating the effectiveness of instructional strategies. Conditions for the successful implementation and maintenance of consultative-collaborative models of service delivery include time to implement them, parity among participants, shared participation, accountability, resources (Friend & Cook, 1990), and knowledge of and experience with the necessary problem-solving and management skills.

We know some ways to assess and evaluate students to better understand their diverse needs. Assessment techniques include norm-referenced assessment procedures (to ascertain students' academic achievements and cognitive abilities), criterion-referenced assessment techniques (to determine students' depth and breadth of knowledge and skills relevant to the curriculum), performance-based assessment measures (to determine students' reasoning and problem-solving skills and evaluate how students approach their learning), curriculum-based assessment methods (to continually probe and estimate students' knowledge and performance in order to better design instructional objectives), and informal techniques such as student observations, questionnaires, and interviews.

One way to get students actively involved in their own learning and development is to collaborate with them in the collection and evaluation of material. This can result in a portfolio of information that is chosen by the students under the guidance of the teacher and that reflects the day-to-day performance of the students in the classroom. This type of collection allows students to be participants in the assessment process and provides a way for teachers to monitor their students' performance in relation to a variety of learning tasks. Moreover, it is one example of how assessment practices can be part of the daily instructional routine.

We know that once we gather information about our students, we can better address their needs. Planning should incorporate long-term goals, short-term objectives, and instructional strategies to accommodate the diverse needs of the students. We also know that good planning should involve the consideration of key concepts to be understood by the students, and the provision of activities that connect students with their real-world experiences.

We know some effective ways for managing and instructing children with diverse needs. For example, all students will learn and behave better in classrooms that are well organized and where behavioural expectations and routines are well established as well as monitored and maintained by the teacher (Englert, 1984). Positive social/emotional behaviour can be created by teachers who demonstrate to students that they care about them and who help them meet classroom expectations.

Social climate as well as academic development can be facilitated by using peer-tutoring arrangements (Jenkins & Jenkins, 1985; Lloyd, Crowley, Kohler & Strain, 1988) where students can instruct and guide one another with respect to various skills. However, materials need to be carefully arranged and structured and sessions should be continually monitored by the teacher. Cooperative learning experiences provide opportunities for students to undertake roles such as leader, encourager, recorder, facilitator, and be significantly involved in group work (Johnson & Johnson, 1986). According to Murray (1993, p. 181) "teachers report that as a result of working in cooperative groups, special students become less hesitant to offer ideas in larger group discussions. They develop more confidence in their ability to think and contribute."

Successful teachers of students with diverse needs prevent problems from occurring. Students need to understand the behavioural rules and routines of the classroom and be helped in making good behavioural choices. Appropriate behaviour is promoted by teachers who make adjustments in the curriculum and in their teaching methods to accommodate student differences. Teachers can maintain and facilitate successful learning and appropriate behaviour by using effective instructional procedures.

We know that many children with learning problems also have social problems that need to be addressed by the teacher in the classroom. Teaching students to become socially skilled and effective social problem-solvers is a challenging task that requires attention to cognitive, affective, and behavioural dimensions. This is another area in which regular and special educators can work together in identifying the social needs of students and providing social skills training for the students. Many programs and strategies are available that have proven to be effective in regular classrooms (see McIntosh & Vaughn, 1993; Vernon & Schumaker, 1993).

Many students do not have the social skills they need to be able to successfully work and interact with their peers. Hence, many teachers are finding it necessary to provide direct social skills instruction. Research has shown that positive peer interactions can be increased and that students can feel better about themselves when cooperative group and peer-tutoring structures have been implemented (Putman, Rynders, Johnson & Johnson, 1989; Delquadri, Greenwood, Whorton, Carta & Hall, 1986). It has also been shown that instructing students in social skills, giving them opportunities to practise these skills, providing feedback with respect to their performance, and providing appropriate behavioural modelling augments sociometric acceptance and status of children (Gottman, Gonso & Schuler, 1976) and helps reduce inappropriate behaviour (Zahvi & Asher, 1978) while increasing conversational behaviours (Bondy & Erickson, 1976). Overall, the literature points out that teachers can effectively teach social skills to their students.

Many children in today's classrooms have second-culture and second-language backgrounds that should be respected and acknowledged in the day-to-day learning activities. The more we are aware of our own cultural values and beliefs, the more likely we can appreciate the variant beliefs and values held by our students and create a community of learners in which there is equality of opportunity and expression.

We know that there are many benefits from the establishment of school-home partnerships (Shea & Bauer, 1991). Along with providing useful information regarding student interests, motivations, behavioural tendencies, and learning styles, parents can be trained to work with their children at home in accordance with classroom directives as well as undertake volunteer roles within the school (Shea & Bauer, 1991; Nystul, 1987).

It is also important to note that students with diverse needs come from families that are unique and diverse. Families differ in terms of culture, religion, belief systems, stress levels, educational background, political affiliations, social status, and other dimensions. Knowing about the characteristics of families can help teachers form more workable collaborative relationships.

We know that the use of technology can play an important role in promoting the academic development of students within the classroom. Advances in computer hardware and software makes individualized instruction more feasible within the classroom. Moreover, computing technology can be used in ways that support collaborative planning and decision making. Computers can also be used by teachers to more efficiently record student progress and prepare learning profiles of students. At the functional level, computer technology can, for example, help students get more actively involved in their writing through the use of word-processing software programs and help them become more proficient in mathematical computations and problem solving. Technologies are also available to assist students with hearing and visual impairments as well as students with physical disabilities to better communicate with others. At the developmental level, computer technology can be used to prepare students for their future in a workforce that will likely require them to be users of advancing computer technology.

Teaching students with diverse learning needs is not easy. It requires hard work, deep commitment, and perseverance. Many teachers are not supportive of the integration of exceptional students into their classrooms (Winzer, 1985) and some are angry and frustrated, particularly if appropriate supports are not provided (Hardman, Drew, Egan & Wolf, 1990). Many teachers worry that their classroom might be disrupted if children with diverse learning needs are placed in regular classrooms (Vacc & Kirst, 1977) and that their programs will be diluted (Bradfield, Brown, Kaplan, Rickert & Stannard, 1973). We know that teachers' attitudes and dispositions regarding teaching children with diverse learning needs are important determinants of inclusive education. In order to facilitate positive attitudes, teachers cannot feel burdened with diversity (Duquette, 1992) and must experience support from the administration within their school, help from their colleagues related to the frustrations and stresses involved in the teaching process, and have positive and successful encounters with their students and their families.

Students with diverse learning needs are unlikely to be taught well by someone who has no desire to develop their teaching skills and who has little interest in learning how to teach students with diverse needs. Teachers should be (among other things) bright, fair-minded, patient, caring, thoughtful, cooperative, inquisitive, resourceful, and willing to learn, grow, and change for the betterment of themselves and their students.

Although we know some things about teaching students with diverse needs there is a lot for us to learn. It seems reasonable to expect that we will always be trying to improve our instructional ability and our students' learning abilities. As we develop over time we will become more knowledgeable about how to teach and manage diverse populations. Hopefully, we can move beyond discussion and debate about where students with diverse learning needs should be taught and focus on how to best achieve excellence while accepting individual differences within the school and community (Gallagher, 1994; Morse, 1994; Pugach, 1990). Integration has not been shown to be flawed (Goetz & Sailor, 1990) and does not preclude the continued investigation of children's learning problems and the resolution of their difficulties. We have moved away from the assumption that children with special needs are the owners of their problems and have come to realize that the school system and the community at large have ownership of children with diverse educational needs (Csapo, 1992). However, we need to continue to research and develop more effective interventions that can expand the continuum of services for children with special needs within community schools and regular classrooms. As noted by Kauffman (1993), we do not want inclusion to exclude remedial assistance for those students who are struggling in their learning. Rather, we want all students to be a part of the educational mainstream that has teachers who are willing and able to accept diversity and who can assess students' needs accommodate these needs in their programming and instruction, facilitate lifelong learning and self-fulfilment, academic and social skills, school-home partnerships, educational quality and equity, and collaboration among all service providers. *Although perfection in these areas is not reasonable, it is reasonable to improve upon the necessary enabling conditions* (i.e., funding, professional development, empirical studies, and administrative leadership and support) *that can promote these worthwhile targets. Moreover, it is reasonable to increase our understanding of what can be done to improve the teaching of students with diverse needs within the classrooms of our schools.*

SUGGESTED RESOURCES

Andrews, J., & Lupart, J. (1993). *The inclusive classroom: Educating exceptional children.* Scarborough, ON: Nelson Canada.

Bowd, A., McDougall, D., & Yewchuck, C. (1994). *Educational psychology for Canadian teachers.* Toronto: Harcourt Brace & Co.

Bos. C.S., & Vaughn, S. (1994). *Strategies for teaching students with learning and behavior problems* (3rd edition). Toronto: Allyn and Bacon.

Crealock, C., & Bachor, D. (1995). *Instructional strategies for students with special needs* (2nd edition). Scarborough, ON: Allyn and Bacon.

Goodlad, J.I., & Lovitt, T.C. (1993). *Integrating general and special education.* Toronto: Maxwell Macmillan Canada.

Mulcahy, R.F., Short, R.H., & Andrews, J. (1991). *Enhancing learning and thinking.* New York: Praeger.

Smith, T.E.C., Polloway, E.A., Potten, J.R., & Dowdy, C.A. (1995). *Teaching children with special needs in inclusive settings.* Toronto: Allyn and Bacon.

REFERENCES

Bondy, A.S., & Erickson, M.T. (1976). Comparison of modelling and reinforcement procedures in increasing question-asking of mentally retarded children. *Journal of Applied Behavior Analysis, 9*(1), 108.

Bradfield, H.R., Brown, J., Kaplan, P., Rickert, E., & Stannard, R. (1973). The special child in the regular classroom. *Exceptional Children, 39,* 384–90.

Csapo, M. (1992). Special education in crisis. *B.C. Journal of Special Education, 16*(3), 249–58.

Csapo, M., & Goguen, L. (1989). *Special education across Canada: Issues and concerns for the '90s.* Vancouver: Centre for Human Development and Research.

Delquadri, J., Greenwood, C.R., Whorton, D., Carta, J.J., & Hall, V. (1986). Classwide peer tutoring. *Exceptional Children, 52,* 535–42.

Deno, E. (1970). Special education as developmental capital. *Exceptional Children, 37,* 229–37.

Dunn, L. (1968). Special education for the mildly retarded—Is much of it justifiable? *Exceptional Children, 35,* 5–22.

Duquette, C. (1992). Integrating mildly and moderately handicapped children: What goes on in a successful school? *Exceptionality Education Canada, 2*(1&2), 139–53.

Englert, C.S. (1984). Measuring teacher effectiveness from the teachers point of view. *Focus on Exceptional Children, 17,* 1–14.

Evans, W.H., & Evans, S.S. (1983). Using parents in behavior management. *Academic Therapy, 19,* 37–41.

Flynn, G., & Kowalczyk-McPhee, B. (1989). A school system in transition. In S. Stainback, W. Stainback, & M. Forest (Eds.), *Educating all students in the mainstream of regular education* (pp. 29–41). Baltimore: Paul H. Brookes.

Freeze, D.R., Bravi, G., & Rampaul, W.E. (1989). Special education in Manitoba: A consultative-collaborative services delivery model. In M. Csapo & L. Goguen (Eds.), *Special education across Canada* (pp. 47–80). Vancouver: Centre for Human Development and Research.

Friend, M., & Cook, L. (1990). Collaboration as a predictor for success in school reform. *Journal of Educational and Psychological Consultation, 1,* 69–86.

Gallagher, J.J. (1994). The pull of societal forces on special education. *The Journal of Special Education, 27*(4), 521–30.

Glomb, N.K., & Morgan, D.P. (1991). Resource room teachers use of strategies that promote the success of handicapped students in regular classrooms. *The Journal of Special Education, 25*(2), 221–35.

Goetz, L., & Sailor, W. (1990). Much to do about babies, musky bathwater, and trickle-down politics: A reply to Kauffman. *The Journal of Special Education, 24*(3), 334–39.

Gottman, J., Gonso, J., & Schuler, P. (1976). Teaching social skills to isolated children. *Journal of Abnormal Child Psychology, 4,* 179–97.

Hardman, M.L., Drew, C.J., Egan, M.W., & Wolf, B. (1990). *Human exceptionality: Society, school, and family.* Boston: Allyn and Bacon.

Jenkins, J., & Jenkins, L. (1985). Peer tutoring in elementary and secondary programmes. *Focus on Exceptional Children, 17*(6), 1–12.

Johnson, D.W., & Johnson, R.T. (1986). Mainstreaming and cooperative learning strategies. *Exceptional Children, 52,* 553–61.

Kauffman, J.M. (1993). How we might achieve the radical reform of special education. *Exceptional Children, 60*(1), 6–16.

Little, D.M. (1992). The muddle of mainstreaming: Cross-Canada currents—policy and practice of inclusive education. *Exceptionality Education Canada, 2*(1&2), 9–48.

Lloyd, J., Crowley, E.P., Kohler, F.W., & Strain, P.S. (1988). Redefining the applied research agenda? Cooperative learnings, prereferral, teacher consultant, and peer-mediated interventions. *Journal of Learning Disabilities, 21*, 43–52.

Lusthaus, E., & Lusthaus, C. (1992). From segregation to full inclusion: An evolution. *Exceptionality Education Canada, 2*(1&2), 95–115.

McIntosh, R., & Vaughn, S. (1993). So you want to teach social skills to your students: Some pointers from research. *Exceptionality Education Canada, 3*(1&2), 39–59.

Mesinger, J.F. (1985). Commentary on Rationale for the merger of special and regular education or Is it now time for the lamb to lie down with the lion? *Exceptionality Children, 51*(6), 510–12.

Morse, W.C. (1994). Comments from a biased viewpoint. *The Journal of Special Education, 27*(4), 531–42.

Murray, L.B. (1993). Putting it all together at the school level: A principal's perspective. In J.I. Goodlad & T.C. Lovitt (Eds.), *Integrating general and special education.* Toronto: Maxwell Macmillan Canada.

Nevin, A., Thousand, J., Paolucci-Whitcomb, P., & Villa, R. (1990). Collaborative consultation: Empowering public school personnel to provide heterogeneous schooling for all or Who rang that bell? *Journal of Educational and Psychological Consultation, 1*(1), 41–67.

Nystul, M. (1987). Strategies for parent-centred counselling of the young. *The Creative Child and Adult Quarterly, 12*, 103–10.

Porter, G.L. (1991). The methods and resource teacher: A collaborative consultant model. In G.L. Porter & D. Richler (Eds.), *Changing Canadian schools* (pp. 107–54). North York, ON: Roeher Institute.

Pugach, M.C. (1990). The moral cost of retrenchment in special education. *The Journal of Special Education, 24*(3), 326–33.

Putman, J.W., Rynders, J.E., Johnson, R.T., & Johnson, D.W. (1989). Collaborative skill instruction for promoting positive interactions between mentally handicapped and nonhandicapped children. *Exceptional Children, 55*(6), 550–57.

Reschly, D.J. (1988). Introduction. In M.C. Wang, M.C. Reynolds, & H.J. Walberg (Eds.), *Handbook of special education: Research and practice* (Vol. 2, pp. 3–5). Oxford, UK: Pergamon Press.

Reynolds, M.C., Wang, M.C., & Walberg, H.J. (1987). The necessary restructuring of special and regular education. *Exceptional Children, 53*(5), 391–98.

Sharan, S., & Sharan, Y. (1976). *Small group teaching.* Englewood Cliffs, NJ: Educational Testing Publications.

Shea, T.M., & Bauer, A.M. (1991). *Parents and teachers of small children with exceptionalities: A handbook for collaboration* (2nd edition). Boston: Allyn and Bacon.

Stainback, S., & Stainback, W. (1992). *Curriculum considerations in inclusive classrooms: Facilitating learning for all students.* Baltimore: Paul H. Brookes.

Stainback, S., Stainback, W., & Bunch, G. (1989). A rationale for the merger of regular and special education. In S. Stainback, W. Stainback, & M. Forest (Eds.), *Educating all students in the mainstream of regular education* (pp. 15–26). Baltimore: Paul H. Brookes.

Vacc, N.A., & Kirst, N. (1977). Emotionally disturbed children and regular classroom teachers. *Elementary School Journal, 77,* 309–17.

Vernon, D.S., & Schumaker, J.B. (1993). Who benefits from social skills instruction in the mainstream classroom? *Exceptionality Education Canada, 3*(1&2), 9–38.

Villa, R.A., Thousand, J.S., Stainback, W., & Stainback, S. (Eds.). (1992). *Restructuring for caring and effective education: An administrative guide to creating heterogeneous schools.* Baltimore: Paul H. Brookes.

Winzer, M. (1985). Teacher attitudes towards mainstreaming: An appraisal of the research. *B.C. Journal of Special Education, 9,* 149–61.

Wolfensberger, W. (1972). *Normalization in human services.* Toronto: National Institute on Mental Retardation.

York, J., Doyle, M.B., & Kronberg, R. (1992). A curriculum development process for inclusive classrooms. *Focus on Exceptional Children, 25*(4), 1–16.

Zahvi, S., & Asher, S. (1978). The effect of verbal instructions on preschool children's aggressive behavior. *Journal of School Psychology, 16,* 146–53.

CHAPTER 2

Becoming a Change Agent in Your Secondary Classroom

Donna Patterson

University of Regina

Introduction

This chapter begins with an example of how a teacher, Dick Robinson, acts as change agent for himself and his students. The remainder of the chapter focuses on what each of us might do to become such agents in our own classrooms and amid the now-occurring merger of special and regular education. Self-care, political astuteness, planning, effective conflict resolution, and a sense of humour are explored as ways to manage the merger successfully.

CASE STUDY

It was the start of the school year and Dick Robinson was preparing to teach a grade-10 class. The class was predominantly male, and Dick suspected most of them would be wearing baseball hats. In this particular school, there was a rule: "no hats in class." Dick could see that he and his students would probably clash over this. So he made a hatrack, put it on the back wall, bought some paint and some brushes, and waited. When the students filed in the first day, Dick explained that in his class hats weren't acceptable, but that there was an "executive" hatrack on the back wall that the young men could use. He suggested they might want to pick a spot and that he had paint and brushes should they want to paint their name under their spot. The "guys" were surprised; there wasn't much discussion, and in the first week or so Dick had to remind them at the start of each class to use the rack. By November, it was a very rare occasion when he had to remind anyone. His quick thinking turned a potentially aggravating situation into fun.

This example demonstrates the difference between being overwhelmed by change, being a change manager, and becoming a change agent. No matter what the situation, or what we would wish:

> *Change must be accomplished by people.*
> (Evans, 1993)

Change is ubiquitous. It is a constant in our lives, affecting families and schools and most certainly students. Fullan (1985) suggests that change is a process whereby we alter our ways of thinking and doing. It is a process of developing new skills and, above all, of finding satisfaction in new ways of doing things. Cantor (1953) goes as far as to suggest that to learn is to change.

Currently, the classroom is changing. Among many other changes, regular and special education are merging. This merging is often framed in a renewed commitment to meeting the diverse needs of students. Frequently, discussion focuses on what educators can and/or should do for students. This is as it should be, for it is this commitment that brings most of us to and keeps us in the teaching profession (Gold & Roth, 1993). Sarason (1990), in his reflections on school reform, suggests that attempts to reform education (and by extension to merge regular and special education) will make little difference until those initiating change understand that the school must exist as much for teachers as for students. Schools will be successful in nurturing students only to the extent that they nurture teachers. The contention in this chapter is that teachers involved in the merger of special and regular education are at the centre of this change (Postman & Weingartner, 1987).

This chapter reflects the belief that change is a process, not an event, that is made by individuals first and then by institutions, and that in the final analysis it's a very personal experience. It focuses on how we can avoid being overwhelmed, and how we can navigate this merger to become effective change managers and agents. Managing this type of change must start with ourselves. It requires self-care if we are to persist, political astuteness if we are to find support and/or renegotiate roles, a systematic, planful approach if we are not to be overwhelmed, an ability to deal with conflict if we are not to get sidetracked, and a sense of humour to get us over the humps.

> *If you want to know how something works, try changing it.*
> (Lewin, 1935, 1948)

Lewin's statement can be adapted to the personal level: if you want to learn about yourself, try changing yourself.

We are more likely to change if we see the change as desirable or feasible (Beckhard & Harris, 1987); when it is espoused by someone we trust; when it is linked to things we hold as important; and when its target is focused and practical. As an individual teacher in a school or school system, you may become involved in the merging of special and regular education in a number of ways. For some, school or provincial policy will dictate their involvement; for others, the merger speaks to their own commitment to equity. For still others, the merger becomes real only when a student with special needs turns up for the first time or when the number of students with special needs increases beyond two or three.

There are a range of responses to the merging of regular and special education. Some teachers carry on as if nothing were happening (Sikes, 1984; Troyna, 1985). Sometimes teachers suggest that changes have taken place, but the gap between what they say and what they do is wide. Going through the motions of presenting an appearance of change prevents real change from occurring.

Some teachers are already "neck deep" in change. They are the ones most encouraged by the merger. They are already committed, initiating changes for their students in their classrooms. It might be said these teachers are "front runners," showing the rest of us what is possible. Sometimes they are so far ahead of the rest of us that we feel left behind, even resentful, and certainly frustrated.

A novice teacher wanting to include parents in decision making about students' educational programs found the most important thing was to communicate with the rest of the school staff about what she was trying to do. She then communicated with the parents of the students in her class, and, in this way, began to build a circle of support. But she had to try not to do everything on her own, all at once. This chapter will discuss these and other strategies for those finding themselves in a similar position.

The rest of us are beginning to grapple or are in the midst of grappling with the merger. We're starting to develop effective ways to work with and meet the needs of all our students. We are willing to foster the merger, but may not yet be totally committed and/or understand all its implications. Our greatest struggle is not to become discouraged. We need to approach this merger with care.

Of course, there are some things that shouldn't be changed and some that can't be changed—at least, not right now, not quickly and not by ourselves. It is important to identify these and try to accept them gracefully. Remind yourself that you cannot solve every problem or fix everything. However, you can solve *some* problems and begin to change *some* things. At the very least, it is possible to make a start. Some of us are ready to take that step and others have taken it; in both cases the question is what to do next.

Finally, there are those who are actively resisting the merger of regular and special education. Some try to change and fail, but think they are succeeding; other refuse to try. At the very least, many teachers are ambivalent about change (Bolman & Deal, 1991). As Marris (1986) has shown, for many of us the primary metaphor for change is loss. The discrediting of the assumptions by which we live and make sense of our world and our work is often filled with pain and sadness. There are usually good reasons for our resistance to any change. Fear of loss, of incompetence, and of disorganization all fuel our resistance to change. We may not be able to find an "adequate" plan or strategy. How we go about the change becomes a critical question both for the school system and the individual teacher. Our expectations may be high and we may expend a lot of energy looking for a "right" or "best" strategy or plan. In the merger of special and regular education, it would be easy to look for one way to achieve this goal instead of trying a number of strategies to see which works best for us and for our students. We may also resist the merger because of an apparent lack of resources or because we perceive that there has been an underestimation of the issues surrounding resources and feasibility. In this case, it's necessary to go back to the drawing board and rethink what is reasonable given existing resources. High expectations and slight resources often lead to frustration.

Continued resistance requires effort and is often exhausting, even if we join a "grumbling clique" (Sikes, 1992, p. 46). Participating in the merger ensures that our needs and those of our students are addressed and that we can live more easily with the form the merger takes in our school or school system. Being involved can give us a sense of continuity, predictability, and control. (See Appendix 2A for another way to frame or understand our response to change.)

Building in Self-Care

If we don't take good care of ourselves,
we will not be able to give anything to anyone else.
(Coloroso, 1994)

Finding a Buddy

For many of us, the joy of teaching lies in being in the classroom, working with our students. While these days there are many people in and out of the classroom (parents, teacher aides, volunteers, other professionals, even students from other classes), no one else really knows fully what we're doing. Even with conferencing, team, and/or staff meetings we are mostly on our own.

A popular teaching strategy is to set up a buddy system—to pair one student with another to work together on reading, or to pair an older student with a student new to a school to help them learn the ropes. This strategy works well for students and, often, for parents. It is one teachers might use for themselves.

In developing such support we would be assisting ourselves in our own professional development. When this kind of support is set up by a school system, Joyce and Showers (1982) and Hord and Huling-Austin (1988) refer to it as "consulting" or "coaching." Their work indicates that change happens most easily when there are at least two people working to effect the change—when we have a buddy.

There is much to be gained from developing support. It provides a safer environment in which to recognize and explore classroom issues and concerns. It can help you think through changes you are attempting in your classroom with your students. It can encourage us throughout the change process by helping us to focus on our successes. Support can help sustain our efforts, clarify our goals, develop strategies, and generate new ones when the ones we are using aren't working as well as we would like.

Finding someone with whom you feel comfortable, who you can talk to, is a first step. It would be easy to turn to a close friend, someone you know and trust. While these people can be helpful in many respects, they may not always be a good choice; perhaps better is someone whom you respect and with whom you share common experiences in teaching. You may want to choose someone who is a little further along the road, but not so far ahead you can't see them (Odell, 1990; Opuni, 1989; Vann, 1989). Usually a support develops over time, as you develop a working relationship with the other person. The relationship grows with thought, attention, and good communication skills. Of course, it is a two-way street and for most of us must include an understanding that what is discussed is held in confidence. This kind of "being with" helps us feel listened to, understood, and accepted and makes the risks of change a little less ominous.

Usually, we need more support than any one individual can provide. Some teachers find support in professional organizations or in a small group of colleagues. It is important to have a variety of sources of support in your professional life to act just as your family and circle of friends do in your personal life. This need for support, for a circle of caring, in both professional and personal life is so strong that the rate for virtually every major cause of death is significantly higher for the lonely. (Hartog, Audry & Cohen, 1980). This need for support is one we often deal with intuitively, without much thought. When support occurs easily, that is wonderful. But sometimes, particularly in new situations, it doesn't hurt to consciously try to establish it, by finding a buddy.

Learning to Encourage

As teachers and teachers in training, we tend to see ourselves as problem solvers. We try to define what is wrong or what is making learning difficult for our students. The more we do this, of course, the better we get at it. We become quick at identifying errors and become critics. We turn this skill on our students, on our colleagues, and on ourselves. What would happen if we concentrated on the positive, on strengths? I often open my classes by asking students to share one positive thing that has happened to them in the past 24 hours. At the beginning of the semester, students often are hesitant and uneasy. Some remain so; others begin to look forward to the activity and actually find it easy to do by the end of the semester.

Many have written extensively on how we can turn our classrooms into inviting, safe, supportive places for our students (Canfield, 1990; Kearns et al., 1990, Purkey, 1991, Purkey & Schmidt, 1990; Purkey & Novak, 1984, to name only a few). Teachers need to use these same techniques for themselves.

We need to look carefully at how we speak to and about ourselves. Perceiving ourselves positively means applying the labels: valuable, able, and responsible to our lives. Try this: make a list of your strengths as a teacher and beside each strength write an example in which you used that strength.

One way to try to increase the number of positive things we say to ourselves is to acknowledge what we do, what we say, and what we try. Often we just don't take the time to notice. We tell ourselves that what we say and what we do doesn't matter, doesn't or didn't make any difference anyway. Simply acknowledging what we have tried, what we have done, and what we have said is a first step in encouraging ourselves. Accepting what we have done means understanding what has taken place and our part in it. We can also go one step further and agree that what we have done, said and tried is OK. This kind of self-talk will not take place by itself. We'll need to practise encouraging ourselves until this kind of talk becomes automatic.

Many of us get too busy to keep a list or to acknowledge our successes. Still we need to talk about, focus on, what succeeds. Often we have five objectives, succeed in four, but because we are rushing and stressed, we focus all our attention on the one objective we haven't reached. It's easy if we ignore our successes to get frustrated. Perhaps we need to build five or ten minutes at the end of the day just to jot down a few notes on what worked that day. Sometimes a tape recorder can be more helpful since often at the end of the day we're tired of paper and writing.

Deboer (1986) deals at some length with what she calls cognitive distortions, illogical and hurtful self-talk. Her advice seems to be not only to avoid being angry, sarcastic or aggressive with our students, but also with ourselves.

Try to treat yourself kindly and with consideration. Think of it as practice for acting positively with your students. Most of us don't need critics, we need friends—we need encouragement. Recognizing and building in supportive self-talk is one way to begin to provide that encouragement.

Sometimes, you can catch yourself speaking harshly to yourself. Saying things like:

"I must be losing it."
"No one else makes these kind of mistakes."
"I'll never get it right. I must be stupid."
"This would have gone better if I'd been more prepared."

These messages are clearly ones that imply "I'm not valuable," "I'm not able," and "I'm irresponsible." When you catch yourself making these statements, say to yourself, "Stop," or "Interrupt," and then replace the rest of what you were going to say with a reminder that "you are valuable," "you are able," and "you are responsible." Think of something that has worked, think of a time when you felt able, and acknowledge that while this time things did not work, they have in the past and they will again.

There are other ways to be encouraging. When you made your list of strengths, did you have difficulty? If so, think back to something in your work in the classroom you felt proud of, something that made you want to celebrate. Did you celebrate? How? Most of us overlook our successes; we are so good at identifying and solving problems, we forget to celebrate when things work. Celebrating our successes is important, and the more ways we put in place to celebrate, the better. Keeping a list of our successes can help encourage us.

A final tip on learning to encourage: learn to build in successes. Most teachers know to do this for their students, but forget or don't think to do it for themselves. The feeling of competence gained through doing something that works cannot be overstated. If you have not experienced any success for a while, perhaps you need to go back to the drawing board and review how you are trying to bring about change in your classroom with your students. Lack of success is often a sure sign that our steps or strategies are too big, too ambitious, and that we are trying to do too much, too quickly.

Encouragement—engaging in positive self-talk, celebrating our efforts, and building in successes—maintains our willingness to work toward merging special and regular education. These strategies can help us to take pride in our teaching, to do our work with care, to finish what we start, and to know our efforts will work if we persist.

Developing Political Astuteness

Finding Support and Reading the Political Current

Most of us think of teaching as something we do with and for students. We see our involvement with parents and other professionals as working on our students' behalf. This is true, but there is another part of the job and many of us overlook it. Letting others know what we are doing, finding out about district initiatives, and building a circle of collegial support are important if we are to manage change and not have it manage us.

I like to tell my students about a first-year teacher. She worked in a special education resource room and many evenings she sat up late organizing materials and designing learning experiences. There were many Saturdays she spent gathering resources, arranging field trips, and contacting speakers for her classroom. At the end of the year, when the principal was asked to make decisions on staffing, he voted to let her go. His explanation was that he wasn't aware she had done anything special for her students. This story highlights the issue that if the other members of the school community don't know what we are trying to do, they can't help us. They may even unknowingly make life more difficult for us.

If you are either new or viewed as an outsider to a school system, you need to be cautious about the amount or degree of change you undertake initially. Using familiar systems, procedures, forms, and/or language can help you seem more a part of the school system. Check out school system policies and try to get a sense of system priorities and/or initiatives. District administrators are on the front line, often coordinating change efforts so that those changes are coherent and well managed.

It is in your best interest to work closely with your principal. This can be done by keeping your principal informed about what's going on in your class. You can use video or audio tapes, short memos, student-created newsletters, and/or short, regularly scheduled meetings to do this. In most situations, principals have little idea what it is you need from them in terms of support. Most would like to be supportive, so it is your responsibility to provide the necessary information so that they can be so.

Parents also like to know what's happening in your class. If in working with parents you focus on how you can both work together to benefit the student, things often go more smoothly. Parents appreciate being acknowledged as caring individuals and as having their child's best interests at heart.

How we get information to parents is a challenge. Parent–teacher conferences are one way. With both parents working, such meetings can be difficult to arrange. Some other ideas that have worked are postcards—notes to parents about something wonderful their child did that day. Writing one of these a day allows 20 of your parents a month to actually get good news from the school. Another idea a teacher used was to videotape occasional classes (one or two a month) and put them on reserve in the public library. The library made available to parents a viewing room and videocassette recorder (VCR). Whatever we do we mustn't isolate ourselves. Sometimes it helps in all our efforts for our students to remember that the other people involved with our students do the best they can with what they have.

You can find allies if you see others striving toward excellence just as you are. Our resources often determine what and how well we do. You may also find it helpful to remember that your schedule is yours and everyone else has their own. If you want to work well with others you need to accept that you can't always set the pace.

Negotiating Roles

With the merging of regular and special education, the classroom is becoming an ever-expanding community. Many people are in and out throughout the day. There are parents and paraprofessionals or teacher associates. There are other students—younger ones and older ones—some acting as tutors and some coming in to be tutored. There are other teachers and other professionals. Coordinating all of these resources so that students' needs are met and the classroom is not disrupted is challenging.

The key to making this kind of situation work for all those involved lies in our working together, in clearly setting out who will do what, and when and where an intervention will take place. Let's look at an example: Johnny is a grade-9 student having some persistent difficulties with mathematics. A consultant is requested to work with him. At the same time, the teacher decides to involve the student in a mathematics buddies program linking grade-9 students with difficulties with more accomplished high school mathematicians. Unfortunately, because there is no discussion about when, where, or how these programs will take place, both the consultant and the buddy turn up to work with Johnny at the same time. This is easily fixed, but as time goes by Johnny does not do better in his mathematics. It seems that the consultant and the buddy are working at cross-purposes. Everyone is frustrated, particularly Johnny, when after two months he has made no progress. It is vital in situations like this that the teacher, the consultant, and the buddy sit down and talk through what exactly they think should be going on, where Johnny is in his efforts to learn to do mathematics, what steps need to be taken to get him on track, and who will be responsible to see that those steps are taken. If we are really honest, we will involve Johnny in this learning process, since learning to do math, in some ways, is largely in Johnny's hands. Involving the student is not always appropriate, but when it is, it can add a helpful dimension to discussions.

Negotiation skills play a large part in these kinds of discussions. Negotiation is simply a means of getting what you want, a kind of back-and-forth communication designed to reach an agreement when you and the other person or people have some common or shared interests and some interests that are not. Fisher and Ury (1981) advise that negotiations be undertaken in a way that allows you to get what you are entitled to and still be decent, to be fair, and still protecting yourself from being taken advantage of by others. (See Appendix 2B.)

Good negotiation is marked by three things:

1. It meets the legitimate interests of both sides as far as possible.
2. It resolves conflicting interests fairly.
3. The resolution is durable and community interests are taken into account.

Of course, no matter how skilful you are, there are limits to what you can achieve through this process.

A big key in most negotiation is to remember you are dealing with other people—people who have deeply held values, come from different backgrounds, and have emotions, hopes, and dreams just as you do. In negotiation, it is always worthwhile to ask yourself, "Have I paid enough attention to the other person?" If both parties see themselves as partners in a difficult search for a solution beneficial to all concerned, negotiation becomes easier.

Often the ongoing relationship with the other person is more important than the particular outcome, so it is a good idea to deal with people directly, not by making compromises or concessions. Behind opposing positions, behind the apparent conflicting interests, are often shared and compatible ones. Kauffman

(1993) suggests that significant agreements can often be found. Nearly all those involved with students (whether those with special needs or those without) want for these students effective instruction in academic and social skills, appropriate education in a supportive but least restrictive environment, parental participation in decision making, and collaboration among all those working with, or on behalf of, the student. These are but a few of the many shared interests possible.

In negotiating roles and responsibilities, there are some questions that it's wise to consider before you begin and/or strategies that may prevent you from grinding to a halt. One question it's important to be clear on is, "Of the interests you bring to the negotiation, which are the most important?" Knowing the answer to this question can help you stay focused or "grounded" in the negotiation.

Perhaps just as important as knowing what is central to you is having some idea of what a successful solution or agreement might look like. Then you can ask yourself what steps need to be taken to get there. You'll want to reshape your vision of an acceptable or workable agreement as you discuss and gather more information. It's also helpful to think about some realistic objectives. "What can we do given the present situation?" "How will we work together to make these things happen?" and "How will we know if our strategies are working?" become useful questions when we try to decide how to implement our solutions. It can also be helpful to generate a number of solutions. Of course, if we generate alternatives, we also need to think of some criteria for deciding among them or devise some "rule of thumb" to help us select one to try.

It's always a good idea to remain open to revisiting your ideas on roles and responsibilities. Listen closely to the person who carries through on a strategy. His or her suggestions are more likely to happen. An effective guideline is that if the person who will provide direct assistance to the student (the doer) makes a suggestion, try it first, as long as the student will not be placed at a disadvantage.

Negotiating roles and responsibilities is really about clarifying who does what under what conditions. In a time when the number of people involved in the classroom is growing on a daily basis, this kind of clarification helps create a classroom where students' needs can be met.

Planning

If we don't change our direction, we are
likely to end up where we are headed.
(Ancient Chinese proverb)

In any undertaking, planning is the key to successful change (Barker, 1992). The emphasis here is on the process rather than the product. It's important to plan, knowing that no matter how good the plan, the future holds surprises.

Planning really has two components: the decision making regarding the steps to be taken to bring about the desired change and the preparation needed to make these steps happen. (It is not unusual in discussions of planning for this last to be overlooked, but if we want the change to succeed it is as instrumental as the first.) To start, we need to define the change we are trying to make. The clearer we can set out what the change is and how things will look when it has taken place, the more likely we are to know if we are making progress. Having a time frame for the change can help us determine how things are going. We also need to decide how long we will or need to take.

Developing a rationale can also be helpful: what are your reasons for choosing this particular change at this point in time? If you honestly believe everything is fine as it is, change will be more difficult. Usually, it's not enough to think things will be better or that the change is for the good. It's important to identify specifically how the change will make things better for you and for the others affected by it.

Often if we try to make too big a change all at once, we get overwhelmed. It's definitely an advantage if the change we undertake is realistic, if it builds on what we are doing already, if it builds on our strengths. Setting a destination that is clear and reasonable is an important first step.

In defining or setting out where you are going, you are wise to involve those who might be affected by the attempted change (Eastwood & Louis, 1992). Students, parents, volunteers, other professionals, even your family, need to know what you are trying to do so that they can be supportive. They may even have ideas about how you could go about the change—ideas you may not have thought of and that may work.

Having set a goal, having involved those around you, it is important then to set out how you will reach this goal. A series of small steps will ensure success and keep frustration to a minimum. If your steps are too large, you will experience little success, and it's important to experience some success if we want to persist.

Reconsider your steps if you are not experiencing any success. See if you can make the steps smaller and more doable. Again, it's a good idea to involve those affected by the steps, reviewing whether or not each of the steps is working. It is also usually a good idea to tackle each of the steps sequentially. Setting out how long you think each step will take can be useful.

Take time to consider carefully the particular setting in which you find yourself and the people with whom you are working. Strategies or steps that may work in some situations and with some people won't always work. History, tradition, and experience play a large part in determining what will work and how long a change takes.

Having a goal and a set of steps to reach that goal strengthens our resolve and helps each of us mobilize our energies for change. Setting out the particular steps can help us see our underlying beliefs and priorities and can be a wonderful opportunity to get in touch with our wishes and dreams.

To truly accomplish all that we can, we must appreciate what constitutes real achievement. We must measure our progress against both our ideal outcome and our actual base line. Real change is always personal, organizational change always painstaking. Success depends both on our striving for the best and our realistic acceptance of the possible.

Dealing with Conflicts

There are no quick fixes.
(Common saying)

It is not possible to try to change things in your classroom, in your students, or even within yourself without running into conflict. Conflict, in itself, is not a bad thing, but if conflict occurs, it is important to try to negotiate a resolution. You may find it useful to share these skills with your students so that they can learn to better manage their own conflicts without needing to involve adults. (See Appendix 2B for a possible way to go about this.)

Most of us have strategies for dealing with conflict. Unfortunately, those strategies are not always constructive. To deal with conflict constructively means turning it into a "win–win" situation. The following four steps may help achieve this:

1. *Establish respect.* Prior to meeting consider outside influences that may affect attempts to resolve the conflict. Ask those involved:

   - "Is this a convenient time to talk?"
   - "Is this a place that is quiet and free of interruptions?"
   - "Has enough time been allotted to discuss the problem and reach a resolution?"

   At the meeting itself, take care in setting the tone. Begin by stating your positive intentions about the relationship and/or the current situation. For example:

   - "I want to resolve this problem."
   - "I want to understand how this problem arose."
   - "I want to hear your point of view."

   Hint: These negotiations will go better if they begin with everyone involved in a calm state.

2. *Pinpoint the issue.* Prior to meeting, some reflection on the following questions may prove useful:

   - What is it that specifically concerns me about the situation?
   - What are my real needs in the situation?
   - How do I view the other person? What are my assumptions and suspicions?
   - What exactly would make the situation better for me?

   At the meeting itself, try to separate the person from the problem—it is important to see yourself as working with, as being on the same side, as trying to attack and resolve the same issue.

   Try to focus on shared interests rather than hardlined positions. If solving the conflict is really important to us, we need to look beyond our initial position to honestly examine our own real interests and needs in the situation. It also helps to think about what the interests of the other person might be.

   Hint: We can find out what has given rise to conflict only by talking and listening to one another.

3. *Explore Alternatives.* Prior to and in the meeting itself, all alternatives for dealing with an issue should be examined.

   In both the work of Deboer (1986) and Fisher and Ury (1981), four common obstacles to generating and exploring alternatives have been identified:

   - Premature judgment or criticism
   - A search for the "one and only," "very best," "perfect" solution
   - The belief that resources are limited and so no new alternative is possible
   - The belief that the responsibility for resolving the issue lies with someone else

   Hint: Brainstorming may help override or prevent this obstacle from occurring. (See Appendix 2C.)

4. *Participate in shared decision making.* There must be a new agreement, those involved must reach a decision that establishes clear lines of responsibility.

   The people in conflict must decide how they will deal with one another from this point on.

   The final decision of what to do must have the active involvement and agreement of those most responsible for carrying through on the decision or it will fail.

The first step in carrying out this decision should be very clear because this is where most resolutions fall apart. The person responsible for the first step is often not sure how to get started. Taking some time on this in the resolution process can help things stay resolved.

An anecdote might be helpful here. Late on Friday afternoon toward the end of the school year, a mother turns up in a school hall looking for Mrs. J., her daughter's grade-11 social studies teacher. The mother probably has been thinking about what has been on her mind all week and only now has been able to bring herself to the school.

The teacher meets her in the hallway and they quickly get into a confrontation. The mother wants her daughter kept behind. The teacher doesn't understand and is quite mystified. She recognizes that the student is behind and experiencing some difficulties. She tries to explain to the parent that she understands that the parent wants the best for her daughter, but that retaining the young woman is not board policy. The parent, seeing the teacher does not understand and will not comply, asks for a meeting with the principal. The teacher agrees that might be best.

A meeting is arranged for the parents, the principal, the teacher, and the teacher associate working with the student. As they talk, it becomes clear that the parents, in particular the mother, see putting the daughter ahead as setting her up for failure. As parents, they care enough to be concerned. The principal says, "We know Sarah isn't able to do the work that is expected of a grade-12 student and what we want to do is work with her at her level." The parents noticeably relax. They ask the principal to repeat the commitment made to dealing with Sarah at her level. They do this to reassure themselves and to check that they have understood.

Only when the underlying concerns have been addressed correctly can positions be discarded, and only then can the team—the parents, principal, teacher, and teacher associate—begin to work out ways to best meet Sarah's needs.

A final comment on conflict. Raspberry (1992) suggests that it's important to distinguish between enemies and problems. Problems persist after enemies are vanquished, and diverting energy into battles with real or imagined enemies often prevents or delays solutions. So let's focus on the issues or problems to find solutions that work for our students, for our parents, for our colleagues, and for ourselves.

Getting Over the Humps

There is a caution I should bring to your attention. There will be rough times. There will be instances when you forget your resolve, when you are overwhelmed. The frequency and extent of these times vary with individuals, but they do happen. (When you are having one of these times, it's important not to get discouraged. Discouragement is one of the most damaging forces against managing change.)

You can also get frustrated when change is not happening fast enough for you. If you feel dissatisfied and think that you are not having the effects you want soon enough, have patience and confidence in yourself and your efforts. A better strategy is to start now to develop your own personal approach to dealing with such moments so that you have a plan of what to do when the need arises.

While this is not how any of us would like it, these humps, these occasions of discouragement, are an integral part of the change process. The new strategies that you are trying to put in place aren't as automatic as the old ones that you are trying to give up. An example may help here. A grade-10 teacher was trying to use cooperative groups. Initially, she paid a lot of attention to grouping the students and observing how they participated. In focusing on these elements, she found it difficult to also look at their grasp of the concepts she was teaching. She was like her students learning a new way to work. She found it hard to focus on the curriculum, the teaching/learning process, and her students all at once. As she became more comfortable with cooperative groups, more practised in using them, not only did she feel more comfortable, but she was again able to pay attention to the many elements necessary for an effective lesson.

When you begin to hear yourself saying, "In my class..." rather than "In my class, I am trying...," you will know you have survived your anxiety and frustration and overcome your moment of discouragement.

Keeping a Sense of Humour

When the first baby laughed for the first time,
the laugh broke into a thousand pieces and
they all went skipping about and that was the beginning
of fairies.
(James Barrie, *Peter Pan*)

Question: What do you get when you cross a monster
with a drip dry suit?
Answer: A wash and wear wolf.

A surprise! An unexpected, weird, funny change. Sometimes when these things happen and sometimes when we make them happen, we laugh.

Conventional wisdom has held that play, laughter, having fun, and especially humour have a positive effect on our daily lives. Most of us can recount numerous anecdotes where humour, aptly used, has helped to diffuse a potentially stressful situation, has helped to break the mould of conventional thinking in problem solving, has helped both psychological and physiological healing, and has helped the communication process.

Humour, laughter, play, and fun are powerful tools to use in any change effort. They convey caring and warmth, and generate feelings of confidence. They prevent burnout, increase productivity, and create hope for future possibilities. Robinson (1986, p. 132) says of humour that it's "the human being's built in mechanism for equilibrium and haemostats."

Humour is one way to stop us from taking ourselves and our situation too seriously. Yet in all the pressures and stresses of merging special and regular education, of doing our best for each of the students in our classrooms, it makes sense to remember to occasionally laugh and to laugh at ourselves. Without laughter there would be no bounce in our lives and, in some cases, no way to keep going.

Summary

> *Grown ups love figures. When you tell them you have made a new friend, they never ask you any questions about essential matters. They never say to you, What does his voice sound like? What games does he love best? Does he collect butterflies? Instead they demand: How old is he? How many brothers has he? How much does he weigh? How much money does his father make?*
> (Saint Exupéry, 1971, p. 16)

Like most grown-ups, discussions on how or even whether to merge regular and special education are well intentioned but misplaced. The wrong questions are asked and the focus is in the wrong place.

There is an old truism that one cannot change anyone but oneself. It follows, then, that efforts to change schooling, to make it inclusionary, to merge regular and special education, cannot start with the community, with the classroom, or even with the students, but must start with ourselves. The question we must each ask ourselves is, "How must I be so I can help each child feel she or he counts, so that every child feels included?"

Please remember: as teachers we often tell our students that progress typically comes through everyday activities or efforts, through small steps taken each day. These steps often seem mundane, inconsequential, but they are necessary for "long-term gain." These small steps need to include some attention to ensuring self-care, to developing political astuteness, to planning in a systematic way, to dealing with conflict, and to using humour when all else fails. Please understand that these steps are only a beginning, are not exhaustive, and so invite additions and adjustments.

We don't come to the merger of special and regular education without resources. Many of the strategies suggested here are those we use with our students. That's what, as teachers, we should capitalize on—using our best teaching strategies not only for our students but for ourselves.

Some Tips and Reminders

1. If what you desire in the way of change is not immediately forthcoming, take your time.
2. Do the best you can and don't stop trying or don't be afraid to make mistakes. Mistakes are human.
3. Remember to take one step at a time and to build in success.
4. Recognize and build on your strengths.
5. The initial stages of any significant change involve anxiety and uncertainty and/or taking a risk.
6. Support is crucial.
7. Change involves learning new skills through practice and feedback.
8. The most fundamental breakthrough occurs when you understand how the new way will make things better for you.

APPENDIX 2A

Stages of Concern: Typical Expressions of Concern about the Innovation

	Stages of Concern	Expressions of Concern
Impact	6 Refocusing	I have some ideas about something that would work even better.
	5 Collaboration	I am concerned about relating what I am doing with what other instructors are doing.
	4 Consequence	How is my use affecting learners?
Task	3 Management	I seem to be spending all my time in getting material ready.
Self	2 Personal	How will using it affect me?
	1 Informational	I would like to know more about it.
	0 Awareness	I am not concerned about it (the innovation).

Notes: These stages of concern are taken from the Concerns Based Adoption Model (C–BAM) project. Research and Development Centre for Teacher Education, University of Texas, Austin. According to this research, most of us approach a particular change with a concern about, "How will using it affect me?" or/"How will I have to adjust my practice?" (stage two). It is a while before we become concerned about, "How is my use affecting students?" (stage four).

Researchers in the project (Hord, 1989; Hord & Huling-Austin, 1988; Hall & Hord, 1987; Hall & Rutherford, 1976) suggest that to fully implement a significant change in our classrooms may take three to five years. So taking our time, moving slowly and steadily, and being patient with ourselves and with others become important skills if the merger of special and regular education is to be successful.

APPENDIX 2B

Teaching Your Students to Manage Conflict

Consider teaching your students to negotiate constructive resolutions to their problems. Students who know how to manage their own behaviour have a definite advantage over those who do not. If students are to learn how to resolve their own conflicts, they must have opportunities to practise conflict resolution, to resolve conflicts, and to follow through on these resolutions.

Johnson and Johnson (1987, 1991, 1992) suggest a useful six-step format:

1. State what you want: "I want my book back now."
2. State how you feel: "I'm frustrated. You had the book for two weeks. If I don't get the book back soon, I won't have enough time to study for the test on Friday. It's frustrating to have to wait."
3. Summarize your understanding of what the other person wants, how the other person feels, and the reasons underlying both.
4. Invent three optional plans to resolve the conflict.
5. Choose one plan and the first step in that plan carefully.
6. Shake hands and take that first step.

Students need to learn a conflict resolution procedure such as the one above, and become skilful in its use in relatively easy situations before they try to use it to resolve real conflicts. The procedure, along with listening and assertive skills, needs to be overlearned so that they are readily available when emotions run high and feelings of fear and anger are intense.

Students should learn to handle conflict one-on-one before learning to mediate someone else's conflict (Roy, 1993). It's easy for these procedures to sound simplistic, but to teach these strategies to students, we need to practise and master the techniques ourselves (Scherer, 1992).

Resources for teachers:

The Canadian Institute for Conflict Resolution, St. Paul University, 223 Main Street, Ottawa, ON, K1S 1C4, promotes and provides educational services in conflict resolution for communities and schools. This nonprofit organization has a newsletter for educators called *Common Ground.*

"From Peer Conflict Resolution through Creative Negotiation" is a program developed by Sandy Kalmakoff and Jeanne Shaw for Public Education for Peace Society, #208–1956 W. Broadway, Vancouver, BC, V6J 1Z2. Phone: 604-736-2918.

APPENDIX 2C

Ground Rules for Brainstorming

1. Rule out all criticism or evaluation of an idea . Ideas are suggested and placed before the group without evaluation or critical analysis.

2. Expect wild ideas when the group suspends judgment. Practical considerations are not important at this point. The session is to be free-wheeling.
3. The quantity of ideas counts, not quality. All ideas should be expressed, and not screened out by an individual. A great number of ideas will increase the likelihood of discovering good ones.
4. Build on the ideas of other group members when possible. Pool your creativity. Everyone should be free to build on to ideas and to make interesting combinations from the various suggestions.
5. Focus on a single problem or issue. Don't skip around on problems or try to brainstorm a complex multiple problem.
6. Promote a congenial, relaxed, cooperative atmosphere.
7. Make sure all members, no matter how shy and reluctant, contribute and get their ideas heard.
8. Record all ideas.

SUGGESTED RESOURCES

Becoming a Change Agent

Dedrick, C.V.L., & Raschke, D.B. (1990). *The special educator and job stress.* Washington, DC: National Education Association. This monograph examines stresses encountered by special educators, ways of coping with professional demands, and reasons why some teachers handle job stress better than others. Symptoms of burnout are reviewed. Ten stress management techniques are discussed.

Friend, M., & Cook, L. (1992). *Interactions: Collaborative skills for school professionals.* New York: Longman Publishing Group. This book is about collaboration. It can be used as a tool to learn skills that have immediate use, such as interpersonal problem solving, resolving conflict, and program planning.

Idol, L., Nevin, A., & Paolucci-Whitcomb, P. (1994). *Collaborative construction* (2nd edition). Austin, TX: Pro–Ed, Inc. This book is intended to stimulate and encourage collaboration among classroom, special education and remedial education teachers, other support staff, and administrators who are jointly responsible for students with special needs. This text provides a detailed six-step process for working together and is perhaps more useful for the more experienced reader or teacher in the field.

REFERENCES

Barker, J.A. (1992). *Future edge: Discovering new paradigms of success.* New York: William Morrow and Co.

Beckhard, R., & Harris, R.T. (1987). *Organizational transitions* (2nd edition). Reading, PA: Addison-Wesley.

Bolman, L.G., & Deal, T.E. (1991). *Reframing organizations: Artistry, choice and leadership.* San Francisco: Jossey-Bass.

Canfield, J. (1990). Improving Students' Self-Esteem. *Educational Leadership, 48*(1), 48–50.

Cantor, N. (1953). *The teaching-learning process.* New York: Holt, Rinehart and Winston.

Coloroso, B. (1994). *Kids are worth it!* Toronto: Somerville House Publishing.

Deboer, A.L. (1986). *The art of consulting.* Chicago: Arturus Books.

Eastwood, K.W., & Louis, K.S. (1992). Restructuring that lasts: Managing the performance dip. *Journal of School Leadership, 2,* 212–24.

Evans, R. (1993). The human face of reform. *Educational Leadership, 51*(1), 19–23.

Fisher, R., & Ury, W. (1981). *Getting to yes: Negotiating agreement with giving in.* New York: Penguin Books.

Fullan, M. (1985). Change processes and strategies at the local level. *The Elementary School Journal, 85*(3), 391–421.

Fullan, M. (1991). *The new meaning of educational change.* New York: Teachers College Press.

Gold, Y., & Roth, R.A. (1993). *Teachers managing stress and preventing burnout: The professional health solution.* London: Falmer Press.

Hall, G.E., & Loucks, S.F. (1978). Concerns of teachers about implementing team teaching. *Educational Leadership, 34*(3), 227–33.

Hall, G.E., & Hord, S. (1987). *Change in schools: Facilitating the process.* (SUNY Series in Educational Leadership). State University of New York-Albany: SUNY Press.

Hall, G.E., & Rutherford, W.L. (1976). Teacher concerns as a basis for facilitating and personalizing staff development. *Teachers College Record, 80*(1), 36–53.

Hartog, J., Audry, J., & Cohen, Y. (Eds.). (1980). *The anatomy of loneliness.* New York: International Universities Press.

Hord, S. (1986). "Recent results of research on school leadership: The principal and beyond." Presentation to the Faculty of Education, University of Calgary (March 14).

Hord, S. (1989). Facilitating change in secondary schools—Myths & management. *NASSP — Bulletin, 73*(516), 68–73.

Hord, S., & Huling-Austin, L. (1988). Curriculum implementation: How to know if it's there (or not there). *Journal of Rural and Small Schools, 1*(3), 23–26.

Johnson, D.W., & Johnson, R. (1987). *Creative controversy: Intellectual challenge in the classroom.* Edina, MN: Interaction Book Co.

Johnson, D.W., & Johnson, R. (1991). *Teaching students to be peacemakers.* Edina, MN: Interaction Book Co.

Johnson, D.W., & Johnson, R. (1992). Effects of mediation training on elementary school students. *Mediation Quarterly, 10*(1), F.

Joyce, B.E., & Showers, B. (1982). The coaching of teaching. *Educational Leadership, 40*, October, 4–10.

Kauffman, J.M. (1993). How we might achieve the radical reform of special education. *Exceptional Children, 60*(4), 6–16.

Kearns, J.R. et al. (1990). "The London project: The implementation of invitational strategies at the secondary school level." Paper presented at the Annual Meeting of the American Educational Research Association, Boston, MA (April 16–29).

Lewin, K. (1935). *A dynamic theory of personality.* New York: McGraw-Hill.

Lewin, K. (1948). *Resolving social conflicts.* New York: Harper.

Louis, K.S., & Milles, M.B. (1990). *Improving the urban high school: What works and why.* New York: Teachers College Press.

Marris, P. (1986). *Loss and change.* London: Routledge and Kegan Paul.

Morris, J. (1994). Pain by the gain. *Principal, 73*(3), 54.

Odell, S. (1990). "Mentor teacher program. What research says to the teacher." Document Eric ED 323185.

Opuni, A. (1989). "The teacher induction program." Document Eric ED 322104.

Postman, N., & Weingartner, C. (1987). *Teaching as a subversive activity.* New York: Dell Publishing.

Purkey, W.W. (1991). "What is invitational education and how does it work?" Paper presented at the Annual California State Conference on Self-Esteem (Santa Clara, CA, February 22–24).

Purkey, W.W., & Novak, J.M. (1984). *Inviting school success.* Belmont, CA: Wadsworth Publishing Co.

Purkey, W.W., & Schmidt, J.J. (1990). "Invitational learning for counselling and development." Ann Arbor, MI: University of Michigan ERIC Counselling and Personnel Services Clearing House.

Raspberry, W. (1992). Address at the Annual Invitational Team Case Competition. University of Virginia, Charlottesville (May 24).

Robinson, V.M. (1986). Humour is a serious business. *Dimensions of Critical Care Nursing, 5*(3), 132–33.

Rossman, G., Corbett, N.D., & Firestone, W. (1988). *Change and effectiveness in schools.* Albany, NY: State University of New York Press.

Roy, I. (1993). Violence is preventable: How some schools are educating students to be peacemakers. *Brock Education, 3*, 116–18.

Saint Exupéry, A. (1971). *The little prince.* New York: Harcourt, Brace and World, Inc.

Sarason, S.B. (1990). *The predictable failure of educational reform.* San Francisco: Jossey-Bass.

Scherer, M. (1992). Solving conflicts—Not just for children. *Educational Leadership, 50*(14), 15–18.

Sikes, P.J. (1984). "Teacher careers in the comprehensive school." In S. Ball (Ed.), *Comprehensive schooling: A reader.* London: Falmer Press.

Sikes, P.J. (1992). "Impose change and the experienced teacher." In M. Fullan & A. Hargreaves (Eds.), *Teacher development and educational change.* London: Falmer Press.

Troyna, B. (1985). The great divide: Politics and practices in multi-cultural education. *British Journal of Sociology of Education, 6*(2), 209–24.

Vann, A.S. (1989). A Principal's guide to the hiring and induction of new teachers. *Principal, 69*(1) 26–29.

CHAPTER 3

Collaboration and Consultation to Meet Diversity in Secondary Schools

Henry Janzen

University of Alberta

Introduction

Collaboration and consultation is a critical component in the delivery of a comprehensive, all-inclusive system of education. This chapter begins with an educational design for inclusive education, which includes four basic quadrants that illustrate intervention strategies that can be done *around, for, with* and *in behalf of* secondary students. The development and organization of one of the most effective teacher team models, namely, Teacher Assistance Teams (TAT), are then described, followed by a detailed eight-step TAT problem-solving collaborative process. Teachers will find the Collaborative Consulting Inquiry Form a most useful, practical device for implementing a collaborative intervention program for students with a range of disabilities, handicaps, and special needs. Furthermore, special comment is offered on how to work collaboratively with parents within the TAT model. The chapter ends with a real-life case study that illustrates the eight-step problem-solving process.

The Role of Collaboration and Consultation

The primary goal of this chapter is to describe the collaborative stages and practical steps secondary teachers can use to provide the best individual services to the learning, social, and psychological needs of their students.

The role of collaboration and consultation has been emphasized in recent writings and in the present text as a critical component in the delivery of an inclusive system for all secondary students (Lifter, 1993; Rotheram-Borus, 1993; Foley, 1994). Whereas **collaboration** involves the willingness of teachers, parents, students, and other school personnel to work together to produce the most appropriate learning environment for every student, **consultation** includes the consideration of asking for advice or guidance from specialists (e.g., school psychologists, counsellors, nurses, social workers, psychiatrists, etc.) to produce the most appropriate individual strategies for effective inclusive education (Paul & Simeonsson, 1993; Janzen, Paterson & Paterson, 1993). In most cases, collaboration and consultation are not distinguishable, since both processes involve problem-solving methods, with team leaders in either case. Collaboration, by definition, involves consultation.

The Canadian Context

The role of collaboration and, in many cases, consultation, has been used quite effectively in many secondary schools in Canada and elsewhere (Janzen et al., 1993). Within the collaborative framework, Teacher Assistance Teams (TAT) have been structured to accommodate a diversity of needs for Canadian students (Janzen et al., 1993; Erchul, 1993; Huebner, 1993). Inclusive education must also recognize the individual learning, social, and psychological needs of these secondary students with learning disorders, attention deficit problems, conduct and behaviour problems, sensory deficits, the mentally challenged, and the emotionally disengaged, to name a few. Erchul's (1993) work and the writings of Idol (1993), Masters, Mori & Mori (1993), and Foley (1994) have clearly shown that teamwork and the use of problem-solving methodologies, within the framework of Teacher Assistance Teams, are the most successful ingredients in implementing practical and innovative classroom strategies for secondary school students. In more practical terms, these collaborative teams began with the following model:

FIGURE 3.1
Inclusive Education in the Secondary Schools

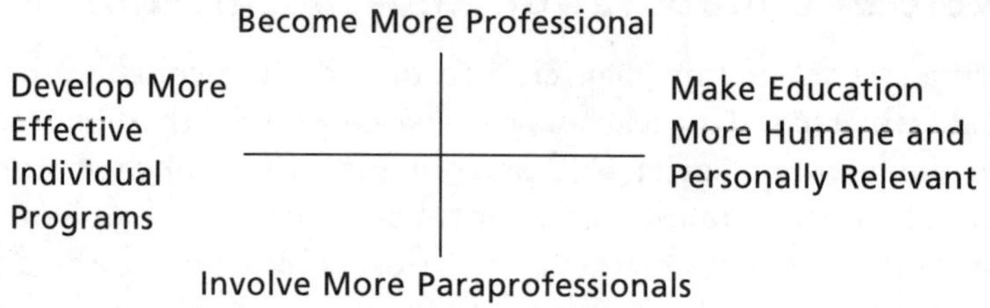

This general framework, with suggested strategies, can be applied to every student who comes to the attention of the Teacher Assistance Teams. Throughout the collaborative and consultation process, the four quadrants would be examined and discussed relevant to the presenting issues, and specific, individual program (IPP) and educational (IEP) plans drawn up.

Teacher Assistance Teams

The use of "teams" is especially relevant in an all-inclusive classroom. Teams are not new to education. In the past 30 years or so, schools have used collaborative teams (and consultation within the teams) as a pre-referral method for deciding what to do in the classroom (Aksamit & Rankin, 1993). Over the years, this process of team collaboration and consultation has been evaluated empirically and found reasonably successful (Idol, Paolucci-Whitcomb & Nevin, 1986; Friend, 1988; Pryzwansky, 1989; Erchul & Chewing, 1990; Hagborg, 1993). Today, it is no longer a pre-referral process, but an ongoing system of collaboration to help each student develop those cognitive, social, and emotional skills that are appropriate to their needs and age level, and that have been adapted to their unique learning style, relevant to the changing world in which they live.

Who is in the team? The composition of the team could likely change, but initially, the following members should be asked to serve on the TAT:

- *Teachers,* who have the most frequent contact and certainly the most important contacts with the students. Those teachers who have the referring student in their class serve on this team.
- *Administrators,* who must provide the necessary administrative support to the teachers and the team, so they can help the students.
- *Parents,* who know their child better than anyone else. Guardians or surrogate parents should be involved where the case arises.

- *Special education personnel,* who can be particularly helpful in deciding on specialized programs and teaching strategies.
- *Specialists,* whose expertise may be urgently needed to provide consultation on corrective/remedial services needed by the student. Most Canadian school teams currently utilize the services of school psychologists, psychiatrists, and social workers, but other specialists may be involved on the TAT as well.
- *Student peers,* who have a vested interest and special knowledge of their friends.

TABLE 3.1
Organizational Chart: Strategies for Helping Students

Strategies for Developing Academic/Intellectual Skills	Corrective/Remedial Interventions
Things that can be done **around** the student: • Program management • Grouping/placement • Structuring	Special things that can be done **for** the student: • Tutoring • Adding Stimulation • Reinforcement • Reducing Stimulation
Developing Humanistic Strategies	**Corrective/Therapeutic Interventions**
Things that can be done **with** the student: • Improving self-concept • Clarifying one's values • Expressing one's feelings • Improving communication skills • Relating with others • Adopting more mature roles • Making appropriate decisions	Special things that can be done **in behalf of** the student: • Working with small groups • Working with individuals

Team Functions

Some practical and very important questions remain: Who calls the team together? Who decides who should be on the team? How does the team actually work? According to the system employed in several Canadian secondary schools at present, the process, in broad terms, would follow a basic pattern as sketched out below:

- *The classroom teacher*, who has an issue or concern about a student, would approach another teacher, a counsellor, a special educator in the school, or an administrator with the presenting problem.
- *The team coordinator or designate* reviews the referral in sufficient detail to decide on additional team members. In most cases, the coordinator or designate would invite a student representative and the parents to the team. If the presenting issue is a behaviour or conduct problem, the school counsellor and/or school psychologist will also be invited.
- *The team coordinator or designate* calls the first meeting (at noon or after school) and a team member is assigned to observe the student. Team members also familiarize themselves with the issues and student's needs.
- *The team coordinator or designate* calls further meetings, following the problem-solving stage-by-stage method as outlined in this chapter, or as described in other chapters of this book.
- *The classroom teacher* who brought a concern to the team, with the possible assistance of an aide, a student peer, and other sources of support, begins to implement the recommended strategies.

At this point, the reader may very well wonder who has the time in a normal school day to do all this. Those school systems in Canada that have tried this collaborative TAT model have found that team meetings do add to their workload. Administrators who have implemented this system have spent many weeks before school started designing a teaching schedule with built-in collaboration and consultation times. Without an appropriate timetable, it truly is difficult for the teams to get together. Nevertheless, for the all-inclusive concept to work and be effective, such basic issues will need to be addressed. The good news is that when Teacher Assistance Teams design appropriate interventions, the teachers' stress levels are reduced and the daily classroom work is made more enjoyable. We are now beginning to appreciate the tremendous power of this approach both in preventing problems and failures and, if properly implemented, in correcting identified learning, social, behavioural, and emotional problems.

Skills Required in the TAT Collaboration Process

If collaboration and consultation among professionals in the schools is to be effective, there will be a need to consider school system changes such as a) decentralization of the organization and governance of schools, b) empowerment of those closest to students in the classroom (e.g., teachers, parents, principals), c) creation of new roles and responsibilities for educators and parents, and d) transformation of the teaching learning process (Huebner, 1993). In addition to these major systemic changes, the professionals involved in the collaboration process will need to have certain competencies in order to reach effective conclusions and implement educational changes. First and foremost, the collaborators will require a **knowledge base**, including understanding of the characteristics of learning and behaviour disorders; evaluation techniques; knowledge of learning styles; models of consultation cross-cultural information; and techniques for individualizing interaction. Second, the collaborators will require **basic skills**, including active listening; developing collaborative relationships; designing in-service training; conducting case conferences; goal setting; conflict resolution and dealing with resistance; problem-solving techniques; ability to identify special-needs students; ability to assist with mainstreaming; and mobilizing resources to assist in providing appropriate educational programs. And finally, the collaborators will require **judgmental competencies** including ability to select appropriate collaboration models given contextual variables; identify needed linkages among individuals, subsystems and systems that link collaboration to resources; develop an awareness of personal systems and vary style based on characteristics of teachers; adapt to cross-cultural concerns; use data from a variety of sources; design and conduct classroom observations to assess teacher and student problems; and deliver in-service training to facilitate the TAT model.

TAT Problem-Solving Steps

The use of collaboration is central to the Teacher Assistance Teams concept (Maher, Illback & Zins, 1983; Reynolds & Gutkin, 1982). No one professional has all the answers. Yet, bringing professionals together in a problem-solving format will add strength to the educational process.

There are numerous approaches, or models, of collaboration/consultation. Four of the most common models identified in the professional literature include: a) mental health consultation (Meyers, Parsons & Martin, 1979), b) organizational development consultation (Maher, Illback & Zins, 1984), c) problem-centred consultation, and d) behavioural consultation (Brown, Pryzwansky &

Schulte, 1991). All these models treat collaboration as an indirect means of providing service to the student. Problem-solving collaboration is defined by the following sequence of steps:

- Step 1: Define and clarify the problem in concrete behavioural terms.
- Step 2: Analyze the ecological forces impinging on the problem.
- Step 3: Brainstorm alternative strategies.
- Step 4: Evaluate and choose among the alternatives.
- Step 5: Specify responsibilities to members of the Teacher Assistance Teams.
- Step 6: Implement the chosen strategies.
- Step 7: Evaluate the effectiveness of the strategies.
- Step 8: Make changes and try again if there is minimal effect.

The TAT Eight-Step Collaborative Process

Step 1: Clarifying the Referral Issues

By far, the most important step is to arrive at a consensus as to the concrete nature of the problem. It is helpful to ask the teacher questions, so as to avoid vague problem statements. It is at this point that assessment data (both normative and curriculum based) as well as an ecological analysis may be made. It would be beneficial to have a special educator, counsellor, or school psychologist involved in the TAT to explain assessment data. If that is not possible, answering the following questions at Step 1 should help.

As a team member, ask the referring teacher and yourself the following questions:

1. Do I understand the implications of the student's previous record and ratings on standardized tests? Did I forecast failure or low grades from information that I was given by the student's previous records?
2. Knowing this student's capabilities, have I adjusted my teaching accordingly and given the student sufficient time to respond?
3. Have I tried a variety of teaching methods to help capture the student's strengths? Have I capitalized on the student's strengths?
4. Did I become acquainted with the student's attitudes or handicaps or were my efforts to establish good rapport absent?

5. Does the student have any serious physical or sensory impairments? Is the student's vision and hearing impaired? Is this child learning disordered? Has a specialist in learning been consulted?

6. What have I used to motivate this student? Have I ever threatened the student with failure? What have we done that proved successful?

One reason why collaboration team efforts fail is the tendency to describe too many problems at once. It is the team coordinator's responsibility to orient the discussion toward a problem definition for the most important component and then describe it in practical, concrete, behavioural terms.

Step 2: Analyzing the Ecological Factors

Vital to identifying the problem is following with a thorough team discussion on the ecological forces impinging on not only the presenting problem but also the selection of intervention strategies. This process, at Step 2, is itself a model of problem solving known as Ecological Evaluation (Knoff, 1986). An example of the basics in ecological terms follows. Study Figure 3.2 to become familiar with the terms used in ecological analysis and the factors that need to be raised in the team meetings. All systems, from micro to macro, are vital to understanding why high school students behave the way they do.

The importance of social and ecological context cannot be understated. Ecological analysis is vital to the team's discussion, because it presents the larger environmental picture impacting on the presenting concern(s). While the classroom teacher, who brings an issue for problem solving to the team, sees what is actually happening in the school environment, the cause may be found in another "system" (see Figure 3.2). In the two classic studies on ecological analysis, Devereux (1977) and Gump and Adelberg (1978) suggest that the following questions be discussed by the TAT:

- What is the student's involvement in the microsystem? Who are the student's friends? What is the structure of the immediate family?
- What factors in the size of the school or neighbourhood impact on the presenting problem? Does the school provide adequate opportunities for activities outside the academic context? Are leadership opportunities available?
- At the meso- and exosystems, does the community have an adequate number of settings for positive student participation? How can the church help? Will community clubs provide financial assistance?

The development of personality, values, and behaviours are functionally related to the ecological systems to which students are exposed. Ecological issues such as crowding, isolation, ethnicity, linguistic pluralism, community values, and so forth, may lead to classroom/school behaviours such as talkativeness, silence, aversion of eye contact, low self-esteem, aggressiveness, and use of drugs and alcohol, which, in turn, may lead to poor academic performance. At Step 2, therefore, the Teacher Assistance Teams may already have suggestions for interventions. Here are a few practical ideas the team can discuss:

- *For Improving Self-Concept:* classroom team-building exercises; role playing I'm OK, You're OK; use of the Magic Circle in several core classes.
- *For Making Appropriate Decisions:* tutoring or improving study skills; enrolment in a community activities program.
- *For Improving Relationship and Communication Skills:* use of class meetings; implementation of a Student Effectiveness Training Program.

FIGURE 3.2
The Systems Involved in Student Assessment and Subsequent Consultation

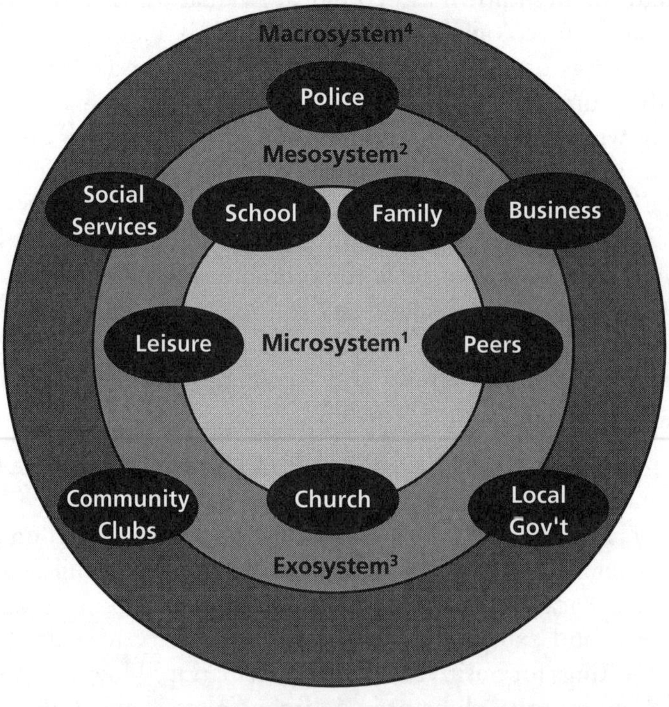

1 Microsystems: Most immediate to the student (e.g., family, peers, school, church, camp, etc.).
2 Mesosystem: Interrelationship and links to the microsystem.
3 Exosystem: Situations in which the student is not directly involved but have a bearing on individual development.
4 Macrosystem: Broad ideological and institutional patterns of a culture or subculture.

High school students in an all-inclusive classroom are a group of individuals with diverse backgrounds, abilities, and personalities. The Teacher Assistance Team needs to keep in mind that different people react differently to the same environment, and the same environment may interact differently with the same person at different times.

Ecological analysis has the distinct advantage to the team collaborative process in bringing about an awareness of the complex interrelationships of all the systems involved and how they impact the student in the classroom. The team's basic task is to describe and determine the proportion of a student's whole life span spent in settings with specific characteristics—settings such as those listed in Figure 3.2. The total system, or "habitat" is more than an additive sum of its parts. Rather, its totality becomes a "meaningful whole," greater in effect than an individual part. For example, the psychological effects on a student who comes from a "permissive" family setting, in consort with an "authoritarian" school setting, will be quite different than if a student comes from an "authoritarian" family setting and goes to a "permissive" school.

In addition to listing and defining the impact of subsystems for an individual student, ecological approaches encourage the collaborative team to examine the relationships of student to teacher, student to student, student to environment, and teacher to the community. Teacher and classroom variables such as the approaches to student feedback, the amount and nature of reinforcement, the subject matter, the teaching techniques, and teacher expectations are all examined in an ecological analysis. Even classroom structure, such as the arrangement of desks, the temperature of the room, and the value of the tasks assigned to be learned, comes under ecological scrutiny. Often, by changing one small part of a subsystem, one can change the behaviour of the student to the whole system.

It is important to keep in mind that it is impossible to assess every factor. Nevertheless, when the basic subsystems are defined and discussed at a team meeting, the impact will be practical.

The concern at Steps 1 and 2 is the assessment of social and environmental systems that interact with individual students, affecting their total life space. Ecological approaches give recognition to the powerful forces working behind the "behavioural scene" in motivated ways. After all, the first law of ecology is that "you can never do only one thing." Intervention must involve more than one subsystem because behaviours, attitudes, values, and expectations are driven by forces within and between systems, especially for students with diverse backgrounds and in their teen years.

Preceding Steps 3 to 6

To assist the process from Steps 3 to Step 6, the completion of the Collaborative Consulting Inquiry Form by all team members may be helpful. If the form, as shown on the following pages, is completed as thoroughly as possible, it will facilitate choice of intervention strategies. In order to complete it, the team may need to involve other school specialists (e.g., school psychologist, counsellor, speech therapist, social worker, school nurse, principal, etc.).

Use of the Collaborative Consulting Inquiry Form should ensure attention to details essential to determining what instructional strategies capitalize on the learning style of the referred student, what has been tried and found wanting, and what has worked in the past. Special attention should be given to instructional features, curriculum suitability, aptitude and achievement patterns, and cognitive assessment data. If a thorough psychological assessment has not been done, the team could refer to the school psychologist for assessment and then reconvene.

Step 3: Brainstorm Alternative Strategies

At Step 3, a number of alternative strategies are placed on the table for discussion, in addition to those already suggested at Step 2 of the problem-solving collaborative model.

For example, let us assume the presenting problem is one of academic failure in core school subjects, with resulting low self-esteem, lack of community involvement, and increased aggressiveness within the classroom and in the community. The psycho-educational assessment suggests above-average cognitive abilities, with auditory short-term attention problems (impulsive, not paying attention, forgets instructions, does poorly on tests).

Alternative strategies might include:

- Peer pairing in the core subjects
- Use of a teacher aide for assistance on seat work
- Parents agree to assist with the homework
- Teacher may use unlimited time to write major tests (to be supervised by the librarian)
- Parents may agree to reward the student for modest grade gains and increase praise
- Teachers call upon the student to repeat instructions at random intervals
- Use of peers to assist with homework assignments
- Teachers use stimulus variation techniques in their lessons to increase attention
- Possible referral for counselling to build self-esteem and reduce aggressiveness
- Teachers may choose to use contingency contracting in the core subjects

FORM 3.1

Collaborative Consulting Inquiry Form

Student: ____________________

School: ____________________

Date of Session: ____________________

Grade: ____________________

Age: ____________________

Present at Conference:

SECTION I—Reason for Referral

1. Discuss why student was referred and by whom.

SECTION II—Problem Identification and Expectations of Student

A. SCHOOL

1. Discuss the current situation. List the concerns specific to the referral question(s).
2. Discuss and list what the parents want the child to do that he or she presently does not do.
3. If the concerns are primarily behavioural, social/emotional/peer-related, etc., obtain an estimate of the frequency, duration, and severity of this behaviour.

B. PARENT(S)

1. Discuss and list the school's perception of the problem (in behavioural/objective terms).

2. Discuss and list what the school wants the student to do that he or she presently does not do.
3. If the concerns are primarily behavioural, social/emotional/peer related, etc., obtain an estimate of the frequency, duration, and severity of this behaviour.

SECTION III—Learning, Behavioural, and Instructional Analysis

---

Environmental/Background Influences

A. HOME

1. Describe and ascertain general family characteristic/medical, behavioural/learning.
2. Discuss behavioural concerns that may be occurring at home.
3. Is there a pattern to the behaviour? What precedes the outbursts or misbehaviours? What action or reaction follows the outburst or misbehaviours?
4. Include pertinent background information related to the problem.
5. Include previous history of schools, success, experiences.
6. List interest areas, extra-curricular activities.

B. SCHOOL

1. Describe the present educational setting, e.g., the make-up of class, size of class, number of concerns/discipline, resources, stress level, teacher directedness/expectations, productivity/homework, social/emotional/peer related, conduct disorder (aggressive, lying/stealing, tantrums, etc.).
2. Is there a pattern to this behaviour? What precedes the outbursts or misbehaviours? What are the child's goals of this behaviour?
3. Are there any observable similarities between home and school behaviours?

Instructional Features

1. Describe the student's ability to benefit from existing instructional processes and curriculum.
2. Comment on the following questions:
    a. Is the student challenged or frustrated?
    b. Time on task as related to time needed? Are assignments/homework completed?
    c. Seat work vs. lecturing. Does student function differently in either situation? Does the student's behaviour affect the instruction?
    d. Organization and study skills.

Curriculum

1. Describe and comment on the following questions:
   a. Curriculum structure, i.e., Are you on target as to where you want to be in math, reading, etc.? What have you done in your curriculum to accommodate the student?
   b. Is curriculum linked to student's needs in the present environment? How is the curriculum monitored (curriculum-based assessments, teacher-made tests)?

Student Attributes (Aptitude/Achievement/Behaviour)

A. COGNITIVE ABILITIES

1. List and discuss any tests administered to the student:
   a. Aptitude: individual/group ability (include psychomotor/visual/auditory) How does student learn best?
   b. Achievement tests: individual/group (reading, written expressive work, math)
   c. Speech and language tests (include informal observations)

B. BEHAVIOURAL CONCERNS

1. Utilize teacher observations and/or child behaviour checklists to obtain estimates of the following:
   a. Frequency
   b. Severity
   c. Duration

C. AFFECTED DOMAIN

1. Self-esteem
2. Intensity and mood changes
3. Distractability
4. Motivation/task persistence
5. Adaptability/flexibility
6. Attention/memory
7. Peer relationships (extent of positive peer group relationships)
8. Locus of control (Does student feel he or she is in control of educational outcomes?)
9. Evidence of lack of effective problem-solving skills. (Note that lack of cognitive processes abilities can underline social behaviour.)

SECTION IV—Group Verification of Problem

Summary (Assessment of educational/behavioural needs):

1. Summarize the data presented.
2. Obtain group consensus of problem.

3. Determine if problem (learning/behaviour) is considered severe according to current definitions.
4. Determine if the expectations are appropriate.

SECTION V—Problem Resolution to Date

---

1. Summarize what has been done to resolve the problem.
2. How difficult is the problem to resolve?
3. Describe what resources, special programs, materials, interventions, and strategies have been utilized in the past to remediate problems.

SECTION VI—Recommendation/Plan Implementation

---

1. Determine if an individual educational plan (IEP) or an individual behaviour plan (IBP) is required.
2. Brainstorm alternatives.
3. Select the most practical solutions and develop the ideas using the following outline:
   a. Identification of educational/behavioural goals and objectives
   b. Identification and selection of resources
   c. Development of educational/behavioural plan
   d. Implementation of educational/behavioural program (limiting factors)
   e. Evaluation of plan/program
   f. Clarification of responsibility and follow-up

Source: Adapted from T. Tomko and E. Spadafora, Learning Disabilities Program Planning Form. Edmonton Catholic Schools (unpublished document; used with author permission, 1993).

At Step 3, all ideas are welcomed. None are rejected. The above 10 ideas are examples of practical and sometimes effective strategies. Nevertheless, implementation and individualization is more difficult. Availability of a long list of possible strategies will make the task of implementation easier, since only those ideas that are "workable" likely will be selected.

If individualizing instruction was difficult at the elementary school level, it is even more so at the secondary level. Gaps between achievement and potential are wider, and the adolescent development in body, emotions, and social environment produce even greater variability in individual characteristics and program requirements. Thus, the more information the team has on cognitive strength, preferred learning style, organization and study skills, curriculum suitability, etc., the greater the range of "alternative strategies" can be brainstormed at Step 3. All ideas should be noted and discussed.

Step 4: Evaluate and Choose Strategies

The TAT, having brainstormed alternative strategies, now needs to choose from the list. Within the inclusive classroom concept, however, the chosen strategies are usually those that can be implemented within the classrooms. However, since peers, parents, and specialists are part of the team, the TAT should not hesitate to involve them, or indeed other community members. The basic task at this step in the problem-solving process is to *evaluate* all the suggestions that best meet the presenting problem and which suggestions could be implemented at a later stage.

A most useful and practical way to evaluate alternative intervention strategies is to examine the organizational chart (Table 3.1) in this chapter and the ideas generated by the team in filling out the Collaborative Consulting Inquiry Form. Depending on the targeted problem areas, the team can list those ideas that can be done *for, with, around* and *in behalf of* the student, perhaps using some of the strategies listed in Table 3.1. Special attention to parts A to D of Section III of the inquiry form should generate more ideas. As a general rule, intervention strategies should be selected that: a) the classroom teacher understands and can implement in the lesson plan, b) focus specifically on the behaviour to be modified, and c) have maximum possibility of generalizability. Chosen strategies should be coordinated between team members who can apply them in two or more subject areas. Nonteaching team members (e.g., peers, parents, principals, counsellors) could also be asked to "back up," monitor, or reinforce the positive effects of the chosen interventions.

Step 5: Specify Appropriate Responsibilities

Step 5 is a logical outcome of Step 4. Once the alternatives have been decided, it will become clear who has responsibility for the interventions. In the TAT format, interventions are usually multimethod. This means that the teacher who presented the concern has the "backup" of student peers, parents, aides, and other people resources. The TAT coordinator, however, has the role of checking with every person involved in the intervention plan.

Everyone on the TAT should be absolutely clear as to their responsibilities. A sample of TAT individual responsibility could be as follows:

- *The homeroom teacher* agrees to modify assignments and the taking of tests in the core subject. The use of verbal praise for on-task behaviour is increased to the rate of one praise every five minutes, or as the on-task behaviour occurs.
- *The principal* agrees to allow the student to write the tests in the library and give unlimited time for testing.
- *The student peer* agrees to assist the targeted student by sitting next to him or her, help the student with assignments, and keep the student on task.
- *Other classroom teachers* agree to modify assignments in the student's subjects and reinforce on-task behaviour.
- *The counsellor* is asked to come to the classroom to observe, record, and have positive informal talks with the student. The recordings will be used at later meetings to evaluate the interventions.

Step 6: Implementing the Chosen Strategies

The value of the collaborative TAT approach to problem solving in the inclusive secondary school classroom is that considerable expertise is represented on the team. Each team member should or could be assigned a specific part of the intervention plan. The decision now to be made is when to begin. Every TAT member should be clear on what they are to do.

By now the reader should recognize the value of Teacher Assistance Teams in the all-inclusive classroom. Teachers with years of experience, and student teachers alike, recognize their limitations in meeting the diverse and unique needs of the secondary student. With the TAT problem-solving collaborative model, however, multiple resources are utilized for effective intervention. Implementation will be more effective if the "intervention plan" is typed and distributed to every TAT member. A specific day for start-up of the plan should be made, and a minimum of *three to four weeks of implementation* allowed before evaluation takes place.

Completing Steps 7 and 8

In the often hurried and harried world of school-based personnel, it is not unusual for some unexpected events to temporarily distract the team's attention from the intervention plan agreed upon at the collaborative team meeting. There is, then, a clear need for additional consultative contacts throughout the intervention process to prevent derailing a potentially effective intervention plan.

Evaluation of the intervention plan can be a complex and time-consuming process, but it is an essential activity. The counsellor, who was asked to observe and record, can present simple charts of the targeted behaviour changes. Next, the teachers on the team should present any increases or decreases in academic performance on tests and quizzes. The peer member can report on how the assignment compilation process is functioning, and the parents can give their impressions of any changes in behaviour, attitude, and study skills in the home environment.

Those strategies that have been found helpful should be continued, others may be abandoned and new strategies suggested. New problem areas can be targeted for intervention and ideas brainstormed one more time. The same plan can now be started for a second or third student in the classroom. If the plan has shown improvement only in the school environment, the TAT can bring other community members to the meeting and ask for their assistance.

Involving Parents in the Collaborative Process

Parents often feel alone when they discover that their child has problems that cripple school progress, frustrate teachers, and damage their child's self-esteem. Bringing parents into the team meeting as collaborators is essential (Hagborg, 1993; Leblanc & Reynolds, 1989). Parents' involvement in the collaboration process is important because they have a primary role in caretaking and are a valuable source for ecological data. Hagborg (1993) has shown that parents exhibit an excellent understanding of the major components of their child's educational and social assessment as presented at the TAT meetings. Whether parents are brought in as team members, or called in for a consultation session with the teacher, the following practical hints should contribute to effective parent collaboration (Christenson & Conoley, 1992).

TABLE 3.2
Reasons for Parent Consults

1. *To explain* to them all data in their child's file.
2. *To gather data* from them regarding any family-related issues that impact the child's social, emotional, and educational opportunities.
3. *To discuss with parents* what goals they have for the child and what they expect of the school or you. Here you need active **listening skills**.
4. *To make them feel accepted,* and welcome, in the school. Here you need **reinforcement-building** skills.
5. *To provide consultation* (not counselling) to them on any questions they might have (e.g., child rearing, behaviour modification, relationship, parenting, discipline, communication skills, stress management, etc.).
6. *To listen* to the parents' concerns, issues, hopes, and dreams. Here you need **empathy** skills as a way to build **congruency**. (Keep Carl Rogers in mind!)
7. *To mediate* between parents and school on any problem or issue that they're concerned about. Here you need **advocacy** and **mediation** skills.

TABLE 3.3
Suggestions on How to Make Parent Collaboration Work

1. Work on your diplomacy skills.
2. Know how to explain specialized data in a practical, yet intellectually honest, way.
3. Place an invitation in the school newsletter of your willingness to meet, or write the parents yourself.
4. Hold an evening meeting where you talk to the parents about the services you provide and the model of service.
5. Be willing to arrange meetings at their convenience.
6. Let other teachers and administrators know that you want the parents involved and are willing to meet with them.

7. Use the telephone for debriefing or just chatting. It lets parents know you care.
8. Build up a file of handouts for distribution.
9. Prepare at least two or three workshop topics for you to give to parents at evening meetings.

Parent involvement is a key component of the TAT model. Working with parents can be quite enjoyable, yet difficult for some of us; hence, its special focus in this chapter. Parents want and need to be fully aware of any strategic changes imparting their child. With the help of the parents, the collaboration process is much more effective.

CASE STUDY

The case study of A.P. (not his real name) will illustrate, in practical terms, the process of collaboration, consultation, and program intervention for a senior high school student, age 16–18, grade 10.

Step 1: Defining the Problem in Concrete Terms

A.P. was referred by the high school principal for an in-depth psycho-educational assessment.

The school psychologist, in this case the designated coordinator, arranged for a meeting with the following individuals: school principal, three regular classroom teachers, high school learning assistance teacher, school counsellor, and vice-principal. The school psychologist requested that all files pertaining to A.P.'s case be brought to the meeting, including the cumulative school file, counselling file, and any previous teacher reports.

The first meeting, which lasted two hours, was organized and chaired by the school psychologist. However, in the collaborative model, it was explained that all team members had equal voice, vote, and expertise. At subsequent meetings, any team member could take the role of chair. It was the objective of this meeting to define, in concrete behavioural terms, the nature of the problem. Upon examination of all the available data and observations of all team members, it was agreed that the following statements clearly defined the nature of A.P.'s learning, behavioural, and social difficulties.

1. A.P. was unable to cope with the grade-10 curriculum, specifically in English 10, Mathematics 10, Social Studies 10 and Science 10. The primary problem was one of delayed reading and comprehension skills, which affected his program in the subjects noted above.
2. A.P. was often truant. The issue was raised as to how the school could improve his attendance record.
3. A.P. was seen as having a short attention span, unable to sit still,

impulsive in his behaviours and frequently getting into fights with other students. Some teachers were afraid of him.

4. Teachers reported that A.P. made disparaging comments about himself (e.g., "I'm stupid." "I'm slow."), which suggested low academic and social self-esteem.

The specific behavioural and academic problems identified were: a) difficulty in passing grade-10 basic subjects, b) not attending classes regularly, c) lowered self-esteem, and d) difficulties in peer relationships.

Step 2: Analyzing Ecological Forces Impacting on A.P.

A second team meeting was called within a week, but this time A.P.'s mother, the home-care social worker, and the assistant superintendent were invited to attend. This meeting brought significant new information to the case that eventually changed the subsequent intervention approaches. At Step 1, the team had learned that A.P. was of average intellectual ability, had a two-grade level deficit in reading, comprehension, and spelling skills, and was diagnosed with attention-deficit hyperactivity disorder by previous assessments, both psychiatric and psychological. It was likely that A.P. was learning disabled as well, but this was not clear.

At the time of this meeting, A.P.'s father was in jail and the mother was recovering from a drug addiction. Social Services had called in a home-care worker to help the mother in home-care duties for A.P., his sister, and herself. A.P. was currently on probation for charges of theft and property damage. These latter activities occurred in a gang activity in this small rural community.

Ecological factors pertinent to this case included the fact that this small rural high school (350 students) had few specialized resources available (at school or in the community), although the town was but a one-hour drive from a large urban city (population one million). Resources were available, if needed. In this small town everybody knew one another, but this family felt ostracized. They had few, if any, friends. The high school students also "stuck together," so that A.P.'s gang was clearly labelled and isolated. The mother was a full-time homemaker, but she had her own problems to solve. Little assistance on school-related interventions, therefore, would be possible in the home. It was the team's decision that any interventions would need to be done at the school, and/or referred to the large urban city for treatment. The assistant superintendent agreed to use school budget funds to assist A.P. Finally, it was decided that an updated psychiatric evaluation would be requested. The mother agreed to take A.P. to a nearby city hospital for this assessment.

Step 3: Brainstorming Alternatives

A third meeting, with two regular classroom teachers, learning assistance teacher, counsellor, and school psychologist was held to brainstorm for educational, psychological, and social/environmental interventions.

This meeting was held after the psychiatric report was forwarded to the school. This report confirmed the diagnosis of ADHD, plus added "Conduct Disorder." The psychiatrist suggested medical (drug) intervention and therapy by a psychologist.

The brainstorming session on intervention alternatives, in brief, included: a) attendance in the high school learning assistance class for remediation in reading, comprehension, written work, and spelling, b) collaboration between teachers in modifying assignments in the regular classroom subjects, c) referral to the school counsellor for self-esteem and social skills training, d) referral to a psychiatrist for medical interventions, e) agreement from the vice-principal to help A.P. finish his homework at school, f) development of a behaviour modification program in all of A.P.'s classes, g) development of an individualized educational plan by the school-based team, h) individualizing all tests to be supervised by the school librarian, i) offering consultation sessions to the mother, at home or in school, by the school psychologist, j) placing A.P. in a residential school in the nearby city

Step 4: Evaluating and Choosing Among the Alternatives

All the suggestions seemed to make sense to the team. However, the suggestion of placement in a residential school was checked out first by the school psychologist. Unfortunately or not, this was not going to be possible. The team members, comprised of the same members as in Step 3, decided upon the following after lengthy discussion and evaluation:

1. A.P. would attend the L.A. class during the regular high school French and health classes. Specific curriculum interventions were to be determined by the L.A. teacher and shared with the regular class teacher, within two weeks.
2. A.P. would be referred to the high school counsellor for self-esteem and social skills building, but the homeroom teacher was asked to step up the rate of verbal reinforcers following any successful completion of tasks.
3. A.P. would be referred to a psychiatrist for medical interventions.
4. The mother would be asked to attend sessions with the school consulting psychologist in order to effect a behaviour management program at home.
5. The regular class teachers would modify the curriculum in English, mathematics, social studies, and science.
6. All tests and quizzes would be taken by A.P. in the library, with the proviso that the librarian could assist A.P. in reading questions to him and giving him unlimited time to answer the questions.

Step 5: Specifying Responsibilities to Team Members

As noted in Step 4, all team members agreed to accept their responsibilities. It was decided to meet within a week to discuss the details of plan implementation (Step 6).

Step 6: Implementing the Chosen Strategies

Implementation was discussed at this meeting. The individual educational plan (IEP) prepared by the English teacher was ready and distributed to all team members before the meeting. Other regular class teachers prepared a "modification plan." While all team members knew what they were to do, the key factor at this meeting was to somehow explain all these strategies to A.P. The school counsellor, who had developed a good relationship with A.P., agreed to present this plan to him.

Steps 7 and 8: Evaluating the Effectiveness of the Strategies: Making Changes

Before the team met again for the sixth time, the school counsellor telephoned the members to report that A.P. had agreed to all the chosen strategies. If this had not been the case, another meeting would be called to make changes to the plan. The team agreed to meet within 12 weeks to evaluate the effectiveness of the interventions.

The team members reported good news and bad. The good news was that A.P. had improved his failing grades by 15%. The bad news was that A.P. was, according to the psychiatrist, a resistant client not complying with taking his medication. Since A.P. was improving in his classroom performance, less truant, and faithful in his visits to the school counsellor, it was decided not to try to get A.P. to take the medication insofar as this would have been possible by the school team.

While the school-based interventions seemed to produce positive results, A.P.'s community behaviours did not improve. In the next year, A.P., was found guilty of another theft charge. The court sent him to a residential treatment centre, a lockup unit where he would serve his two-year sentence, attend school, and receive the necessary psychological treatment.

Conclusions

Admittedly, this was a rather "serious" case, a difficult situation requiring involvement from all members of the large school community as well as the community agencies.

It would require an entire textbook or more to outline all the details, factors, questions asked, and specific plans in order to fully prepare the reader for collaborative problem solving. The information presented in this chapter, however, will give the reader the basic processes necessary. This case study does show that A.P. could be accommodated in the inclusive classroom, although specialist resources were clearly required. This case also illustrates the limitations and range of successes and failures teachers can expect.

Summary

The implementation of a Teacher Assistance Team concept within a problem-solving collaboration framework has been found particularly effective in the all-inclusive secondary classroom, since no one teacher has the time or all the needed skills for the myriad issues faced from day to day. Within the TAT design, and assisted by an eight-step problem-solving process, secondary students experiencing academic, behaviour, social, and other problems can achieve reasonable success. The message, either explicit or implicit, in this chapter is that the emergence of consultation and collaboration as a process for facilitating the delivery of appropriate all-inclusive education for secondary students grew out of a need for improved communication between parents and professionals. The benefits of the processes described are increased interaction and problem solving, greater ownership and commitment to all students, and increased knowledge of the role of interdisciplinary personnel in the delivery of education. Collaboration, through Teacher Assistance Teams, may be a critical factor in the delivery of an inclusive quality educational service.

APPENDIX 3A

FORM 3.2

Distribution of Responsibilities of Child Study Team Members

Responsibilities	Assigned to
1. Organize a district child study team	
2. Recommend persons for team membership	
3. Provide in-service training for team(s)	
4. Provide resource materials needed by team members	
5. Provide information on local district eligibility criteria and placement options	
6. Facilitate total team process	
7. Organize all forms and team materials	
8. Chair team meetings	
9. Assign team tasks and monitor their completion	

Responsibilities	Assigned to
10. Facilitate group decision making	
11. Supervise record-keeping procedures	
12. Ensure due-process procedure	
13. Carry out all parent/child contacts required by law	
14. Conduct home visits	
15. Make recommendations for comprehensive evaluation	
16. Provide comprehensive evaluation of student within area of expertise and submit written report	
17. Provide specific information describing student's strengths and weaknesses	
18. Provide information on current classroom performance	
19. Provide information concerning home situation	
20. Outline capabilities and limitations of placement options	
21. Make suggestions for development of IEP	
22. Write the IEP	
23. Monitor student's progress after implementing the IEP	
24. Write the individual instruction plan	
25. Monitor the individual instruction plan	
26. Provide specific recommendation for placement	
27. Submit reports of student progress	
28. Keep an accurate record of team meetings	
29. Maintain appropriate files	
30. Make arrangements for team meetings	

APPENDIX 3B

FORM 3.3

Name of Student: ______________________________

Program Goal: ______________________________

Objective(s) and Criterion Level	Materials and Resources / Instructional Strategies	Date Started	Date Reviewed	Evaluative Comments

SUGGESTED RESOURCES

Programs/Materials

Collaboration in the schools: Inservice and Preservice Curriculum for Teachers, Support Staff and Administrators (West, Idol & Cannon). PsyCan Corp., Box 290, Stn. V, Toronto, ON, M6R 3A5. Explains the problem-solving collaborative process, with lesson plans and assessment devices.

Collaboration in the Schools Videotape (45 minutes, colour, VHS). PsyCan Corp., $330 Cdn. Instructional videotape on collaboration.

Effective Instruction of Difficult-to-Teach Students: Inservice and Preservice Professional Development Program (Idol & West). PsyCan Corp. A training base program for classroom, remedial, and special educators.

Self-Esteem Teacher Power (Video 1 with Video Guide). PsyCan Corp., $190 Cdn. Building self-esteem resources.

Self-Esteem Teacher Strategies (Video 2 with Video Guide). PsyCan Corp., $190 Cdn. Includes a handbook on in-class strategies.

STET: Systematic Training for Effective Teaching (Dinkmeyer, McKay & Dinkmeyer). PsyCan Corp., Package kit: $370 Cdn. K-12 practical approach to understanding students with special needs, and working with parents. Includes books and four cassettes.

Paraprofessionals: Training for the Classroom (Hank & McKenzie). PsyCan Corp., Kit: $450 Cdn. Four-session video and handbook training material, for paraprofessionals such as teacher aides.

Responsible Kids in School and at Home: Six Video Series (K-12). PsyCan Corp. Six video series: $500 Cdn. Perfect for viewing at PTA meetings, school improvement programs.

STEP/teen: Systematic Training for Effective Parenting of Teens (Dinkmeyer & McKay). PsyCan Corp. Audio kit: $300, Video kit: $575. Two videocassettes or five audiocassettes, plus Activities Training Book.

Social Skills Intervention Guide (Elliott & Gresham) (Grades 3 to High School). PsyCan Corp., Intervention Guide: $140 Cdn. Actual case studies plus 43 training lessons for teaching social skills in any setting.

Tools for Transition: Preparing Students with Learning Disabilities for Postsecondary Education (Aune & Ness). PsyCan Corp., Complete kit: $240 Cdn. Includes teacher's manual, student workbook, 46 Blackline masters, and videocassette.

Options and Consequences: Six-Video Set Series for Middle School Use. PsyCan Corp., Complete six-video set: $460 Cdn. Dramatic, live-action episodes shot in school to deal with stealing, lying, cheating, and gossip.

Contemporary Concerns of Youth (Schwarzrock & Wrenn) (Grades 7 to 12). PsyCan. Corp. Complete kit: $110 Cdn. Complete with manual, 85 Blackline masters, and communication cards. Explores self-image, handling responsibilities, and goal setting.

Sack-Yourman Study Skills Program (Grades 9 to 12). PsyCan. Corp. Complete kit: $200 Cdn. 12 cassette tapes, teacher manual, and student workbook to improve notes.

Strategies: Alternative Approach to Integrated Language Arts (Braun, Goepfirst & Siamon) (Grades 4 to 8). PsyCan Corp., Books and tapes as well as manuals individually priced. Audiocassettes, story books, teacher and student books on integrating language into any school subject.

Lifeskills Instruction for All Students with Special Needs (Cronin & Patton). PsyCan Corp., $50 Cdn. A resource text with "how-to" material for students at risk for failure.

Collaborative Consultation: Second Edition (Idol, Nevin & Paolucci-Whitcomb). PsyCan Corp., $65 Cdn. A resource text for enhancing collaboration between classroom teachers.

The Educational Consultant: Helping Professionals, Parents, and Mainstreamed Students, 3rd Edition (Heron & Harris). PsyCan Corp., $62 Cdn. A resource text on consultation models and designing intervention assistance teams.

Academic Skills Problems: Direct Assessment and Intervention (Shapiro). Guilford Pub., 72 Spring St., New York, NY 10012 $19.95 U.S. Step-by-step instructions for establishing intervention strategies and for determining the success of remedial efforts.

Severe Behaviour Problems: A Functional Communication Training Approach (Durand). Guilford Pub., 72 Spring St., New York, NY 10012, $17.95 U.S. Provides step-by-step instructions for teaching students how to replace their challenging behaviours.

Thinking, Feeling & Behaving: An Emotional Education Curriculum for Adolescents (Vernon) (Grades 7 to 12). Research Press, 60 Rankin St., Waterloo, ON, $36 Cdn. A comprehensive curriculum to develop self-acceptance, learn problem solving and decision making.

The Peer Mediation Video: Conflict Resolution in Schools (Schrumpf & Crawford) (Grades 6 to 12). Research Press, $455.00 Cdn. VHS 28-minute video, training secondary students in peer mediation skills.

Diversity and Teaching: Teacher Education Yearbook 1 (O'ttair & Odell). Harcourt, Brace Canada, 55 Horner Ave.,Toronto, ON M8Z 4X6. A resource book linking research and teaching for diversity in the classroom.

REFERENCES

Aksamit, D.L., & Rankin, J.L. (1993). Problem-solving teams as a prereferral process. *Special Services in the Schools, 7*(1), 1–25.

Allport, J.L. (Ed.). (1982). *Psychological consultation in educational settings: A casebook for working with administration, teachers, students and community.* San Francisco: Jossey-Bass.

Brinchenhoff, L.C., Shaw, S.F., & McGuire, J.M. (1993). *Promoting postsecondary education for students with learning disabilities.* Toronto: PsyCan Ltd.

Brown, D., Pryzwansky, W.B., & Schulte, A.L. (1991). *Psychological consultation: Introduction to theory and practice* (2nd edition). Needham Heights, MA: Allyn and Bacon.

Christenson, S.L., & Conoley, J.C. (1992). *Home-school collaboration: Enhancing children's academic and social competence.* Silver-Spring, MD: National Association of School Psychologists.

Cronin, M.E., & Patton, J.R. (1993). *Life skills instructions for all students with special needs.* Toronto: PsyCan Ltd.

Devereux, E. (1977). "A critique of ecological psychology." Paper presented at the Conference on Research Perspectives in the Ecology of Human Development, Ithaca, NY.

Erchul, W.P. (1993). Selected interpersonal perspectives in consultation research. *School Psychology Quarterly, 8*(1), 38–49.

Erchul, W.P., & Chewing, T.G. (1990). Behavioural consultation from a request-centered relational communication perspective. *School Psychology Quarterly, 5*(1), 1–20.

Foley, R.M. (1994). Collaboration activities and competencies of special educators serving students with behaviour disorders. *Special Services in the Schools, 8*(2), 69–90.

Friend, M. (1988). Training special educators to be consultants. *Teacher Education and Special Education, 8,* 115–20.

Gump, P., & Adelberg, B. (1978). Urbanism from the perspective of ecological psychologists. *Environment and Behaviour, 10,* 171–91.

Hagborg, W.J. (1993). Parental understanding of their child's psychological evaluation findings conference. *Special Services in the Schools, 7*(2), 59–69.

Heron, T.E., & Harris, K.C. (1993). *The educational consultant: Helping professionals, parents and mainstreamed students* (3rd edition). Toronto: PsyCan Ltd.

Huebner, E.S. (1993). Psychologists in secondary schools in the 1990's: Current functions, training and job satisfaction. *School Psychology Quarterly, 8*(1), 50–56.

Idol, L. (1993). *Special educator's consultation handbook* (2nd edition). Toronto: PsyCan Ltd.

Idol, L., Nevin, A., & Paolucci-Whitcomb, P. (1993). *Collaborative consulting* (2nd edition). Toronto: PsyCan Ltd.

Idol, L., Paolucci-Whitcomb, P., & Nevin, A. (1986). *Collaborative consultation.* Rockville, MD: Aspen Systems.

Janzen, H.L., Paterson, J.G., & Paterson, D.W. (1993). The future of psychology in the schools. *Canadian Journal of School Psychology, 9*(2), 174–80.

Knoff, H.M. (Ed.). (1986). *The assessment of adolescent child and adolescent personality.* New York: Guilford Press.

Kratochwill, T.R., & Bergan, J.R. (1990). *Behavioural consultation in applied settings: An individual guide.* New York: Plenum Press.

LeBlanc, R., & Reynolds, C.R. (1989). Accordance of mothers' and fathers' ratings of children's behaviour. *Psychology in the Schools, 26*(3), 225–29.

Lifter, K. (1993). Implementation of the consultative approach in the classroom in support of related services. *Special Services in the Schools, 7*(1), 145–66.

Maher, C.A., Illback, R.J., & Zins, J.E. (Eds.). (1984). *Organizational psychology in the schools: A handbook for professionals.* Springfield, IL: Charles C. Thomas.

Martens, B.K., & Kelly, S.Q. (1993). A behavioural analysis of effective teaching. *School Psychology Quarterly, 8*(1), 10–26.

Masters, L.F., Mori, B.A., & Mori, A.A. (1993). *Teaching secondary students with mild learning and behaviour problems: Methods, materials, and strategies* (2nd edition). Toronto: PsyCan Ltd.

Meyers, J., Parsons, R.D., & Martin, R. (1979). *Mental health consultation in the schools.* San Francisco: Jossey-Bass.

Paolucci-Whitcomb, P., & Nevin, A. (1985). Preparing consulting teachers through a collaborative approach between university faculty and field-based consulting teachers. *Teacher Education and Special Education, 8*, 132–43.

Parsons, R.D., & Meyers, J. (1984). *Developing consultation skills.* San Francisco: Jossey-Bass.

Paterson, J.G., & Janzen, H.L. (1993). School counseling in the social, political and educational context of Canada. *International Journal for the Advancement of Counselling, 16*, 151–68.

Paul, J.L., & Simeonsson, R.J. (1993). *Children with special needs: Family, culture and society.* Toronto: Harcourt Brace Jovanovich.

Pryzwansky, W.B. (1989). School consultation: Some consideration from a cognitive psychology. *Professional School Psychology, 4*(1), 1–14.

Reynolds, C.R., & Gutkin, T.B. (Eds.). (1982). *The handbook of school psychology.* Toronto: John Wiley & Sons.

Rotheram-Borus, M.J. (1993). Multicultural issues in the delivery of group interventions. *Special Services in the Schools, 8*(1), 179–88.

Witt, J.C., Elliott, S.N., Kramer, J.J., & Gresham, F.M. (1994). *Assessment of children: Fundamental methods and practice.* Madison, WI: Brown & Benchmark.

CHAPTER 4

Classroom-Based Assessment for Instructional Planning at the Secondary Level

Claudio Violato
Anthony Marini

University of Calgary

Introduction

While the scientific approach based on experiments has its roots in antiquity and has undergone rapid advances in the 20th century, the science of educational assessment is only now beginning to emerge as a unified field. This is because some necessary developments for the growth of this science—statistical and mathematical theories, test theory, microcomputers and optical readers, social and political policy—have emerged only in the last two or so decades (Violato, McDougall & Marini, 1992). Currently, the field is undergoing rapid development and change bringing exciting possibilities and challenges.

Assessment, Testing, and Evaluation

Assessment involves the assignment of numbers, quantities, or characteristics to some dimension. Evaluation is the process of interpreting or judging the value of the assessment. Testing as used in the usual sense is a subset of assessment—in the classroom it is assessment of educational outcomes (Wiggins, 1993). In recent years, the focus for classroom-based assessment has been on **performance assessment**. This sort of assessment involves "real life," open-ended activities intended to measure aspects of higher-order thinking (Resnick & Resnick, 1992).

Evaluation involves value judgments. To make an evaluation, you interpret a measurement according to some value system. For example, a measurement may be a teacher reporting Jason's score on his biology test as 19. If the teacher interprets this score and concludes that Jason has excellent achievement in biology, then this is an evaluation.

Assessments generally serve as measurements or attempts to quantify some aspect of pupil educational functioning. The letter grades ("A," "B," "C," "D," "F") or adjective descriptions (excellent, fair, poor) associated with these numbers are evaluations based on these test scores. Evaluation, therefore, is assessment plus value judgments. The quality of the evaluation depends on both the quality of the assessment and the care with which this result is interpreted. A careless interpretation of good quality data is likely to lead to a poor evaluation just as a careful interpretation of shoddy data would.

The Role of Assessment in Teaching and Learning

All teaching has some goal or objective as its purpose. The objective may be implicit or explicit. Teaching, then, is for the purpose of having pupils reach some intended learning outcome (objective). The only sound means by which a teacher can determine the extent to which pupils have achieved the objectives is to measure performance. The outcome of the assessment, therefore, is an evaluation of not only pupil performance, but the effectiveness of the teaching itself as well. The main function of assessment is to measure the extent to which the instructional objectives have been met (Gronlund & Linn, 1990). Tests and assessments also have a number of other functions in teaching and learning.

Motivation

Any technique that teachers can use to motivate students is desirable, and tests and impending assessments motivate students to work and study harder than they might otherwise. Frequent short assessments will also motivate pupils to sustain a consistently higher effort than long-term infrequent tests.

Enhance Learning

Increasing student motivation to work will also increase their learning. When students anticipate a forthcoming test, they will attend to material more closely, increase their study time, and work harder to learn the relevant material (Sadler, 1983). The anticipation of a test also improves students' learning strategies so that they increase their memory capacities for the material (through rehearsal, elaboration, organization).

Testing also promotes overlearning, which occurs when you systematically study and prepare for a test. Of course some of the material learned for the test will be forgotten afterwards (hence the term overlearning), but more material will be retained in the long run than if overlearning had not occurred.

Feedback

Assessment results provide feedback for both the teacher and student. The teacher can evaluate the efficacy of instruction based on the pupils' performance. If, for example, no pupil in the class is able to correctly solve the long division problems on the test, then the teacher can conclude that his or her teaching of long division failed.

Feedback can also be provided directly to the student. Based on performance the student can evaluate progress as a whole or in specific subareas measured by the test.

Teaching

Students may learn substantially merely from writing a test since they will have to formulate answers to questions. In a recent study Foos and Fisher (1988) gave students a short essay to read about the American Civil War. Half of the students were then given an initial test and half were not. Two days later, all the students took a final common exam—those students who took the initial test generally did better than those who did not. It may very well be that the act of retrieving the information for the original test may have altered and strengthened the knowledge of that information (McDaniel & Masson, 1985).

Summative, Formative, Placement, and Diagnostic Assessment and Evaluation

The following types of evaluation refer to the way assessment results will be used.

- *Summative.* This is a "summing up" of all assessments and measurements in order to determine final performance. Assigning the letter grade ("A," "B,"... "F") is a form of summative evaluation.

- *Formative.* This is monitoring the situation. This usually involves quizzes, mid-term tests, anecdotal records, portfolios, etc.
- *Placement.* Sometimes it is necessary to determine where in the educational sequence (i.e., grade level) the pupil should be placed. Teachers and the principal may be uncertain, for example, in what grade to place a student coming from another country. Placement evaluation might be conducted using previous records (if any), test data, and interviews.
- *Diagnostic.* When pupils have persistent learning problems, it may be necessary to diagnose the problem. Psychological, medical, and educational data are frequently necessary to make a diagnostic evaluation.

Important Characteristics of Assessments

There are three critical elements of any classroom assessment: validity, reliability, and usability. Reliability has to do with the consistency of measurement and usability deals with the practicality of using an assessment. Validity has to do with the extent to which the assessment measures whatever it is supposed to measure—that is, validity focuses on the question of how well an assessment carries out its intended function.

Reliability is a precondition to validity. An assessment must be reliable to be valid. A reliable test, however, is not necessarily valid. Reliability therefore, is a necessary but not sufficient condition for validity. Finally, neither validity nor reliability can guarantee usability or practicality. The polygraph illustrates an instrument with low practicality under some conditions. This device measures physiological arousal on various modalities such as the electroencephalograph, Galvanic skin response, heart rate, and so on. It is highly reliable and valid for measuring arousal responses in laboratory learning situations. The polygraph is not very practical or usable for the same assessment under naturalistic conditions such as classroom learning, however, because the pupil must be strapped into electrodes and other equipment. This limitation greatly reduces the use value of the polygraph as an assessment of arousal for classroom learning. Similarly, many current attempts to institute wide scale performance-based classroom assessment have floundered because of the high cost and impracticality of the proposed assessments (Popham, 1993).

The Nature of Validity

When examining the validity of an assessment, there are four levels of analysis:

1. Face Validity
2. Content Validity

3. Criterion-related Validity
    a) predictive
    b) concurrent
4. Construct Validity

These levels are generally regarded as hierarchical, thus a higher level incorporates those levels below it. It is not always necessary to analyze every level of validity for every situation or use of an assessment. Indeed there are some useful rules of thumb for classifying the validities and procedures for establishing them. These are summarized in Table 4.1.

When teachers undertake assessments, they are primarily concerned about the first two levels of validity, face and content, which are not empirical in nature. The other two levels, criterion-related and construct, which are empirical in nature, are more relevant to standardized and formal educational assessments. In short, face and content validity can be established without recourse to data while criterion-related and construct validity require data for their demonstration.

Face Validity

Face validity can play a crucial role in many assessment situations. Face validity has to do with appearance—does the test *appear* to measure whatever it is supposed to measure?

In conventional discussions, three forms of validity are generally recognized (content, criterion-related, and construct). Face validity is not regarded as a form of validity, per se. A joint committee of the American Psychological Association, National Council on Measurement in Education, and the American Educational Research Association has prepared a document, *Standards for Educational and Psychological Testing* (Washington, D.C.: American Psychological Association, 1985), which describes validity and sets standards for test use. In this treatment, face validity is not regarded as a form of validity. Many textbook writers also do not discuss this form as a separate kind of validity. Nevertheless, in the present text, it is discussed as a separate type of validity because it influences classroom climate or rapport between psychologist and testee. Therefore, for present purposes, face validity is considered a form of validity. It involves pupils perceptions. From the testee's perspective, does the test look right and fair? Why is this so important?

Besides providing an initial impression of an assessment, face validity can be crucial in establishing rapport, motivation, and setting classroom climate (Violato, 1986). There is little that makes a group of students hostile as quickly

TABLE 4.1
Four Types of Validity

Type	Definition	Importance	Evidence	How to Establish
Face	The appearance of test	Teacher-made tests	Non-empirical	Make the test appear appropriate
Content	The adequacy with which the test samples the domain of measurement	Teacher-made tests	Non-empirical	Construct a table of specifications
Criterion-related	The extent to which the test relates to some criterion of importance	Standardized tests (e.g., Scholastic Aptitude Test)	Empirical (correlation)	Correlates the test scores to some criterion of performance
Construct	The psychological mental processes that underlie performance on a test	Standardized psychological tests (e.g., IQ tests)	Empirical (correlation)	Manipulate test scores through experimental procedures and observe results

as a test that is perceived to be inappropriate or unfair. However, face validity plays a secondary role to content validity.

Content Validity

Content validity concerns the extent to which an assessment adequately samples the domain of measurement, the content. If in grade-9 science, for example, 17 new concepts have been introduced and pupils are required to know them, then the domain of measurement refers to the understanding of all the concepts. You would probably not want to include all of these on a test, however, as it would be too long and tedious. Thus you might randomly select 7 concepts from the total domain of 17 concepts to include in the test. The extent to which the 7 concepts selected adequately represent the total domain of concepts determines the content validity of the test. Content validity is usually the most important consideration in classroom assessments.

Content validity, involves sampling or selecting. The domain of measurement, therefore, must be clearly defined and detailed. Not only must the content areas or subject matter be identified, but so must the cognitive processes involved. The cognitive processes refer to the levels of Bloom's Taxonomy (Bloom, 1956) (knows, comprehends, applies, analyzes, synthesizes, evaluates). You must determine not only the subject matter to be assessed but, as well, the cognitive outcomes that have been specified by the instructional objectives. Enhancing content validity may be achieved most directly through the use of a table of specifications. An example of a table of specifications is provided in Table 4.2.

Table of specifications. A table of specifications is a blueprint of the assessment device or procedure (Worthen, 1993). Just as an engineer develops a detailed plan of a bridge that is to be built and an architect draws a blueprint of the building that is to be erected, so too the teacher begins with a plan for the test. This plan *specifies* the content areas to be assessed as well as the cognitive outcomes and skills that are to be measured, thus it is called a table of specifications.

The table of specifications is a chart where, by convention, the content area to be measured is itemized along the vertical axis, while the cognitive outcomes are specified along the horizontal axis. Use the following steps to construct the table of specifications:

1. Prepare a heading on a blank sheet of paper. Write the subject, date, and grade level of the test.
2. Identify all of the content areas to be tested and list these on the left-hand margin in the order they were taught.
3. Across the horizontal, specify the levels of learning outcomes described in the instructional objectives.
4. Determine the total number of items that will be on the test.
5. In the right-hand margin, write the number and percentage of items that will be devoted to each specified content area and do the same for the objectives.
6. In each cell (intersection of content area and level of learning outcome) write the number of items and percentage of the total test that these items represent (some cells may be blank).
7. Carefully consider the percentage of test items in each cell and ensure that this accurately reflects the emphasis and time spent in the teaching and learning of this content.
8. Each item should be carefully checked to ensure that it indeed measures at the intended cognitive outcome.

A well-designed and carefully developed table of specifications will provide a sound plan for your assessment. The closer the match between the assessment in its accurate sampling of both the content and learning outcomes, the higher the content validity.

TABLE 4.2
Table of Specifications for Grade 11 Biology Test

	Level of Understanding				
Content	**Knowledge**	**Comprehension**	**Application**	**Higher**	**Total**
1. History	1	1	—	1	(3)6%
2. Cells	3	2	—	—	(5)10%
3. Development	2	2	—	—	(4)8%
4. Ecology	1	2	2	2	(7)14%
5. Evolution	1	1	2	1	(5)10%
6. Heredity	2	2	1	—	(5)10%
7. Morphology	3	2	1	—	(6)12%
8. Physiology	3	1	—	—	(4)8%
9. Ethology	1	1	3	1	(6)12%
10. Taxonomy	2	2	1	—	(5)10%
Total	(19)38%	(16)32%	(10)20%	(5)10%	(50)100%

Criterion-related Validity

When we are interested in how performance on an assessment correlates with performance on some other criterion, we are concerned about criterion-related validity (Cronbach, 1984). The criterion may be any performance on some other assessment. There are two subcategories of criterion-related validity: a) predictive, and b) concurrent. Predictive validity refers to how current performance correlates with some *future* performance on a criterion and thus involves the problem of prediction. Concurrent validity refers to how performance correlates *concurrently* with some criterion.

Construct Validity

Construct validity focuses on the truth or correctness of a construct and the assessments that measure it. A **construct** is an "*entity, process*, or *event* which is itself not observed" but which is proposed to summarize and explain facts, empirical laws, and other data. In the physical sciences, gravity is an example of a hypothetical construct. Gravity, defined as a process or force, cannot be directly observed or measured; only its effects can be identified and quantified.

In psychological and educational measurement, examples of constructs include intelligence, scholastic aptitude, anxiety, honesty, impulsivity, verbal fluency, and creativity. These constructs have been proposed to explain, summarize, and organize empirical relationships and response consistencies. Intelligence, like gravity, cannot be directly observed or measured; its existence must be inferred from behavioural assessments (Sternberg, 1992). In any case—whether gravity or intelligence—construct validity requires the gradual accumulation of information from a variety of sources. In effect, it is a special instance of the general procedure of validating a theory in any scientific endeavour. The ultimate purpose of validation is explanation, understanding, and prediction.

Cronbach (1984) has proposed that *all* forms of validity are really construct validity. Content and criterion-related evidence are pieces of the puzzle on which we can focus our attention. In many assessments, it follows that all forms of validity should be considered and synthesized to produce an explanation and understanding. The particular kind of validity that is of interest will depend on the specific use of a test. An illustration of validity concerns for the various purposes of a verbal reasoning test is given in Table 4.3.

Reliability

Reliability has to do with the consistency of measurement. It is a necessary condition for validity. While reliability is a precondition for validity, it does not guarantee it—a reliable assessment device is not necessarily valid. A simple example can help to clarify the nature of reliability. Suppose that you measured the length of your kitchen table with a ruler and it turned out to be 100 cm long. Later that day, you began to doubt this measurement, and next morning you measured the table again. This time it turned out to be 82 cm long. What is the problem here? There are two possibilities: 1) the table keeps changing length every time it is measured, or 2) something is wrong with your measurement instrument.

Under normal conditions, of course, tables do not change length so in this case the problem must be the measurement instrument. Upon closer examination you discover that your ruler is made of rubber and the differential results are due to the inconsistency of the measurement.

This example is not merely unlikely or trite, though, as many educational assessments do in fact behave like rubber rulers, as they produce inconsistent results or unreliable measurements. The concern with reliability in educational and psychological assessment is paramount because of the difficulty of producing consistent measures of achievement and psychological constructs.

Reliability is a multifaceted concept rather than a singular idea. Indeed, there are several ways of thinking about and discussing reliability. Four methods of establishing reliability are usually recognized.

TABLE 4.3
Validity of a Verbal Reasoning Test for Various Purposes

Purpose of Test	Validity	Information Rendered
Achievement test in elementary school reading	Content	Amount of verbal learning that Ashley has achieved
Aptitude test to predict performance in high school	Criterion-related: predictive	Jason's potential for future learning in a literature course
A procedure for diagnosing learning disabilities	Criterion-related: concurrent	Specific disabilities of Jerrod's performance
A measure of verbal reasoning	Construct	The nature of Trista's cognitive processes

Four Methods for Determining Reliability

The four methods or techniques for determining the reliability of a measurement instrument are listed below.

1. Test-retest
2. Parallel Forms
   a) given at the same time
   b) given at different times
3. Split-half
4. Internal Consistency

These techniques are not only different methods for establishing reliability, but each type produces a somewhat different type of reliability as well. While all forms of reliability focus on consistency, there are different aspects of the testing to which the consistency is relevant. The consistency on the test-retest method, for example, focuses on time. Does the test produce consistent results from one measurement to another at a different time?

A second type of reliability is estimated by parallel forms or equivalent forms method as it is also called. Here the focus is on the consistency of measurement across different forms (parallel or equivalent) of the same test. Because the different forms can be given either simultaneously or at different times, stability of the assessment over time can also play a role in this method.

The third type of reliability that is estimated both by split-half method and the internal consistency method deals with the internal consistency of the assessment or the consistency of measurement across different items within the test. Split-half is a special version of internal consistency. Here we are concerned about the extent to which each item (or group of items) consistently measures in the direction of the other items on the test. Each method and type of reliability is compared and summarized in Table 4.4.

TABLE 4.4
Various Methods of Estimating Reliability

Method	Measure	Procedure
Test-retest	Stability over time	Give the exact same test to the same group of pupils at different times
Parallel forms (same time)	Form equivalence	Give two forms of the same test to the same group at the same time
Parallel forms (different time)	Form equivalence and stability over time	Give two forms of the same test with a time interval between the two forms
Split-half	Internal consistency	Split the test into odd-even halves and correlate the resulting scores. Adjust with the Spearman-Brown formula
KR20, KR21, Cronbach's alpha	Internal consistency	Give the test once and apply the Kuder-Richardson formula or Cronbach's alpha coefficient formula

Grading and Reporting

Central to instructional planning in the classroom is the need for grading and reporting. Grading and reporting provide several functions including feedback, accountability, directing pupil effort, as well as rewarding and motivating effort, and providing information for instructional planning.

Grades (also called marks) provide feedback on performance to the pupil, parents, future teachers, and prospective employers. This information is usually provided via report cards and parent-teacher conferences, which keep parents informed and involved in their child's education. Such information can indicate areas of strength, weakness, or deficit that require attention. Based on this feedback, appropriate action may be suggested and taken to improve the teaching and learning that the pupil is engaged in.

Grading and reporting also provides a form of accountability. Since periodic reporting is done, this holds the teacher, school, and pupil accountable for their educational activity. These reports provide analogous functions in education that financial statements play in business. Without such formal reporting systems, there would be no mechanism to hold all those involved in the educational enterprise accountable for their actions. Such accountability ultimately helps to improve education as it requires planning, thought, and review of the outcomes of education.

Weaknesses, deficits, and strengths are identified by grades and are communicated by reporting. This helps to direct future efforts and interests. Exceptional achievement in mathematics, for example, may be identified by grading and therefore affect decisions about future efforts in mathematics. Deficits in reading may also be identified by grading and the reporting to parents may help the child direct their efforts to overcome the problem.

Grades can motivate pupils to work hard. High grades also serve to reward hard work and effort. Conversely, poor grades can motivate effort to improve performance.

There are, however, a number of real or perceived problems with grades. The main problem lies in the meaning of grades. Marks may have different meanings across teachers, schools, and school districts. This lack of universal meaning for grades is a problem that can be at least partially solved by more valid assessment procedures.

The discrepancy of grading among teachers, schools, and school districts, is directly due to the lack of universal objective evidence for assigning grades. There is no universal scale to which teachers can refer to assign these letter grades, thus teachers are left to their own judgment as to what is the meaning and the evidence for assigning the marks. While this problem can never be completely solved, it can be mitigated by using as reliable and valid measuring instruments as possible.

Another criticism is that pupils are motivated to work for grades rather than for significant educational outcomes or important learning. This is more a perceived problem than a real problem with grades. The solution to this problem is make the grades more valid and thus reflect important learning outcomes. Then the pupil will work for both grades and important learning.

Teacher-assigned grades have been shown to be notoriously unreliable (Educational Testing Services, 1963; Starch & Elliot, 1912, 1913). When the grade is assigned largely or wholly on subjective grounds, numerous irrelevant factors such as pupil appearance, politeness, gender, attractiveness, honesty, and so on, influence the grade. The solution to the problem is to use data (e.g., assessment outcomes) that are objective and reliable.

A final problem frequently identified with grades is that they are responsible for a variety of detrimental side effects such as anxiety, self-concept problems, hostility, cheating, and producing negative attitudes toward learning and education when low grades are received. That some pupils have low self-concepts, are anxious, cheat, and are hostile to learning, is undeniable. These problems, however, are not caused by grades.

Letter Grades

The most widely used symbol system is the traditional letter grade ("A," "B," "C," "D," "F"). While this system is concise, readily understandable, and familiar, it does have some difficulties. First, as we have seen, these letter grades lack universal meaning from teacher to teacher and from school to school. Second, the letter grade alone tells us nothing about other important educational matters such as effort, attitude and interests. Third, the letter grade may have different meanings across subject matter itself.

Numerous attempts have been made to improve the shortcomings of the traditional letter grade. This usually takes the form of using different symbols and reducing the number of categories.

These attempts are not really improvements over the letter grades as they have the same problems and introduce new ones as well. Parents and pupils tend not to like these systems as they are not as familiar as the letter grade. As well, the reduction of the number of categories reduces the reliability of the grades. (Crocker & Algina, 1986; Hopkins, Stanley & Hopkins, 1990). For this reason it is important to use a system with several categories (at least five). Thus despite the shortcomings of the traditional letter grade system, it is likely to continue to be widely used in the foreseeable future.

Numerical Grades

There are two generally used numerical grading systems: 1) percentages, and 2) numerals between 1 and 10. In the percentage system, the total achievement scores for the reporting period are summed and converted to a percentage value. To increase meaning, percentage ranges are frequently assigned adjective descriptors (90–100 = excellent, 80–89 = very good, etc.). In the second numerical system, a number between 1 and 10 is assigned with 1 indicating very poor and 10 indicating outstanding.

The main problems with these systems is their lack of familiarity and their deceptive nature. These numerical systems have not been used as widely as have the letter grade and therefore are not as widely known. Does 100% indicate a complete knowledge of the subject matter? Does 50% indicate half knowledge? What does 7 mean? These numerical grades obviously offer no advantage over the letter grade especially when adjective descriptors are required to interpret them.

Pass-Fail System

This system provides only two categories of grading, namely either a pupil passes or fails a course. While there was some initial enthusiasm for this system in the 1960s and 1970s, and it became used at various levels of education from elementary to graduate school, it never really became widespread for at least three reasons. First, it is not as familiar as the letter grade system, which is generally preferred by pupils and the public. Second, it reduces substantially the information communicated to the pupil. Third, the system would be quite unreliable since it reduces the number of categories to the bare minimum—two.

For the above reasons it is unlikely that this will ever become the preferred grading system although it has found some accepted use in specialized applications. For example, courses which taken as electives, for example, and are not to be included in the grade point average calculation might profitably employ this system. As well, courses taught strictly as mastery learning could employ this grading system.

Anecdotal Records

Anecdotal records or narrative reports are detailed reports that contain statements about effort, attitudes, behaviour, and achievement of each pupil. Narrative descriptions have the advantage of allowing the teacher to include much more information in reporting the pupil's performance than would otherwise be possible. These reports also tend to reduce norm-referenced comparisons and focus instead on a more comprehensive picture of the child.

Anecdotal records have a number of problems associated with them. First, while parents, teachers, and school administrators generally favour them, they still want the traditional letter grades in the reports. Second, the collection of information and composing of the reports represents a tremendous amount of work for the teacher. Third, the amount of information that would accumulate over the course of a month or two would make summarizing and compiling the actual narrative report a huge undertaking. Fourth, most teachers have little or no training in making and recording behavioural observations. Fifth, at the secondary and even upper elementary level, teachers generally have many more pupils and generally do not know their students as well as primary teachers know their pupils.

Perhaps narrative reports alone could be justified for the primary grades if parents are given a convincing rationale for the lack of letter grades. The anecdotal report could also be useful with special education groups that might otherwise receive persistently low grades and thus discourage pupils. Finally, the anecdotal record is probably most useful as an addendum to letter grade (or other) reporting systems. Here it would enrich and elaborate the traditional mark.

Checklists of Objectives

In this scheme, a checklist of objectives or educational outcomes is used and each pupil is rated as to whether they have met the objective. This method has the advantage of providing very specific and informative reports about the pupils' behaviour and what they can and cannot do. Such information has obvious use for educational decision making and for undertaking remedial action. Moreover, it assesses pupil progress on specific and relevant educational objectives rather than against peer performance or some numerical standard.

Despite their obvious advantages, checklists of objectives have not flourished as the sole method of grading. The main reason for this is that parents still want to know the letter grade performance that meeting the objectives represents. A second difficulty with checklists of objectives is that they can become so long and extensive with very specific objectives in every subject matter, that evaluating every objective for each pupil can become an onerous task for teachers. Checklists of objectives are most useful and informative when they are used in conjunction with traditional letter grade systems.

Letters to Parents

Letters to parents in lieu of other more traditional grading systems have also been tried. They are only useful if the descriptions of pupil performance are based on extensive and valid information. As sole methods of grading, however, this system suffers from the same flaws as do anecdotal records and narrative reports. They are best used as addenda to letter grade systems for communicating additional information or elaborating the grade.

Grading Assignments and Homework

Assignments such as reports, essays, arithmetic problems, book reviews, and other homework activities are not primarily assessment activities. Their primary purpose is for teaching and learning. As we have seen, tests and other assessments are intended primarily as measurement instruments. It is these that should be used as the components for deriving grades. Assignments ideally should not be included as components in the grade.

If assignments and homework are not assigned a value or a mark, however, it is unlikely that pupils will consistently do them and work as hard as the teacher would like. As a rule of thumb, assignments and homework should account for no more than 25% of the total value of the grade. Keeping the value of these components that are low in validity and reliability to a maximum of 25% will tend to limit the extent to which they can reduce the reliability and validity of the final grade.

The primary problem with grading assignments and homework is that the expectations of the teacher and the criteria by which the assignment will be evaluated are not clearly laid out and communicated before the assignment is done. Scoring criteria, just as in scoring essay tests, should be developed and guide the evaluation of the assignments. First, grading can be done more efficiently because of a clear-cut set of criteria and expectations. Second, the feedback to students can include diagnostic statements indicating specific problems and deficiencies. Third, extraneous factors such as the length of response, penmanship, and clarity of writing, are less likely to influence the scoring since clear criteria are specified. Fourth, when the expectations and criteria are presented to the pupils at the same time of the assignment, there is less possibility of misunderstanding and the nature of the assignment is made clearer.

Moving Beyond Traditional Assessment Models: Performance Assessment

Assessment in secondary classes has in the past been primarily characterized by paper–pencil testing. More recently, secondary teachers have begun to implement a variety of performance assessments. In part, this action addresses the demands of educational critics who argue that assessment must reflect the complex behaviours that students are required to demonstrate outside the school setting. As Figure 4.1 suggests, performance assessments are not altogether new forms of assessment activities. What is new is the degree to which such

FIGURE 4.1
The Many Faces of Performance Assessment

- DIRECT WRITING ASSESSMENTS
- PORTFOLIOS
- EXHIBITIONS
- DEMONSTRATIONS
- EVALUATIONS OF STUDENT PRODUCTS
- OLYMPICS OF THE MIND
- SCIENCE FAIRS
- MUSIC COMPETITIONS
- SIMULATIONS
- WORK SAMPLES

Source: Richard J. Stiginns, Assessment Training Institute (Portland, OR).

types of activities have come to play an important role in the assessment programs of many schools.

As you examine the list of possible assessment activities in Figure 4.1, you may recognize that the key features of performance assessment involve teacher observation and judgment. While much of educational measurement attempts to maximize objectivity in assessment, performance assessment clearly involves subjective decision making. However, as you shall see in the examples that follow, subjective assessment decisions can be informed by a clear set of well-thought-out scoring criteria. Students need to know exactly how they will be evaluated. These criteria once developed, are shared openly with the student and are designed to guide student effort and provide clear instructional feedback.

The examples found in Boxes 4.1 to 4.4 provide evidence that this form of assessment can been applied across a wide range of grade and ability levels. Each of the examples attempts to clearly define the specific learning behaviour the student is to display. Describing performance at three levels (e.g., superior, average, and weak) is a common characteristic of performance assessment. In fact, many educators have argued that students should be able to examine models of actual work that has been judged to be excellent; after all, how can one strive for excellence when one is unclear about what constitutes excellent work?

BOX 4.1

Examples of Performance Assessment Devices Developed by Classroom Teachers

Subject: Art

Skill: Life Drawing

Rationale: As student's end-product is representational of his/her understanding of abstract concepts and theories, and his/her ability to translate these into concrete form. Evaluation in art is best reflected in a performance-based assessment.

Definition: Life drawing is the ability to generate images that are representative of the form being drawn. This includes proportion, volume, depth, and movement.

Levels of performance:

5 Superior

1. The student's drawing has used basic shapes to produce a proportional drawing.
2. The student is able to describe, discuss, and use the concept of depth and volume.
3. The student is able to translate his/her knowledge to create action and movement in their drawings.

3–4 Developing/emerging

1. The student uses basic shapes in a drawing that reflect the basic concepts of proportion but are not fully proportional.
2. The student is able to verbalize an understanding of volume and depth, yet is not totally successful in producing the concept on paper.
3. The student understands the idea of placing basic shapes to create movement in their drawing, but is encountering difficulties when applying this knowledge to pencil/paper tasks.

2–3 Partial

1. The student uses basic shapes in his/her drawing, but their work is not proportional.
2. The student identifies the difference between 2–D and 3–D figures, but does not transfer the knowledge to the task.

BOX 4.1 *(continued)*

3. The student's drawing does not reflect an understanding of body movement.

1. Weak

1. The student's drawing does not use basic shapes and is not proportional.
2. The student cannot verbalize nor demonstrate understanding of volume or depth.
3. The student's drawing is stiff, flat, and does not depict movement.

Source: Karen Aasen, Beth Novak, & Beverly Sequin (product of informal workshop), Calgary Academy.

BOX 4.2

General Topic: Essay Organization

"Organizing an essay includes the ability to focus the topic around a *thesis statement*, and to develop the thesis in a *sequential* and *ordered* manner."

Subtopic: Thesis Statement

5 Superior Thesis Statement

1. The student's thesis is expressed in one sentence.
2. The student's thesis consists of one idea only.
3. The student's thesis is expressed in introduction, and reiterated in conclusion.
4. The student's perspective has a specific qualifying statement. i.e., Calgary is the best city in Canada.

3 Average Thesis Statement

1. The student's thesis is expressed in more than one sentence.
2. The student's thesis consists of more than one idea.

BOX 4.2 *(continued)*

3. The student's thesis is not expressed in both introduction and conclusion.
4. The student's perspective has a general qualifying statement, i.e., Cities are all around us.

1 Poor Thesis Statement

1. The student's thesis does not exist.
2. The student does not express his point of view
3. The student has no apparent focus to the essay
4. The student's perspective has no qualifying statement. i.e., I live in Calgary.

Subtopic: Sequencing

5 Superior Sequencing

1. The student's essay contains an effective introduction and conclusion
2. The student's essay contains one topic per paragraph
3. The student's essay is developed in a logical progression (e.g., compare/contrast, general/specific, chronological, least to most important).

3 Average Sequencing

1. The student's essay contains an unclear introduction and conclusion.
2. The student is inconsistent in expressing one idea per paragraph.
3. The student's essay contains inconsistent logical progression.

1 Poor Sequencing

1. The student's essay does not contain an effective introduction and /or conclusion.
2. The student's essay contains more than or less than one idea per paragraph.
3. The student's essay has no apparent order.

Source: Betty Braithewaite, Rob Tolsma, Krista Thiesen, & Judy Rose (product of informal workshop), Calgary Academy.

BOX 4.3

Topic: Lab Performance

Lab performance involves the ability to cooperate with peers in a safe manner while following given procedures.

5 Superior Lab Performance:
Student demonstrates lab performance required of them in an efficient and effective manner.

1. The student cooperates fully with peers/teacher.
2. The student follows/demonstrates all safety guidelines.
3. The student accurately follows given procedures in a step-by-step manner.

3 Average Lab Performance:
Student displays development in lab performance.

1. The student attempts to cooperate with peers/teacher.
2. The student demonstrates some, but not all, safety procedures.
3. The student begins an appropriate procedure, but is unable to carry it out completely.

1 Inadequate Lab Performance
Student lacks ability to follow proper lab performance.

1. The student infrequently cooperates with peers/teacher.
2. The student infrequently follows (ignores) safety guidelines
3. The student has difficulty following procedures in a sequential manner.

Source: Betty Braithewaite, Rob Tolsma, Krista Thiesen, & Judy Rose (product of informal workshop), Calgary Academy.

BOX 4.4

Activity: Volleyball

Rationale: It is an observable physical skill, that is assessed based on performance.

Definition: Volleyball includes:

service

bump

set

spike

block

The above skills performed at the appropriate time.

Specific Skill : Forearm Pass (Bump)

5	toes pointed to target weight on inside of the ball of feet one foot ahead weight transfer from foot to foot bent knees arms are relaxed and in front of the body contact the ball every time correctly
3	basically the pass is successful with only some minor difficulty e.g., knees not bent arm swing limited weight transfer foot position incorrect
1	V—ball doesn't reach the target due to minimal or no contact with ball knees aren't bent wrong foot position not facing target no weight transfer

Source: Dean Sawatsky, Christine Giles, & Jon Beatty (product of informal workshop), Calgary Academy.

Developing Performance Assessment Devices

Now that we have examined a number of performance assessments developed by classroom teachers, let's turn our attention to how such devices are developed. Figure 4.2 outlines the basic steps in this process. Perhaps the most challenging of these three phases involves defining the performance to be assessed.

FIGURE 4.2
Phases of Performance Assessment Development

Phase 1: Defining Performance

Phase 2: Designing Performance Exercises

Phase 3: Scoring and Recording Results

Source: Richard J. Stiggins. Student-Centred Classroom Assessment (New York: MacMillan College Publishing, 1994).

Steps in this process as they might relate to developing a performance assessment device for assessing effective teaching are identified in Figure 4.3. The first phase, Reflecting and Brainstorming, tends to be the most instructive activity in the process. Teachers begin by asking some very basic but critical questions in relation to the domain they are trying to assess. While such brainstorming activities can be done individually, having teachers working in groups tends to be much more effective.

FIGURE 4.3
Defining Performance

Reflecting and Brainstorming (factors contributing to effective teaching)

Condensing (reducing the factors to 3 to 5 underlying categories or dimensions)

Defining (defining each of the underlying categories or dimensions)

Contrasting (finding words and examples to describe the range of possible performance within each dimension and describing what ineffective teaching looks like on this dimension and how that changes as it moves towards outstanding teaching)

Describing Success (what technique to quantify the levels of effectiveness, e.g., Checklists, Rating Scales, Anecdotal records)

Revising and Refining (e.g., apply your assessment device to evaluate teaching effectiveness.) Does it need refinement?

Another important aspect of performance assessment devices is their ability to address issues of grading. Scoring systems for performance assessment devices frequently take on a "5" for superior, "3" for average, and "1" for weak performance format. A teacher may choose to assign a value of a score of "2" or "4" to signify that the student is in a transition stage of achievement. This type of scoring does not represent the only method available but is, in fact, one of the most popular methods in use.

Advantages of Performance Assessment for the Diverse Classroom

As the composition of the regular classroom increases in diversity, the classroom teacher will need to have a wider range of assessment devices than those traditionally found in most secondary settings. Moreover, the need to make the assessment process even more explicit will increase as students with a variety of learning difficulties become part of the regular classroom. Performance assessment is particularly well suited to address these two issues.

Increasingly, we are becoming aware of the importance of different learning styles as well as different performance abilities. For many students, having a range of assessment tasks, each requiring a different set of skills, provides a more comprehensive picture of their achievement levels than relying on primarily a single approach. Moreover, the open explicitness of performance assessment sends a clear message to students that our assessment activities are not characterized by trickery or guarded secrets but rather they are clear objectives we wish our students to achieve.

Achieving a Balance in Our Assessment Approaches

While performance assessment has much to offer, it also has a number of limitations. First, performance assessment is labour intensive. While the rewards of such devices can be substantial in addressing issues related to student learning and instructional strategies, the issue of time investment and its associated costs is perhaps the greatest barrier to the wide-scale adoption of performance assessment. Second, questions regarding the reliability of the instruments must be raised. Because reliability is influenced by the adequacy of the sample size of assessment items, the use of a performance assessment that focuses on relatively narrow aspects of learning may not give a teacher a sufficient understanding of the student's overall ability levels. Third, just as there are students who encounter test anxiety, some students will undoubtedly experience performance anxiety in an assessment context.

In the everyday experience of the classroom, it is reasonable to use a combination of both traditional and performance assessment activities. When attempting to assess whether your students have a mastery of the knowledge component of a large area of study, a paper–pencil test may be the best choice. However, when the objective of the assessment is to determine whether a student can perform a particular task (e.g., focuses a microscope, delivers an oral critique, engages in a debate, uses a foreign language), a performance assessment would clearly be the best choice.

Conclusion

Educational assessment and evaluation play a central role in all aspects of classroom planning and instruction. Educational decisions can be well-informed by sound assessments. Accordingly, teachers must ensure that assessments meet the critical criteria of adequate validity and reliability. Usability will determine the practicality and cost of any assessment practice. The results from the assessment must be graded and reported in order to effectively plan instruction, provide feedback, and enhance motivation.

SUGGESTED RESOURCES

On the Internet

There are a number of sites on the Internet that can provide you with some very useful information related to assessment activities. The examples sited below are among the most interesting.

The Centre for Research on Evaluation, Standards and Student Testing (CREST) provides educators with information on current trends in assessment and descriptions of resources such as books, videos, articles and technical reports on assessment (some of these are downloadable) aimed at creating a productive assessment environment. The World Wide Web address for CREST is:

http://www.cse.ucla.edu/CRESTHOLME.html.

ERIC/AE Test Locator: This resource assists educators in locating educational tests. In addition, test selection tips are provided and the site contains a searchable database of test descriptions and reviews. The gopher site for this resource is:

gopher://vmsgopher.cua.edu./11gopher_root_eric_ae:[_tc].

Software

TRAC: Teacher Records and Comments is a software package designed to assist the classroom teacher with the recording and organizing of classroom assessment data. Along with the typical grade generation options the program is designed to make anecdotal entries easier and provides complete search and printing capabilities for the anecdotal database. Information regarding TRAC may be obtained from the publisher, Detselig Enterprises Ltd., P.O. Box 399, Calgary, AB T3A 2G3.

Journals

One of the most useful journals for educators interested in issues related to student assessment is *Educational Measurement: Issues and Practice* published by the National Council on Measurement in Education. The journal addresses all aspects of assessments across the entire educational spectrum. Some of the more recent articles have addressed issues relating to the impact of standardized testing on teachers and students, the impact of testing on instruction, an examination of alternative forms of testing, and factors related to the fair assessment of students with disabilities.

REFERENCES

Anastasi, A. (1988). *Psychological testing* (7th edition). New York: Macmillan.

Bloom, B.S. (ed). (1956). *Taxonomy of educational objectives, the classification of educational goals.* New York: David McKay.

Crocker, L., & Algina, J. (1986). *Introduction to classical and modern test theory.* Toronto: Holt, Rinehart & Winston.

Cronbach, L.J. (1984). *Essentials of psychological testing* (5th edition). New York: Harper & Row.

Educational Testing Services. (1963). *Multiple-choice questions: A close look.* Princeton, NJ: ETS.

Foos, P.W., & Fisher, R.P. (1988). Using tests as learning opportunities. *Journal of Educational Psychology, 80,* 179–83.

Gronlund, N., & Linn, R. (1990). *Meaurement and evaluation in teaching* (6th edition). New York: Macmillan.

Hopkins, K., Stanley, J., & Hopkins, B. (1990). *Educational and psychological mesurement and evaluation* (6th edition). Englewood Cliffs, NJ: Prentice-Hall.

McDaniel, M.A., & Masson, M.J. (1985). Altering memory representations through retrieval. *Journal Experimental Psychology: Learning, Memory and Cognition, 11,* 371–85.

Popham, J. (1993). Circumventing the high cost of authentic assessment. *Phi Delta Kappan, 74,* 470–73.

Resnick, L., & Resnick, D. (1992). Assessing the thinking curriculum. In B. Gidford & M. O'Connor (Eds.), *Changing assessments.* Boston: Kluwer.

Sadler, D.R. (1983). Evaluation and improvement of academic learning. *Journal of Higher Education, 54,* 60–79.

Starch, D., & Elliot, E. (1912). Reliability of grading high schoolwork in English. *Scholastic Review, 20,* 442–57.

Starch, D., & Elliot, E. (1913). Reliability of grading high schoolwork in Mathematics. *Scholastic Review, 21,* 254–59.

Sternberg, R. (1992). Ability tests, measurements and markets. *Journal of Educational Psychology, 84,* 134–40.

Stiggins, R.J. (1994). *Student-centered classroom assessment*. New York: Macmillan College Publishing Co.

Violato, C. (1986). Canadian versions of the Information subtest of the Weschler Tests of Intelligence. *Canadian Psychology,* 27, 69–74.

Violato, C., McDougall, D., & Marini, A. (1992). *Educational measurement and evaluation.* Dubuque, IA: Kendall/Hunt.

Wiggins, G. (1993). Assessment: Authentic, context and validity. *Phi Delta Kappan, 75,* 200–14.

Worthen, B.R. (1993). Critical issues that will determine the future of alternative assessment. *Phi Delta Kappan, 74,* 444–57.

CHAPTER 5

Holistic Program Planning: Adapting the Secondary-Level Curriculum

Vianne Timmons

St. Francis Xavier University

Introduction

This chapter focuses on the unique needs of secondary teachers in facilitating the inclusion of adolescents with exceptional learning needs. The emphasis is on planning strategies the secondary teacher can implement to accommodate learners with diverse needs.

The Secondary Teacher

Inclusion of students with special needs has become an area of concern for secondary teachers. The focus of instruction in our secondary schools has traditionally been curriculum oriented. For example, the methodologies taught in teacher education programs have centred around the subject areas rather than child-centred approaches. In recent years, initiatives such as destreaming in Ontario and Nova Scotia and the inclusion model in New Brunswick have increased the numbers of teenagers with special needs in the regular classroom.

Teaching students in an inclusive classroom is a challenge for secondary teachers. They are often required to teach a large amount of content to students with a wide range of abilities. They are also responsible for teaching a greater number of students than the elementary teacher, who has the responsibility of educating a small group of children throughout the day. There may be anywhere from four to seven teachers who are involved in the education of a teenager with special needs in a secondary school. The coordination can be difficult if the communication of information does not occur. The orientation of secondary schools has been heavily academic. It has also been highly resistant to change (Gajar, Goodman & McAfee, 1993). Teachers trained in secondary education need to develop strategies and attitudes that can help them modify classroom instruction to accommodate all students. Teachers need to collaborate with their colleagues to develop ways to adapt planning for students with exceptionalities within their curriculum. There are some general strategies that secondary teachers can utilize in their planning and instruction that provide greater ease and flexibility in accommodating students with special needs. The focus now becomes the learner rather than the curriculum, and this shift does not happen easily.

> I became a secondary teacher to teach high school English not to teach children with special needs.
> (Quotation from a pre-service secondary teacher)

This quotation reflects what can happen when students see curriculum and students as separate. Curriculum needs to be viewed as a guide to instruction. Emphasis on how to ensure learner fit with the content is important for successful integration. Planning for instruction has to move beyond the curriculum and be applied to individual learners.

Teachers in the secondary system are requesting and looking for methods and ways they can accommodate students previously served in special education. Regular classroom teachers should be actively involved in the individualization to ensure that the curriculum expertise is part of the process. The school may have special education personnel or people designated to provide support within the school or the district to provide learner characteristics. The classroom teacher may require information on the child's special needs, learning style, family background, and educational history. The special education personnel may also be involved in team planning, team teaching, and evaluation of instruction. Collaboration where all participants have a valued role is essential for success.

Gathering of Information

The first step in comprehensive planning is the gathering of information. This would usually be initiated by the homeroom teacher or subject area teacher. A special education support person, or a guidance counsellor may also be appropriate personnel to fulfil this role. There needs to be organization of the data collection prior to the planning meeting. Typically, a number of sources are investigated for information.

One of the first sources would be a perusal of the student's school records. Any medical information, such as type of syndrome or disability, should be explained to the school staff. An overview of previous assessments and the results should also be collected. Other important information is the result of previous attempts at inclusion and the results of those endeavours.What were the main objectives for the student and was there success? What strategies were previously attempted and what were the results of these strategies.

One of the goals of the gathering of information is to ensure consistency of techniques between school settings wherever possible. The communication between the student's previous school and/or previous class could be essential for the child's success.

Other sources of information can be gathered from the family and any specialists involved with the family.

The student may also be involved in the planning. Inquiries regarding the student's interests, preferences, and desires may be a key to the instructional adaptations that a teacher can make. In studies looking at quality of life of people with disabilities, it was found that the participants were aware of areas they needed to work on and had realistic aspirations (Goode, 1988; Brown, Bayer & MacFarlene 1988; Timmons, 1993).

The reason for the interview should be explained to the student so that he or she can assist wherever possible. The classroom teacher or special education personnel would be an appropriate person to explain the process to the student. The student should not only be given the opportunity to understand what is happening, but should also give consent.

The Planning Team

The next step is the setting up and format of the planning team.

The planning team may vary in format; however, there are some consistencies that tend to be maintained in most schools. The planning team is school based and fluid in nature, changing for different students. Each student's needs and requirements are unique and therefore may require different support personnel. For example, planning for a teenager with a spinal cord injury may require the presence of a physiotherapist at the planning session, while a student with cerebral palsy may require a speech therapist.

The team in the secondary school could look like this:

- The counsellor
- The homeroom teacher
- The parent
- The student
- Relevant subject teachers
- Support personnel (i.e., special education teacher, physiotherapist, teacher aide, etc.)
- An administrator

If all the subject teachers are not represented, there needs to be a plan of communication established from the onset. A designated person becomes responsible for ensuring that all parties are informed of the outcome of the planning session.

The research reinforces the value of parental involvement in the collaborative process (Van Reusen & Bos, 1994). Parents who participate in team planning contribute a wealth of information that can contribute to their children's success in the classroom (Lazzari, 1992). Research indicates that parental involvement in planning is minimal. However, when parents are involved there is a greater chance for success (Gartner & Lipsky, 1987). Teachers need to encourage the parents to participate in the planning process.

Many students at the secondary level can also contribute to the planning session. Involving the students in the planning process can empower them by allowing them to be part of the decision-making process (Van Reusen & Bos, 1994). The student should be given direction on how he or she can best contribute. It would be reasonable for the team to prepare a draft document for the student to review before the meeting. This could be an overview of suggested objectives for the individualized educational plan.

The Individual Educational Plan

A unique challenge the teachers at the secondary level face is the development of a plan that is specific, clear, and measurable, yet flexible in its application to a number of different subjects.

The plan should be a resource to the classroom teacher and be able to be adapted to a regular lesson plan without too much difficulty. The versatility of the plan is what sets it apart from the elementary setting. Plans at the elementary level are developed for fewer personnel to implement due to the difference in the school scheduling and structure. The secondary plan should focus on coping strategies rather than remediation.

The individual educational plan (IEP) session should be clear and to the point. Classroom teachers need to know the focus of the planning session ahead of time and be presented with an opportunity to review the information that was gathered for the meeting.

One of the difficulties with planning sessions is that they tend to be scheduled after school and all relevant personnel may not be able to attend. There should be ample notice of meetings or have the administration look at flexible planning time during the school day.

A group facilitator should be selected to lead the meeting and coordinate the planning. The mandate of the meeting must be clear. Time should not be spent debating whether or not the student should be included in the regular classroom, but rather how best can the teachers accommodate the student.

The facilitator should also be a skilled group leader, experienced in IEP planning. If a school is undertaking this planning for the first time, an outside person could be appointed who can train the school staff to carry on with other sessions on their own. Although there may be a designated facilitator, the focus needs to be on all the participants contributing their expertise.

The planning should be done in a comfortable setting with few distractions. The group must be able to work effectively and efficiently so that teachers continue to be interested in maintaining involvement with further sessions.

This individual educational plan provides the information for a regular classroom teacher to plan for instruction of the student with special needs. The policies of some school districts may not recommend or enable IEPs to be developed for every student. This does not mean the process for developing an IEP is not valuable for all teachers to know. The individualization of a program can also be done by the classroom teacher if the team is not available. The process begins with the establishment of long-range goals.

Long-Range Goals

Long-range goals need to be established for the students to set the tone and direction for the planning session. They typically span the year; however, they can be biannual. These goals are of a general nature.

Short-Term Objectives

Short-term objectives are derived naturally from the long-range goals. Short-term objectives are organized by domains, which are areas of learning. They can be designated by types of learning such as the cognitive, affective, and social domain. The domains may also be considered subject areas such as English, science, and social studies. They could also be organized by skill acquisition (i.e., new skills, maintenance of skills, and generalization of skills). The classification of the domains should be developed by focusing on the student's strengths and needs.

Short-term objectives should be specific; however, they also need to be easily incorporated into a teacher's lesson plans. The objectives should be written so that they are clearly understood, easily implemented, and measurable. A definite relationship must exist between the purpose of the instruction and the assessment components. This should give the teacher an indication of how to adapt his or her instruction to meet the student's needs. The part of the IEP document that has the objectives for each subject area should not be more than one page in length so that the teacher can implement them with ease. Each subject teacher should leave the planning session with a working IEP for his or her subject area with no more than eight objectives.

Examples of short-term objectives for the student with ADD are: a) the student will stay on task for a minimum of twenty minutes each class, or b) the student will add five minutes to the length of his on-task behaviour each week.

The Individual Educational Plan Form

The planning team may need to set up as a means of evaluating the incorporation of IEPs into lesson plans. This ensures adequate support for the teacher. A supplementary follow-up meeting should be arranged (possibly two weeks later) with the mandate to review the initial implementation of the IEP and assess the applicability to the classroom situation.

Wood (1993) prepared guidelines that the teachers need to consider in the planning:

1. Realize that modifications to the regular class lesson plan may be necessary.
2. Be specific in listing what will occur in each component of the lesson plan.
3. Allow time for teachers to review the lesson plan and develop appropriate modifications.
4. Be flexible when an adaptation or modification does not work.
5. Be prepared to develop an alternate modification.
6. Realize that when a modification is made to the lesson plan, the plan is still valid and not watered down.
7. Be as flexible in modifying the student assignment or evaluation section as you are in modifying the objective and strategies sections.
8. Realize that you are always modifying the lesson plan for the student success and attainment of objectives.

The team facilitator needs to check that each member follows through on the area for which he or she is responsible. There also needs to be a meeting time set for evaluation of the IEP. This should be established at the initial planning meeting. The IEP needs to be easily accommodated into lesson plans.

This form is one possible sample of an IEP form. School districts usually develop their own form.

FORM 5.1

Sample Individual Educational Plan for Secondary Teachers

Date: ________

Team Facilitator: ______________________________

Team Members:	Name	Title/Role
	______________________	__________
	______________________	__________
	______________________	__________
	______________________	__________
	______________________	__________

Assessment Summary:

Tests	Date	Results
____________________	__________	__________________________
____________________	__________	__________________________
____________________	__________	__________________________

Long-Range Goals:

1. ____
2. ____
3. ____

Short-Term Objectives: Domain:	Techniques/Materials	Evaluation
1. ____________________	____________________	__________
____________________	____________________	__________
2. ____________________	____________________	__________
____________________	____________________	__________

FORM 5.1 (*Continued*)

3. ______________________ ______________________ __________
   ______________________ ______________________ __________

Domain: ________________ ______________________ __________

4. ______________________ ______________________ __________
   ______________________ ______________________ __________

5. ______________________ ______________________ __________
   ______________________ ______________________ __________

Domain: ________________ ______________________ __________

6. ______________________ ______________________ __________
   ______________________ ______________________ __________

7. ______________________ ______________________ __________
   ______________________ ______________________ __________

8. ______________________ ______________________ __________
   ______________________ ______________________ __________

Date for Revision: ______________________

Person Responsible for Setting up Meeting: ______________________

The Modification of Lesson Plans

The team needs to be aware of the different levels of learning students engage in when planning the modification of lesson plans. The teacher or team's identification of the student's level of cognitive functioning helps direct the differentiation of the curriculum.

Identifying key concepts is a modification to the lesson that could be of benefit to teachers in their planning. The teacher identifies three key concepts for the student to learn and then ensures that the student has understood these concepts. By providing the student with the focus of the lesson, the teacher is better prepared to direct the student's learning. Consider it bringing the students onside.

The teacher needs to be creative in the lesson modification. Curriculum guides and classroom textbooks may not provide the teacher with specific suggestions on how to meet the different needs of students. Parmar and Cawley

(1993) found in a review of science textbooks that the texts did not recommend modifications for a wide range of learning disabilities, the recommendations made did not actually address the needs of the students for which they were intended, and there was no consistency in the nature of the recommendations. These authors concluded that teachers need to monitor the usefulness of published materials and develop their own supplementary resources.

These modifications may seem challenging; however, teachers are used to working with heterogeneous groups of students in the secondary level and they often have acquired skills to facilitate success. Wood (1993) suggested a format to assist teachers in the adaptation of lesson plans. The model presented on the following page is modified slightly from the original suggested by Wood.

Wood's suggested format is recommended to be a) used by the regular classroom teacher with adaptations made by the special education personnel, and b) completed in total by the regular classroom teacher.

TABLE 5.1
Format to Assist Modifications of Curriculum

	Objective	Strategies	Materials/ Resources	Evaluation/ Assignments
Date:_________ Cognitive Level Adaptations		Teaching Techniques	Adaptations	Evaluation Test
				Student Assignment

Techniques

There are a number of instructional techniques that teachers have found useful in the inclusion of students with special needs in the regular classroom. Some of these techniques were identified by the Roeher Institute in a report that looked at educational practice in Canada for children and youth with disabilities (1992). They found that integrated curriculum practices at the secondary level provided more opportunities for success for students with special needs. This means that teachers who broaden the curriculum boundaries have more opportunities to differentiate the instruction. English classes that incorporate spelling, grammar, writing, and the study of literature can incorporate modifications with relative ease.

In addition, teachers who incorporate various means of instruction can consciously plan for a variety of learning. An important skill teachers require in the teaching field today is flexibility within a structured environment. Teachers who accommodate visual, auditory, and tactile learners are aware of different learning styles.

All the strategies discussed are teacher facilitated rather than teacher directed. This important distinction enables teachers to direct the learning that occurs in the classroom rather than take the total responsibility for the instruction. Andrews and Lupart (1993) identified the changing roles of teachers as one from directive thinking to facilitated thinking. This facilitated learning should be incorporated with direct teaching. Stewart (1993) emphasized facilitated learning and yet cautioned teachers not to abandon direct instruction. Students with special needs can benefit from the direct instruction with the activities, participation, and evaluation differentiated.

Multilevel Instruction

Multilevel instruction allows for different levels of learning within the classroom curriculum. The focus of this strategy is the understanding of key concepts rather than assimilation of content. The teacher would include all the students in the lesson while planning for individual differences. The students are expected to understand and grasp the material in a variety of ways.

Collicott (1991) describes multilevel instruction through a four-step process:

1. Identify the underlying concepts of the lesson or unit.
2. Determine the teacher method of presentation or how concepts will be presented.
3. Determine the student method of practice or how the student will indicate understanding of the concepts.
4. Determine the method of student evaluation.

This will vary depending on the cognitive level of the student. For example, Jane, a student with exceptional reading comprehension abilities in grade 10 who is working with the novel, *Julius Caesar* by Shakespeare, may be asked to identify the historical events that may have impacted on the writing of this novel while the rest of the students are asked to identify the significant events in the novel that impacted on the outcome. Jane may be required to interview an historian, do library research, and write a report. The rest of the class is asked to write a report with diagrams reflecting the events in the novel. Jane is not asked to do more work, but rather has different expectations.

Cooperative Learning

Cooperative learning is the organization of students into small groups for assigned tasks and/or activities. These groups should not exceed three students and the students should have a clear understanding of what they need to accomplish. Hymel, Zinck, and Ditner (1993) found in a review of three different types of classroom learning activities (cooperative, competitive, and individualistic) that cooperative learning structures enhanced learning and improved interpersonal relations. There are five important components that must be part of cooperative learning (Johnson, Johnson & Holubec, 1986; Hymel et al., 1993).

1. *Positive Interdependence:* All groups must contribute to and feel responsible for the success of the group and each member in the group.
2. *Face-to-Face Interaction:* Students must participate in direct, verbal interactions with one another.
3. *Individual Accountability:* There are two elements of individual accountability that are important: a) the fair, equitable distribution of labour and effort, and b) the independent evaluation of learning for each member of the group.
4. *Social Skills Training:* This training needs to be ongoing and incorporated.
5. *Group Evaluation Opportunities:* It is vital that children learn how to self-evaluate the group and discuss the group dynamics. The teacher should also participate in group evaluation.

In cooperative activities, the teacher should not just ask students to move into groups and do a task. The groups need to be carefully selected and the students taught how to work cooperatively. The teacher may have to play around with the composition of groups until the best combination is found. If the students are having difficulty communicating and cooperating because of different personalities, the learning may take second place to the relationships.

The most successful grouping for inclusive practices is heterogeneous groups. This means that the students in the group are of different ability levels. Jenkins, Jewell, Leicester, O'Connor, Jenkins & Trountner (1994) found in a study on grouping of students for instruction that teachers who restructured classrooms utilizing heterogeneous groups were able to accommodate individuals of different ability levels without significant difficulty.

The groups should have designated time limits for the tasks they are assigned. These time lines help teach time management and keep the group on task. At the end of the cooperative learning activity, the group should have a finished product such as ideas recorded or a plan of action written.

In cooperative learning, each person in the group is assigned a specific role. Typical roles are group leader, recorder, and presenter. Kohn (1987) presented an overview of cooperative learning that identified three as an ideal group size. This enabled all participants to be active.

Peer Support and Peer Tutoring

Peer tutoring and support, which focuses on the students in the class as active participants, is becoming a common practice in many secondary schools across the country.

In peer tutoring, one student works with another student to assist the learning of a new skill. The peer tutor may monitor the practice or maintenance of a newly acquired skill. Salend (1994) provides suggestions to teachers supporting or overseeing peer-tutoring programs:

1. Establish specific goals for the sessions.
2. Plan particular learning activities to meet the identified goals.
3. Select tutors who demonstrate proficiency in the content to be taught.
4. Train students to function as successful tutors.
5. Schedule sessions for no longer than 30 minutes and no more than three times per week.
6. Monitor the tutoring process and provide feedback to both students.
7. Inform parents of the purpose and the value of peer tutoring.

Peer tutoring is a strategy that must be carefully planned. It should supplement the classroom teaching, not replace it. It requires time to organize and monitor. Many schools have peer support groups for the entire school. These peer support groups are also trained in peer counselling. A classroom teacher may find it more manageable to focus on peer tutoring rather than peer counselling.

Partial Participation

All students are not expected to participate in all levels of the inclusive classroom. There could be different levels of participation, which should be agreed upon during the planning process. The most common example of partial participation is the level of involvement in group work (Collicott, 1991). Ferguson and Baumgart (1991, p. 219) wrote that:

> The principle of partial participation was proposed to ensure that even those students who might never be able to acquire a full complement of functional skills to completely participate in the activities of their lives would still be able to learn enough to partially participate.

Teachers can define the participation level by simply having shorter assignments or having students presenting personal experiences that are connected to the lesson topic rather than writing a report. Partial participation is a viable way to support inclusive education and keep students with special needs involved in the curriculum.

Reciprocal Teaching

Reciprocal teaching is an instructional technique approach that features "guided practice." It is used as an approach to improve a student's understanding of text. This approach is generated from theories of guided learning, such as Vygotsky's zone of proximal development (Vygotsky, 1978). He believed that children had two developmental levels: the actual and the potential. The actual reflects the level at which children work independently successfully. The potential is the level at which children succeed with assistance or collaboration. The zone of proximal development is the area between these levels and where instruction should take place.

> In reciprocal teaching (a) the focus is upon teaching students specific, concrete, comprehension-fostering strategies which they can apply to the reading of new text and (b) this instruction takes place primarily in the context of a dialogue between the teacher and the students. (Rosenshine & Meister, 1994, p. 480)

The teacher may find that, at times, homogeneous grouping is required to utilize this strategy. For example: the class is working on a novel in English class and has to summarize the chapters. The teacher may wish to have a small group who is experiencing difficulty work with him or her on the summarization activity. The teachers uses prompts, such as why and how questions, to lead the students to identify the essential elements. Eventually the students themselves could learn the questions and prompts that direct their own learning.

Modification of Curriculum for Different Subject Areas

There are ways specific subject teachers can view the differentiation of curricula for various subject areas.

English

If a student has difficulty with reading the required content for the secondary program, suggest a comprehensive reading assessment. The information from this assessment should be made available to the classroom teacher so that he or she has the information required to modify the reading expectations.

There are a number of strategies a teacher can plan for to assist the student in grasping of the content:

1. Taping the text for the student to listen to as he or she reads.
2. Having the student watch a video of the story or play being discussed in class.
3. Having a buddy read along with the student.
4. Identifying specific key concepts you want the student to understand.
5. Having discussions or lectures dictated and recorded for the student to refer to at home.
6. Identifying the key vocabulary in the text the student is reading.
7. Ensuring the student interacts with the written material through discussion and self-regulating strategies such as questioning and predicting.
8. Assigning assignments that challenge the student with advanced comprehension skills such as research into elements that impact on the written text.

The secondary school program also requires writing in all subject areas. If the student has an orthopedic disability, such as cerebral palsy, the teacher will have to look at handwriting aids. The school should solicit the cooperation of an occupational therapist for this advice.

Technology has opened the doors for many students who had difficulty with fine motor control. Computer for word processing should be encouraged for all students at the secondary level, especially students who find the writing process tedious.

Some suggestions for classroom teachers to consider while planning are:

1. Provide an outline for the student to assist him or her with the organization of the written assignment.

2. Allow for a variety of presentation styles such as oral, taped, and videotaped reports.
3. Encourage students to use editors for their work.
4. Vary the length of required projects for students who find writing difficult.
5. Provide different types of projects geared for different learning levels.

These modifications are not limited to English as they cut across curriculum boundaries.

Mathematics

For most students, the ultimate goal of mathematics "is the mastery of problem solving skills necessary for independent living and career success" (Wood, 1993, p. 326). For students who have learning difficulties, the priority for math instruction may be skills needed for independent living. Some strategies that math teachers may find helpful are:

1. Encourage the use of aides, such as calculators, in the secondary classroom. Recognize the student may require instruction on the use of the calculator.
2. Have the students use manipulatives to develop concrete representation of concepts being taught.
3. Use materials for student activities such as money, bills, newspapers, and chequebooks.
4. Relate the activities to everyday activities, such as budgeting, banking services, measurement.
5. Match the math assignment to the student's skill level.
6. Teach the math vocabulary to the student before each math activity and review the vocabulary after.

Social Studies

Wood (1993) presented ways to adapt the social science and science curricula for students with special needs. Social studies instruction is focused on providing information and developing an informed student around community life. Some suggestions that may be of benefit to the social studies teacher when planning for inclusion are:

1. Acquire supplementary texts at different reading levels.
2. Identify the key concepts the students should acquire.
3. Review terms prior to the instruction.
4. Use concrete material, such as maps, photographs, videos, and newspaper clippings, as much as possible.
5. Vary the presentation of charts and graphs so that students can present simplified projects.
6. Allow for alternate ways to complete assignments, such as tapes, videos, shorter reports, and photographic reports.
7. Relate the topics to students' experiences as much as possible.

Science

Science instruction utilizes a variety of instructional techniques. There are some suggestions science teachers may want to keep in mind when planning for the inclusion of students with disabilities.

1. Students with learning difficulties strive in structured, well-organized settings.
2. Clearly present and adhere to the rules regarding safety.
3. Students with physical handicaps and aspects such as mobility, sight and fine motor control require special consideration in lab procedures.
4. Outlines and key words help the students grasp the concepts being taught.
5. For students with significant reading disabilities, emphasize learning through doing and acquire texts of varying reading levels for students to read.
6. Provide simplified lab reporting procedures and data collection sheets.
7. Plan for generalization by relating activities to everyday situations.

Summary

The inclusion of students with special needs takes planning and collaboration as the secondary school is set up differently than an elementary school. This difference makes communication and consistency more difficult, yet just as vital.

The first important component of planning is the collection of relevant information. This needs to be organized to ensure that teachers can focus on important and key information.

The planning team needs to be student centred. It should vary according to the subjects the student takes. The student and the parents should be encouraged to be involved as much as possible.

The planning team develops an individual educational plan for teachers to implement. This plan is a working document that assists the teacher in the modification of lesson plans. It needs to be general enough to be applied to all subject areas, yet specific enough to be evaluated. The IEP consists of long-range plans, short-term objectives, strategies, and evaluation procedures.

Planning for inclusion requires organization, collaboration, and commitment on the part of the teachers. Once teachers are comfortable with the procedures, they become part of the basic school functions.

SUGGESTED RESOURCES

Adapting Instructional Materials for Mainstreamed Students. Jane Burnette (1987). CEC: To order call 1-800-CEC-READ. ($5.00).

ADHD: Inclusive Instruction and Collaborative Practices. Sandra F. Rief. (VC) 38 min. CEC: To order call 1-800-CEC-READ. ($110.00 U.S.).

Chance to Belong: A Story of School Integration. (VC), 20 min., colour. (1987). Roeher Institute, 4700 Keele St., North York, ON, M3J 1P3. ($65.00).

Facing Inclusion Together. (VC) 50 min. (1993). CEC: To order call 1-800-CEC-READ. ($99.00, U.S.).

Jenny's Story. (VC) 15 min. colour. (1987). Roeher Institute, 4700 Keele St., North York, ON, M3J 1P3. ($55.00).

Literacy in Motion. (1993). Roeher Institute, 4700 Keele St., North York, ON, M3J 1P3.($18.00).

Salend, S.J. (1994). *Effective Mainstreaming: Creating Inclusive Classrooms.* Toronto: Maxwell Macmillan Canada.

Teaching Gifted Kids in the Regular Classroom. Susan Winebrenner (1992). CEC: To order call 1-800-CEC-READ. ($19.95).

Winzer, M. (1989). *Closing the Gap News.* Toronto: Copp Clark Pitman.

REFERENCES

Andrews, J., & Lupart, J. (1993). *The inclusive classroom: Educating exceptional children.* Scarborough, ON: Nelson Canada.

Baker, J.M., & Zigmond, N. (1990). Are regular education classes equipped to accommodate students with learning disabilities? *Exceptional Children, 56*(6), 515–26.

Brown, R., Bayer, M., & MacFarlane, C. (1989). *Rehabilitation programmes: Performance and quality of life of adults with developmental handicaps.* Toronto: Lugus Production Ltd.

Collicott, J. (1991). Implementing multi-level instruction: Strategies for classroom teachers. In G. Porter & D. Richler (Eds.), *Changing Canadian schools: Perspectives on disability and inclusion.* Toronto: Roeher Institute.

Ferguson, D.L., & Baumgart, D. (1991). Partial participation revisited. *The Journal of the Association for Persons with Severe Handicaps, 16*(4), 218–27.

Gajar, A., Goodman, L., & McAfee, J. (1993). *Secondary schools and beyond: Transition of individuals with mild disabilities.* Toronto: Maxwell Macmillan Canada.

Gartner, A., & Lipsky, D. (1987). Beyond special education: Toward one quality system for all students. *Harvard Educational Review, 57,* 367–95.

Goldstein, M.T. (1982). "Curriculum: The keystone to instructional planning in special education." Paper presented at the annual meeting of the Association for Educational Communications and Technology, Dallas.

Goode, D.A. (1988). *Principles and recommendations from the quality of life project.* New York: Mental Retardation Institute.

Hymel, S., Zinck, B., & Ditner, E. (1993). Cooperation versus competition in the classroom. *Exceptionality Education Canada, 3*(1&2).

Jenkins, J.R., Jewell, M., Leicester, N., O'Connor, R.E., Jenkins, L.M., & Trountner, N.M. (1994). Accommodations for individual differences without classroom ability groups: An experiment in school restructuring. *Exceptional Children, 60*(4), 344–58.

Johnson, D.W., Johnson, R.T., & Holubec, E.J. (1986). *Circles of learning: Cooperation in the classroom* (Revised). Edina, MN: Interaction Book Co.

Kohn, A. (1987). It's hard to get left out of a pair. *Psychology Today,* October, 53–57.

Lazzari, A. (1992). Mainstreaming: A shared responsibility. In J. Wood (Ed.), *Adapting instruction for mainstreaming and at-risk students* (pp. 67–95). New York: Merrill/Macmillan.

Parmar, R.S., & Cawley, J.F. (1993). Analysis of science textbook recommendations provided for students with disabilities. *Exceptional Children, 59*(6), 518–31.

Roeher Institute. (1992). *How it happens: A look at inclusive educational practice in Canada for children and youth with disabilities.* North York, ON: Roeher Institute.

Rosenshine, B., & Meister, C. (1994). Reciprocal teaching: A review of the research. *Review of Educational Research, 64* (4), 479–530.

Salend, S.J. (1994). *Effective mainstreaming: Creating inclusive classrooms.* Toronto: Maxwell Macmillan Canada.

Stewart, D. (1993). Teaching or facilitating: A false dichotomy. *Canadian Journal of Education, 18*(1), 1–3.

Timmons, V. (1993). "Quality of life: Teenagers with special needs." Ph.D. thesis, University of Calgary.

Van Reusen, A.K., & Bos, S.C. (1994). Facilitating student participation in individualized education programs through motivation strategy instruction. *Exceptional Children, 60*(5), 466–75.

Vygotsky, L.S. (1978). *Mind in society: The development of higher psychological processes.* (M. Cole, V. John-Steiner, S. Schribner, & E. Souberman, Eds. and Trans.). Cambridge, MA: Harvard University Press.

Wood, J.W. (1993). *Adapting instruction for mainstreamed and at-risk students.* (2nd edition). Toronto: Maxwell Macmillan Canada.

CHAPTER 6

Instructional Strategies for Meeting the Learning Needs of All Students in the Classroom

Margaret Brown
James Fasano

Acadia University

Introduction

The 1980s witnessed a growing interest in improving educational outcomes for children with various disabilities in Canadian schools. Educating all students together in the regular classroom was seen as a rational approach in preparing all children to be fully participating, valued members of their community. Historically, secondary schools used an organizational model whereby learning needs among the students were relatively homogeneous, teaching was subject/content centred, and little communication among teachers was required. Practice has shown us that these classes were not as homogeneous as once thought and that teachers needed and used some variation in instructional approaches (Goodlad, 1984).

Establishing a successful model of full inclusion in secondary schools poses different and perhaps more complex, but not insurmountable, problems. This requires an adaptation to the manner in which secondary teachers organize their classrooms, present the curriculum, evaluate learning outcomes, and relate to other professionals. Fortunately, the mechanisms for change do not have to be invented, as these new roles and responsibilities require a conscious consolidation and some modest extension of established best practices. The secondary teacher facing the inclusive classroom should be reassured in the knowledge that the key lies in the extension of flexibility, not the discovery of new mystical techniques.

Individualization Strategies to Facilitate Inclusion

The increasing diversity of learning needs among students in secondary classrooms requires careful attention to individualization within the framework of the general instruction. To accomplish this, teachers build on a foundation of principles for inclusive classrooms, attend to the learning styles of the students present in the classroom, and adjust the curriculum accordingly.

Strategy 1: Utilize Principles of Inclusion

To prepare for teaching in inclusive secondary classrooms, keep in mind the following principles:

1. Include the whole class in the lesson.
2. Focus on understanding concepts rather than covering content.
3. Expect that not all learners will derive the same type or amount of learning from any lesson.
4. Identify the specific purpose for each student in the lesson.
5. Incorporate individual learning objectives into the lesson.
6. Employ a variety of flexible instructional strategies.
7. Integrate lessons across curriculum-thematic units.
8. Employ a variety of flexible evaluation strategies.

Lesson preparation is based on the assumption that all students will participate. While the amount of content to be covered in secondary schools is important, the primary focus of the teacher's attention needs to be on underlying concepts and their application to the real world. It is not possible, nor would it be desirable, for all students to derive exactly the same type or amount of learning from any particular lesson. Expect different learning outcomes depending on a student's background knowledge, interest, ability, and motivation, as well as the cognitive or psychomotor demands of the learning tasks.

Initially, the teacher identifies a lesson to be taught and decides on instructional strategies for the range of learning styles normally found in the class. Individual learning objectives, derived from formal individualized plans or from informal teacher assessment, are then incorporated into the lesson plan for those students who need them. Evaluation of student learning is accomplished by the teacher using a variety of assessment strategies that permit students to demonstrate their knowledge in their most efficient and effective manner.

Strategy 2: Accommodate Learning Styles

The diversity of learning needs found in heterogeneous classes can best be described in terms of learning styles rather than labels. Naturally occurring numbers in an inclusive class will likely have no more than one student with some type of severe disability (e.g., mental handicap, autism, deafness, legal blindness), several students experiencing difficulty with reading, writing, communication, numbers, behaviour (e.g., learning disability), the majority of students experiencing no obvious difficulty mastering the curriculum (e.g., typical learner), and a few students requiring enrichment or extension of the curriculum (e.g., giftedness). Ability/disability labels serve little purpose in assisting the teacher in the design and delivery of the appropriate instructional program.

Consideration of learning styles during lesson preparation provides increased opportunities for all members of the class to benefit from the instruction (Gamoran, 1987; Samples, 1992). The traditional methods of lecture and discussion, practice through reading and writing activities, and evaluation by means of a written test impede full access to the curriculum for a large segment of the class. Most of us receive information through a variety of modes, though a particular mode or combination of modes can be identified as the preferred learning style of each individual. Although a particular disability may interfere with learning through one or more modes, we must not assume that we know which of the other unaffected learning modes is the preferred learning style for that individual student. For example, among three students who are blind, Jennifer learns best through the auditory channel, while Darren learns best through the tactile and manipulative/hands-on mode, and Katrina seems to learn best through multisensory input. Regardless of the labels that might be used to identify a certain student or disability, the preferred learning style may have little to do with the disability itself. Teachers, therefore, need to be primarily concerned with delivering a curriculum via varied and flexible learning activities that incorporate visual, auditory, motor, kinesthetic, and tactile approaches.

The effectiveness of a multimodal approach to teaching is supported by recent research. For example, as part of a curriculum modification research project (SCAMP) in a Canadian secondary school attempting inclusion (Brown & Fasano, 1990), interviewed teachers indicated that curriculum materials originally intended for a student with particular learning needs were found to facilitate learning for a number of other students as well. That is, teachers were surprised to discover improved learning outcomes for students considered "average" or "typical" learners, because at least some part of the instruction matched their preferred, or most efficient, learning style (Fasano & Brown, 1992).

Strategy 3: Individualize Curriculum

To promote optimal learning for each student in the class, the teacher participates in the development of individualized plans for specific students and incorporates the individual learning objectives into the class lessons. To accomplish this, the following steps are taken:

1. Assess the specific student's learning characteristics.
2. Assess the classroom learning environment.
3. Identify learning goals and objectives for the specific student.
4. Incorporate the student's learning objectives into the class lessons.

Typically, some form of individualized plan is prepared for students with exceptional learning needs to assist in the delivery of an appropriate program. Some teachers get the individual student's portion of their overall plans from formal individual educational plans (IEPs), or from McGill Action Planning System (MAPS) (Lusthaus & Forest, 1987; Vandercook, York & Forest, 1989), or from less formal ongoing problem-solving activities with colleagues. Having primary responsibility for all students in the class, the teacher participates in the gathering and coordination of appropriate information to generate a detailed profile of the student and the learning environment.

The profile contains all relevant information regarding the student's learning characteristics, style, strengths, and interests, as well as the areas of difficulty and needs within the present learning environment. Where a student is approaching a transition stage, from middle school to high school, or from high school to community, the demands of the next learning environment will also be a consideration in the planning. To ensure that the profile is a rich description of the student, all possible sources of information must be tapped. The essential input comes from the student, the parents, and the homeroom and subject teachers, who collectively generate the necessary information on the student's strengths and needs in all the present learning contexts. Others, such as the principal, resource teacher, speech and language specialist, physiotherapist, occupational therapist, or other support personnel will be included when appropriate.

The development of a student profile occurs most easily at the elementary level where the majority of class instruction is in the hands of one teacher. In the typical secondary school, where teachers are in daily contact with scores of students, the development of such profiles is more difficult if no one person has the responsibility of acquiring a holistic view of the student.

Successful inclusion at the secondary level utilizes organizational strategies, commonly found in the modern middle-level school, which permit the student to be well known by an individual staff member. This may be accomplished in a number of ways. For example, team planning time, when teachers teaching the same group of students meet together, provides opportunity to share information and ideas concerning a student. Meeting students in advisory groups, organized in some schools as homeroom periods, or in adviser-advisee session, also provides teachers with a more intimate knowledge of individuals. In addition, counsellors assigned the same group of students each year, perhaps alphabetically A–L or M–Z, accumulate knowledge on the same students and their siblings. Another model schedules three periods per cycle for the homeroom teacher to meet with individual students for guidance and counselling. Such students are called back individually from the classes of other teachers (Fasano, 1984). Thus in the secondary school, while many people need to be involved in the development of individualized plans, the person having the primary responsibility for producing a student profile may be any of a number of the teachers who have contact with the student in question.

The next task is one of translating and embedding individualized goals and objectives from the profile into the generic lessons and units of instruction. Each subject teacher begins by examining the unit of instruction and engages in a form of "curriculum cruelty." For any group of students, teachers must be ruthless with their content to determine a) what is critical, b) what is important, and c) what is desirable (Pratt, 1994). The teacher determines the appropriate learning objectives for the various groups and individuals in the class. For example, students identified as gifted in the particular subject area will be exposed to a wider range of objectives than those students experiencing some type of learning difficulty. In each case, the learning objectives are designed to appropriately challenge the student.

The learning activities to be used are designed to suit the learning styles and needs expected to be present in the class. The teacher then further adjusts the instructional approach and learning activities by accommodating the specific individualized learning style and needs of the profiled student(s).

Organizational Strategies to Facilitate Inclusion

To facilitate successful teaching in inclusive secondary classrooms, consider the following organizational strategies.

Strategy 1: Organize the Physical Setting

Consideration needs to be given to the best location for each student within the classroom. Because of variations in vision, a student might be placed near the front of the room, or away from the glare produced by an outside window. Consider placing a student with a hearing impairment near the front of the classroom to be in closer proximity to the speaker's voice and to provide a clear view of the speaker's face for visual cues and support in accessing the auditory information. If an interpreter is used, the student might best be placed at the front and to one side. For independent work, a student who is distracted by visual and/or auditory stimuli might be provided with a three-sided study carrel to be used while engaged in independent or partner work. If the class includes a student who uses a wheelchair or walker, aisle space in the classroom must be sufficiently wide to permit access to all areas of the room. Desks, tables, lab benches, and bookshelves must be of a suitable height. Sometimes aisle space is required to permit a student to work with a peer or with a teaching assistant. While there are no hard and fast rules, as each student's needs will be different, it is important to be flexible and creative in organizing the classroom.

Strategy 2: Organize Classroom Routines

Classroom routines can be established that facilitate access to, and management and storage of, learning materials by the students. Such individual or group materials as instructions for written assignments, values clarification exercises, learning activities and games, and the like can be organized in learning activity packets and learning centres. Providing specific locations for the submission and return of homework and assignments is accomplished through something as simple as in/out baskets. Managing permission for students to leave the room can be regulated by providing a single "permission to leave" or "hall" card placed by the door, which students access and return independently, thereby limiting the number of requests as well as the number of students leaving the room at one time. These organizational strategies not only facilitate the efficient operation of the classroom, but, more importantly, provide a stable structure for those students who require organizational support to effectively manage their time and materials.

A second source of stability for students in the classroom is a well-understood and appropriate code of conduct. Student understanding is promoted by involving them in the development of a clear statement of student rights and responsibilities. Keeping the agreed-upon rules to a minimum, in addition to explaining and posting them in the classroom, can help minimize confusion and reduce lost instructional time. Being generous with praise for abiding by the rules, and ensuring that consequences for failure to respect the rules are logical and consistently applied, promotes a positive learning atmosphere. Remember that the most powerful means for teaching the rules of appropriate conduct is the behaviour modelled by the teacher.

Strategy 3: Organize the Students

How students are organized will vary depending upon the nature of the lesson or learning experience and where the learning is taking place. Regardless of the location and the activity, Ferguson and Fairchild (1992) suggest three basic principles that should always be applied when creating student groups:

1. Maximize variation across student characteristics.
2. Maximize positive interdependence.
3. Maximize individual accomplishments.

Structuring the learning activities to facilitate learning the material, working together, building peer relationships, and maximizing positive interdependence, teachers organize the students within each group so that they can see one another, share materials, and help one another. The learning activity is organized so that the efforts of all members of the group are required to complete the activity successfully. Roles, such as recorder, encourager, data collector, checker, reader, helper, reporter, etc., need to be assigned and periodically rotated among group members to enable each student to play a part in the successful functioning of the group, and to learn to take a leadership role (Ferguson & Fairchild. 1992). Where appropriate, an assigned role can be matched to a particular IEP objective for a student. For example, one objective for Douglas is to learn to address classmates by name. His assigned role in his group is the helper passing out the work material and using the person's name as he gives each one the material. On the other hand, one of Mark's objectives is to learn to identify main ideas. His assigned role in his group is summarizer, writing down the main ideas on a prepared organizer sheet. Objectives must be stated for and understood by individuals and the groups, and any necessary support can be provided by the teacher as progress is monitored. Groups need to be acknowledged and rewarded for developing strategies for helping one another, involving everyone in the group, and solving interpersonal difficulties (Ferguson & Fairchild, 1992).

Given that specific goals and objectives will vary according to each student's learning needs, maximizing individual accomplishments needs to be facilitated by the organization of student groups. By combining learning tasks that are related and require similar time and location, the amount of learning expected to be mastered by each student can vary and yet be achieved through a common learning activity. Using a cooperative approach rather than a competitive one allows teachers to evaluate on the basis of individual improvement, group project, and/or individual learning objectives (Johnson, Johnson, Holubec & Roy, 1988).

Strategy 4: Organize Support Personnel

Support personnel in an inclusive classroom primarily includes educational assistants, resource teachers, team teachers, and parent or community volunteers. Decisions regarding level of support are made by the teacher in collaboration with the student, parents, and principal, considering the following factors:

A. Determine teacher support required. The amount and nature of support required by the teacher varies according to the size of the class, the nature of the diversity represented in the class, and the background, skills, and experience the teacher brings to the teaching situation. An inexperienced teacher may well require more support than a teacher who has had several years' experience in an inclusive classroom. Similarly, an experienced teacher may require more support if the class is larger than usual, or if the learning needs of one or more of the students is more complex than usual. More support may be required for specific periods of time, such as at the beginning of the term, or during a complex unit of instruction in a lab. Support can best be provided in a flexible structure, accessed as needed and reallocated when not needed.

B. Determine student support required. The amount and nature of support required by individual students varies according to the particular needs of the learner and by the demands of the learning task. A student is likely to require more support when a new task is introduced, however, as the skill develops and becomes fluent, the student will succeed with support reduced or removed. Teachers must strive to provide only the minimum amount of assistance essential for student success. The primary support for all students remains with the teacher who decides when and how support will be provided by others. It is important that students requiring support look for and receive it from a variety of sources: teacher, educational assistant, classmates, and other school personnel. Being tied to a single support person limits the learning environment to the particular style of the support person, and limits the students' opportunities to learn and practise social interaction behaviours in varied contexts.

C. Utilize existing structures as supports. Some teacher support exists, or has the potential to exist, within the typical organizational structures of the school. For example, tapping the experience and expertise of other teachers within the school through the use of collaborative teams provides substantial assistance to teachers creating responsive learning environments for students with diverse learning needs. Types of collaborative teams would include teachers meeting as grade level or interdisciplinary teams to focus on cooperative planning for a particular student or curriculum issue, or as subject teams to focus on a particular element of subject matter. In the past, problem-solving teams of various types have been in place to deal with general items of concern raised by teachers requesting assistance or were created to assist with particular types of schoolwide student difficulties, such as behaviour, discipline, motivation, and the like. The role of such teams may be expanded to include matters related to improving inclusion. For example, MacKinnon and Brown (1994) describe one Nova Scotia junior high school with a teacher team in place known as the Mod Squad (modification team). This pre-inclusion volunteer structure had existed for years, and met weekly at noon to deal with concerns raised by individual teachers. When the school became a fully inclusive school, the Mod Squad team proved to be a most effective means of providing support to teachers and of devising creative ways to improve the inclusive learning environment for the whole school.

Two other school professionals have a direct support function. The principal, as the curriculum leader of the school, plays a leadership role in the initiation and development of support teams. Administrators can also put in place structures that facilitate teaming, such as timetables with common team time. Further, the principal may take an active role in accessing specialist and community supports outside of the school. Resource teachers are a valuable support in providing teaching ideas, locating materials, or acting as another set of eyes to observe the classroom.

The students in the classroom are an often overlooked source of teacher support. In one situation, the student with exceptional learning needs may be the best source of information, while in other situations classmates may provide helpful ideas. Students' perception of schooling is very different, though no less valuable, than the teachers' perception of the same experience. Given the opportunity to participate in meaningful problem solving with teachers, students' fresh perspectives frequently result in very creative solutions to difficult problems (Glasser, 1986; Johnson et al., 1988; Villa & Thousand, 1988, 1992).

D. Utilize specialists as support. Outside specialist support is sought when the nature of a specific student's learning needs cannot be satisfactorily met by resources typically found within the school. Using the chain of command established by each school board, the teacher's role is to access the necessary support to be able to appropriately meet the needs of all students in the class. The role of the outside specialist is to provide the assessment and intervention advice required to improve the learning outcomes for particular student(s) and to assist with embedding the interventions within the regular curriculum.

E. Understand the effects of support. Teaching is characterized as an involved, complex, sometimes frustrating, but rewarding task at any time. Teacher support is crucial in classes of students with widely diverse learning needs. With the appropriate type and amount of support, the experience is a positive one as teachers learn new skills, find satisfaction in their teaching, and become better teachers overall (York Giangreco, Vandercook & Macdonald, 1992). However, proper balance is essential as there is danger in both undersupport and oversupport. Insufficient support can lead to teacher frustration and burnout, lowered achievement for all students, and dissatisfaction expressed by parents, administrators, and school board. However, oversupport also has negative effects as teachers become dependent upon the expertise of others, relinquish their responsibility for some of their students, and fail to learn new skills.

Pedagogical Strategies to Facilitate Inclusion

Students learn from everything that happens in the classroom. Teachers must consciously be aware of the total learning environment and ensure that it promotes positive growth for all students in the inclusive classroom.

Strategy 1: Model Attitudes and Values

Not surprisingly, the teacher is a powerful force in the classroom whose actions communicate important values and attitudes. When speaking to or about students, teachers convey respect by always referring to students by their names rather than by their characteristics, and especially not by their disability or exceptionality.

Inclusive classrooms means more than including students with exceptionalities. The words and actions used by teachers can convey the presence or absence of gender bias. To prevent inadvertently expressing, and thereby teaching or condoning, gender bias, teachers can be sensitive to the fact that the quick and open responses typical of male students may interfere with the opportunity to receive the more reticent and reflective responses typical of the female students. Consciously providing sufficient wait time for all students to prepare a response, and asking for answers and opinions from females and males equally, creates a positive learning environment for all students. Gender role stereotyping, such as "girls are no good at math" or "boys are such ruffians," is avoided as such statements set up inappropriate expectations (Bowyer, 1990).

In recent years, high schools have taken on a more human face by becoming more student centred while continuing to value quality content. Such simple acts as being in the classroom to greet your students as they enter, and making positive comments not only about their academic achievements but social activities and personal accomplishments as well, form the basis of a warm, trusting relationship between teacher and student. Just being available in the classroom during recess, lunch, and after school times provides a welcome opportunity that many students will use for informal chats and formal appointments.

The Welcoming Classroom

1. Speak to or about students by name.
2. Place equal value on all parts of the curriculum.
3. Create a gender fair learning environment.
4. Create a welcoming classroom with your presence.
5. Be available to students for informal chats.
6. Recognize the social nature of acquiring knowledge.
7. Model collaborative problem solving and learning.

Teachers teach a more powerful lesson about the social nature of acquiring knowledge by the way they permit students to treat one another in the learning process than by the words teachers use to describe it (Bricker, 1989). Both social and academic objectives can be addressed by structuring learning experiences in ways that contribute to the students' abilities to learn the material, to work cooperatively, and to build relationships with one another. Letting go of the traditional role of "teacher as information giver," and adopting a role of "teacher as problem solver" and "teacher as lifelong learner" helps to create a collaborative and welcoming learning environment for students.

Strategy 2: Provide Structure

Most students benefit from some measure of structure to facilitate their learning. For some, the structure needs to be explicit, tangible, and consistent, but need not interfere with normal routines and learning activities, nor make a particular student stand out. For students to transfer their learning to real life, it is essential that the teacher structure learning activities to foster the use of natural cues, rather than having students learn to be dependent upon teachers or teaching assistants. For example, homework instructions, written in the same place on the board each day, help the student with organizational problems learn to find it. Designating one notebook, perhaps of a specified colour, for recording all homework helps prevent loss or misplacement of homework assignments. Schedules to be followed, organizational charts for completing the assigned tasks, and colour coding materials according to purpose may provide unobtrusive support for a number of students in the class.

All students need structure for learning the social behaviours necessary for requesting or offering and/or giving or receiving peer support. Clear expectations and evaluation procedures can be provided in a standards booklet listing what constitutes an essay at each grade level, cooperation at each grade level, a research paper at each grade level, and so on.

Strategy 3: Vary Basic Instructional Approaches

When preparing for instruction, each lesson is planned for the whole class, with individual learning objectives interwoven into class objectives, so that the lesson has a specific purpose for every student (Collicott, 1991). Subsequently, the teacher decides on an appropriate instructional approach.

Expository

When disseminating oral information to students, and when providing comprehensive explanations, consider a number of strategies. The teacher can provide headings on the board or overhead, and copies of notes for an individual student where necessary. When utilizing board space, a left-to-right sequence needs to be employed in order to be logical and predictable, and results in notes being left on for longer periods of time. When speaking to a class, the teacher should face students directly so that they can access facial cues. Developing a pattern of consistency in presenting key concepts, etc., can be achieved by delivering vital information from the same location in the classroom utilizing an established visual or auditory cue. Such a cue might be: "Listen up," shutting off the overhead, lowering one's voice, and/or standing on "the spot."

Expository presentations become more meaningful to many students when accompanied by outline organizers. Such organizers can be verbal or graphic, and may be used on overhead by the teacher a) at the beginning of the class to indicate the overall nature of the topic to be covered and the various parts that comprise it, b) periodically throughout the class to indicate where a part of the discussion fits into the overall topic, and c) at the end of the class to review what has been learned in the class.

Inquiry

The inquiry mode includes seeking information, solving problems, and conducting investigations or experiments. These formats are particularly useful for students who have difficulty with auditory input or processing, or who have a strong preference for the tactile or manipulative learning modes.

A frequent application of the inquiry mode is the asking of questions. Some students find questions asked by the teacher intimidating. Tension can be reduced for the student if the teacher asks only questions that the student can answer, asks the question slowly and in clear, simple language, and allows sufficient wait time for the student to formulate the response. For students who have difficulty responding to questions in class or who have learned from previous experience to be fearful of responding, the teacher can privately arrange to cue the student, for example, by asking the student a question only when standing directly in front of him or her. This allows the student to concentrate on the discussion, rather than worrying about being called upon as each question is asked. Having students ask one another questions in small, cooperative groups provides a safe environment for learning, practising, and reviewing the instructional material.

Demonstration

Demonstration is especially suitable for students who need to be shown or engage in the activity themselves to learn. Within any subject, teacher modelling, student modelling, and simulations are typical forms of demonstration. Visual cues are an essential part of demonstration; however, auditory cues may or may not be helpful.

Activity

Activity-based instruction is a "learning by doing" approach best used with small, cooperative groups of students, although individual or whole class variations may also be used. Hands-on manipulations, such as constructing models or exhibits, and drama and role playing, provide excellent learning opportunities for all students engaged in science, mathematics, social studies, and languages. Instructions need to be given orally and in written form for students to understand, to follow the steps, and to complete the activity. Interdisciplinary instructional units, which involve such activities as projects and field trips, provide an overall structure for numerous facts otherwise unrelated, and furnish many different perspectives on the same concepts.

Activity-based instruction is particularly suited for multi-ability groups of students, as all learning styles and abilities can easily be accommodated. For example, in a drama activity some students play a major role, others a minor role, and others will be involved in preparing sets, costumes, advertising posters, or programs.

Strategy 4: Provide Learning Modality Support

While the section above examined teaching methods, this section details ways of providing additional student support, focusing on each of the learning modalities.

Visual Supports

When the instruction is primarily oral, either through lecture or discussion, visual support can be provided with pictures, photographs, diagrams, charts, maps, globes, and constructed models to assist student comprehension. Using overheads with key points underlined, circled, or written in a different colour ink provides additional support. For students who are beginning readers, non-print visual supports such as pictures and photographs are particularly important, although they should never be used in the absence of the crucial vocabulary words related to the topic. Bulletin boards can be used to display important images and vocabulary or to provide an interactive activity relevant to the instructional unit.

Structured organizers are essential for many students to comprehend expository information and learn to develop organizational skills that are transferable to other areas of learning. These organizers contain all or part of the information, or are left blank for the student to add all the relevant information in the appropriate structured spaces. Graphic organizers, in vertical (top-down or bottom-up) format or in horizontal (sequential) format, can be prepared to demonstrate a sequence, cause and effect, comparisons, illustrated design to be labelled, or points leading to a conclusion.

Auditory Supports

Students experiencing any level of difficulty with reading can be supported by having the text on audiotapes to be used in conjunction with the text. Further, material written on the board needs to be read aloud. Providing opportunities for brief discussion, either in small groups or the whole class, helps consolidate information difficult to obtain only through visual or written information.

Tactile Supports

Tactile learners need to be able to touch objects to fully understand them. For any unit of instruction, providing real-life objects or artifacts and engaging students in projects involving construction of models can be very helpful. For example, when studying geology, students will benefit from being able to feel the different textures of various rocks. When studying the production of wheat on the prairies, having samples of seeds, green and dried wheat, cracked wheat, and/or natural and refined flour helps comprehension.

Manipulative Supports

Mathematics and science particularly lend themselves to the use of manipulative supports. Some students benefit from using sticks or string to form the structures studied in geometry.

Kinesthetic Supports

For some students, using the whole body is a means of understanding concepts. While not all instructional content lends itself to this form of learning, much of it can. For example, to help understand the position and movement of planets in the solar system, have students physically position themselves appropriately and walk through the rotations around a simulated sun. Or to help understand the construction or analysis of a particular type of writing, for example, try the use of alliteration, where students identified as specific letters arrange themselves in the appropriate sequence.

Technological Supports

Computer technology is fast becoming a standard learning tool in the classroom. In its simplest form, computers offer support to students having difficulty with writing, as it avoids the visual-motor activity of handwriting per se, and provides spelling and grammar editing support and easy correction of errors. Use of these basic modifications accommodate many learning needs. Computer adaptations such as modified keyboards, alternate keyboards and overlays, braille input and output, voice input and output, single switches, and touch window open up many new avenues for students with diverse learning needs.

Multimedia, particularly with videodisc or CD-ROM components, provide access to a multitude of visual and auditory information in interactive formats.

Strategy 5: Vary Evaluation Strategies

Evaluation of student progress involves decisions about how and when evaluation will take place. Giving students some choice of learning activities and assignments provides teachers with important information about how each student learns best. Progress needs to be evaluated taking individual differences into account; therefore, choices regarding method of demonstrating knowledge need to be available.

For evaluation procedures conducted in a specific time period, such as tests or examinations, adjustment must be made for students who require extended time. Accommodations also may be made for students who a) perform best when questions are presented orally, either by a teacher, assistant, or on audiotape, or b) experience difficulty with the writing process and perform best when questions are answered orally, on audiotape, or on computer.

Strategy 6: Provide Recognition

Students need recognition not only for academic success but for such nonacademic activity as participation in sports, helping others, social activities, drama, yearbook, and the like. Placing student work on display improves self-esteem, sparks creativity and motivation, and increases sense of ownership toward school. School and classroom award programs can be employed that recognize real achievement on the part of each student.

Curriculum Material Strategies to Facilitate Inclusion

Modifying curriculum materials to suit a particular student has long been recognized as a traditional task of teachers. The few existing studies typically focus on a particular disability and/or the elementary classroom. One recent study addressing secondary curriculum for a wide range of student needs is the Secondary Curriculum Adapted Materials Project (SCAMP) at Acadia University in Nova Scotia (Fasano & Brown, 1992). This project identified modification strategies for instructional materials to complement the standard curriculum, suitable for the full range of diversity and intervention intensity encountered in inclusive secondary classrooms. The following strategies address all levels of learning needs, have their origins in the SCAMP project (Fasano & Brown, 1992), and are intended as starting points for the creative teacher.

A. Principles for curriculum materials modification. In addition to lecture and discussion, such learning strategies and activities as modified reading materials, photo study, paper–pencil activities, board and card games, and speaking and movement activities may all be used in the following ways:

1. In the early stages of a lesson as an introduction or as motivation.
2. As the main vehicle of content delivery in the body of the lesson.

3. In the latter stages as part of review and/or practice.

4. For testing or evaluation of learning.

Thus, modified learning activities in the classroom, when viewed as an integral part of ongoing lessons, offer unique ways to vary and extend educational experiences for heterogeneous groups of students. In cooperative learning settings, they encourage students of widely diverse abilities to engage in a common activity, learn together, and support one another.

The modification strategies and learning activities presented here can be used to support reinforcement of past learning, review and practice of new learning, and evaluation of student progress. For some students, it is a challenging opportunity to go beyond the *desirable* curriculum content and expand vocabulary, answer complex questions, use abstract thought, solve complex and cryptic clues, engage in independent research, extend the application of discipline-specific vocabulary, or develop a second language. For others, the activities focus on *important* content, may utilize fewer words and less complex reading, may provide visual support in the form of pictures, diagrams, graphs, etc., may have varying complexity of questions and clues, and may avoid the use of cryptic clues. Experience has taught us that students encountering extreme difficulty with print and who are at the very early stages of beginning reading can benefit from modified activities. For these students, the activities provide interesting avenues for presenting new, *critical* curriculum content material, introducing high-frequency content-related vocabulary and concepts, and posing questions by means of simplified text, minimal reading, short sentences with words selected from target vocabulary, Cloze technique (fill in the blanks), scrambled answers, and substantial visual support in the form of pictures or word lists of correct answers.

B. Development of modified materials. Whether learning activity resources are developed by the teacher, by teaching assistants, by school volunteers, or by students, time and effort are required. Teachers are encouraged to develop a collection of adapted materials over the years that can be updated and revised for ongoing use in the classroom.

Teachers developing modified learning materials and activities may find the following steps helpful:

1. With colleagues, brainstorm activities and games you have engaged in or observed.

2. Assume any curriculum content can be presented in any format.

3. Choose a challenging topic, even if it might be difficult to adapt.

4. List and prioritize—as critical, important, or desirable—the facts, concepts, and principles to be learned, practised, and expanded.

5. Consider the range of reading and ability levels to be included.
6. For board games, sketch out your plan on paper.
7. Be creative in design, e.g., a game designed in basketball format having question cards shaped like basketballs, or question cards for a concentration game based on electricity shaped like light bulbs.
8. Consider ease of storage of materials while at design stage.
9. Wherever possible, provide an answer key for students to self-check their responses.
10. Pilot test it outside the classroom or at home to identify the needed improvements.
11. Modify and complete the finished product.
12. Protect the materials with suitable coverings, clear plastic envelopes, lamination, etc.
13. Use with your students after specifying ground rules.

Strategy 1: Include Paper-and-Pencil Learning Activities

Crossword Puzzles

Crosswords for students with any type of reading or writing difficulty might benefit from a somewhat smaller number of words, with perhaps seven words across and five words down, in a large and open crossword frame limiting the number of distractors. Clues can be short statements written in simple language that incorporate the most important vocabulary, facts, and concepts. They can be written in the form of a list of definitions or simply as a list of answer words. Clues written as a "fill in the blank statement" provide more contextual support for identifying the target words, which are then transferred into the appropriate spaces in the crossword puzzle.

Crossword puzzles for some students who experience difficulty with reading, verbal language, or who do not use speech may be limited to as few as three critical content words in either an open or closed frame. Open frame uses no outside boundary for the puzzle and no black squares, but simply places the blank squares for each target word on the page with only one or two intersections. If a student has difficulty with fine motor skills, the crossword might be filled in by using letter stamps or paper squares each with a letter printed on it. Clues can be in the form of a list of definitions or target words to be used. Additional support is provided by having one or more of the correct letters already in place.

Crossword puzzles may be made more challenging by placing words in unusual patterns, densely compacting words by eliminating black squares, and by increasing the number of complex words and phrases drawn from the desirable curriculum content. Alternatively, cryptic crosswords may be generated using cryptic (logical but disguised) clues and any size of standard crossword frame. (See Illustration 6.1.)

Word Searches

Word searches for students with any type of reading or writing difficulty can best be presented in a matrix with the hidden words in a left-right horizontal or top-bottom vertical orientation only. Backward and diagonal orientations are avoided to prevent exacerbating an already present reading difficulty. The size and complexity will vary according to student need. Clues may take the form of questions or definitions for the hidden words in the matrix.

Word searches for some students who experience difficulty with reading, verbal language, or who do not use speech have a matrix with a limited number of rows and columns with critical content words found only in left-right orientations. Using enlarged print is helpful, as is using bold print to indicate the first letter of the words in the matrix. Enclosing the word search in a plastic sleeve or envelope and using grease pencils or washable markers of various sizes provides support to students needing fine motor support and/or additional practice.

ILLUSTRATION 6.1

Clue Strategies for Cryptic Crosswords

Cryptic clue strategies for instructional words in a science unit on pressure might include "pressure," and "pump."

Clue: 1. *Iron not finished certainly.* (8) **(pressure)**

***Strategy*:**
a. Words with same meaning (iron/press).
b. Indicate part of word is missing ("not finished" indicating last letter of "press" is absent, therefore "pres"). Other similar indicators might include "headless," "beheaded," "incomplete," "almost all," etc.

Clue: 2. *Inflate half of pumpkins.* (4) **(pump)**

Strategy:
a. Word with same meaning (inflate/pump).
b. Half of the word "pumpkins" (pump-kins).

Word searches may be made more challenging by using large numbers of complex words and phrases drawn from the desirable curriculum content. Further, students can be challenged to create new versions of this activity for themselves and their classmates.

Matching Activities

Matching exercises for students with any type of reading or writing difficulty most often use columns of equal length. For example, seven important vocabulary words can be listed in one column with seven simple descriptive phrases in another, requiring the student to draw lines between matched pairs.

Matching activities for some students who experience difficulty with reading, verbal language, or who do not use speech may require matching two columns that contain the same critical content words but in a different order. Alternatively, the task may consist of matching a word to different descriptor words or phrases, or matching word to picture, or picture to related picture. Visual support may be provided in the form of dashed lines drawn between one or two pairs of matching items to get started. Larger print and/or enclosing the activity in a plastic sleeve may be helpful as well.

Matching activities may be made more challenging by including columns of varying lengths where excess items have to be eliminated or where two items in one column must be matched with one item in the other column. Students may also be asked to create new matching activities for themselves and their classmates.

Cryptograms

Cryptograms for students with any type of reading or writing difficulty consist of important content statements with selected words replaced by a cryptogram frame containing numerical or pictorial symbols, such as arrow, star, dollar sign, etc., to represent the missing letters of the alphabet. Illustration 6.2 provides an example of a cryptogram for a social studies instructional unit.

Cryptograms for some students who experience difficulty with reading, verbal language, or who do not use speech include a variety of supports. A letter/symbol key is provided and distractors are limited by using only non-alphabetic symbols, such as arrows, stars, and dollar signs. Hidden messages can be simple, critical content sentences with as few as one or two words to be completed. Using enlarged print is usually helpful, as is enclosing the cryptogram in plastic and providing washable markers of various sizes. Alternatively, printed letters may be provided for pasting into the appropriate spaces.

Cryptograms may be made more challenging by presenting complex sentences drawn from desirable curriculum content, presented totally in code format. Codes are created from the usual alphabet, or Greek hieroglyphics, the phonetic alphabet, braille, signing symbols, or other keyboard symbols.

ILLUSTRATION 6.2

Cryptogram Strategy

"Did you know? The capture of # $ % * % ε brought

about the end of the ¿ Π % Σ ε ¥ % Δ □ ≈ Π %

in Σ √ Π ∞ ¥ + Δ % Π ≈ ε + ."

The key is as follows:

a b c e f h i m n o p q r t u

\+ * ε % ¿ ¥ ≈ Δ Σ √ □ # Π ∞ $

Other Paper and Pencil Activities

Activities such as Hangman, Graph-it, Cloze/Fill in the Blanks, and scrambled words may be modified in a similar manner to vary the complexity of content or presentation in order to accommodate any range of diversity of learning needs among the students.

Strategy 2: Include Game-Structured Learning Activities

Board Games

Board games are an interesting and fun way for two or more individual students or teams to engage in learning the curriculum content. Fashioned after common family games, they usually involve an element of chance with the roll of dice or a number spinner to determine movement around a game track, and most follow a question-and-answer format. This category includes such easily modified games as Trivial Pursuit, Clue, Monopoly, Snakes and Ladders, Jeopardy, and Mythology. Game boards can be designed and crafted for specific games or a generic game board can be created that is suitable for several games. (See Illustration 6.3.)

Bingo-type and Tic-Tac-Toe games are created with various words or phrases placed in the squares of the game cards. Questions, definitions, synonyms, or antonyms, etc., are written on small cards and drawn one at a time by the caller who reads them aloud (and perhaps also presents them on overhead) to the players. Each student uses a marker or chip to cover the correct answer if it is present on the game card.

ILLUSTRATION 6.3

Generic Game Board

A generic game board can be created that easily lends itself to modifications and is a valuable addition to the teacher's curriculum materials. The flexibility of a generic board enables the teacher to update existing content or change to new content quickly and easily simply by preparing a new set of question cards.

A generic game board has a basic colour-coded path with periodic bonus and penalty spaces for game piece movement around the board and locations outlined for the placement of one or more sets of question cards.

The decor for the board is interesting and colourful, and can either be relatively neutral in design or can exhibit symbols representing many areas of the curriculum. Alternatively, using stick-and-peel materials, the decor can be changed as necessary to reflect specific curriculum content and/or to provide visual support for students.

A Wheel of Fortune format provides a Cloze technique activity that can be similarly varied in content difficulty and presentation complexity. A spinner or dice determines movement around the track, with each square on the track identifying a) either a vowel or consonant, and b) the point value to be awarded if the letter selected by the player is used in the Cloze statement. Visual and memory support can be provided by posting an alphabet and marking or removing letters as they are selected.

A Scrabble format uses letters to form curriculum content words to fit on a board in crossword style. Students blindly select a specified number of letters to begin with, equal to one less than the total number of letters in the longest word being used, and at the end of each turn the student draws new letters to replace the number of letters used. Scoring can be as simple as 10 points for each word completed on the board plus 5 points for each word intersected by the new word, or as complex as varying the value of individual letters and designating certain places on the board to be worth double, triple, or bonus points. Increasing the size of the letters and the squares on the board is helpful for students with visual or fine motor difficulties. Visual and memory support can be provided by posting the list of words used in each game.

Card Games

Blank playing cards can be used to prepare verbal content cards for knowledge-based, classification, and matching games. Card games using typical playing cards with numbers and suits facilitate enjoyable and motivating mathematical manipulation.

Using a Memory or Concentration game format, where prepared cards with important content are spread out face down and each player in turn picks up two cards at once in an attempt to find a matching pair, is the most flexible type of game. Any content can be used and in almost any form, such as pictures, words, phrases, titles with authors, quotations with speakers, definitions, antonyms, synonyms, analysis, interpretation, fractions, decimals, algebra, geometry, and the like, for a variety of learning purposes. For example, in an instructional unit on Shakespeare, one set of cards is prepared with words or phrases from the text of a play written in Shakespearean English, and the second set with the modern English translation.

A similar game, particularly for students experiencing fine motor difficulties, avoids the problems associated with manipulating playing cards. A simple Battery Board game is constructed so that students can select answers to questions or check matching items as described above by simultaneously touching the question and the answer terminal with probes. A correct match causes a light to go on.

Concentration or Memory games played with regular playing cards are used for number recognition, addition, subtraction, multiplication, and division. A spinner, dice, or a separate set of prepared cards can be used to provide the solution. All playing cards are spread out face down in the centre, and each player, in turn, draws two playing cards and decides whether the two cards match the required solution when the designated mathematical operation is applied. For example, suppose the operation is multiplication, and the number drawn on the prepared solution card is 48. The player must draw 8 and 6, or 4 and King (valued at 12), from the playing cards in the middle, and recognize them as the correct elements for the solution to keep the cards and take another turn. If a successful pair is not drawn, the cards are replaced face down, and the turn passes to the next player. Students can work as individuals, in pairs, or as cooperative teams. Popular card games, such as War, Eights, Crazy Eights, dominoes, and cribbage, can be similarly modified for classroom use.

Classification games, similar to the commercial game Scategories and the popular card games, rummy and Fish, use prepared cards with pictures, words, phrases, statements, or numbers, to be sorted into the appropriate category or class. Students are dealt a specified number of cards, perhaps five, and group them into designated categories. Rules are agreed upon, where at each turn the player either asks another player for a card needed for a particular category or draws a card from the pack, or both. As a player completes a category, the cards are placed face up on the table. For example, in a biology instructional unit on anatomy, categories could include muscles, bones, fluids, and nerves, with the names and/or functions of various anatomical parts having to be appropriately classified. Most classification games are played by pairs or cooperative teams of players, but each can easily be modified to be played by an individual student for practice, review, or evaluation.

Strategy Games

Games involving strategy and planning, primarily for challenging students already familiar with the desirable curriculum content, are well suited for heterogeneous cooperative student teams. Typically, a game board is used where a number of scenarios are possible with the cards provided, and players reach one of several outcomes depending upon the decisions made during the game. Decisions are based on knowledge, critical analysis, and logic. (See Illustration 6.4.)

Strategy 3: Include Oral-and Motor-Type Learning Activities

Oral-Type Learning Activities

Activities such as Toastmasters and games such as Talk About and Liar's Club all concentrate primarily on the students' abilities to express themselves verbally. These are most suitable for auditory and verbal learners.

Toastmasters activities provide an opportunity for students to research and prepare a speech on an assigned topic to be delivered in a public speaking forum, such as the class or a school assembly. Some students with good research and organizational skills require little structure, while other students require narrower topics, more support in locating material, and more editorial assistance from peers, parents, or teachers.

Talk About, similar to the popular television game show, is easily modified for instructional use, played either as two individuals or two teams competing in front of a class. The teacher prepares an overhead divided into 10 or 12 blocks, each block containing a word or phrase related to a selected instructional topic, such as Canadian poets, interest rates, blood circulation, etc. Each block on the overhead sheet is covered with a piece of paper having the word or phrase visible only to the game leader who operates the overhead. As each block is identified by the players, the paper is removed from that block, allowing the class to see the "board." A coin toss determines which team plays first. For example, Red Team is sent away while Blue Team is given a topic to brainstorm out loud, trying to identify all 10 (or 12) pieces of information

ILLUSTRATION 6.4

Strategy Game

A game board could present a map of the west coast of North America marked off in squares, with two target locations identified—one where the salmon begins its life and, another, the farthest point the salmon travels from its birthplace.

A set of risk factors, such as a storm causing a shipwreck, increase in water temperature killing salmon, oil spill killing all fish, etc., is prepared for each of a number of grid outlines. That is, each grid outline has different squares with specific dangers, such as E-10 storm, and H-4 water temperature 20°C. The particular risk grid outline used for each game is known only to the referee, not to the players.

Various routes are possible for the life journey of the salmon. One player or team represents the salmon, the other player(s) represents various predators, such as other fish, mammals, humans, and so on.

Rolling dice can determine the number of spaces to be moved, with the player deciding the direction of movement. Play can also be determined by drawing a coordinate card to indicate the next location, with the player deciding whether to accept the move. Alternatively, two identical boards can be used with each team unable to see the moves being made on the other's board.

After each turn, a referee records the move and signals when a) two game pieces have landed on the same square, indicating the destruction of a predator or capture of the salmon, and b) a game piece has landed on a risk square that is lethal to it. The game ends when all remaining salmon have returned to their spawning ground or when one team has no game pieces left.

on the overhead. If successful, they win the round. If unsuccessful, the Red Team comes back and, from the information exposed on the board, tries to guess the topic. If successful, they win the round; if not, the Blue Team keeps the points.

Liar's Club is a game played by two teams who are initially designated either as truthful or as liars by the "role" cards they are given by the teacher. Speech topics are identified from curriculum content. All truthful stories are based on factual information, and all liars' stories contain one piece of misinformation along with factual information. At the end of the time limit, the teacher asks various students in the class to identify the untruthful team by indicating the misinformation. For example, the two teams could present two versions of Prime Minister Pierre Elliott Trudeau speaking on the topic of the repatriation of the Constitution of Canada. On another occasion, the two teams represent a fungus speaking on the topic of its food sources. Each team speaks for a specified time.

Motor-Type Learning Activities

For students whose preferred style is motor learning, alternatives to print material must be available. Students may learn and communicate their knowledge through such fine motor activities as drawing, sketching, painting, sculpting, and model building.

Model building is an excellent hands-on activity for students to deal with curriculum content. Similarly, painting, sculpture, drawing, or sketching can serve a similar function where a variety of instrument sizes, textures, and materials are used. Game formats providing similar fine motor and tactile avenues of learning include those based on such commercial games as Pictionary or Win, Lose or Draw. (See Illustration 6.5.)

Charades, pantomime, drama, and dance provide opportunities for gross motor learning and expression. Further, Statues and Tableaux have students create motionless representations to depict people such as Marie Curie, things such as water molecules, and events such as the expulsion of the Acadians. All of these games and activities are purposely designed to exclude the use of speech, which accommodates students who have difficulty with speech and helps develop creativity in all students.

Combined Oral-Motor Learning Activities

Activities that combine oral and motor activities are also valuable learning experiences for many students. As with the activities above, role playing and

ILLUSTRATION 6.5

Fine-Motor Game Strategy

In a Pictionary-type game, a set of cards is developed by the teacher for an intended unit of study; for example, a science unit on simple machines. Topics presented on the cards in print form could include pulley, fulcrum, lever, etc.

With students grouped in teams, one student selects a card and draws a picture of the selected topic on a small sheet of paper, and teammates attempt to identify the topic. Team points are awarded for correct identification only, with no penalty for incorrect responses. Following an attempt by one team, the turn passes to the other team regardless of success.

simulations, drama, and dance can easily incorporate curriculum content. The following examples illustrate these activities.

1. Role play allows the study of distinct events, such as the creation of the United Nations.
2. Simulation may show the effects of acid rain on life in a pond.
3. Re-enactment of a courtroom drama facilitates the understanding of the issues and tensions around the assisted suicide of a person with a terminal illness.
4. Dance created and performed by students can portray the shifting of the jet stream by seasons or the path of food through the body.

Photo study adds a strong visual component that can be used as a stimulus for writing activities, but can also initiate any of the oral or motor activities noted above. Students extending their learning beyond the desirable curriculum can examine a photo of a relevant event, process, or product. Students are challenged to interpret and predict in a different time frame, to develop the text for a play, to describe their experience as if they were in the scene, to prepare a speech for the central figure, to design clothes for the opposite season, and so on. Important curriculum can be examined through pictures that stimulate various levels of oral discussion, and can be used in conjunction with a tape recorder to provide a record of the student's interpretation. This record allows the student to review and/or add to his or her own work, and provides the basis for a written report.

Description, interpretation, and prediction can also occur with varying complexity and sophistication. Photo study can be used for identifying the critical curriculum components within a picture for discussion or for story development. Students can be asked to interpret the events and feelings of people in the photo, to describe what led up to the photo, and to predict what might happen next. To illustrate, students are presented with a dramatic scene depicting ships leaving Halifax Harbour and headed overseas during World War II, or the floor of the stock market on the day of the 1929 crash, or an operating room during heart transplant surgery, or the granting of citizenship ceremony for a group of new Canadians. Challenging questions or statements can accompany the photo, asking students to examine the roles of the characters in the picture, to put themselves in the shoes of an individual in the picture, or to create a dialogue for two or more of the people depicted. Student responses can be written or oral, and completed either individually or in small groups, thereby accommodating varying ability levels.

Strategy 4: Include Reading Activities

For most students, reading is the most efficient method of obtaining the volume of information required to learn the curriculum content in secondary schools. Not surprisingly, textbooks are written with the so-called average reader in mind. However, some students master the desirable content very easily and welcome the challenge of supplementary reading or related independent research projects.

For students experiencing reading difficulty, one or more of the following strategies can be used.

1. Additional time to complete the reading.
2. Rewritten texts using simplified language.
3. A companion audiotape to listen and read simultaneously.
4. Enlarged print.
5. Supporting pictures, graphs, and diagrams.
6. Working in mixed-ability cooperative learning groups.

Illustration 6.6. furnishes modification strategies used in the preparation of reading activities for a social studies instructional unit on the Battle of the Plains of Abraham, which are designed to accommodate the needs of students with very low reading and verbal skills.

ILLUSTRATION 6.6

Social Studies Reading Strategies

A colourful picture book containing captions is prepared using simplified text with critical concepts and vocabulary words enlarged and highlighted. Colour coding provides additional support with words related to the British printed in red to match the colour of their uniforms, while words related to the French are shown in blue. The text describes the main events of the battle in simple terms, providing a relatively easy reading activity. To facilitate independent reading, an audiotape accompanies the book, which is bound on three snap rings, allowing pages to be used separately.

A duplicate picture book without captions allows for sequencing based on pictorial information only. Each page is mounted on a different colour backing, and the matching captions are mounted separately on the corresponding colour. The left and right edges of the coloured backing of the caption strips are each shaped in unique, self-correcting, interlocking puzzle forms to enable the learner to link the text together in the correct sequence. This allows the student to use both colour clues and puzzle clues to support reading skill development. An additional set of the captions on plain backing affords a more challenging activity for students to match caption to picture or to sequence the story based on written information only.

The New Frontier

The preceding strategies for modifying curriculum materials have been typically applied using concrete materials such as cardboard, glue, etc., as paper-and-pencil activities, or as card and board games. More recently, most of these strategies for modifying curriculum materials have been applied using a computer authoring program (HyperCard) to create similar learning activities that utilize standard word processing, graphics, and paint programs. With the addition of adapted computer input-output devices, such computer versions become accessible to all learners (Brown, 1994).

Summary

Inclusive education is much more than simply placing students in a regular classroom. It is the provision of rich and flexible learning environments accessible to all students. Given that all students learn in unique ways, understanding learner characteristics and individualizing the curriculum are essential. All learners can work toward the same educational outcomes, but the degree of emphasis placed on each and the levels at which these outcomes are achieved will differ according to the particular learning needs of each student (Schrag & Burnette, 1994.)The teacher's task is to set up the optimal conditions in the classroom to facilitate learning and achievement for every student. Teachers know their students experience curriculum in many ways, visually, auditorally, through movement, or by multisensory means. Modifying the language and presentation methods used in delivering the curriculum allows more students to profit from some aspect of each learning activity. The greater the variety of strategies, the more all students are likely to benefit.

Teaching in today's secondary classrooms is a more challenging and potentially a more rewarding experience for teachers. Much has been learned in the past decade about instructional methods, curriculum materials, students with exceptional learning needs, and specialist and support services. Students, teachers, schools, and the community are already experiencing the benefits of inclusive education. As we continue to learn and improve educational practice, inclusive secondary schools will become a more widespread reality.

SUGGESTED RESOURCES

Retish, P., Hitchings, W., Horvath, M., & Schmalle, B. (1991). *Students with mild disabilities in the secondary school.* White Plains, NY: Longman. In Chapter 5 (pp. 89–112), entitled "The Process of Using What Works: Strategies for Implementation," these authors provide instructional strategies, organizational skills, and modifications. Chapter 9 (pp. 190–215), entitled "Resources," provides a list of further reading in curriculum and effective teaching, as well as an extensive list of information sources for hardware and software for technology and computer users with special needs.

Salend, S. (1990). *Effective mainstreaming.* New York: Macmillan. Chapter 6 (pp. 225–314), entitled "Modifying Instruction for Mainstreamed Students," describes methods of modifying groups, print, instruction, classroom behaviour, and classroom design. Chapter 7 (pp. 315–82), entitled "Modifying Content-Area and Instruction," examines general strategies in six content areas applicable to all grade levels.

Smith, T., Polloway, E., Patton, J., & Dowdy, C. (1995). *Teaching children with special needs in inclusive settings.* Needham Heights, MA: Allyn and Bacon. Chapter 12 (pp. 348–77), entitled "Classroom Organization and Management" examines fundamentals and components of effective classrooms. Chapter 14 (pp. 412–43), entitled "Curricular and Instructional Accommodations: Secondary Level," addresses secondary school curricula and program and methods for secondary schools.

Wang, M. (1992). *Adaptive education strategies: Building on diversity.* Baltimore, MD: Paul H. Brookes. Two chapters in this book provide support resources for developing instructional strategies for inclusive classrooms. Chapter 4 (pp. 119–44), entitled "Curricular Resources for Implementing Adaptive Education," and Chapter 5 (pp. 145–68), entitled "Instructional Management," are particularly relevant to the task.

Wood, J. (1992). *Adapting instruction for mainstreamed and at-risk students* (2nd edition). New York: Macmillan. Chapter 6 (pp. 153–85), entitled "Adapting the Physical Environment," addresses the preparation of a master schedule and physical organization of the classroom. Part Three, "Adapting Planning and Teaching," includes Chapter 7 (pp. 187–208) on lesson planning, Chapter 8 (pp. 209–44) on adapting teaching techniques, Chapter 9 (pp. 245–84) on adapting format of content, and Chapter 10 (pp. 285–310) on adapting media.

REFERENCES

Biederman, G., Davey, V., Ryder, C., & Franchi, D. (1994). The negative effects of positive reinforcement in teaching children with developmental delay. *Exceptional Children, 60*(5), 458–65.

Bowyer, J. (1990). Women in science. In L. Trowbridge & R. Bybee (Eds.), *Becoming a secondary school science teacher* (5th edition) (pp. 126–27). Toronto: Collier Macmillan Canada.

Bricker, D. (1989). *Classroom life as civic education: Individual achievement and student co-operation in schools.* New York: Teachers College Press.

Brown, M. (1994). *Inclusion of students with diverse educational needs: Adapting an 11th grade literature unit of instruction.*" Paper presented at TAM '94 Technology—The Equalizer Conference, Technology and Media Division of the Council for Excpetional Children, St. Paul, MN (February).

Brown, M., & Fasano, J. (1990). SCAMP: Secondary curriculum adapted materials project. Paper presented at Atlantic Educators Conference. Halifax, NS (October).

Collicott, J. (1991). Implementing multi-level instruction: Strategies for classroom teachers. In G. Porter & D. Richler (Eds.), *Changing Canadian schools: Perspectives on disability and inclusion* (pp. 191–218). Downsview, ON: Roeher Institute.

Fasano, J. (1984). "Survey of middle school models in Canada." Unpublished document. Wolfville, NS: Acadia University.

Fasano, J., & Brown, M. (1992). Facilitating inclusive secondary classrooms through curriculum adaptation. *Exceptionality Education Canada, 2*(1&2), 155–79.

Ferguson, D., & Fairchild, L. (1992). It's not a matter of method: Thinking about how to implement curricular decisions. In S. Stainback & W. Stainback (Eds.), *Curriculum considerations in inclusive classrooms: Facilitating learning for all students* (pp. 159–74). Baltimore: Paul H. Brookes.

Ford, A., & Davern, L. (1989). Moving forward with school integration: Strategies for involving students with severe handicaps in the life of the school. In R. Gaylord-Ross (Ed.), *Integration strategies for students with handicaps* (pp. 11–32). Baltimore: Paul H. Brookes.

Gamoran, A. (1987). The stratification of high school learning opportunities. *Sociology of Education, 60*, 135–55.

Glasser, W. (1986). *Control theory in the classroom.* New York: Harper & Row Publishers.

Goodlad, J., & Lovitt, T. (Eds.). (1993). *Integrating general and special education.* Don Mills, ON: Maxwell Macmillan Canada.

Johnson, D., Johnson, R., Holubec, E., & Roy, P. (1988). *Circles of learning: Cooperation in the classroom.* Alexandria, VA: Association for Supervision and Curriculum Development.

Lusthaus, E., & Forest, M. (1987). The kaliedoscope: A challenge to the cascade. In M. Forest (Ed.), *More education integration* (pp. 1–17). Downsview, ON: Roeher Institute.

MacKinnon, D., & Brown, M. (1994). Inclusion in secondary schools: An analysis of school structure based on teachers' images of change. *Educational Administration Quarterly, 30*(2), 126–52.

Pratt, D. (1994). *Curriculum planning: A handbook for professionals.* Orlando, FL: Harcourt Brace College Publishers.

Rainforth, B., York, J., & Macdonald, C. (1992). *Collaborative teams serving students with severe disabilities: Integrated therapy in educational programs.* Baltimore: Paul H. Brookes.

Reis, S., & Renzulli, J. (1992). Using curriculum compacting to challenge the above-average. *Educational Leadership, 50*(2), 51–57.

Samples, B. (1992). Using learning modalities to celebrate intelligence. *Educational Leadership, 50*(2), 62–66.

Schrag, J., & Burnette, J. (1994). Inclusive schools. *Teaching Exceptional Children, 26*(3), 64–68.

Vandercook, T., York, J., & Forest, M. (1989). The McGill action planning system (MAPS): A strategy for building the vision. *Journal of the Association for Persons with Severe Handicaps, 14,* 205–15.

Villa, R., & Thousand, J. (1988). Enhancing success in heterogeneous classrooms and schools: The powers of partnership. *Teacher Education and Special Education, 11,* 144–54.

Villa, R., & Thousand, J. (1990). Administrative supports to promote inclusive schooling. In W. Stainback & S. Stainback (Eds.), *Support networks for inclusive schooling: Interdependent integrated education* (pp. 201–18). Baltimore: Paul H. Brookes.

Villa, R., & Thousand, J. (1992). Student collaboration: An essential for curriculum delivery in the 21st century. In S. Stainback & W. Stainback (Eds.), *Curriculum considerations in inclusive classrooms: Facilitating learning for all students* (pp. 117–142). Baltimore: Paul H. Brookes.

Wood, J. (1992). *Adapting instruction for mainstreamed and at-risk students.* Don Mills, ON: Maxwell Macmillan Canada.

York, J., Giangreco, M., Vandercook, T., & Macdonald, C. (1992). Integrating support personnel in the inclusive classroom. In S. Stainback & W. Stainback (Eds.), *Curriculum considerations in inclusive classrooms: Facilitating learning for all students* (pp. 101–117). Baltimore: Paul H. Brookes.

C H A P T E R 7

Behaviour and Procedures of Secondary Teachers in the Integrated Classroom

Cheryll Duquette

University of Ottawa

Introduction

With the passage of PL94-142 in the United States and various provincial legislation in Canada, handicapped children across most of North America have the right to a free and appropriate education (Duquette, 1992). The objective is to have a greater number of children with handicaps educated in the regular classroom rather than in a segregated setting. It involves a partnership between special education and regular education in which their combined knowledge is used to support the education of pupils with learning difficulties. While it is one thing to have exceptional children in the school in segregated classes, for a regular classroom teacher it is entirely a different thing to be expected to be accountable for the learning of an exceptional child.

Among some teachers there is an attitude of reluctance to make accommodations for children with special learning needs. In a study conducted in elementary and secondary schools, teachers commented on the importance of not treating students with handicaps differently, expecting the same from them as other pupils (Bacon & Schulz, 1991). However, in the 1990s, teachers are accountable for the learning of all students in their classes and should be prepared to make adjustments in lesson planning and teaching techniques to meet the learning requirements of handicapped students that they teach.

Teaching Behaviours and Characteristics of Secondary Teachers

Traditionally, secondary teachers who are successful at integrating students with handicaps demonstrate excellent teaching practices in the areas of lesson planning, teaching behaviours, and classroom management (Duquette, 1992; Larrivee, 1982). They also make a point of accessing the special education personnel to report an exceptional child's academic achievement and behaviour and to discuss modifications to program and teaching techniques that might be made to enhance a pupil's performance (Bacon & Schulz, 1991; Duquette, 1992; Larrivee, 1982). Secondary teachers who are successful at integrating handicapped pupils into their classroom definitely do not treat them exactly as other pupils. These teachers have learned that modifications to program and teaching techniques may be necessary, and these teachers are willing to spend the extra time to make them.

The attitude of equal treatment seems to be more prevalent among secondary teachers than in elementary teachers (Reed, 1983). This attitude may be reinforced by the organization of secondary schools in which pupils are streamed for instruction to produce relatively homogeneous groupings. The general belief held by secondary teachers is that if all students are well taught, then so are the handicapped ones (Bacon & Schulz, 1991). However, most secondary teachers recognize that these groupings, particularly at the lower achievement range, are anything but homogeneous. They are a mixture of underachieving pupils, slow learners, and handicapped children. Generally, these classes have fewer pupils than those in the academic stream and are taught at a slower pace. Teachers rely on their interpersonal skills and their ability to explain the lesson on a one-to-one basis to pupils. However, Pritchard (1984) expresses the need for all secondary teachers to be sensitized to the differences in students' abilities and styles of learning. McCormick (1983) furthers the point by stating that high school teachers should accommodate these differences in their lesson planning and teaching strategies.

Studies of secondary teachers who successfully integrate handicapped pupils show that, like their elementary colleagues, they are aware of individual learning needs and do make adjustments in curriculum and teaching methods

(Bacon & Schulz, 1991; Larrivee & Algina, 1983; Munroe, 1982; Munroe, 1984). These high school teachers select appropriate content and activities for the abilities and interests of students (Larrivee & Algina, 1983). They also make use of advance organizers, such as pre-reading questions and explanation of new vocabulary (Bacon & Schulz, 1991).The teachers begin the lessons with an overview, then they break the content into components that are understandable to the pupils, and at the end of the lesson the parts are summarized. These high school teachers plan a variety of learning activities that include teacher-led, group-work, and hands-on activities (Bacon & Schulz, 1991; Munroe, 1984). Visual, auditory, and concrete aids are used, as well as manipulatives (Bacon & Schulz, 1991; Munroe, 1984). Teachers who successfully integrate handicapped students also use differentiated assignments, such as a basic one with one or more advanced options (Bacon & Schulz, 1991; Johnson, 1982; Munroe, 1984). They also permit the use of oral tests and assign marks for effort and participation (Bacon & Schulz, 1991).

The successful teachers demonstrate specific teaching behaviours. They explain material clearly and state academic expectations. These teachers use content and probing questions (Munroe, 1984). They provide 5 to 10 seconds of wait time, restate the question if necessary, and give supportive responses for incorrect answers (Larrivee & Algina, 1983; Munroe, 1984). Pupils are motivated through positive feedback for correct oral answers, written work, and behaviour (Larrivee & Algina, 1983, Munroe, 1984). The teachers also use repetition and review of concepts and skills, as well as verbal markers (e.g., "This is important.") (Bacon & Schulz, 1991; Munroe, 1982). Finally, the successful teachers teach study skills (e.g., how to read a text, how to take a test) and show the students how to remember the material (e.g., mnemonic devices) (Munroe, 1984).

The classrooms of secondary teachers who successfully integrate handicapped students are well managed. The teachers establish patterns of behaviour and standards of acceptable behaviour through the routines, procedures, and rules that are known to their students (Munroe, 1984). Seat work and small-group work is supervised, and there is generally a low incidence of off-task behaviours (Brady et al., 1988, Munroe, 1984). Transitions from one activity to another are smooth and there is a low incidence of organizing by the teacher during activities (Brady et al., 1988, Munroe, 1984). Intervention by the teacher is minimal (Larrivee & Algina, 1983).

These high school teachers also possess personal qualities that contribute to their success in integrating handicapped students. They are, on one hand, businesslike, task oriented, punctual, consistent, and convey to students their high standards (Munroe, 1984). They are also friendly, warm, courteous, and supportive teachers who take an interest in individual students (Munroe, 1984).

In sum, the secondary teachers in these studies clearly model excellent teaching practice, show awareness of the needs of all their students, and demonstrate a willingness to spend time making adjustments in the program to meet individual learning needs.

Observations of Successful Inclusion

Mainstreaming refers to the practice of teaching exceptional pupils in the regular classroom for more than 50% of the school day. For this chapter, the terms **mainstreamed** and **integrated** will be used interchangeably. As this chapter focuses on the integration of exceptional students who are not gifted, the terms **exceptional** and **handicapped** will also be used interchangeably.

The three teachers discussed in the rest of this chapter are employed by a separate school board in the eastern Ontario region. This particular board of education is moving toward total integration of exceptional students.

The school is located in a middle-class suburb of the Ottawa-Carleton region, and houses 396 grade 7 and 8 pupils and 990 grade 9 to OAC students. This is a semestered secondary school that operates on a five-day cycle. There are four periods a day, each of which is 75 minutes long. The school has two full-time resource teachers, a .5 resource teacher who works with the transition classes (grades 7, 8, and 9), and two teacher aides who are assigned to particular students. The resource teachers provide traditional "pull-out" types of programs and in-class assistance for students. The resource room has four computers, and some senior students who have been identified as exceptional come to use the computers. Occasionally, the resource teacher will take a group of the students (exceptional and nonexceptional) from the class for some extra work on a particular concept. The school also has a Multidisciplinary Team (MDT), consisting of a psychologist, an educational psychologist, an educational consultant, a social worker, and a behavioural specialist.

Exceptional students in this secondary school generally have been identified in their elementary years. The resource teachers are assigned approximately 30 identified students who range between grade 9 and OAC. The progress of these students is monitored closely by the resource teachers, who also provide the necessary support. The resource teachers also support the classroom teachers who are integrating the exceptional students. During the first week each semester, classroom teachers receive a list of exceptional students in their classes. For each pupil there is a two-page summary containing information on strengths, weaknesses, monitoring strategies, program objectives, teaching strategies/methods, and student responsibilities. The resource teachers and classroom teachers both make telephone calls to parents on a regular basis.

Administrators with the board view this secondary school as a model for integration. The administration perceives three teachers at this school as being very successful in integrating exceptional students. These teachers teach science, math, history, and English courses. None of these teachers had taken special education courses.

The classes of these teachers ranged in size from 13 to 28 pupils, including 1 to 9 mildly and moderately exceptional students. The types of exceptionalities were as follows: learning disabilities, attention deficit disorder, visual impairment, behavioural disorders, and low academic achievement.

Each of these teachers was observed teaching for five hours on different days to determine their teaching behaviours. They were all interviewed individually to discuss curriculum adaptations and attitudes. The findings are described and grouped under three headings: behaviours, personal characteristics and attitudes, and support for integration.

Behaviours

Thirty-one common behaviours were observed among the three classroom teachers who were mainstreaming the exceptional students (see Table 7.1). These behaviours are divided into four groups: lesson planning, instructional behaviours, classroom management, and behavioural management.

The teachers displayed so many common teaching behaviours and yet their teaching styles were very different from one another. The science teacher was very calm, composed, structured, and methodical. The most frequently observed teaching approach used was question and answer. The math teacher exhibited a very active style; he constantly moved from student to student. His approach was to provide a lot of individual assistance to students who may have been having difficulty with the assignments. The English/history teacher was relaxed. The approach used most frequently during observation was teacher-directed class discussion. The differences in teaching style may be a result of the subject matter that is being taught and the teachers' personal preferences.

TABLE 7.1
Common Teaching Behaviours

Lesson Planning

1. Variety of learning activities
2. Motivational exercises
3. Slower pace

4. Variety of media
5. Visual, auditory, and tactile components
6. Concepts are defined and linked to students' lives
7. Summary notes
8. Reduced amount of writing for daily assignments
9. Frequent review of previously taught concepts and review activities before tests
10. Differentiated evaluation strategies
11. Teacher-centred lessons with some group work
12. Adjustments to meet the learning needs of exceptional students

Instructional Behaviours

13. Content questions, wait time, restated questions, other questions asked to direct to correct answer
14. Questioning pattern: question, name of student, answer, positive feedback
15. No lecturing
16. Student responses provide most of the content of the lesson through teacher questioning and teacher-directed discussion
17. Involvement of most students in the class
18. Conscious effort to involve exceptional students in activities
19. Positive feedback
20. Teacher indicates important points
21. Well-paced lessons with no "dead" spots

Classroom Management

22. Written agenda
23. Rows of desks
24. Smooth transitions
25. Time spent with each student monitoring and assisting
26. Efficient tracking system
27. Frequent marking of assignments/quizzes

Behavioural Management

28. Eye contact, proximity, stating student's name and behavioural expectations
29. High level of "with-it-ness"
30. Present in classroom at all times
31. Students greeted and dismissed with a positive comment

Lesson Planning

Previous studies have shown that teachers who are successful at integrating use a variety of learning activities (Bacon & Schulz, 1991; Munroe, 1984). These teachers also planned different activities throughout a period. They all used motivational exercises, such as crosswords, word searches, and special exercise sheets. All the courses observed being taught by the teachers were at the general level. Therefore, the rate in which new content was presented was at a slower pace than for advanced classes. The three teachers used a variety of media during each lesson: blackboard, overhead projector, exercise sheets, textbooks, and videos. For each lesson, the teachers incorporated oral, visual, and tactile components in the form of question and answer, discussion, visual aids, blackboard diagrams, examples on the blackboard, and note taking. In addition, all of these teachers presented concepts through explanation and by relating the concept to previous work or to the students' lives. For the exceptional students, the teachers would copy the notes for the student (required by a visually impaired student), give the students the teacher's copy of notes to copy, and reduce the amount of writing by making special notes for a student in which he or she had to fill in the blanks. The science and math teachers organized the notes for each unit according to topic and a coding system. The coding consisted of two numbers: one representing the unit and the second the lesson. For example, a lesson might be labelled "The Human Digestive System" and coded 5.6. The coding helped the students to keep their notes in order. Before tests, the teachers conducted reviews of the material to be tested. This was done through question and answer/discussion or by review sheets. Generally, the three teachers chose structured, teacher-directed approaches. In sum, all three teachers were conscientious about lesson planning and were willing to make adjustments in the lessons to accommodate the needs of exceptional students.

Instructional Behaviours

The teachers in this study most frequently used content-oriented questions. This finding supports previously reported results (Larrivee & Algina, 1983; Munroe, 1984). If the student gave a wrong answer, the teacher continued the questioning by asking other questions that led the student to the right answer. These teachers also asked probing questions, gave 5 to 10 seconds wait time, and restated the question if required, which support the results of Munroe (1984). The general questioning pattern for the three teachers was: a) question, b) name of student, c) answer, and d) positive reinforcement.

In none of the classes that were observed did the teachers lecture. The students themselves furnished most of the content of the lessons through the process of question and answer and by discussion of concepts. The teachers motivated the students through the positive feedback and praise that they used repeatedly after student answers. This result has also been reported by Larrivee and Algina (1983) and Munroe (1984). During the lesson, these teachers would indicate important points to students, thereby helping them to focus on the key concepts and ideas.

Classroom Management

The teachers began each period by reviewing the agenda for the lesson that had been written on the blackboard. This technique helped the students to organize the flow of the lesson. In addition, the rules and procedures also helped to organize the students' behaviour.

The teachers also organized the students' desks into traditional rows. The science room had lab stations on the perimeter of the room and single rows of desks in the middle. The English/history teacher was located in a portable classroom and had arranged the desks in single rows. The desks could be grouped for discussion. The math teacher was also in a portable classroom, which was equipped with tables that each seated two students. These tables were arranged in three rows. As indicated previously, there were between three and five activities per lesson. The transitions between activities were smooth and marked by little off-task behaviour. This result supports a similar finding by Munroe (1984) regarding transitions.

Another finding was the amount of time the teachers focused on individual students that conveyed an attitude of caring about their academic performance. During the activity/assignment portion of the lesson, the teachers were involved with each student through monitoring progress and providing individual assistance. Munroe (1984) has previously reported a similar result. These teachers also had tracking systems that permitted them to know exactly what assignments each student had submitted. They were all able to manage the administrative side of teaching and pay attention to the achievement of individual students.

Behavioural Management

Larrivee and Algina (1983) reported that in classrooms where exceptional students at the secondary level were mainstreamed there was a low incidence of teacher intervention. Teachers wasted little instructional time attending to discipline problems in the classroom. The results of this study supported the previous finding. During the 15 hours of classroom observation, the students exhibited no prolonged disruptive behaviours or defiant behaviours. The only off-task behaviour that was observed was talking. In all cases, the teachers swiftly corrected it through eye contact, proximity, and stating the student's name and behavioural expectations. In addition, the teachers exhibited a high level of "with-it-ness." They were present and seemed to know what was going on in all parts of the classroom at all times. They greeted the students when they arrived, and also dismissed the classes with a pleasant comment, such as "Have a good day," "See your tomorrow," or "Thanks for coming."

The teaching behaviours used by the three teachers who are successful at integrating exceptional students demonstrate lesson planning that is conscientious and thorough, instructional behaviours that invite student involvement, classroom management strategies that support academic achievement, and behavioural management techniques that ensure a high level of academic learning time.

Personal Characteristics and Attitudes

Munroe (1984) reported that secondary teachers who were successful at integrating exceptional students were at the same time task-oriented and supportive of students. She found that they were consistent and conveyed high standards to their students. They were also friendly and took an interest in individual students (Munroe, 1984). The three secondary teachers in this study also demonstrated these behaviours and characteristics.

These teachers were also calm, relaxed, and confident in the classroom. The science teacher, who had been teaching the grade-10 general-level science course for three years made the following comment:

> Knowing the material helps you to know what has to be taught and what the time lines are. It allows me to feel more relaxed about what has to be taught and what strategies work.

She further commented that feeling comfortable with the material and knowing which strategies work with the students help her to focus on student learning instead of on her own delivery of content.

These teachers were very well organized in terms of the lesson planning and administrative aspects of their jobs. All teaching aids (e.g., videos, concrete aids, work sheets) and notes were ready at the beginning of the class. The three teachers were able to keep track of assignment completion and the progress of individual students. Near the end of the semester, the math teacher even gave each student a printout of his or her average mark for the course.

The teachers also had a good rapport with the students in their classes. The students were observed discussing personal and school matters with the teachers during homeroom period, before and after class. The positive relations these three teachers had with their students also indicated a sense of caring about the adolescents with whom they were working.

A final characteristic that was common to the three teachers was their flexibility in regard to making changes to curriculum and teaching approaches to meet the needs of the exceptional students in their classes. All three teachers permit extra time for students who require it on tests and exams. The teachers also demonstrated their flexibility through their ability to work with the resource teachers in the classroom. The classroom teacher and his or her designated resource teacher work as a team in monitoring and assisting the exceptional pupils and in providing feedback to parents through telephone calls.

To summarize, the classroom teachers in this study maintained orderly classrooms, focused on the academic tasks of the curriculum, and gave attention to the students as individuals. Through personal attention and continuous feedback to the students, the teachers were able to develop positive relationships with each student. Interestingly, most of the exceptional students in the classes of the three teachers were successful in the courses taught by these teachers.

The teachers all expressed positive attitudes toward the integration of exceptional students. They believe that the exceptional students have a right to be in their classrooms. They also want the handicapped pupils to do well academically and to prove to themselves that success is possible. The teachers in this study demonstrated this positive attitude through the number of modifications they made to curriculum and teaching approaches. However, the teachers all expressed their frustration at exceptional students for whom they had made particular adjustments and who have not applied themselves to meet the academic behavioural requirements.

Support for Integration

Administration

In a previous study on integration at the elementary level, it was found that the principal played a very active role in supporting the teachers and exceptional students (Duquette, 1992). At this secondary school, the administration provided strong moral support. The administrative team was only involved with the students when they exhibited behavioural problems. This level of involvement by the secondary administrative staff was acceptable to the three teachers who did not expect the principal and vice-principals to become involved at the instructional level. Therefore, the administration of the school generally provided moral support to teachers who were mainstreaming.

Curriculum Documents

Curriculum documents may also support the teacher in providing useful ideas for lesson planning, instruction, and adjustments that may be made for exceptional students (Duquette, 1992). The teachers in this study did not only rely on board or ministry documents to provide a complete range of useful approaches. Academic background and teaching resources gave the teacher confidence when teaching subject matter.

Resource Staff

In this secondary school, the resource staff provides much of the support for the teachers and handicapped students. For the 990 students attending the school, there are 2.5 resource teachers and three teacher aides. The resource teachers work with teachers and students in the classrooms, and they provide pull-out programs. The teacher aides are assigned to a specific student and assist him or her in regular classes. Whenever possible, they also provide assistance for other students in the class.

At the beginning of the semester, the resource department provides detailed information to all teachers about the exceptional students in their classes. The resource teachers will also provide further information on specific disabilities upon request. The resource teachers are paired with the teachers who are integrating the exceptional students and work in the teachers' classrooms. When in the classroom, the resource teacher monitors the progress of the exceptional students, reteaches the material if necessary, and assists the students in completing the assignments. For a portion of the class, either at the beginning or ending of the period, the resource teachers take the exceptional students (and nonexceptional students) to the resource room to work on the assignment or to reinforce a concept. Full period pull-out programs are run for senior exceptional students who are timetabled into the resource room for assistance.

The teachers in this study were very comfortable with the presence of another adult in their classrooms. In addition, the classroom teachers and resource teachers regularly share information about the progress of the students because they see each other almost every day.

The teachers were very positive about this model of integration, but did express some concerns. One teacher questioned whether it was as efficient as the pull-out model because the resource teacher had to come to the classroom instead of remaining in the resource room. Two of the teachers wondered if the extra support was actually doing the exceptional students a disservice in the long run because it seemed to encourage dependence. The resource teachers agreed that some of the grade-9 students required more support than others. However, by the time the exceptional students were in the senior grades the amount of direct academic assistance was minimal.

In sum, the most important support for the secondary teachers in this study was the resource teachers who assisted them and the exceptional students in the classroom. Classroom teachers and resource teachers believed that this model was an effective way to support the students in their academics and to assist the teacher in the instruction of the pupils.

Summary

Previous studies on integrating exceptional students at the secondary level have focused on teacher behaviours (Bacon & Schulz, 1991; Munroe, 1982; Munroe, 1984). The observations of the three teachers described earlier in this chapter show that teaching excellence and the resource teacher are important variables for successful integration of secondary students. In this school, the resource teachers provided support for individual students through direct classroom monitoring and assistance, as well as through traditional pull-out programs. They also provided support for the classroom teacher by distributing information on the exceptional students and by assisting in the classroom. The latter function was particularly important in the math class when the exceptional students all seemed to require assistance with the assignment at the same time. The resource teachers and the classroom teachers worked efficiently to assist the students with their work. The result was that the wait time for assistance was reduced, and the academic learning time was increased. In all classes, the resource teachers and the classroom teachers worked as a team to ensure the learning of all the students in the class.

The resource teachers and the classroom teachers met each other every day in the classroom and used the opportunity to share information and observations about the exceptional students. This scheduled and regular time for communication about the students was important for monitoring progress. Therefore, the direct involvement of the resource teachers, in combination with the excellent teaching behaviours and positive attitudes of the classroom teachers, provided formidable support for the exceptional students in this secondary school.

SUGGESTED RESOURCES

Books, Articles, and Papers

Alexander, W., & Caldwell, M. (1983). *Characteristics of special needs learners.* New Jersey: Trenton State College.

Brown, G.M., McDowell, R.L., & Smith, J. (1981). *Educating adolescents with behavior disorders.* Columbus, OH: Charles E. Merrill.

Ernst, M. (1982). Tapping literature's language growth potentials for the secondary school hearing-impaired student—The study guide. *Volta Review, 84*(2), 109–20.

Grosse, S.J. (1993). Become a part of the mainstream process. *Strategies, 7*(1), 16–19.
Jones, V. (1980). *Adolescents with behavior problems: Strategies for teaching, counselling and parent involvement.* Boston: Allyn and Bacon.
Kise, J., & Darr, A.D. (1982). "A conceptual framework and practical applications to help regular teachers accommodate special students." Paper presented at the Annual Meeting of the Association of Teacher Educators, Phoenix, AZ.
MacMillan, B., & First, C. (1990). "The progressive/collaborative high school: A model program." Paper presented at the 68th Annual International Convention of the Council for Exceptional Children, Toronto (April 23–27).
Manus, R. (1990). *The skillful teacher's handbook: Effectively teaching regular and special students.* Springfield, IL: Charles C. Thomas.
McDonnell, J., Wilcox, B., & Hardman, M.L. (1991). *Secondary programs for students with development disabilities.* Boston: Allyn and Bacon.
Morse, W.C., Ardizzone, J., MacDonald, C., & Pasick, P. (1980). *Affective education for special children and youth.* Reston, VA: Council for Exceptional Children.
Nagel, R., Peat, F., & Wayne, D. (1981). *Not alone: teaching the secondary student with special needs.* Toronto: Ontario Secondary School Teachers' Federation.
Pearpoint, J., Forest, M., & Snow, J. (1992). *The inclusion papers: strategies to make inclusion work: A collection of articles from the center.* Toronto: Inclusion Press.
Pritchard, R.J. (1984). Special students in regular secondary classes: Selected annotated bibliography. *Journal of Teacher Education, 35,* 51–54.
Project Change. (1993). "Assessing your school climate for integration and developing strategies for change and from vision to commitment." Paper distributed following a presentation at the 71st Annual Convention of the Council for Exceptional Children, San Antonio, TX (April 5–9). Winnipeg School Division Number 1, Manitoba.
Putnam, J. (1993). *Cooperative learning and strategies for inclusion: Celebrating diversity in the classroom.* Toronto: Paul H. Brookes.
West, L. (Ed.). *Functional curriculum for transitions: A resource guide.* Missouri University, Columbia: College of Education.
Woodward, D. (1981). *Mainstreaming the learning disabled adolescent: A manual of strategies and materials.* Rockville, MD: Aspen Systems.
Woodward, D., & Peters, J. (1983). *The learning disabled adolescent: Learning success in content areas.* Rockville, MD: Aspen Systems.

Information Centres

Center for Integrated Education and Community, 24 Thorne Crescent, Toronto, ON, Canada, M6H 2S5. Phone/fax: 416-658-5363. (Videos and books).

ERIC Clearinghouse on Disabilities and Gifted Education, 1920 Association Drive, Reston, VA, 22091-1589.

National Clearinghouse for Professions in Special Education, 1920 Association Drive, Reston, VA, 22091-1589.

National Information Center on Deafness, Gallaudet University, 800 Florida Avenue, N.E. Washington, DC, 20002-3695.

NICHCY (National Information Center for Children and Youth with Disabilities), P.O. Box 1492, Washington, DC, 20013. Phone: 1-800-695-0295.

Audio-Visual

Mainstreaming in Action. (Takes viewers into several classrooms on the elementary or secondary level to watch and listen as teachers work with handicapped students. 26 minutes. Color no. 3626. Visual Education Center.)

REFERENCES

Bacon, E., & Schulz, J. (1991). A survey of mainstreaming practices. *Teacher Education and Special Education, 14,* 144–49.

Brady, M., et al. (1988). Differential measures of teachers' questioning in mainstreamed classes: Individual and classwide patterns. *Journal of Research and Development in Education, 22,* 10–17.

Duquette, C. (1992). Integrating mildly and moderately handicapped children: What goes on in a successful school? *Exceptionality Education Canada, 2,* 139–53.

Larrivee, B., & Algina, J. (1983). "Identification of teaching behaviours which predict success on mainstreamed students." Paper presented at the Annual Meeting of the American Educational Research Association, Montreal. ED232362.

McCormick, M. (1983). The handicapped experience project: Preparing the secondary teacher for mainstreaming. *Journal of Teacher Education, 34,* 45–47.

Munroe, M. (1982). "Teaching behaviors effective in mainstream classrooms." Paper presented at the Annual State Conference of the Arizona Federation Council for Exceptional Children, Tucson. ED213679.

Munroe, M. (1984). "Effective teaching: Commitment to learning in the mainstream classroom." Paper presented at the Greater Edmonton Teachers' Convention Association, Edmonton. ED242667.

Pritchard, R. (1984). Special students in regular secondary classes: Selected annotated bibliography. *Journal of Teacher Education, 35,* 51–54.

Reed, P. (1983). Mainstreaming in secondary schools: A shared professional responsibility. OATE-OACTE Monograph Series No. 7. ED242722.

CHAPTER 8

Promoting Social Development and Social Acceptance in Secondary School Classrooms

Nancy L. Hutchinson

Queen's University

Introduction

There is considerable evidence to suggest that, with the growing diversity in inclusive secondary classrooms, many students lack the social development necessary to handle the social demands. This chapter presents a case study of a teacher thinking aloud about her actions to ensure that John, a student with learning disabilities, experiences inclusive education in her classroom. Her thinking can be used as a model by teachers who are including any exceptional adolescent.

John walks into the grade-9 classroom where he will meet his home-room classmates for the first time. The classroom is quiet. He looks around. There are only two other students in the room. Most students are still shouting to their friends in the halls and catching up on the news about summer vacations. John is relieved that he met his teachers last week. His tutor from the learning disabilities program at his elementary school had encouraged him to do that.

Students like John, those who have disabilities or have experienced learning difficulties, want to succeed in secondary school. Exceptional adolescents also frequently experience low levels of acceptance by their peers. Exceptional students are more likely to lack social development and social acceptance. This seems to be true whether they have, for example, learning disabilities (Gresham, 1993; Sabornie, 1994), communication disorders (Lass, 1991), behaviour problems (Sabornie, Kauffman, Ellis, Marshall & Elksnin, 1988), or hearing loss (Jaussi, 1991).

Social Development and Social Acceptance: Definitions

Social development and social acceptance are complex phenomena with behavioural, social, cognitive, and metacognitive aspects. **Social development,** or social competence, is defined as "the ability to implement developmentally-appropriate social behaviours that enhance one's interpersonal relationships without causing harm to anyone" (Schneider, 1993, p. 19). **Social acceptance** refers to the response and evaluation, by peers, of students' social behaviours. Do peers approve of their behaviours, consider them to be members of the group, and include them in social and learning activities (Dodge, 1985)?

After welcoming John to his new homeroom, his teacher thinks to herself:

"I am glad I read John's file. Now that I see him in a busy school, I understand better what the reports mean by 'some delay in social development' and 'not socially accepted.' While everyone else is socializing, John is in the classroom early; he is probably more comfortable talking with me, like a younger kid, really. I guess the other kids are not sure how to relate to him; maybe because he responds in ways they're not expecting. They may not ask him to eat lunch with them, or to be in their group for learning activities."

Both social development and social acceptance are important for all adolescents, in the classroom and beyond. "Affection, intimacy, and a sense of reliable alliance are primarily obtained in close friendships, particularly preadolescent and adolescent ones, whereas feelings of inclusion are likely to result from peer group relations" (Furman & Robbins, 1985, p. 45). Social skills and competencies are acquired in both close friendships and general peer-group relationships. Intimacy skills are more likely to develop in friendships and skills like leadership in peer relations. Research suggests that children and adolescents with poor peer adjustment are at greater risk for criminality and dropping out of school (Parker & Asher, 1987). Social skills are also increasingly important to successful participation in the workplace (McLaughlin, 1992; Tennant, Hutchinson & Freeman, 1992).

Promoting Constructive Social Relationships

Research conducted by Tanis Bryan (1991) and Sharon Vaughn (1991) suggests that it is important to enhance both social development of youth with exceptionalities and social acceptance by peers, because neither alone is sufficient. This combination of factors places demands on secondary teachers for formal instruction of social development and social acceptance with the entire class. In this formal teaching, teachers provide instruction that promotes collaborative learning and interdependence among heterogeneous groups of students (Baron & Brown, 1991; Hutchinson & Freeman, 1994). For such collaborative learning to be effective, it must take place in a context where cooperation, community, and peer support are a part of everything that happens. This means teachers must engage in informal teaching of social development and acceptance of diversity with the entire class. Such informal teaching takes place in the way teachers conduct their classrooms, express their expectations, and model social acceptance.

Informal Teaching

Teachers create positive and inclusive climates in their classrooms by showing respect for all members of the class, and making all students feel that their presence counts. Teachers communicate high expectations—that they expect students to be successful—and provide a high degree of support to enable students to reach those high expectations. John's teacher thinks:

"What should I say to ensure John is accepted by his classmates? There are many different ways I can introduce all the students to my expectations for the course and indicate how I expect them to interact with one another. I will show them the way I expect them to treat John, that is, like all other members of the group. The more he is accepted, the more opportunity he will have to grow socially."

Students learn their manner of referring to and treating their fellow students from the teacher. This means that teachers can provide good models, and demand that students behave similarly. When they make their thinking apparent to students, teachers provide a model of deciding, acting, and explaining, which promotes both social development and social acceptance, without patronizing (McIntosh & Vaughn, 1993).

Formal Teaching: Collaboration and Social Interdependence

Researchers have argued that enhancing social development and acceptance requires not only the acquisition of cognitive and behaviour skills to succeed in interpersonal situations, but also sufficient opportunities to practise these skills in a reinforcing environment (Vaughn, 1991). Adolescents prefer to focus on learning and refining social skills within the context of learning "relevant and practical information" (Hutchinson, Freeman & Quick, in press). All of these perspectives point to integrating social skills enhancement into ongoing curriculum within the secondary school, with the teacher acting as the primary change agent. John's teacher has decided:

"Today, I will get John started positively with paired learning activities. Who should I have John work with to ensure that he and his partner collaborate? The new emphasis in homeroom on career development and acquiring academic goals will be ideal. It is easier to foster interdependence with questions and topics for which there are many good answers and many good explanations."

The perspective on teaching and learning that dominated much of this century was teaching as transmission and learning as passive absorption of facts and skills. Recently, much has been written about the current perspectives, cognitive and social constructivism. According to constructivist views, learning consists of learners building on what they bring to the situation and restructuring or recasting initial knowledge as increasingly complex understanding (Marshall, 1992). Whereas cognitive constructivists emphasize that learners construct knowledge (often with guidance), social constructivists place greater emphasis on the role of social interaction in meaning construction. Learning and thinking are situated in social contexts rather than solely in the individual's mind (Rogoff & Lave, 1984). For social constructivists, teaching means creating challenging tasks that require active involvement by students and provides opportunities for students to learn together. Meaningful tasks are emphasized that are related to needed real-world knowledge and skills (Brown, Collins & Duguid, 1989). Collaborative learning methods allow teachers to capitalize on the social nature of learning and promote social development and acceptance, as well as cognitive growth.

Collaborative learning methods include cooperative learning, problem solving in pairs and groups, and peer tutoring. These grouping methods usually involve students of varying abilities and skills, that is, heterogeneous groupings rather than homogeneous groupings. Collaborative learning methods have been successful in improving academic performance of students of varying ages, grades, subjects, and abilities (Scheid, 1993). Students, in general, are more likely to be successful when a) they are instructed in well-structured, cognitively oriented programs (Cohen, Kulik & Kulik, 1982), and b) they are required as part of their group work to give and receive explanations for answers and ideas suggested in discussion (Webb, 1985).

Collaborative learning makes sense in inclusive classrooms because it builds on heterogeneity and encourages and formalizes peer support. Collaborative learning methods improve social development and acceptance in groups containing exceptional and regular students, as well as engaging student thinking.

Planning for Formal Teaching of Collaboration

Teachers should not infer that they must use collaborative groups as an exclusive approach to learning. A collaborative strategy should be chosen when the teacher intends to promote positive peer support and systematic development of social acceptance and social skills, and when the knowledge can be best learned through the contributions of many learners. There are three types of collaborative strategy groups. The first type is base groups or home groups, which serve as small, long-term support structures. These are often the peers with whom the student sits in homeroom or at the beginning of each class session. The second type is informal groups, which the teacher puts together for a short period of time to complete a particular activity. The third type is formal groups, that the teacher assembles with great attention to composition to work together over a sustained period of time, perhaps throughout a unit (Johnson & Johnson, 1989).

After deciding to adopt collaborative learning, the teacher makes a number of planning decisions. (A sample graphic planner appears in Table 8.1.) First, for every lesson a decision must be made about the academic goals for the group as a whole and any modifications of goals for learners with special needs. Second, the social goals must be set. Both types of goals should be communicated to students, and social skills taught rather than assumed. Then the

TABLE 8.1
Sample Planning Form for Inclusive, Collaborative Learning

Lesson Name: ____________________

Date: ____________________ Time: ____________________

Academic goals:

Modified academic goals (for students with special needs):

Social goals:

Modified social goals (for students with special needs):

Social skills to pre-teach:

Interaction between students:

Collaborative learning technique:

Group composition:

Room arrangement:

Positive interdependence:

- in process:
- in products:

Student roles in groups:

Monitoring:

Intervening:

Individual accountability:

Evaluation:

Teacher reflection:

Parts of the lesson

Introduction:

Activities in groups:

Closure on the content:

Group reflection on the process:

teacher chooses the type of interaction between students to meet these goals, and chooses the collaborative learning technique that will promote such interaction. Teaching decisions are made about monitoring student performance and guidelines set for intervening in poorly functioning groups (with the proviso to intervene as little as possible, and with questions rather than answers). Individual accountability can be observed during monitoring or in the products. The teacher must decide how to introduce the lesson, foster the collaborative learning, and help students to obtain closure on the content and feedback, and then to reflect on the social skills. Finally, the teacher evaluates the learning and reflects on the process.

There are many examples of lesson plans for collaborative learning in various content areas at the secondary level (Clarke, Wideman & Eadie, 1990; Johnson, Johnson & Holubec, 1987; Lincoln County Board of Education, 1993; Villa & Thousand, 1994). These sources contain forms teachers can use for all aspects of the planning and execution of collaborative teaching. There are also excellent models of planning collaborative teaching for classes that include students with special needs at all levels from primary to adult education (Nevin, Thousand & Villa, 1994), for techniques ranging from simple to complex.

TTYPA

Fogarty (1990) suggests a simple method that punctuates a lecture, film, or reading: TTYPA or "turn to your partner and..." The teacher stops and tells the students to "turn to your partner and...introduce yourself (or describe a time when you...) then switch roles."

John's teacher recalls the lesson plans she has made:

"Today, I will introduce the class to collaborative learning by explaining what it is, why we do it, and what I expect. I will use the simple technique of TTYPA (turn to your partner and...) to help the students get to know one another, and get used to asking questions and giving explanations. The desks are set in pairs, so I will ask each student to turn to the person beside and consider that person partner for the day. The student with the shorter hair in each pair will start by turning and introducing himself or herself. Then the second person in the group will do the same. In the next switch, the first will ask two questions about what the partner likes to do and why. The second student in each pair will, then, do the same. I will eavesdrop on the pairs to get enough sense of these students to make pairings for tomorrow's activities. I will form heterogeneous pairs for tomorrow as best I can on the basis of what I know from the records and today's class. We will change partners often so I can re-pair and give them choices as we go along."

TTYPA is helpful for students to make connections between their prior learning and the topic under study. TTYPA is good preparation for more complex collaborative activities.

Think-Pair-Share

Another simple but powerful technique is called Think-Pair-Share (Kagan, 1992). A problem is posed, usually by the teacher, and students think alone about the question for a specified amount of time. Then students Pair with a classmate to discuss the question. During Share, a few students are randomly chosen to share their classmate's thoughts (or the thoughts of both members of the pair).

Paired Partners: Think Aloud

Another approach for partners that works especially well with mixed-ability pairs is Partners Thinking Aloud. The teacher has to model thinking aloud and ensure that the students understand what is expected of them. Whimbey and Whimbey (1975) piloted this technique: one student becomes the problem solver and the other student becomes the monitor. The problem solver thinks aloud throughout the task, telling his or her thoughts, strategies, and ideas for solving the problem. The monitor cues the "self-talk" of the solver by asking questions like, "What is your goal, does this makes sense, why?" Then they switch roles. Students can become reflective about their own thinking and highly interactive when thinking aloud with partners. Hutchinson (1989) demonstrated the effectiveness of this technique for teaching math problem solving to grade-8 students from an inner-city school, in mixed-ability pairs.

Pathways

Pathways (Hutchinson & Freeman, 1994), a program recently developed and tested in Canada, has shown benefits in social development and social acceptance for individual adolescents in mixed-ability groups (Hutchinson, Freeman & Quick, in press). This program was judged by adolescents to be relevant and practical, and to teach that "two heads are better than one." Teachers judged the materials to be easy to use, clear, and specific.

Pathways consists of five modules that can be used independently, or all five can be used as a course of study:

1. Knowing about Yourself, Knowing about Careers
2. Succeeding with the Résumé and the Application
3. Succeeding with the Interview
4. Solving Problems on the Job
5. Anger Management on the Job

John's teacher is looking forward to starting *Pathways.*

"This group of ninth graders will work on the module, 'Knowing about Yourself, Knowing about Careers.' That will help me get to know the students and begin to provide some guidance about course choices, programs, and goals for high school—the focus of our homeroom program. They work with a partner, taking turns, thinking out loud in these activities. I think out loud, to model, before they work in pairs."

In the career awareness module, students work with a partner to think about their personal needs and values, sort cards to learn about clusters of careers, and match want ads with personal characteristics. The module on application forms and résumés is structured so that students spend equal amounts of time in written and oral activities. Among the oral activities, students discuss employment rights, evaluate employment applications, and practise asking for assistance. Active practice is one aspect of the module on employment interviews. Students develop answers in groups, trace routes to interviews, rate each other's interviews, and develop a strategy for discussing personal strengths and weaknesses. Another module focuses on problem solving on the job. Working individually, in pairs and in groups, students tackle problems they find relevant. They engage in discussing, role playing, and recording radio advertisements. The module on anger management enables students to develop and practise a strategy for controlling anger.

The modules from *Pathways* have been integrated into curriculum in a number of courses. All modules emphasize communication and have been taught in English courses. The problem-solving module has been taught in mathematics courses, and the module on résumés in a keyboarding course. The entire program has been taught in cooperative education in grade 11, and in destreamed or mixed-ability classes at the grade-9 level.

Cooperative Learning

An approach that has been used extensively to promote interdependence in mainstreamed classrooms is Cooperative Learning (Johnson & Johnson, 1989). These authors describe three classroom structures. The first structure is individual, in which students' learning outcomes are independent of one another. The second structure is competitive, in which students work against one another to accomplish a goal that only one or a few students can achieve. The third is cooperative, in which students work together to accomplish shared goals. In Cooperative Learning, students are assigned to small groups and instructed to learn the assigned material and ensure that all members of the group master the assignment. Johnson and Johnson argue that five elements are necessary for successful Cooperative Learning:

1. It is necessary for students to see themselves as interdependent.
2. They must meet face-to-face.
3. Tasks require the efforts of all members for group success.
4. Students must know how to collaborate.
5. They must receive feedback about and reflect on the group's functioning.

Often teachers accept one product from the whole group so that all students in the group receive a grade based on this product. Roles are frequently assigned to keep the group functioning and to ensure that everyone participates.

John's teacher is thinking about how she has used cooperative groups in the past for reading activities. Students predicted and justified the outcome in a five-minute mystery (Weber, 1988).

"I think I will bring in a mystery later this week to get the students working in groups. That means that I must introduce them to the roles of encourager, checker, and reporter. Three in a group will be enough for the first time. The whole activity can be done in about 10 minutes. First, I will give the students a quick introduction to the roles, and read most of a brief mystery. Each group will receive a copy of what I read. I will save three clues, giving one clue to each student in each group. Then the groups will discuss for four minutes, putting their clues together with what I read. They will predict and justify the solution to the mystery, with the encourager and checker expected to fill their roles at least once. Finally, the reporter for each group will give a one-sentence prediction and one-sentence justification to the class. I must remember to tell them the social goals: remembering the names of the other two people in the group and carrying out their individual roles."

In a review of the internal dynamics of Cooperative Learning groups, Johnson and Johnson (1985) conclude that the processes that promote higher achievement and liking among students may include the promotion of high-quality reasoning strategies, constructive management of conflict over ideas, and feelings of psychological support and acceptance. However, only 1 of the 42 studies included in the review investigated an academic subject in grades 8 to 12. Nevin, Johnson, and Johnson (1982) found that over a 17-day intervention in grade-9 mathematics, cooperative groups of three—heterogeneous in sex, ability, and handicap (learning disabled, emotionally disturbed)—showed greater achievement and interpersonal attraction than students in the individualistic condition. The majority of their studies have been conducted in elementary school classrooms and a few in college settings.

Jigsaw

The ultimate cooperative interactive design is Sharan and Sharan's (1976) Group Investigation Model. It is a variation of the Jigsaw strategy (Aronson, 1978). This highly cooperative approach highlights the sink-or-swim-together elements, which means that all members must be able to work with others effectively. The teacher places students in base groups, often threesomes. First, each member of the threesome selects or is assigned a piece of the group work. Each member gathers and organizes information about one piece of the "puzzle." Sometimes all the number ones work together to learn their part of the "puzzle"; the twos work together, and the threes work together. Part of the task of these expert groups is to devise a plan to teach what they have learned to the other members of their base group. Then the original base groups reassemble and the members each teach their critical findings to the others so they all know all the pieces of the jigsaw as well as they know their own. To perform Jigsaw effectively, students need explicit instruction in how to effectively share information so others will learn.

John's teacher knows that near the end of the *Pathways* module on self-awareness and awareness of careers, she will form base groups that include one student interested in each of the job clusters. She thinks:

"I am glad I decided to wait a few weeks before trying the Jigsaw about career clusters. Each group can interview someone from the community who has a job in their cluster. I will work closely with the expert group researching jobs that involve the use of tools and hand skills, because a number of them may have difficulty with research skills. I think I will help them line up a number of visitors to talk about apprenticeships, their training as tradespeople, and their experiences on the job. When these students teach their base group about that hands-on job cluster, maybe they can each show part of a videotaped interview with one of the visitors. Or perhaps they can do a hands-on demonstration."

There are many examples of Jigsaw activities used in content area classes in the secondary classroom. Lazarowitz and Karsenty (1990) implemented a biology unit on photosynthesis in 19 grade-10 classes using a Jigsaw approach. The learning material was divided into five subunits. Each base group consisted of five students, heterogeneous with regard to gender and ability. Each student in the base group received a different subunit to study, chosen by the teacher to match students' abilities with task difficulties. Once everyone was familiar with the topics and sequence, the students who received the same subunit formed an expert group. Their role was to study the topic assigned to them through reading, identifying problems, performing experiments, and collecting and arranging data in tables and graphs. (Students were allowed to present experiments in the base group that they had conducted in the expert group.) They explained to one another the answers to questions, discussed their findings, and drew conclusions. The last two sets of activities in these expert groups involved a) making teaching plans for the return to the base groups, and b) checking to ensure that everyone knew the content of the subunit and was well prepared for the next step. In the return to the Jigsaw base groups, each student taught his or her part as it had been studied in the expert group. They posed questions, presented experiments that they had conducted, and showed data in tables and graphs. Finally, students checked the comprehension of the others on the subunits they had taught before the final test.

The 10 control-group classes studied the same topic in a traditional approach, using laboratory experiments conducted by teachers, and working alone during the learning process.

The students in the Jigsaw approach demonstrated higher achievement scores on the two tests of content and the four process skills: measuring, reading graphs, interpreting data, and designing an experiment. The Jigsaw class reported "experiencing more cooperation and cohesiveness in their classrooms and feeling more satisfied." They also judged their learning material to be less difficult and their classes to have less competition and less favouritism. Lastly, they reported "less apathy and cliqueness among their peers" (Lazarowitz & Karsenty, 1990, p. 140). In general, the Jigsaw students expressed slightly higher levels of self-esteem. There were two gender differences. In the cooperative mode of instruction, girls emerged with higher self-esteem than their male counterparts. In the traditional condition, girls expressed lower self-esteem than the boys in their group and than the girls in the cooperative condition.

Overall, this study demonstrates that the Jigsaw approach can be used for an entire unit in a secondary content class with positive outcomes for academic achievement and social climate. In this case, instruction was designed so that students of varying abilities could be successful in their expert groups and in the subsequent teaching. Heterogeneous groups were used and activities were designed to encourage discussion and explanation.

Summary of Formal Teaching: Collaboration and Interdependence

In formal teaching to promote collaboration and interdependence, teachers and students engage in "intentional" talk as well as "contingent responsiveness" (Wells, Chang & Maher, 1990). Teachers and students model for one another the range of thinking, sense making, and problem solving that could be used. They respond to one another's thinking aloud, and pursue tasks that require individuals to work together. The main focus is benefits (cognitive and social) for the individual learner within the group.

Getting Started with Formal Teaching for Collaboration

How can students learn to cooperate well with others, particularly with those who are different from them in some way? Teachers should ascertain through observation the behaviours and social skills that students most need. For the most important social skills (like giving everyone a chance to talk, listening actively, and giving an explanation), students need practice in a facilitating environment, guidance through effective role models, and teachers who help them persist in the face of deterrents. In her book, *Designing Groupwork: Strategies for the Heterogeneous Classroom,* Elizabeth Cohen (1986) provides several examples of activities and games to help students acquire group-work skills.

It is often helpful to begin with simple, short activities that provide frequent occasions for participation in the class. Teachers can start with participation in pairs through TTYPA, Think-Pair-Share, and Think Aloud pairs, and progress to short Cooperative Learning activities like 10 minutes of group work on a 5-minute mystery. Later, teachers will be ready to implement longer collaborative programs like Jigsaw in grade-10 biology (modelled on Lazarowitz and Karsenty, 1990) or programs modelled on *Pathways* to promote social problem solving, communication, or career education. They will know how to form groups and intervene effectively after practice with simple, short collaborative activities. The students will have had considerable practice with collaboration and may be able to recommend preparatory activities to ensure social interdependence.

Challenges to Formal Collaboration

Collaboration has been shown to enhance social development and social acceptance in many studies with children (Johnson & Johnson, 1985) and adolescents (Lazarowitz & Karsenty, 1990). However, there are a number of challenges to collaborative learning. Cooperative activities in which all students in a group receive the same grade can result in unfair evaluation outcomes if some students have failed to contribute, or if some knew all the content before the unit began. Occasionally, a student may become dependent on the more able members of a cooperative group. Exceptional students and gifted students in inclusive classrooms are more likely to experience these drawbacks than their peers. It may be necessary to provide alternate evaluation criteria for some students. (See Chapter 4.) It may be necessary to modify or adapt the goals and curriculum for some students with special needs. (Nevin, Thousand, and Villa, 1994.)

Other strategies to meet the challenges include monitoring group interaction closely, and focusing specifically on the needs of exceptional students in the inclusive classroom when deciding about the composition of groups. They can challenge one another when they pursue tasks with content much more advanced than their classmates. When the gap is very large between them and the rest of the class, they may be too impatient to be supportive and good models for the lowest achievers. Although the general guideline is heterogeneous groups, the teacher must decide when planning each lesson or unit about the best group composition for meeting the academic and social goals.

In the context of the departmentalized, curriculum-driven secondary school, teachers frequently feel pressure to "cover the curriculum" and "keep up" with the pace at which other teachers are progressing through the curriculum (Hutchinson, Freeman & Quick, in press). Many argue that the gains in motivation, reasoning, and self-directedness more than compensate for the time required to teach students to work collaboratively (e.g., Bellanca & Fogarty, 1991). In upper years, students may be competing for grades, entry to post-secondary education, and scholarships. These characteristics may make it more difficult for teachers in secondary schools than teachers in elementary schools to adopt formal approaches to collaboration. However, the mandate for inclusive schooling heightens the need to promote social development and social acceptance, and formal and informal approaches to enhancing collaboration appear to be among the best ways to accomplish these goals.

Collaborative learning approaches may be particularly challenging with adolescents who tend to have a low tolerance for diversity (Rice, 1987) and view conformity as an important requirement for popularity (Sebald, 1981). These approaches can focus the frustration of group members on students who contribute less than their share when the collaborations are unsuccessful (Scheid, 1993). Cohen, Lotan, and Catanzarite (1990) suggest that when mixed-status groups are engaged in collective tasks, they can be dominated by high-status members and not pay attention to the contributions of low-status members. Because these techniques depend on interaction for their desirable effects on learning, differing access to interaction according to the status of students is a practical concern. Cohen et al. (1990, pp. 226–27) make a number of recommendations for minimizing the impact of status problems:

1. Train students in listening to one another, taking turns talking, and assuming various roles in the group. Use collaborative activities, for this training, that emphasize process as much as content. As students improve at the process, shift the balance to activities that emphasize learning of content.

2. Use learning materials that are rich and stimulating but not entirely dependent on reading. Such learning materials may supplement textbooks with diagrams and illustrations, videotapes, audiotapes, case studies and realistic tasks containing authentic documents. Sometimes recorded speeches may communicate more effectively than history books.

3. Draw on a wide range of knowledge and experience, beyond that typically used in the classroom, with authentic tasks. Point out to the students how these activities are different. Point out the varied successes of a number of students.

4. Teachers may need support through in-service in implementing collaborative approaches consistently. Secondary schools often use part of their professional development time each year to respond to teacher needs. A department in a secondary school might propose collaborative learning (or any other group of teachers who feel they can support one another) for themselves or the whole school. Inclusion and collaborative learning challenge teachers to make use of available information, strategies, and programs and to keep an account of their experiences to share with colleagues (Gaskins & Elliot, 1991).

Summary

This chapter uses a continuing case study of a secondary teacher thinking aloud about the actions she will take to ensure that a student with learning disabilities experiences inclusive education in her classroom. Her thinking can be used as a model by teachers who are including any student who would benefit from the promotion of social development and social acceptance.

There are two major approaches to promoting social development and social acceptance. First, teachers can promote a climate of acceptance and respect by interacting this way with all members of the class and setting the standard they expect of students. When there are difficulties, they can "seize the moment" to teach and negotiate what is expected.

Second, teachers can adopt formal teaching approaches that foster collaboration and interdependence in learning. Some of the techniques include having students work with a partner, Thinking Aloud, a program like *Pathways,* Cooperative Learning, and Jigsaw. These methods usually involve heterogeneous rather than homogeneous grouping. They are more successful when they are well structured and when students are required as part of their group work to give and receive explanations for answers and ideas suggested in discussion.

Working in a group, giving and receiving explanations, and sharing responsibilities for problem solving are essential to success in inclusive schools, employment, and life in general for all students. Teachers and students are positive about the experiences and outcomes of collaborative learning for social development and social acceptance, when the approach is implemented thoughtfully and consistently (Scheid, 1993).

SUGGESTED RESOURCES

Books for Teachers

Blueprints for Thinking in the Cooperative Classroom. James Bellanca & Robin Fogarty (1991). Skylight Publishing, 200 E. Wood Street, Suite 274, Palatine, IL 60067. Phone: 708-991-6300. A thorough handbook with three lesson plans in each chapter, one for each of elementary, middle, and high school. Contains forms, checklists, and activity sheets for students.

Cooperative Learning. Spencer Kagan (1992). Kagan Cooperative Learning, 27134 Paseo Espada, Suite 302, San Jaun Capistrano, CA, 92675. Phone: 714-248-7757. Kagan describes the structures he has developed for encouraging collaborative learning. There are lesson designs, teacher tools, and student handouts. He also provides a rationale for this practical approach to teaching.

Cooperative Learning: Where Heart Meets Mind. Barrie Bennett, Carol Rolheiser-Bennett & Laurie Stevahn (1991). Educational Connections, Station "P", 704 Spadina Avenue, P.O. Box 249, Toronto, ON, M5S 2S8. This Canadian source is set up like a workshop manual for teachers to work through in a workshop or in a group. It provides many reproducible student activity pages and forms for record keeping, evaluation, etc.

Creativity and Collaborative Learning: A Practical Guide to Empowering Students and Teachers. Jacqueline S. Thousand, Richard A. Villa & Ann I. Nevin (1994). Paul H. Brookes, P.O. Box 10624, Baltimore, MD, 21285-0624. One chapter (pp. 131–225) of this edited book contains thorough examples of lesson and unit planning for collaborative learning in inclusive classrooms with curricular modifications to meet the needs of exceptional learners. This makes it a unique resource for teachers.

Designing Groupwork: Strategies for the Heterogeneous Classroom. Elizabeth Cohen (1986). Teachers College Press, New York. In this book, Cohen provides several examples of activities and games that can be used to help students acquire group work skills. These emphasize acquisition of knowledge about process or "how-to" work in a group rather than content knowledge. This book is generally thought to be the best source of ideas for dealing with issues related to the differing status of group members.

Designs for Cooperative Interactions. Robin Fogarty (1990). Skylight Publishing, 200 E. Wood Street, Suite 274, Palatine, IL, 60067. Phone: 708-991-6300. Fogarty outlines a series of increasingly complex cooperative learning techniques, beginning with simple approaches like TTYPA ("turn to your partner and") and paired problem solving, working through to Jigsaw and other activities that are sustained over a unit of instruction. This is a practical source with clear guidelines.

Growing Collaboratively. Lincoln County Board of Education (1993). Prentice-Hall Canada, Scarborough, ON. This resource prepared by teachers of the Lincoln County Board of Education in Ontario includes guidelines for modifying curriculum for collaborative learning, sample forms, and complete lesson plans from primary to the senior grades, including reproducible activity masters. The pages are crowded, but this resource is packed with helpful information.

Helping Students Become Strategic Learners: Guidelines for Teaching. Karen Scheid (1993). Brookline Books, P.O. Box 1046, Cambridge, MA, 02238-1046. Chapter 5 of this practical book provides teachers with strategies for implementing collaborative learning in the classroom. Although some strategies may be more suited to elementary classrooms, there are many ideas that will be helpful to secondary teachers, like checklists to determine whether learning materials support collaborative learning.

Perspectives on Small Group Learning: Theory and Practice. Mark Brubacher, Ryder Payne & Kemp Rickett (1990). Rubicon Publishing, Inc., Oakville, ON. This collection of papers, many by secondary classroom teachers, was edited by three Canadians with extensive experience teaching secondary English. Teachers describe their experiences implementing collaborative and small-group learning in drama classes, poetry units, collaborative writing with computers, and mathematics classes.

Together We Learn. Judy Clarke, Ron Wideman & Susan Eadie. Prentice-Hall Canada, Scarborough, ON. The original edition of this excellent Canadian production was prepared cooperatively by a consortium of school boards in the Toronto area. It is practical, but also contains thoughtful discussion on topics like informing parents about cooperative learning and how to start group work. Contains sample lesson plans for all grade levels and evaluation strategies and forms. A video program that complements this handbook is available from the Metropolitan Toronto School Board.

Instructional Programs

The ACCESS Program: Adolescent Curriculum for Communication and Effective Social Skills. Hill M. Walker, Bonnie Todis, Deborah Holmes & Gary Horton (1988). Pro-Ed, 8700 Shoal Creek Blvd., Austin, TX, 78758. Phone: 512-451-3246. ACCESS is designed to teach peer-to-peer skills, skills for relating to adults, and self-management skills to students at middle and high school levels. It is designed for use by both regular and special educators and may be taught in small-group or large-group formats. It contains teaching scripts, instructional procedures, and a student study guide.

ASSET: A Social Skills Program for Adolescents. J.S. Hazel, J.B. Schumaker, J.A. Sherman & J. Sheldon-Wildgen (1981). Research Press, Champaign, IL. The ASSET program teaches eight social skills, including giving and receiving feedback, negotiation, and conversation. The lessons include teacher explanations, opportunities for student practice of the skills, and homework assignments for students to obtain practice outside school. This program has less emphasis on authentic tasks than programs developed more recently. It is more suited to use with groups of students with learning disabilities rather than inclusive classrooms.

Pathways. Nancy L. Hutchinson & John Freeman (1994). Nelson Canada, 1120 Birchmount Road, Scarborough, ON, M1K 5G4. Phone: 1-800-268-2222. This highly interactive Canadian program uses collaborative learning methods particularly well suited to mixed-ability groups and inclusive and destreamed classrooms. It consists of an overview booklet and five modules that can be used singly or in combination for a unit or a course of study. It contains teacher scripts, and includes modelling, thinking aloud, group and pair work, and involves students in solving authentic social problems.

REFERENCES

Aronson, E. (1978). *The Jigsaw classroom.* Beverly Hills, CA: Sage.

Baron, J., & Brown, R.V. (Eds.). (1991). *Teaching decision making to adolescents.* Hillsdale, NJ: Erlbaum.

Bellanca, J., & Fogarty, R. (1991). *Blueprints for thinking in the cooperative classroom.* Palatine, IL: Skylight Publishing.

Brown, J.S., Collins, A., & Duguid, P. (1989). Situated cognition and the culture of learning. *Educational Researcher, 18*(1), 32–42.

Bryan, T. (1991). Social problems and learning disabilities. In B.Y.L. Wong (Ed.), *Learning about learning disabilities* (pp. 195–229). San Diego, CA: Academic.

Clarke, J., Wideman, R., & Eadie, S. (1990). *Together we learn.* Scarborough, ON: Prentice-Hall Canada.

Cohen, E. (1986). *Designing groupwork: Strategies for the heterogeneous classroom.* New York: Teachers College Press.

Cohen, E., Lotan, R., & Catanzarite, L. (1990). Treating status problems in the cooperative classroom. In S. Sharan (Ed.), *Cooperative learning: Theory and research* (pp. 203–29). New York: Praeger.

Cohen, P., Kulik, J., & Kulik, C. (1982). Educational outcomes of tutoring: A meta analysis of findings. *American Educational Research Journal, 19,* 237–48.

Dodge, K.A. (1985). Facets of social interaction and the assessment of social competence in children. In B. Schneider, K.H. Rubin & J.E. Ledingham (Eds.), *Children's peer relations: Issues in assessment and intervention* (pp. 3–22). New York: Springer-Verlag.

Fogarty, R. (1990). *Designs for cooperative interactions.* Palatine, IL: Skylight Publishing.

Freeman, J.G., & Hutchinson, N.L. (1994). "Teachers' views of what makes good instructional materials: Using teacher focus groups in developing an instructional program." Paper presented at the annual meeting of the Canadian Society for the Study of Education, Calgary, AB.

Furman, W., & Robbins, P. (1985). What's the point? Issues in the selection of treatment objectives. In B. Schneider, K.H. Rubin & J.E. Ledingham (Eds.), *Children's peer relations: Issues in assessment and intervention* (pp. 41–54). New York: Springer-Verlag.

Gaskins, I., & Elliot, T. (1991). *Implementing cognitive strategy instruction across the school.* Cambridge, MA: Brookline.

Gresham, F.M. (1993). School-based social skills training: Implications for students with mild disabilities. *Exceptionality Education Canada, 3*(1&2), 61–78.

Hutchinson, N.L. (1989). "Now I can do it! Now they can do it! Implementing strategy instruction in an inner city school." Paper presented at the annual meeting of the Canadian Society for the Study of Education, Quebec City, QC.

Hutchinson, N.L., & Freeman, J.G. (1994). *Pathways.* Scarborough, ON: Nelson Canada.

Hutchinson, N.L., Freeman, J.G., & Quick, V.E. (in press). Group counseling intervention for solving problems on the job. *Journal of Employment Counseling.*

Iannaccone, C.J., Wienke, W.D., & Cosden, M.A. (1992). Social skills instruction in secondary schools: Factors affecting its implementation. *High School Journal, 75,* 111–18.

Jaussi, K.R. (1991). Drawing the outsiders in: Deaf students in the mainstream. *Perspectives in Education and Deafness, 9*(5), 12–15.

Johnson, D.W., & Johnson, R.T. (1985). The internal dynamics of cooperative learning groups. In R. Slavin et al. (Eds.), *Learning to cooperate, cooperating to learn* (pp. 103–24). New York: Plenum Press.

Johnson, D.W., & Johnson, R.T. (1989). Cooperative learning and mainstreaming. In R. Gaylord-Ross (Ed.), *Integration strategies for students with handicaps* (pp. 233–48). Toronto: Paul H. Brookes.

Johnson, R.T., Johnson, D.W., & Holubec, E.J. (Eds.). (1987). *Structuring cooperative learning: Lesson plans for teachers.* Edina, MN: Interaction Book Co.

Kagan, S. (1992). *Cooperative learning.* San Juan Capistrano, CA: Kagan Cooperative Learning.

Lass, N.J. (1991). Adolescents' perceptions of normal and voice-disordered children. *Journal of Communication Disorders, 24,* 267–74.

Lazarowitz, R., & Karsenty, G. (1990). Cooperative learning and students' academic achievement, process skills, learning environment, and self-esteem in tenth-grade biology classrooms. In S. Sharan (Ed.), *Cooperative learning: Theory and research* (pp. 123–49). New York: Praeger.

Lincoln Board of Education. (1993). *Growing collaboratively.* Scarborough, ON: Prentice-Hall Canada.

Marshall, H.H. (1992). Seeing, redefining, and supporting student learning. In H.H. Marshall (Ed.), *Redefining student learning: Roots of educational change* (pp. 1–32). Norwood, NJ: Ablex.

McIntosh, R., & Vaughn, S. (1993). So you want to teach social skills to your students: Some pointers from the research. *Exceptionality Education Canada, 3*(1&2), 39–59.

McLaughlin, M. (1992). *Employability skills profile: What are employers looking for?* Ottawa, ON: Conference Board of Canada.

Nevin, A., Johnson, D.W., & Johnson, R.T. (1982). Effects of group and individual contingencies on academic performance and social relations of special needs students. *Journal of Social Psychology, 116,* 41–59.

Nevin, A., Thousand, J.S., & Villa, R.A. (1994). Introduction to creative cooperative group lesson plans. In J.S. Thousand, R.A. Villa & A. Nevin (Eds.), *Creativity and collaborative learning* (pp. 131–225). Baltimore: Paul H. Brookes.

Parker, J.G., & Asher, S.R. (1987). Peer relations and later personal adjustment: Are low-accepted children at risk? *Psychological Bulletin, 102,* 357–89.

Rice, F.P. (1987). *The adolescent: Development, relationships, and culture.* Newton, MS: Allyn and Bacon.

Rogoff, B., & Lave, J. (Eds.). (1984). *Everyday cognition: Its development in social context.* Cambridge, MA: Harvard University Press.

Sabornie, E.J. (1994). Social-affective characteristics in early adolescents identified as learning disabled and nondisabled. *Learning Disability Quarterly, 17,* 268–79.

Sabornie, E.J., Kauffman, J.M., Ellis, E.S., Marshall, K.J., & Elksnin, L.K. (1988). The bi-directional and cross-categorical social status of learning disabled, behaviorally disordered, and non-handicapped adolescents. *Journal of Special Education, 21,* 39–56.

Scheid, K. (1993). *Helping students become strategic learners: Guidelines for teaching.* Cambridge, MA: Brookline Books.

Schneider, B.H. (1993). *Children's social competence in context: The contributions of family, school, and culture.* Oxford, UK: Pergamon.

Sebald, H. (1981). Adolescents' concept of popularity and unpopularity. *Adolescence, 16,* 187–93.

Sharan, S., & Sharan, Y. (1976). *Small group teaching.* Englewood Cliffs, NJ: Educational Testing Publications.

Sproles, E.K. (1988). Research indicates new approaches in counseling vocation-education students. *School Counselor, 36,* 18–23.

Tennant, B., Hutchinson, N.L., & Freeman, J.G. (1992). Employers' expectations of adolescents with learning disabilities in cooperative education. *Exceptionality Education Canada, 2*(3&4), 129–42.

Thorndike, E. (1932). *Fundamentals of learning.* New York: Teachers College Press.

Vaughn, S. (1991). Social skills enhancement in students with learning disabilities. In B.Y.L. Wong (Ed.), *Learning about learning disabilities* (pp. 407–40). San Diego, CA: Academic.

Villa, R.A., & Thousand, J.S. (1994). One divided by two or more: Redefining the role of a cooperative education team. In J.S. Thousand, R.A. Villa & A. Nevin (Eds.), *Creativity and collaborative learning* (pp. 79–102). Baltimore: Paul H. Brookes.

Vygotsky, L. (1978). *Mind in society.* Cambridge, MA: Harvard University Press.

Webb, N. (1985). Student interactions and learning in small groups: A research summary. In R. Slavin, S. Sharan, S. Kagan, R. Hertz-Lazarowitz, C. Webb, & R. Schmuck (Eds.), *Learning to cooperate, cooperating to learn* (pp. 147–72). New York: Plenum.

Weber, K.J. (1988). *Five minute mysteries.* Philadelphia: Running Press.

Wells, G., Chang, G.L.M., & Maher, A. (1990). Creating classroom communities of literate thinkers. In S. Sharan (Ed.), *Cooperative learning: Theory and research* (pp. 95–121). New York: Praeger.

Whimbey, A., & Whimbey, L. (1975). *Intelligence can be taught.* New York: Innovative Science.

CHAPTER 9

Maintaining and Fostering Sociocultural Awareness in a Community of Secondary School Learners

David Piper

Saint Mary's University

Terry Piper

Memorial University

Introduction

The question that frames the discussion in this chapter is: What is sociocultural awareness in secondary schools? In other words, what kind of learning environment are we striving for? To answer this question, we will begin with a description of the "culture" of secondary schools, a culture that differs in a significant way from the culture of elementary schools. We will then attempt a definition of culture that is appropriate for educational purposes, a definition that we will apply in a discussion of the attitudes that people have to their own and to other cultures, the judgments they make about those cultures, and the impact they have on classroom environments. Language is an aspect of culture that is not only extremely evident, but which causes the most conspicuous policy and practical problems for schools. We will examine how culture and language are interrelated and the impact that has on schooling. We will conclude the chapter with a set of practical recommendations for merging these various ideas to create classroom environments that are welcoming, sustaining, and effective for all the young people who populate them.

Culture of the Secondary School

Any discussion of how to foster sociocultural awareness must be cast within an understanding of the institutional environment of Canadian high schools. There are several factors that contribute to the fundamental differences between the environment of the elementary school and that of the secondary school. Age of the learners is, of course, a major one that has sociological as well as cognitive, and thus pedagogical, consequences. While it is common practice in Canada for the provinces to certify teachers to teach at all levels from kindergarten to grade 12 (or 13) no matter the level for which they were prepared, teachers quickly realize that the training they received for the primary or elementary years has little applicability to older learners. In the next few pages, we will look at how the institutionalized culture of the high school differs from that of the elementary school and how it is possible to work within this culture to bring about a greater and more facilitative level of sociocultural awareness among all members of the educational community—for teachers and principals as well as students.

Teaching and learning are subject based. While curricular content is a central organizing principle of both elementary and secondary schools, high schools are organized around individual and largely independent subject areas. Teachers are subject specialists, teaching English, social studies, physics, mathematics, and sometimes two subjects but rarely, outside the very small rural schools, more than two. During the school day, students move from teacher to teacher and, more importantly for our purposes here, from membership in one group to membership in another, according to which of these subjects they are taking. Students have four, five, six, or more teachers rather than the one or two they had in elementary school.

The students are adolescents! Most people depend on several group memberships for their sense of identity. These include nationality, race, language group, gender, and age. At different points in our lives, we place different importance on these groups in figuring out who we are. Adolescents are in the midst of working out just where they fit in each of these groups, but age plays a greater role than it does at any other time in life. There is tremendous pressure to conform to peer values, and social relationships begin to take precedence over family relationships.

The purpose of schooling becomes more immediate. In part, there is a feeling that the high school years are the "last chance" to provide whatever knowledge or skills may be required for university, trade school, or community college admission, attaining a job, parenting, being a consumer—in short, life. This sense of purpose is very much culturally determined because attitudes to education are based in the belief systems of individual societies, a fact we must remember as we think about the culturally inclusive classroom. Not every student, nor even every teacher, will share the same beliefs and, thus, goals. Another important effect of age is that all the ever-present pressures and dangers of the society (substance abuse, family breakdown, etc.) become greater threats to the security of individual adolescents and, thus, have greater impact on their learning potential.

A third consequence of age for the current and coming generations is that they have grown up in an age of information, supertechnology, and the global village. Growing up in a world made smaller by a variety of telemedia, today's adolescents may have experienced the conflicting effects of increased awareness of other cultures and simultaneously increased insularity as they struggle to find their own identities.

There are more men teaching high school than elementary school. Ideally, men and women would be equally represented on the faculties of both elementary and secondary schools. In fact, the elementary (and especially the primary) years are dominated by females, while far more men find their way into high school teaching. Researchers have observed that women teachers interact with their students in ways that are derived from the ways in which they were mothered (Mitchell & Watson, cited in Seelye, p. 229). There is bound to be a shift in climate and, possibly, pedagogical approach between the elementary and secondary years.

Group Membership and Identity

Knowing more about culture, about what it means to belong to a culture, and about the emotions associated with cultural membership is especially important to all educators. The groups to which individuals belong include nation, smaller (i.e., provincial) or larger (i.e., North American) geographical regions, race, gender, family, school, or age. Individuals devolve much of their identity from their membership in these cultures.

There are many kinds of emotions and behaviours associated with cultural identity in adult life, and there are many potential reasons for adults, and thus adolescent near-adults, to feel either secure or insecure in their everyday negotiations with others.

When a specific cause, such as language, religion, or territory becomes the focus for a political and cultural movement, the search for identity may be a more abstract battle over symbols. Symbols, whether they come in the form of images, buildings, or documents that have particular historical or ethnic significance, can all engender feelings of defensiveness, outrage, and aggression if they come under threat. This is true because, in a very real sense, when an individual's identity is partly defined by membership in a group which the symbol represents, an attack on that symbol is an attack on the individual's sense of self.

Any threat to the feeling of secure group membership, whether imagined or real, tends to lead to strong defensive reactions on the part of those who feel threatened. When families emigrate to another country, individuals who have grown up with a sense of belonging to a number of social groups suddenly find that many of these groups are absent. The most severe forms of detachment are likely to be experienced by refugees who may quite suddenly lose their membership in national, linguistic, religious, and professional groups, and who may find even their family membership changed. Adolescents, already struggling to discover their own individual identities, are usually more greatly affected by loss of group memberships than older or younger immigrants.

The matter of an individual's cultural identity is more complex than the mere listing of the groups to which he or she can claim membership. More than anything, it involves a sense of belonging and identification with others in various groups.

Adolescence is a time of dynamic transition, and young people have to find a workable balance between their family identities, on the one hand, and their identities as members of peer-group subcultures, on the other. Adolescent subcultures differ from those of adults mainly in relation to the particular norms, values, and concerns that underlie their shared experiences. These experiences, and the social bonds that are formed through them, can be shaped in a number of ways. One obvious way is through the feelings of group solidarity that arise from adolescents' frustration with the adult authority around them. Adolescents often feel powerless in the face of the adult authority that confronts them both at home and at school, and they crave greater control over their own lives. Not surprisingly, feelings of resentment about this lack of control are typical components of subcultural solidarity among groups of adolescents. The rapid growth of sexual identity at this stage of life leads to the formation of many new social relationships and subcultural networks. Feelings relating to sexual attraction and rejection are typically stronger during adolescence than they are at any other age, and adolescents face many difficult challenges of social adaptation. Bonding with their peers in subcultural groups provides a necessary and effective way of dealing with these challenges, and sharing experiences with others provides an essential framework for social learning. Another way in which adolescents form subgroups is on the basis of their shared responses to cultural developments—especially those relating to music, style, and fashion. Adolescents' preferences for particular types of music or styles of dress can become the basis for forming strong bonds with others who feel the same.

The school is the primary setting in which adolescents find new groups with which to identify. It has a dual responsibility: to provide the potential for a number of new group memberships, one of the most important of which is language, and to be sensitive to the fact that all teaching and learning take place against the background of cultural, political, and emotional dynamics.

Definitions of Culture

A definition of culture that serves to further our discussion of culturally inclusive classrooms centres on group membership and the shared values, experience, and beliefs of those who belong. Culture is most usefully viewed as a compendium of attributes that, taken together, constitute an educationally relevant definition of the term.

1. *Culture is a dynamic process through which individuals living in groups collectively develop rules, norms, and values according to which they think, feel, and live.* Most of these mores evolve slowly over time and without the conscious awareness of those who hold them, a fact that in no way diminishes their effects on the group or the group's willingness to adhere to them. In fact, most people follow the "laws" of their culture without even being aware of them. Some of these rules relate directly to education.

Although the general aims of schooling may be very much the same across most cultures—the aims of academic learning and social development—cultures appear to have evolved quite different modes of achieving these ends.

2. *These constituent elements are arbitrary and conventional in kind as are the language terms used to express them.* Cultural meaning is developed in each society and within cultural subgroups and individuals. "Arbitrary," used in this sense, does not connote irrationality, inconsistency, or capriciousness, but means simply that there is nothing inherently right or correct about the beliefs, values, or symbols of any one culture in comparison with any other. Rather, they are a matter of convention.

3. *Individual thoughts and actions are to some extent conditioned by existing rules and norms, although this conditioning does not imply uniform reaction and behaviour.* It implies, instead, that the norms provide reference points for feelings, choices, actions, and the experience of cultural identity. Just because cultures embody systems of rules and conventions, this does not mean that everybody blindly follows them, or even that they understand them in the same way. The situation is far more complex and interesting than this. It is quite clear, in fact, that people do not think or behave in the same ways in a given culture, and that disagreements, disputes, and misunderstandings are all just as much a part of cultural life as are shared rules.

It is clear that cultural norms and constitutive rules do not work in any simple or direct way. Rather, they are the source of constant negotiation. In the case of immigrants, we sometimes find that children, caught between the distinct cultures of home and school, are in constant negotiation with both. Moreover, the outcome of these negotiations may differ radically from individual to individual even from the same original culture. Some young people will shun their native culture in a somewhat desperate attempt to "become Canadian" while others will resist the pressure toward Canadianization and cling protectively to the values of the home, rejecting those of the new culture as represented by the school. Either extreme is nonadaptive and must be met with great care by educators.

Often, members of a culture will want to test or push the limits of their culture's rules. In our culture, adolescents are perhaps more prone to this behaviour than younger or older people, but it is not restricted to them.

4. *Communication across cultures naturally requires a deliberate effort to view other cultures in terms of their own norms and conventions.* It is much easier—and will almost invariably lead to the wrong conclusions—to view other cultures in terms of our own. In the school setting, we have to remember that this is a two-way street. Teachers are as apt to misunderstand behaviour of their students as students are to misinterpret theirs. The onus, at least at the beginning, is on teachers and other adults in the school to learn as much as possible about their own cultural norms as well as those of the students who come to their classes.

Judgments, Attitudes, and Cultural Distance

Although attitudes change over time, they can be thought of as relatively stable modes of thinking that play an important part in cultural interaction. Over the years, social psychologists have conducted a great deal of research on attitudes, particularly negative ones, and having some understanding of what they have discovered helps us to discern more about our own emotional reactions and behaviours in more depth. It also helps us to understand better the dynamics of multicultural societies and schools.

The attitudes we hold have far-reaching and powerful social and cross-cultural consequences. The metaphor of cultural distance captures the idea that individuals feel "near" or "far" to cultures depending on a number of factors, including whether people in another culture speak the same language, whether they appear "friendly" or "hostile," and so on. Understanding more about how cultural distance comes about, how it can be increased or decreased, and its effects on individuals may lead us to greater empathy with students from other cultures.

A good place to start a discussion of these issues is to look more closely at our own attitudes. We have posed 10 questions as a vehicle for focusing our attention on our own attitudes and beliefs. Try to answer each question honestly before reading your response. You should recognize at the outset that we are all likely, at one time or another, to put the interests of our own cultural groups above those of others and that all of us may have discriminated against people from other groups at some point in our lives.

QUESTION 1: If an immigration officer of a foreign country handed you a blank piece of paper and asked you to describe as fully as possible your "cultural status," giving you no further clues about how to reply, how would you respond?

In answering this, you probably responded to the imaginary immigration officer by listing at least your nationality, gender, and occupation. You might also have added your skin colour or ethnic background if you or your family emigrated to the country whose passport you are using at the time. You might also have added your age, your socioeconomic status, and your religious affiliation, if you have one. What you list in response to the immigration officer is likely to be a function of our feelings and thoughts on several issues. First, it reflects what you happen to think the most basic categories are in your cultural identity. Second, it reflects what you believe it is that the foreign authorities really want from you. Third, it reflects what information you think it might be best to leave out. Fourth, it reflects your own personality and what you feel about the situation of being at the gates of a foreign country.

Many people feel that they should not have to give a "full disclosure" of themselves, especially when they feel themselves to be part of a culture that is in some sense "superior" to the one represented by the immigration official. If you are able to compare your answer with someone else's, you might consider why you thought it significant to include or exclude certain information.

QUESTION 2: Would your answer be different if you were asked the same question by the president of some social or sports club in your own culture that you wanted to join? If not, why not?

It is more likely that you responded to the question by assuming that only certain information was pertinent. You might have mentioned your job, your marital and family status, and your interests.

What we learn from our responses to this question is that our cultural self-image and the image of ourselves we are prepared to give to others may vary with the social and cultural contexts in which we operate. This forces us to realize how chameleonlike we are much of the time, changing our cultural colours to suit the social "vegetation" around us.

QUESTION 3: How many cultural groups do you belong to? List all the ones you can think of.

Answering this question reminds us that no individual has a single cultural status or definition; that is, membership in a number of groups defines a slightly different cultural composite for each of us. Our affiliation with family, school, club, work groups, friends, political interest groups, religious organizations, etc., provide many points of reference for determining our cultural make-up.

QUESTION 4: List the names of any two other individuals whom you believe to have exactly the same cultural profile as yourself.

Few, if any, people will share exactly the same cultural profile as the one we sketch for ourselves. Answering the fourth question makes it clear that cultural identities have movable boundaries. In some ways, we all seem to be slipping in and out of different roles and identities like character actors. The central point to emerge here is that large cultural groups, such as nations, are far from being unitary in nature. They are formed from the spectrum of subgroups to which individuals have multiple and variable membership.

QUESTION 5: Have you ever felt excluded from a cultural group? When and where? What do you think were the reasons for your exclusion and how did you feel about it?

Here, we begin to learn about how we are likely to react to immigrant students as they struggle to adjust to their new cultures and about their reactions to us. Most of us, in responding to this question, can recall numerous instances of having felt excluded from various groups. As adolescents just beginning to confirm our identities, not being invited to a party could lead to agonizing feelings of exclusion. A key idea here is that for every in-group there is also an out-group, a group of people who are kept out and whose exclusion may even contribute to the sense of solidarity within the in-group.

But what does it feel like to be excluded? Usually, a person who feels excluded believes that she or he was at least eligible to be part of a certain group. A female corporate executive might well feel excluded if she were not permitted to join a club for male corporate executives because on a crucial criterion she clearly qualified for membership. This kind of exclusion constitutes discrimination. Discrimination occurs when individuals reflect some deliberate bias against groups as a whole on grounds such as skin colour, race, class, religion, or gender. In many cases of cultural exclusion, there at least remains the opportunity for excluded individuals to redress their feelings of rejection—either they can hope for later inclusion or they can reassert their self esteem in alternative cultural settings. There is, of course, little chance of changing skin colour, race, or gender, and discrimination on the basis of these permanent attributes leads to the sense of outrage and bitterness unless the attitudes about them are changed.

QUESTION 6: Have you ever played a part in excluding anyone else from any group or activity? What were the reasons for your rejection? How do you feel about your behaviour? How do you think the person who was excluded felt?

In answering the sixth question, we start to come to terms with our own potential for racial discrimination. Racism is not just something that is exhibited only by "extremists"; it has a far wider scope. There are, in fact, several types of racism. The following list of four is based on the categories identified by Brislin (1981):

1. **Extreme prejudicial racism** is the behaviour of people who believe that some races are actually inferior to others. Examples of extreme racism are to be found in the behaviour of the Ku Klux Klan, Nazis, and other extremist groups (not all of them Caucasian, incidentally).

2. **Symbolic racism** occurs when individuals in one group feel that members of another group or groups are intruding or interfering with their own rights or goals. When individuals are asked in surveys, for example, to agree or disagree with statements like, "Over the past few years, [name of racial group] have gained more economic benefits than they deserve," researchers find that they will respond in the affirmative even though they exhibit few, if any, traits of the extreme racist.

3. **Tokenism** is a level of racism that is more difficult to recognize. It finds expression in behaviours such as the hiring of a single member of a race into a large corporation (or university or school district) or when individuals give some other outward show of support for another racial group without being willing to interact with them socially.

4. Related to tokenism is **arm's-length prejudice** in which individuals will interact positively with people from another race in one situation but not in another, controlling the extent of their involvement with the other group.

The existence of various levels of racism make it clear that there are more subtle and dangerous forms of thought and behaviour that are difficult to recognize. While individuals may not be overtly racist in their behaviour all the time, they may become racist whenever they feel threatened. This type of reaction is especially evident when immigrants are competing with longer-term residents for jobs during hard economic times. Symbolic racism, then, is a form of suppressed racism that only comes out into the open at certain times. Tokenism and arm's-length prejudice also represent forms of behaviour that are more widely prevalent than many are prepared to admit. An absence of overt and easily recognizable signs of racism by no means implies that it does not exist.

Even if you do not fall into any of the categories of racism identified above, if you gave an honest response to the sixth question, it is likely that you identified at least one occasion on which you excluded other individuals. Not all exclusion is racially motivated or unjustified. As long as you know the reasons for your actions and as long as they do not reflect unreasonable, unjust, or arbitrary decisions, you need not worry unduly that you have caused injury.

Racism and other parallel forms of discrimination demand an active response, particularly in education where any form of discrimination against students from other cultures is likely to have negative impact on their lives and, indeed, on the lives of the cultural majority. Ultimately, discrimination, since it reduces chances of any cultural negotiation of values, has a negative impact on the society at large and thus affects all our lives. We have to learn to work against certain forms of exclusion in order to create a community of learners in which there is true equality of opportunity to succeed.

QUESTION 7: When travelling to another country, have you ever experienced some shock at not knowing how to satisfy basic needs such as food and hygiene, or not knowing how to ask for something in a foreign language? What were these needs and how did you feel when you found it was difficult or impossible to satisfy them?

In answering the seventh question, most people will realize that they have experienced some form of culture shock. Usually, tourists find a way of making do, either by prior preparation, departing the situation early, or just muddling through. Tourists are very different from immigrants, however, who are thrust, often with little advance preparation, into the midst of everyday living. They have to come to terms with a new language, a new currency and banking system, strange foods, strange places for procuring food, unfamiliar medical practices and systems, and educational, postal, telephone, utility, and social services that differ from those familiar to them. We should not underestimate the adjustment difficulties of people moving into a new culture and understand that if they do not get sufficient support from members of the majority culture, the consequences can be severe. When such misunderstanding threatens their very survival, immigrants experience especially acute anxiety.

The feelings associated with culture shock include rejection, fright, anxiety and panic, frustration, and depression. The most typical reaction when things seem overwhelmingly difficult is social withdrawal, a reaction that cuts off the flow of negative events that immigrants may be experiencing, and gives individuals the time to regain strength, to gather resources, and to regroup.

In extreme cases, withdrawal may become complete, and an immigrant student, or an entire family, may completely withdraw from the society they see as a threat, reducing opportunities for more positive contacts and further learning. One of our central tasks in multicultural education is to counteract the forces that lead to these kinds of conclusions.

QUESTION 8: When travelling to another country or to a different area of your own country, what have been some of your feelings about how members of the local community treat you? Have you ever felt unwelcome or that people were looking at you in a strange way? Did you ever feel you were trespassing on someone else's property? Conversely, have you ever felt that someone was trespassing on your property?

These questions address the issue of territoriality. Taylor (1988) points out that cultural and social factors are two principal predictors of territorial functioning, and that different cultures develop quite different sets of territorial behaviour.

How does the notion of territoriality fit into our discussion of culture, identity, inclusion, and exclusion? Although the setting of territorial boundaries is a natural, though variable, part of cultural behaviour, the feelings and defensive reactions associated with territoriality can all too readily combine with racist sentiments to become the basis for discrimination. In educational settings, classrooms, playgrounds, corridors, libraries, and even lockers and desks can become territorial and cultural battlegrounds.

QUESTION 9: What do you feel about immigrants in your own country? Whom do you think should be admitted (everyone or just certain groups)? Do you think there should be a limitation on the numbers admitted? Should immigrants be told where to live?

Territoriality is likely to play a part in your response to the ninth question, about immigration policy. As numerous governments have found out, it is very difficult to develop an immigration policy that is fair to everyone and that avoids the pitfall of appearing racist. Territorial arguments concerning who should be admitted into a country typically involve pointing out that the country in question is already "overpopulated," or that cities are already becoming "overcrowded" and "more violent" than they used to be. These kinds of social changes are often blamed on immigrants when they may, in fact, be the result of migrations across states or provinces, or of other kinds of factors altogether. Another reason given for rejecting new immigrants is the nonavailability of suitable housing or that present members of a culture need no further competition from outsiders for homes. Although it is difficult to take any of these arguments seriously in a country as underpopulated as Canada, we have to remember that they are articulated more often and more loudly during times of high unemployment or general economic recession.

Few people will have responded that immigrants should be told where to live, for this violates some our most deeply entrenched beliefs about individual freedom. There are constitutional and other legal sanctions against such discrimination. In subtle ways, however, we do control where immigrants live by restricting access to jobs and professions that would give them the means to live in any neighbourhood or part of the country of their choosing and, even more surreptitiously, through attitudes of inclusion and exclusion discussed earlier.

In the end, though, all countries do have to place limitations on the number of newcomers they admit and doing so entails developing principles for excluding certain people. One of the primary ones is financial; most governments insist that applicants have the means to support themselves and accompanying family members, in short, that they not place any financial burden on public resources. While it may be argued that such insistence is discriminatory and not reflective of the humanitarian principles that we would like to think we uphold, exclusion on the grounds that the citizens of a country should not and cannot bear greater financial burden is one with which many Canadians have some sympathy. Many of you likely stated this as one of the grounds for decision making. There are, of course, many others.

Broadly speaking, there are two general directions in which arguments can be formulated, and these directions reflect static versus creative-dynamic views of culture. Arguments related to economics, population, and social problems all concentrate on the past or the present. They take the view that immigration threatens the status quo. If we take the view that society as it is now constituted is not the only, nor necessarily the best, configuration, then we begin to think about future possibilities. One argument in this more optimistic and less exclusive vein relies on the observation that nation states depend for their material wealth on taxpaying workers. The argument that wealth and security are dependent on more people paying more taxes, to put it somewhat simplistically, is more typical in countries pursuing a genuinely multicultural vision and where there is no fear of changing historical patterns of immigration. We are reminded that cultures are essentially dynamic and that groups of individuals have the power to change norms and values. The attitude most likely to foster successful social and educational progress in the lives of immigrants, once they do manage to filter through the immigration process and come to the West, is, of course, the one emphasizing future possibility rather than historical limitation.

QUESTION 10: Should immigrants from ethnic or racial minorities be encouraged to pursue their own cultural interests to the exclusion of those of the host culture?

Question 10 further explores the notion of what is meant by a truly pluralistic society and how one is created. There is a growing realization in a number of English-speaking countries, and most notably Great Britain, that the mere writing of multicultural manifestos and the provision of funds for multicultural or multi-ethnic recognition (through festivals, exhibits, etc.) does little to expunge racist practices. An official policy of multiculturalism, unless it addresses and deals directly with the deeper issue of racism, may just serve to lull us into a false sense of accomplishment and proactivity and thereby actually prevent us from doing anything about the far more invasive and profound problem of ethnocentrism. Moodely has observed, for instance, that the ideal of a multicultural state to some extent represents a utopia that "obfuscates the reality of wealth, differential power and political conflict generally." She continues:

> The image deflects criticism away from the dominance of the few and the manipulation of the many to the false sentiment that everyone is equal if he or she is only made to feel welcome. Despite the professed concern for more active political involvement, the ideology of equal opportunities and harmonious partnership...in fact depoliticizes...newcomer (1984, p. 797).

How, then, is a truly pluralistic culture created? The hidden danger in multiculturalism is that it leads to cultural fragmentation, to the proliferation of cultural groups living in isolation both from one another and from the larger society in which they are embedded. We have come to the view, along with many other educators, that the answer lies in finding a middle ground between complete assimilation of other cultures in accordance with a "melting pot" metaphor and the total preservation of ethnic or racial group identity. The model that seems best to represent that middle ground is referred to as an acculturation model.

Acculturation is the process by which immigrant groups are permitted and encouraged to maintain elements of their own original cultures while assuming some of the constitutive characteristics of the adopted culture. Accordingly, a "politically correct" and positive answer to the tenth question is one that both reflects the rights of minorities to pursue their own cultural interests and that recognizes the unacceptability of cultural fragmentation of a kind tending to alienate minority and majority groups from one another. It is important to recognize, though, that the ways in which minority cultures are treated, and the ways in which members of those cultures are encouraged to maintain and develop their own identities within the host culture are all issues that demand the creative negotiation of cultural values.

Cultural Distance

How can we predict who is likely to be adversely affected by the experiences associated with cultural distance? Clearly, many of the negative attitudes we have discussed above tend to increase distance. Schumann (1978) suggests that the major causes of cultural distance can be reduced to a number of psychological and sociological factors, several of which relate to topics already touched upon. Based on his research on immigration into the United States, his analysis centres on the argument that reduction of cultural distance improves chances for language learning. Schumann also finds that the ideas immigrants have about their intended length of residence affect cultural distance and motivation to learn; the longer an individual plans to stay, the less the apparent distance and the greater the motivation to learn.

While distance models such as Schumann's provide us with a useful framework for discussion and analysis, they should not be used uncritically. The danger in reducing complex cultural matters to neat underlying factors is that they, too, will become stereotypical categories, not moving with the cultural times and leading to inaccurate overgeneralization. Cultural distance is a useful metaphor as long as it does not detract from our understanding the complex feelings about identity underlying the processes of cultural interaction.

Culture, Language, and Education

One of the most obvious ways in which we signal to others who we are is through the language we use. It might appear that the increasing globalization of the planet would mean that we would all start speaking the same language. In many ways, though, the reverse seems to be true. Despite the increasing impact of radio and satellite television, people appear to be intent on maintaining their cultural and linguistic identities through languages and dialects.

How does the fact that culture, language, and identity are closely related affect the way in which people learn second languages? By the time immigrants enter the educational system of a new country they have already established an identity in their first culture together with all the protective feelings that accompany that identity. An individual's success in adapting to a new culture and in developing a new second cultural identity depends on a number of factors including age, culture of origin, and socioeconomic circumstances.

One of the most important facts about second-language learning is that relatively few, if any, second-language learners ever become indistinguishable in all respects from native speakers. Their language learning appears to fossilize when no further cultural, material, or other kind of gain seems possible. But just how and at what point in second-language learning the learner loses motivation to learn further will depend to some degree on how teachers and others treat learners in their new cultural surroundings. The point at which learners fossilize is clearly related to many aspects of cultural identity. It is especially closely related to measures of cultural distance, which also tend to reduce motivation to further learning of a second language.

Cultural distance, together with all its consequences, including culture shock, obviously has great significance for multicultural teaching and learning. Fortunately, there are many ways in which teachers can work against premature fossilization of second-language learning and against severe forms of individual withdrawal. These all involve helping students to build their feelings of cultural security, their motivation, and their self-esteem.

Perhaps one of the most damaging assumptions of all about second-language learners has been that immigrant language learners will do best if they are simply put in the mainstream classroom and left to "sink or swim." When it comes to the practice of placing children directly into mainstream classrooms, however, this mistaken belief often amounts to mere "dumping." It is comparable to placing a Canadian adult in a Chinese university classroom and telling him or her to learn Chinese *and* physics. For this reason, the practice is sometimes referred to as submersion, reflecting an image of a learner being drowned.

The practice of submersing second-language learners appears to have been supported by educators who have mistakenly equated mainstreaming or inclusive streaming with immersion. They assume that if immersion works so well, it should be possible to put immigrant language learners into similar situations with the same effect. In immersion programs, children learn content and the new language simultaneously. This assumption rests on a mistaken view of what is involved in immersion. In the first place, teachers are competent in both languages, allowing them to speak to the children in French, for example, and to understand the children's responses in English (in the beginning stages). Second, immersion teachers are specially trained in methods appropriate for teaching content to children who do not speak the language of instruction. It is rare for mainstream classroom teachers to have received specialized training in integrating second-language learners into their classes or in planning instruction for both proficient native speakers and non-native speakers with limited English proficiency. Third, the children's native language is usually the dominant one of the community and, hence, under no threat. Children in immersion move confidently back into their mother tongue after the school day with the full support of the community. Immigrant children, on the other hand, receive no institutional or societal validation of their first language. In addition, with its targeted government funding, immersion is something of an elitist program in schools, enjoying the support of parents and educators alike. Finally, there are seldom any native speakers of the "immersed" languages in the classes; all the children are second-language learners. In other words, all children in immersion classes are at roughly the same level of proficiency in the new language; there are seldom any native Francophones in the class. In contrast, immigrant learners may find themselves among classmates from many different linguistic backgrounds, including English, the language of instruction. The dissimilarities for immigrant children placed in mainstream classes without assistance are obvious. All second-language learners need a more sensitive understanding of their cultural adjustments than that reflected by submersion policies.

Fostering an Effective Learning Environment

It is becoming increasingly clear that all forms of submersion and the lack of care and attention to individual cultural needs that go with them have the potential for causing a great deal of harm. Fortunately, there are many positive alternatives to the practice of submersion. In describing some of these alternatives, we will begin to outline the requirements of an inclusive environment. These include reception classes and various kinds of withdrawal classes in which immigrant students are given the special help and encouragement they need.

Reception classes, as the name implies, provide students with entry-level exposure to the language and culture of their new country. Such classes are held, ideally, in the same school as the student will be attending, but limited budgets and small numbers of immigrant students will sometimes force school administrators to have a centralized reception centre. Typically, students spend from a few weeks to six months in full-time reception, depending on their progress.

In the secondary school, withdrawal may be synonymous with partial mainstreaming, a program that allows students to integrate into school life as they become able. This approach means that students can continue to develop cultural identity and self-esteem in certain school activities even before they are able to handle all the demands of the school curriculum.

The purpose of language is communication. A sustaining environment conducive to the learning of all children relies very heavily on the ability of teachers to create and sustain effective cross-cultural communication in their classrooms.

In a landmark book on pragmatics, *How to Do Things with Words*, Austin (1962) argued that the way meaning is built up in conversations has much more to do with the underlying purposes and intentions of speakers than it does with what they actually say. He observed that individuals typically "do" things with language and, for this reason, used the term **speech acts** to cover many forms of expression. The use of the term emphasizes the idea that when we speak, we are generally not just simply "describing" the world around us or "telling" others what we think, but that we are also acting to get things done. According to Austin, what matters in communication is not so much the strict truth or falsity of what is said as whether the interchanges are successful. Success depends on whether the participants understand what each other is getting at, whether they trust and believe in each other's honest attempts to speak meaningfully. Austin called these aspects of successful communication **felicity conditions**.

Another philosopher, Grice (1957), developed more specific principles that he believed were followed in successful communication. He suggested that in order to be successful, participants follow a cooperative principle by which they speak only at the appropriate time and listen carefully to responses. According to the principle, speakers must also maintain the "quality" of what they say — they must say what they believe to be true and they must also be aware of quantity, saying neither too little nor too much.

These ideas of Austin and Grice are relevant to cross-cultural communication. The first thing to realize is that although some form of felicity conditions and cooperative principles appear to occur in all languages, their forms and the ways in which they are interpreted are distinct.

Given the different communicative conventions that exist between cultures, it is not surprising that miscommunication occurs—miscommunication that does not result from the use of the wrong words or limited understanding of their meaning but from a mismatch between the speaker's and the listener's expectations about language use and communication.

The success of language teaching policy and practice and attempts to foster effective cross-cultural communication depend on broader educational policy. That is, they must be embedded within an inclusive pluralistic philosophy of education and of teacher education that is accepted by all school personnel as well as students and their parents—all students and parents, not just immigrants. In formulating such a philosophy, educators must remember that people from other cultures bring with them very different cultural beliefs about the relationships between students and teachers and about education in general.

In our interpretations of the attitudes and reactions of students from other countries, however, we should take care not to be blinded by our own cultural expectations. It is important to remember that the relationships between teachers and their students are established in much larger contexts of cultural norms and values.

Fundamental differences in beliefs about the educational process often bring with them significantly different communicative styles. It may be the case that students from other cultures who are silent in class are actually taking in a great deal—perhaps even more than some of those doing the talking. The first step in greater cross-cultural understanding, however, lies in recognizing some of these potential barriers to learning and causes of communicative breakdown.

Any discussion of cross-cultural discourse makes it clear that communication involves many kinds of skills and not merely knowledge of the grammar and the vocabulary of a language. The notion of **communicative competence** is especially useful in pointing to ways in which all students can be helped in learning how to interact with others since it defines many of the different types of knowledge used in successful communication. The term refers to a learner's ability to handle the broader demands of communication, and specifically to discourse, sociolinguistic, and strategic competence.

The **demands of communication** mean that topics have to be kept in mind for extended periods, switches of topic have to be recognized, and the internal structures of longer expressions have to be understood. **Discourse competence** refers to the language user's ability to deal with chunks of discourse that are larger than sentences. It includes the ability to relate subordinate to main ideas and the ability to follow the logical flow of arguments or narratives. **Sociolinguistic competence** refers to the ability to take various aspects of social context into account during communication. It includes the ability to make appropriate shifts of register and the ability to recognize other people's moods, intentions, and roles. **Strategic competence** involves the use of deliberate strategies to ensure communicative success, strategies such as encouraging others to give more information.

Strategic competence can be particularly useful for second-language learners because it can lead to immediate benefits that are dependent on learning new languages. If teachers make students aware of these strategies, they can be used to facilitate communication both in and out of class.

Understanding how to communicate effectively with students from a variety of different cultural and linguistic backgrounds takes us a long way toward creating the kind of environment needed to sustain growth and learning for all learners. Effective classroom communication is only a first step, however, and one that depends for success on broader educational policies and, perhaps, shifts in the thinking of the society in which schools are embedded.

Guidelines for Teacher Educators

The question is not so much how to find a common core of values and goals to guide us, for we can probably agree on fundamental principles of true equality of opportunity and treatment, but how we can realize those values and achieve those goals. In the broadest sense, what we are striving for is to formulate educational policies that will, when put into practice, create environments of true respect and tolerance for individual and group identities. As teachers and teacher educators, we believe that we have to begin with the pre-service education of teachers in order to ensure that teachers understand principles of equality of educational opportunity and have a number of concrete strategies for creating effective learning environments in a pluralistic society and for teaching children from a variety of cultural and ethnic backgrounds.

1. *Admit more nonmajority teacher candidates.* The place to begin in teacher education is right at the beginning, in the selection of candidates for admission. We believe that it is extremely important that members of all cultural groups participate actively in the life of the school and that the most visible participant is the teacher. What we are arguing for goes beyond "representation," or admitting minorities in the same proportion that they exist in the society. Rather, we advocate committing a number of spaces in each class—anywhere from 10% to 50% or even more depending on the ethnic make-up of the region—to nonmajority candidates.

Further, we would recommend that institutions develop active recruitment strategies if they do not currently receive an adequate number of applicants from qualified minorities. We would also advocate that these recruitment strategies be used to redress the gender imbalance, that is, to increase the number of males in primary/elementary schooling and the number of females in secondary schooling, especially the nontraditional fields of mathematics and science.

2. *Globalize our attitudes.* Curriculum for teachers must be culturally proactive. Cognition, as Seelye pointed out, "is not culture free...not a trait but a process" (p. 230). Every aspect of the teacher education curriculum has to be sensitive to this truth if we are to create environments that generate and sustain learning for everyone in the society. While some teacher education programs have made significant curricular advancements by adding or adapting courses to include topics such as global education, critical pedagogy, gender equality, and cultural awareness, many of these have been add-ons to a very traditional curriculum.

3. *Prepare every teacher to teach ESL.* Twenty-five years ago, there was a slogan popular among educators: Every teacher is an English teacher. This saying recognized the centrality of language in the teaching and learning of all subjects. While we do not believe that it is necessary for every teacher to be an ESL specialist, we do believe that every teacher should have an idea about how to deal with an ESL student no matter the level or subject matter.

4. *Dare to teach about culture and cultural differences.* Fortunately, most curricula for educating ESL teachers include a strong culture component, but whether or not teachers receive extensive ESL training, they should have exposure to and experience in dealing with cross-cultural differences. Robinson (1985) recounts her 12-year journey into other cultures during which she lived with people who spoke different languages and who were racially and ethnically different and from different socioeconomic classes. She tells of becoming a teacher, "committed to the idea of teaching languages for the purpose of helping students empathetically understand people who spoke the languages, as well as helping students of the diverse cultures represented in the classroom to understand each other better" (p. 2).

> On the first day, the blacks sat on one side of the room, the whites on the other, with each group subdivided by sex....The task difficulty seemed clear! To my surprise, seating patterns gradually began to change. By the end of the class, the seating pattern was like a chequerboard. Black and white students tutored each other, exchanged notes and even rides to outside events. Not only did they appear to understand each other better, they surpassed the other classes in Spanish achievement based on the standardized departmental exam, including those particular black students who had been designated as "borderline cases" by the previous professor (p. 2).

Robinson's achievement is the goal we all strive for and her account of her experience and what she learned from it led her to devise four key principles for achieving cross-cultural understanding. They are:

> **1.** On a one-to-one basis, the differences between people divided them; commonalities brought them together.
> **2.** Understanding, in the sense of smooth interaction, was probably least affected by awareness of how people were going to act, or the ability to anticipate culturally different events.
> **3.** Neither [the teacher] nor the learners were a cultural tabula rasa. Understanding of another culture did not seem to happen independently of the learner's or my own culture.
> **4.** Understanding—getting over the barriers to communication—did not happen suddenly; it took place gradually. Understanding took time (p. 3).

Understanding also takes effort. Robinson identifies a number of issues that educators must confront as they come to terms with cultural differences and accommodating them in their classrooms. An important one is the effects of cultural experience on perception in general. This is an important one for, as she points out:

> Students...whose previous experience relates to a cultural context which differs from that represented in instruction, may not perceive the target stimuli as intended by the instructor or textbook writer. In a film, learners from different cultures may not be seeing what you expect them to see. Therefore, draw learner attention to those aspects or interpretations which are the intended goal of instruction, be it a particular sound within a word or a particular category of phenomena within a film, such as psychological themes, body language as in greetings, cultural issues, etc. (p. 18).

It is also important for teachers to explore how cultures and cultural roles are acquired. Robinson argues that analyzing the process by which people acquire their cultural understandings will aid teachers in the same way that studying second-language acquisition assists second-language teachers in planning and teaching languages. She identifies three factors that govern cultural acquisition and transmission:

> **1.** Culture is transmitted and acquired through all the perceptual modes, verbally as well as non-verbally.
> **2.** Culture is transmitted within an integrated context, i.e., when signals through various senses or modes send the same message.
> **3.** Culture is acquired gradually, through repeated exposure to similar stimuli or events (p. 26).

These factors provide a framework for educators to explore with future teachers the acquisition and transmission of their own cultures. Such insight is certain to lead to heightened sociocultural awareness, which will have a marked impact on the classroom environments teachers ultimately create.

5. *Do not deny the reality of racism.* A teacher education curriculum that has the components sketched above is a necessary and positive step toward creating the kinds of educational environments that are maximally effective. Racism is a reality in our society and will likely find its way occasionally into even the most enlightened classroom. The teacher education program should confront this possibility and provide new teachers with concrete strategies not only for preventing but for dealing with racism when it rears its ugly head. Fortunately, there is a growing resource base available to assist them in adding an antiracism component to the curriculum.

Guidelines for School Personnel

Teachers, of course, are largely responsible for creating the school environments in which learning occurs, but they do not do so in a vacuum. We conclude, therefore, with recommendations for school policies that will help them to realize the attitudes and effect the goals they have set for socioculturally sensitive education.

1. *Broaden the notion of community of learners.* Some of the most successful schools in Canada are the true "community" schools. A great many schools call themselves "community" schools, but often this means only that the population of the school is drawn from a local community; in other words, the school is not a district or consolidated school drawing students from a

broad geographical area. What we mean by a community school, however, is one that encourages and welcomes the active participation of the entire community in the life of the school. One such school is I.J. Samson, a junior high school in St. John's, Newfoundland.

CASE STUDY

A large urban school, I.J. Samson had, at one time, a reputation for poor attendance, poor discipline, poor educational quality, poor facilities, etc. The principal and teachers at I.J. Samson decided to embark on a school improvement process. The task could have been overwhelming, but the principal and vice-principal wisely decided that it could be achieved as long as they could marshal sufficient resources. Unfortunately, financial resources were extremely limited, but they had an extremely valuable human resource base in the teaching staff who saw the necessity for change. The administrators realized, however, that even with the commitment of the teachers, the school would need help; it would need a maximum number of partners or shareholders to support and to participate in the process. In discussion with the teachers, they took a view that was, in retrospect, perhaps obvious, but seemed bold at the time. That was that the "negative" energy within and around the school might be redirected toward more positive outcomes. The energy that had been used to destroy and to complain could be used productively to create an environment in which everyone might benefit.

That kind of transformation does not just happen, however. It requires the willing labour of all those from students and parents to community and government working together to effect the kinds of changes that the principal and vice-principal envisioned for I.J. Samson. They looked around them, identified the local "stakeholders" in their school, and began to talk to them. They consulted with students, parents, the neighbourhood, businesses, the local university—in short, everyone who had a stake in the educational outcomes of the school. What they found was that there was more help available than they dreamed possible. They were also blessed with good timing. As it happened, both the Fortis Education Foundation and Newfoundland Power were looking for appropriate initiatives in education. Both eventual partners believed that by focusing their resources and energy on a single school rather than spreading them across many, they could have an impact that would serve as a model for other schools in the province. At the same time, teachers in the school had indicated a need to learn more about how to integrate what they were teaching in various curricula with "real world" demands. Newfoundland Power worked with teachers to identify points in the curriculum where teachers could demonstrate the actual uses of material that had previously seemed irrelevant.

The school also contacted the education faculty at the Memorial University of Newfoundland, an obvious partner in the change process. Memorial undertook to assess student attitudes to education and to business before, during, and after the transformation process. Findings from the initial survey were used to identify possible targets for the partnership process. One of those targets turned out to be in technology. Here both business partners responded in tangible ways. The Fortis Foundation augmented the school board's budget for allocating computers, and Newfoundland Power developed the electrical and data network specifications and monitored construction throughout the project.

Newfoundland Power also provided funding, and six employees delivered a program called "Economics of Staying in School," offered by Junior Achievement. The goals of the program were to have students reflect on the advantages of staying in school to acquire the kinds of knowledge, skills, and attitudes they would need to establish a successful career. The benefits to the students are obvious; for Newfoundland Power, the benefit was the potential of better-educated and skilled employees as well as a more positive business environment in which to work in Newfoundland.

No transformation is ever complete. The nature of change, particularly educational change at the end of the 20th century, is that it is ongoing. Nevertheless, there are many successes of which I.J. Samson can boast. Perhaps the recreation of the school into a global community school is best illustrated anecdotally.

On an especially cold snowy morning last winter, the students in a home management class at I.J. Samson baked and delivered hot muffins to elderly residents who lived in the neighbourhood. This was a far cry from the days when the main contact the residents had with the school was to complain about the litter left on their lawns. Some of these same residents drop by the school for lunch and stay on to volunteer to help with the clearing up or to give the teachers a hand in preparing teaching materials or coaching students who need extra attention. When the school held a reception to mark the opening of its refurbished resource centre, the gymnasium was packed with parents and their children, local business leaders, government officials, and university professors. Two years earlier, teachers complained that they couldn't even get parents to attend parent-teacher conferences.

I.J. Samson's success resulted from the vision of the staff of what the school could be and of their sharing that vision and insisting on the participation of all those who had a stake in the accomplishments of the students. By sharing ownership of the entire educational process with all the stakeholders, they distributed the responsibility and gained a much richer resource base than they would otherwise have had. Although cultural pluralism was not their main goal, it was a positive outcome of their participatory approach. As the principal said, it is hard to think about people as "us and them" when we're all "us" and we're all engaged in a common mission.

I.J. Samson now calls itself a "global" school, and in the best sense of the term, it is. Its urban corridors and classrooms represent an educational dwelling place for students from across Canada and the world who often welcome their local neighbours to share in the experience of truly community-based learning. In a school where the student attendance was low and teacher burnout high, neither is a problem. Students will show visitors their school with pride and when the time comes for them to move on to one of the local senior high schools, they leave with regret and some trepidation that their next experience may not be as positive as the last.

2. *Remember that a policy of cultural pluralism should govern everyone's behaviour.* All of the policies listed below are everyone's responsibility to implement and uphold. Teachers are not the only important people we have in schools, nor are they exclusively responsible for the school's success in creating a positive nurturing environment. All school personnel, counsellors, principals, librarians, consultants, superintendents, secretaries, custodians, volunteers, students, and their parents are responsible for upholding the pluralistic policies of the school. There are two immediate implications of this fact. The first and most obvious is that, as much as possible, they should participate in the formulation of the policies. The second is that all personnel hired to work in the system should be chosen for their cultural experience, inclusive attitudes, and, possibly, their potential as role models.

3. *Adopt zero tolerance for racism.* It should be clear to everyone in the school, indeed in the community, that racist behaviour is simply unacceptable. With this tough policy goes a special responsibility to deal fairly with offenders and, more importantly, to get to the bases for the problem and to deal with them to prevent further incidents.

4. *Work to globalize the curriculum—all of it!* We talked above in the section on teacher education about the importance of globalizing the curriculum, of broadening our perspective on educational content and process. A global perspective is equally important in the school curriculum and not only in the obvious areas of geography and foreign language instruction. One of the best ways to globalize the curriculum, of course, is to require that everyone become proficient in at least one language other than their native one. We would even go so far as to recommend that every high school graduate be functionally competent in at least two languages.

5. *Adopt principles of cooperative learning.* Traditional methods of teaching that focus on the teacher as expert and dispenser of knowledge are not likely the best ones in which to build group rapport. Educators have begun to discover that employing the pedagogical practices of cooperative learning approaches reaps many benefits. As its name implies, cooperative learning takes the teacher out of the "expert" role, exchanging it for the facilitator role. The teacher organizes, guides, acts as a resource, and evaluates, but students are responsible not only for their learning but also for determining how they will learn. Cooperative learning entails working with others in groups to find solutions to problems that may be identified either by the teacher or by the learners themselves.

The intent of cooperative learning is to give learners control of and responsibility for their learning. This empowerment of learners can have astounding results; learners tend to stay in school and participate more meaningfully in learning when they can see the purpose and exercise some control over the speed and manner and level of mastery. Another advantage of cooperative learning is that it teaches cooperation and is more effective for students who do not thrive in a competitive atmosphere.

6. *Remember that a school consists of individuals.* In making policies to govern the behaviour of many, it is easy to forget the individual, but we must remember the importance of instilling a sense of self-worth in every child. Success in school and a secure sense of self are closely related; each depends on the other. Students who are successful in school are more likely to develop self-esteem and, conversely, students with high self-esteem are more likely to succeed in school. We must remember that individual identity arises out of harmonious group membership, and the harmony of the groups that form the school is something over which we have a great deal of influence.

Summary and Conclusion

One way of writing a chapter on sociocultural awareness in secondary schools might be to present a list of "things to do" in the classroom. In this chapter, however, we have tried to show that simple recipes for action are inadequate to the challenge of providing positive cross-cultural communities and consistent cross-cultural learning environments. As we have seen, even following so-called "multicultural" principles by no means guarantees success either in the classroom or in society more generally. We have argued, on the contrary, that truly multicultural teaching depends on a much deeper understanding about the nature of cultural identity. It also depends on an understanding of how all individuals develop their social identity within specific cultural and subcultural contexts, and on an understanding of what it means for individuals to move across cultural and linguistic boundaries.

We also emphasized that adolescence is a particularly challenging time for cross-cultural learning. Adolescents from second or minority cultures, many of whom also face the challenge of learning curriculum content in a second language, are particularly at risk for the negative effects of cultural shock, racism, and insensitive educational practices such as submersion. The risk is especially severe when we consider, too, that adolescents face these challenges of cross-cultural adaptation at a time when they are also trying to deal with the complex feelings relating to the emergence of sexual identity, and with peer-group dynamics. Our main conclusion is that fostering sociocultural awareness and good cross-cultural teaching practice in a community of secondary school learners crucially depends on some critical examination of our own culturally based feelings and experiences. Teachers are unlikely to foster sociocultural awareness in others unless they are first prepared to foster it in themselves. It is only in this way, and through our own continuing commitment and will to learn more about cultural identity and interaction, that we can truly join the cross-cultural communities in which it is our role to provide leadership.

SUGGESTED RESOURCES

Allport, G.W. (1954). *The nature of prejudice.* Garden City, NY: Doubleday Anchor.

Anderson, A.B., & Frideres, J.S. (1981). *Ethnicity in Canada.* Toronto: Butterworths.

Appleton, N. (1983). *Cultural pluralism in education: Theoretical foundations.* New York: Longman.

Arnot, M. (Ed.). (1985). *Race and gender: Equal opportunities policies in education.* Oxford, UK: Pergamon.

Banks, J.A., & Lynch, J. (Eds.). (1986). *Multicultural education in Western societies.* London, UK: Holt, Rinehart and Winston.

Banton, M. (1987). *Racial theories.* Cambridge: Cambridge University Press.

Bock, P.K. (Ed.). (1970). *Culture shock: A reader in modern cultural anthropology.* New York: Alfred A. Knopf.

Bock, P.K. (1980). *Rethinking psychological anthropology: Continuity and change in the study of human action.* New York: W.H. Freeman and Co.

Bolaria, B.S., & Li, P.S. (1988). *Racial oppression in Canada* (2nd edition). Toronto: Garamond Press.

Brandt, G.L. (1986). *The realization of anti-racist teaching.* London: Falmer Press.

Brislin, R.W. (1981). *Cross-cultural encounters: Face-to-face interaction.* New York: Pergamon.

Brislin, R.W., Cushner, K., Cherrie, C., & Yong, M. (1986). *Intercultural interactions: A practical guide.* Newbury Park, CA: Sage Publications.

Chan, K.B., & Indra, D.M. (Eds.). (1987). *Uprooting, loss and adaptation: The resettlement of Indochinese refugees in Canada.* Ottawa, ON: Canadian Public Health Association.

Cole, M., & Scribner, S. (1974). *Culture & thought: A psychological introduction.* New York: John Wiley & Sons.

Curtis, J., Grabb, E., Guppy, N., & Gilbert S. (1988). *Social inequality in Canada: Patterns, problems, policies.* Scarborough, ON: Prentice-Hall Canada.

Dovidio, J.F., & Gaertner, S.L. (Eds.). (1986). *Prejudice, discrimination, and racism.* New York: Academic Press.

Elliott, J.L. (Ed.). (1983). *Two nations, many cultures: Ethnic groups in Canada.* Scarborough, ON: Prentice-Hall.

Friere, P. (1973). *Education for critical consciousness.* London: Sheed and Ward.

Furnham, A., & Bochner, S. (1986). *Culture shock: Psychological reactions to unfamiliar environments.* London: Methuen.

Garcia, O., & Otheguy, R. (Eds.). (1989). *English across cultures: Cultures across English.* Berlin: Mouton de Gruyter.

Gardner, R.C., & Kalin, R. (Eds.). (1981). *A Canadian social psychology of ethnic relations.* Toronto: Methuen.

Gumperz, J.J. (Ed.). (1982). *Language and Social Identity.* Cambridge: Cambridge University Press.

Kallen, E. (1982). *Ethnicity and human rights in Canada.* Toronto: Gage.

Krauter, J.F., & David, M. (1978). *Minority Canadians: Ethnic groups.* Toronto: Methuen.

Li, P. (1988). *Ethnic inequality in a class society.* Toronto: Wall and Thompson.

Mallea, J.R. (1989). *Schooling in a plural Canada.* Clevedon, England: Multilingual Matters.

Mallea, J.R., & Young, J.C. (1984). *Cultural diversity and Canadian education: Issues and innovations.* Ottawa, ON: Carleton University Press.

Moerman, M. (1988). *Talking cultural: Ethnography and conversation analysis.* Philadelphia: University of Pennsylvania Press.

Nieto, S. (1992). *Affirming diversity: The sociopolitical context of multicultural education.* New York: Longman.

Paige, R.M. (Ed.). (1986). *Cross-cultural orientation: New conceptualizations and applications.* Lanham, MD: University Press of America.

Phinney, J.S., & Rotheram, M.J. (Eds.). (1987). *Children's ethnic socialization: Pluralism and development.* Newbury Park, CA: Sage Publications.

Piper, D. (1989). Socio-political influence on cultural identity in Canada. Implications for cross-cultural communication in English. In O. Garcia & R. Otheguy (Eds.), *English across cultures: Cultures across English. A reader in cross-cultural communication.* Contributions to the Sociology of Language 53: Series editor, Joshua Fishman. New York: Mouton de Gruyter.

Piper, T. (1993) *Language for all our children.* Toronto: Maxwell Macmillan.
Rex, J. (1986). *Race and ethnicity.* Milton Keynes, England: Open University Press.
Rex, J., & Mason, D. (Eds.). (1986). *Theories of race and ethnic relations.* Cambridge: Cambridge University Press.
Richard-Amato, P.A., & Snow, M.A. (1992). *The multicultural classroom: Readings for content-area teachers.* White Plains, NY: Longman.
Robinson, G.L.N. (1985). *Crosscultural understanding.* New York: Pergamon Press.
Seelye, H.N. (1988). *Teaching culture.* Lincolnwood, IL: National Textbook Co.
Sherwood, R. (1980). *The Psychodynamics of Race: Vicious and Benigh Spirals.* Brighton, Sussex: Harvester Press.
Skutnabb-Kangas, T., & Cummins, J. (Eds.). (1988). *Minority education.* Clevedon, England: Multilingual Matters.
Smith Layton, M. (1991). *Intercultural journeys through reading and writing.* New York: Harper Collins.
Tierney, J. (Ed.). (1982). *Race migration and schooling.* London: Holt, Rinehart and Winston.
Ulin, R.C. (1988). *Understanding cultures.* Austin, TX: University of Texas Press.
Valdes, J.M. (Ed.). (1986). *Culture bound: Bridging the cultural gap in language teaching.* Cambridge: Cambridge University Press.
Young, J. (Ed.). (1987). *Breaking the mosaic: Ethnic identities in Canadian schooling.* Toronto: Garamond Press.

REFERENCES

Austin, J.L. (1962). *How to do things with words.* Oxford: Clarendon Press.
Blum-Kulka, S., & House, J. (1989). Cross-cultural and situational variation in requesting behavior. In S. Blum-Kulka, J. House, and G. Kasper (Eds.), *Cross-cultural pragmatics: requests and apologies, Vol. 31 in Advances in discourse processes.* Norwood, N.J.: Ablex Publishing Corp.
Brislin, R.W. (1981). *Cross-cultural encounters: Face-to-face interaction.* New York: Pergamon.
Grice, P. (1957). Meaning. *Philosophical Review* 66: 377–88.
Gumperz, J.J. (Ed.). (1982). *Language and social identity.* Cambridge: Cambridge University Press.
IRI (Intercultural Relations Institute). (1982). *Take two.* Videotape. Palo Alto, California.
Moodely, K.A. (1984). The predicament of racial affirmative action: a critical review of 'equality now.' *Queen's Quarterly,* 91: 795–806.
Robinson, G.L.N. (1985). *Crosscultural understanding.* New York: Pergamon.
Schumann, J.H. (1978). *The pidginization process, a model of second language acquisition.* Rowley, Mass.: Newbury House.

Seelye, H.N. (1988). *Teaching culture.* Lincolnwood, IL: National Textbook Company.
Tannen, D. (1980). A comparative analysis of oral narrative strategies: Athenian Greek and American English. In Wallace Chafe (Ed.), *The pear stories: cultural, cognitive and linguistic aspects of narrative production.* Norwood, NJ: Ablex.
Taylor, R.B. (1988). *Human territorial functioning.* Cambridge: Cambridge University Press.

CHAPTER 10

Teachers, Parents, and Students in Inclusive Education: Working Together Throughout the High School Years

Evelyn Lusthaus and Charles Lusthaus

McGill University

Introduction

In today's high schools, general education teachers are finding their classrooms filled with students from diverse backgrounds and cultures, with different values, interests, styles, and abilities. The challenges before them are great!

Within these heterogeneous classrooms are students with disabilities; for many high school teachers, this is a new experience. Inclusive education is recent at the secondary level, and many classroom teachers have little experience with students who previously have been educated in special schools and classes. This chapter is written to assist them in working with these students and their families.

The right of students with disabilities to have access to an appropriate education is now part of our educational ethos. During the past two decades we have explored ways of creating effective inclusive educational practices, and we have learned that developing good relationships with students and their parents is an important ingredient for success. This is sometimes called "building partnerships."

The idea of creating partnerships is not unique to education; rather, it is a part of a larger societal orientation. Today, we create partnerships between social workers and clients, professional managers and customers, managers and unions, and, increasingly, schools and families.

In general terms, a partnership is a mutually beneficial relationship between individuals or groups. The partners in the relationship have joint rights, responsibilities, and obligations. They share values and a willingness and ability to work together toward a common goal.

Educational researchers indicate that parent-teacher partnerships contribute to student learning and ultimate success (Elliot & Sheridan, 1992; Evans, Okifugi, Engler, Bromley & Tishelman, 1993; Moore & Littlejohn, 1992; Shea & Bauer, 1991; Sheridan & Kratochwill, 1992). As early as 1987, Henderson noted: "The evidence is now beyond dispute: parent involvement improves student achievement. When parents are involved, children do better in school" (1987, p. 1).

Partnerships between parents and teachers take many forms. Moore and Littlejohn (1992) indicate that "parents as partners" means parents are involved in a number of different roles—as volunteers, teachers, learners, or decision makers. "Parents as partners" is not a prescription for how parents "should" be involved in school. Some parents will be partners by participating actively in many roles; for others, partnership will mean simply being interested in their son's or daughter's education.

This chapter explores parent and teacher partnerships from the time students enter high school through to their graduation. It is divided into two main parts: part one examines the context for family-school partnerships; part two provides activities for developing these partnerships.

Context for partnership. Secondary education is a cyclical system that takes place within three important contexts: the society at large, the educational system, and the family system.

Activities for partnership. The secondary system has macro- and microcycles within it. At the macrolevel, students enter secondary school, go through the various grades, and then exit. At the microlevel, there is a yearly cycle: students begin anew each year, go through the activities of a school year, and then exit into the next year.

The Context of Family and School Partnership: Societal, School, and Family Systems

Partnerships between teachers, students, and parents take place within a larger context that includes the society at the broadest level, the school system that operates within the society, and the specific family system to which the student and parent belong.

The Societal System and Inclusion

Values, beliefs, and attitudes play a central role in guiding the behaviour of people and their institutions. Throughout the century, changing societal values and beliefs about people with disabilities have created changes in their education and treatment (Taylor & Searl, 1987; Roeher Institute, 1994; Wolfensberger, 1975).

During the first part of the 20th century, children and adults with mental disabilities were treated as subhumans, locked away in institutions, uneducated, neglected, and abused (Wolfensberger, 1975). During this period, they were considered a threat to social well-being, and viewed as the source of illiteracy, poverty, and crime. Because social and public policy reflected this value system, people with disabilities were sterilized and forced into lifelong segregation.

This situation began to improve in the 1950s, when institutional conditions were exposed to public scrutiny. Reformers concerned with human rights succeeded in establishing legislation that protected the rights of people who had been institutionalized (Martin, 1978). The society realized that individuals with a disability had been victims of social abuse rather than causes of social upheaval.

In the 1970s, advocates argued forcefully for the vision of normalization and community integration. Today, many people with mental and physical disabilities enjoy opportunities to play valued roles in society: community participant, citizen, learner and contributor (Lusthaus, 1987).

As **community participants**, individuals with disabilities have access to the community and are involved in the day-to-day functions of normal community life (Nisbet, Clark & Covert, 1991). As **citizens**, they enjoy the rights to be educated, work, vote, marry, have children, and be represented in court (Endicott, 1990; Roeher Institute, 1991). They are now recognized as **learners** who have potential to grow and develop, when given opportunities to learn (Halvorsen & Sailor, 1990). Finally, individuals with disabilities are becoming recognized as valuable **contributors**: they enhance the sense of values within their families, schools, communities, and society (Lusthaus, 1986; Turnbull, 1985).

The Educational System and Inclusion

The evolution to inclusive education has spanned approximately four decades of school change. In the 1960s, with the belief that regular education could not meet the needs of children with exceptionalities, school systems developed special schools and special classes. Reynolds and Birch (1982) named this model of education the "two box" model—one box for "normal" children and another box for "disabled" children.

During the 1970s and 1980s, professionals altered this model and created a continuum of education services that ranged from total segregation (institution) to full integration (regular class). Educators placed students with special needs into the setting where they "fit" (Gearheart, 1974). Professionals, parents, and advocates supported this "cascade model" because it made possible more integration than the existing "two box" model.

During the 1980s, many parents and educators advocated a new model of education, the "integration model"; their goal was integration of students with disabilities in ordinary schools with needed support (Lipsky & Gartner, 1989; Stainback, Stainback & Forest, 1989). In Canada, movement to this ideal was empowered by three main forces: the passage of the Canadian Charter of Human Rights and Freedoms in the 1980s, the development of integrated school systems that provided inspiration and practical strategies, and the ground swell of advocacy by parents and educators for a more excellent and equitable education for students with special needs (Crawford & Porter, 1992; Porter & Richler, 1991; Smith, 1994).

Since the beginning of the 1990s, the integration concept has evolved into the image of "full inclusion"; that is, the inclusion of all students—those with diverse abilities, cultural backgrounds, learning styles—into one community of learners (Baker, Wang & Walberg, 1995; Barry, 1995; Crawford & Porter, 1992; Lusthaus, Gazith & Lusthaus, 1992; Stainback & Stainback, 1990b). Today, many school boards across North America are implementing fully inclusive schools with creativity and commitment (Crawford & Porter, 1992; Giangreco & Putnam, 1991; Scruggs & Mastropieri, 1994; Villa, Thousand, Stainback & Stainback, 1992).

For students with a disability, full inclusion in school means that a) the students are educated for all or most of the day in ordinary classrooms with their peers, b) the educational program is adapted to meet their social and academic needs, and c) the students and teachers receive the assistance they need to succeed. Full inclusion *never* means placing a student with challenging needs in an ordinary classroom without adaptations or supports.

To actualize inclusive education, change must occur at the school system, school, and classroom levels.

The School System: Policy and Resources for Inclusion

The school system has the responsibility for ensuring quality education for all its students. It is useful for parents and teachers to learn their school system's policies and practices about inclusive education.

Ideally, the school board has a clear policy statement that explicitly supports this model of education, although this is only a starting point. School boards create structures and job categories to implement policies. In recent years, as a more inclusive perspective has been introduced, many boards have dismantled the old special education system, replacing old structures with new ones.

Within new structures are new jobs, with names such as integration coordinator, community animator, resource teacher, materials and support teacher, and transition coordinator. Procedures that support inclusion include training personnel, modifying roles of special educators, and merging special and regular education into one unified system. School boards also allocate financial resources for books, materials, and equipment, all intended to provide the supports teachers need to carry out their role.

The School and Classroom: Where Inclusion is at Work

The educational system may identify what "ought to occur," but it is the school that must figure out how to "make it happen." What are some ingredients that make partnerships work? Partners must want to be involved with one another; they must also recognize that they may have varying degrees of commitment to the partnership. Partnerships vary in their duration and degree of personal contact.

As educators develop partnerships with parents, both groups need the knowledge and skills that make partnerships work. For teachers, above all is the need to respect differences among parents in their interest and ability to be involved. To achieve this goal, understanding the dynamics of family systems is critical.

The Family System and Inclusion

All families, regardless of size or composition, comprise a system in which each member and event influences the other (Turnbull & Summers, 1985). It is obvious that events of importance—birth of a child, loss of a job, death of a family member—affect everyone in the family. Less obvious is the effect that small, seemingly inconsequential events can have on family members. When a homework assignment is unfinished, when a student arrives late to school—do these events reflect a student's irresponsibility, or is something happening within the family, leading to these outcomes? Educators who view students within a family system are better able to empathize with them.

Educators who recognize the family as a system are also more aware of the impact of their suggestions. If a teacher encourages a parent to work with her adolescent daughter nightly on homework assignments, how does that affect her time with her two younger children or her husband?

Teachers need to be sure that their suggestions are "consistent with the families' priorities and are reasonable in light of the many competing demands they face. Anything we ask families to do, whether it's a school meeting or a home training program, must be important enough to be worth their valuable time" (Turnbull & Summers, 1985, p. 17).

The Diversity of Families

Families vary in every possible way—in number of members, culture, language, religion, and belief system. They differ in income level, occupation (or no occupation), educational background, working hours, community involvement, and expectations. In the past, the educational system tended to define families as white, middle class, and nuclear; today, educators are aware of the tremendous diversity and complexity of families (Fine, 1990; Moore & Littlejohn, 1992; Smith, 1993; Turnbull & Turnbull, 1990).

It is ineffective to relate to diverse families as a homogeneous group. Teachers need to treat families as individually as they treat students. When they know the family's characteristics, needs, and feelings about school involvement, they can develop meaningful, realistic relationships.

Families of Students with Disabilities: Special Issues

Like all other families, families of students with disabilities are diverse and each is unique. They have a number of common realities, however, that increase their stress (Paul, Porter & Falk, 1993; Vitello & Soskin, 1985).

Caretaking. When children with a disability are young, they usually require more physical care than nondisabled children. They are more susceptible to illness and require more frequent hospitalization and surgery.

Services. As the children grow, parents sometimes devote years obtaining the services their child requires—medical, therapeutic, educational and vocational services.

Earnings. Parents also face the added cost of special goods and services their child needs. Often they put their time, money, and energy into family adjustment and child care, rather than career enhancement or achievements, resulting in diminished earning power.

Reactions of others. Sometimes parents must cope with negative reactions of others toward their child; this can happen in the family, neighbourhood, and school. Parents also may face negative reactions from professionals, including teachers. Parents of adolescents with emotional disorders are particularly vulnerable, because they are often blamed for causing their children's problems (Gross, 1994).

Future. Finally, every parent of a child with challenging needs is deeply concerned about the future, and this pressure becomes more pronounced as the child enters adolescence (Campbell & Essex, 1994). Sarason (1985) explained that parental concern for the future is the most persistent of all family needs. Parents ask themselves: What will happen when high school is over; what services and options will be available? What will happen when we are no longer able to provide love and care; will our grown child still be included in the family and community?

In addition to these difficult questions, parents are plagued with emotional and complex legal decisions about wills, guardianship, and trust funds. Because there are no clear guidelines to follow, these concerns are not easily resolved.

Contributions. In spite of the reality of these important stresses, children with disabilities also bring joy and pleasure to their families, a fact that is often overlooked. Researchers indicate that many families are enriched by their child's presence, their family relationships are stronger, and their quality of life is improved (Behr, 1990; Meyer, 1993; Turnbull, 1985; Wikler, Wasow & Hatfield, 1983).

Therefore, when teachers work with families, it is essential to be sensitive to the many pressures and demands upon them, but it is also important to recognize the strengths and gifts their children bring. Teachers who are sensitized to both aspects of the students can appreciate their gifts as well as work on their problems.

Families of Students with Disabilities: Roles Played Vis-à-Vis the Educational System

In their book *Families, Professionals, and Exceptionality: A Special Partnership* (1990), Turnbull and Turnbull outline eight roles parents have played in relation to professionals.

1. *Parents as the problem source.* Although causation theories have declined in the past 20 years, parents are still sometimes blamed erroneously for their children's learning and behavioural problems.
2. *Parents as organization members.* Due to lack of services for their children, parents began organizing for their children's education as early as the 1930s.

3. *Parents as service developers.* Parents have been the initiators of educational, recreational, residential, and vocational services.

4. *Parents as recipients of professionals' decisions.* For many years, professionals expected parents to defer to their professional decisions about where and how their children would be served. When parents disagreed with professional advice, they were thought to be "in denial" or "unrealistic."

5. *Parents as educational decision makers.* Today, rather than leaving the decision making to professionals, most parents participate actively in shaping educational programs.

6. *Parents as learners and teachers.* Beginning in the 1960s, educators and psychologists began training parents to teach their children at home, to reinforce gains made at school.

7. *Parents as political advocates.* Parents have been successful advocates for their children's rights to education, community services, employment opportunities, and residential programs.

8. *Parents as family members.* Parents are individual members of a family system.

Another important role that parents play, implied but not directly mentioned above, is **parents as partners** with educators. In this role, parents and teachers work together to develop a mutually beneficial relationship. Teachers may gain increased job satisfaction, experience, and professional growth; parents may gain satisfaction, recognition, and improved knowledge and skills.

O'Brien and Forest (1989), in their handbook *Action for Inclusion: How to Improve Schools by Welcoming Children with Special Needs into Regular Classrooms,* suggest specific activities for parents and educators to consider as they work together for quality inclusive schooling. They outline five steps for welcoming a new student to school and building an individualized support system:

Step 1: Clarify the family's intention to include their son or daughter in the neighbourhood school.

Step 2: Enlist the principal's help in including the student.

Step 3: Enrol the classroom teacher in including the student.

Step 4: Involve the student's classmates in welcoming the student and getting to know their new class member.

Step 5: Gather the people involved to create a process whereby the student becomes a member of the class and the student's gifts are developed.

Partnership in Action: Working Together Throughout the High School Cycle

High school consists of two types of cycles: the overall macrocycle (entrance into, progress through, and graduation from high school), and the yearly micro-cycle (entrance into, progress through, and exit from each grade).

Macrolevel Cycle: Transition to High School

The move from elementary to high school is a transition of great importance to adolescents and their families. It represents a new phase of development and marks the beginnings of maturity—students make more of their own decisions and accept increased responsibility for their own lives.

Life Cycle Transitions: Stress on Families

Transition to secondary school is an uncertain time for all families, and researchers tell us that transitions are especially challenging for parents who have an adolescent with a disability (Dragan, 1994; Ludlow, Turnbull & Luckasson, 1988; Thorin & Irvin, 1992). Most life cycle passages (e.g., entering or exiting school, moving away from home, getting married or finding a job) create stress for these families. Transitions are poignant reminders of the limitations their children face and the ways in which they are different from others.

Sometimes it is the *lack* of transition that causes difficulty; for example, families with a severely disabled child may have to accept that they will never see an evolution to a job, or marriage, or independent living. Sometimes it is the *level of readiness* for transition that increases strain; for example, a child with a disability is not "ready" academically to move ahead to the next level, or a parent is not "ready" psychologically to let their adolescent move to a new, more independent phase.

It is important for educators to understand that parents feel especially vulnerable during their adolescent's movement to high school. A teacher's (or school principal's) overall attitude of support and encouragement are extremely beneficial in reducing the pressure parents and students may be experiencing.

Selecting a High School

Parents find it difficult to select a high school for their son or daughter with a disability, especially if they are seeking an inclusive high school in a community where special schools and classes are the norm. In most school boards across Canada, inclusive education is more of an ideal than a reality, so searching for an appropriate high school is time-consuming and confusing.

Parents may be besieged by perplexing questions: should they try to register their son or daughter in a local high school; does the school have adequate support services; does it welcome students with disabilities or accept them only under pressure; does it provide a good quality education? The "bottom line" concern for parents is: what is the best environment for my child?

Meyer and Eichinger's *Program Quality Indicators* (1994), summarized in Meyer (1993), can be a helpful guide. Intended for use by both parents and educators, the Quality Indicators checklist is a summary of "what is known" about achieving success in inclusive schooling. The assessment contains 38 indicators, organized into four sections: a) school system indicators, b) building indicators, c) placement and related services indicators, and d) individual student and program indicators. Parents can use the checklist in selecting schools, and educators can use it as a needs assessment for improving their programs.

Students with special needs and their parents may make numerous visits to potential high schools (both "regular" and "special"), take tours, have interviews, and make applications before they are satisfied that they have chosen the best setting. As much as possible, students should be part of this decision-making process.

During this uncertain time, secondary teachers can be supportive by showing empathy for the parents' concerns, answering questions respectfully and honestly, displaying a sincere interest in the special needs of the student, and responding openly about the school's ability to meet these needs.

Planning the Transition to High School

Once a high school location has been selected for a student with a disability, it is important for the family and school members to plan for entry. This usually takes the form of a meeting, in the spring or late summer, before the fall term begins.

Who attends? Ideally, the meeting includes the student, family, and educational team: the principal or vice-principal, special education support staff, homeroom teacher, and teacher(s) who will be involved with the student once school begins. It is also wise to invite a teacher or principal from the elementary school: this provides continuity in the student's program.

What is accomplished?

1. The student, family, and staff get a chance to meet.
2. The student and family get an orientation to the school and the first-year program.
3. The student, family, and staff can begin to identify overall goals for the year: what are the priorities for the first year in high school?
4. A plan for the first few days of school is established, particularly if the student requires significant support from staff and other students.

5. Teachers can ask about the family's preferred type of communication. Many can be used! Written communication includes letters, newsletters, notes, log books, and checklists—daily, weekly, or as needed.

Brown's Elementary-to-Secondary School Transition Strategy

Brown and his colleagues (1988) offer an elementary-to-secondary school transition strategy with three phases: a) gathering information, b) planning the transition, and c) designing and implementing an individual transition plan (ITP).

In phase 1, data are collected about the student, the elementary school, and the secondary school. In phase 2, general plans are made about the student's program and the parents' involvement. Finally, in phase 3, the specifics of the plan are laid out, including: a) transition team, b) curricular content, c) involvement of parents, special education teachers, related services personnel, regular education teachers, and nondisabled students.

School staff need to use their judgment regarding planning; a student with low support needs would not require an extensive process like Brown's, above. Although otherwise comprehensive, Brown's work neglects to mention the involvement of the students in their program planning, a necessary component for building student decision making, self-assurance, and self-advocacy.

Microlevel Cycle: The Yearly Cycle

In this section, we explore four phases of each year's cycle, from the perspective of you, the teacher: a) beginning the year, b) implementing the program, c) evaluating and reporting student progress, and d) planning the transition to the next year. For each phase, we suggest activities teachers can do with students and with parents, to enhance student-teacher relationships and promote parent-teacher collaboration.

Phase 1: Beginning the School Year

Most teachers are excited about the beginning of the school year. They also have many questions: will they have students with special needs, changes in curriculum, changes in administration, adequate support? You can gain confidence and control over the uncertainty of the new year, and the students with special needs you will be teaching, by doing some footwork right at the beginning of school.

First, meet with special consultants or resource teachers in your school who provide support to students and teachers. Discuss expectations and clarify roles so you know how to get their assistance.

Second, seek out the students' teachers from the previous year. This is beneficial in learning about the students' strengths and needs, and what worked well in the past.

Finally, review the curriculum and develop common-sense ways to make modifications for students with disabilities.

Activities with students: Students anticipate the opening of school with excitement and insecurity, especially if it is their first year of high school. Teachers can make them feel more confident! The following suggestions are made for all students, not just those with disabilities:

1. *Greet students with enthusiasm.* Welcome students with warmth and sincerity. Among students' basic needs is the need to belong (Curwin & Mendler, 1988; Jones & Jones, 1995; Mendler, 1994). Take time to tell the students how pleased you are to have them in your class.

2. *Learn about your students.* Get to know the students as quickly as possible. Share information about yourself: what is important to you; what do you like to do; why did you go into teaching? To get to know your students and earn their trust, express interest in their activities, spend time with them during school when possible (e.g., take an occasional lunch together), communicate positively with them, and listen nonjudgmentally when they share problems or issues with you.

3. *Explain requirements and expectations.* Set out clearly your course content, schedule of topics, expectations about academic work and homework, class schedule, and class structure.

4. *Establish classroom rules and guidelines.* Work with the students to develop a set of guidelines and rules for classroom behaviour, as well as a process to be followed when there is a problem. Curwin and Mendler (1988) and Mendler (1994) indicate that students who develop their own classroom rules are much more likely to follow them than students who are presented with rules laid down by the teacher.

Emmer and his colleagues (1994) present practical "how-to" information on developing rules and procedures. They found that effective teachers at both the elementary and secondary levels spend time teaching students (all students, not just those with learning problems) classroom rules and procedures.

5. *Build peer relationships and social skills.* Take time to nurture relationships, especially between students with disabilities and other class members.

Creating a "circle of friends" for students can be an effective way to build relationships (Forest & Lusthaus, 1989). In this exercise, students are sensitized to the importance of a circle of friendship in everyone's life.

A big-brother/big-sister relationship helps new students develop friendships and "learn the ropes," and it is easy to develop. The big brother or sister assists the entering student in meeting others, learning about the school's expectations and practices, and just being available as a new friend.

Activities with parents: During the first few days and weeks of school, try to communicate with families who have a student with special needs in your class:

1. *Communicate about the student's transition.* Although the extent of communication may vary among parents, it is safe to say that all parents with special-needs students will welcome a call or note indicating that things are going well.
2. *Give clear information about classroom expectations.* Parents should also learn your expectations for general classroom work and behaviour. Use a format for communication that is not time-consuming, such as an introductory letter or a brief newsletter.
3. *Keep parents informed.* Also, parents should be kept fully informed if you are requesting additional special services or creating a friendship network for their son or daughter.
4. *Seek additional information.* You might wish to speak with parents to gain more information about students so you can make realistic modifications for them.
5. *Remain open to parental concerns and suggestions.* Be sure to hear concerns parents express; for example, they might wonder whether their son or daughter with special needs will get adequate support in the general classroom.

Phase 2: Implementing the Program

Once the school term has begun and students are settled into their schedules and routines, the ongoing work of instructional and curricular implementation begins.

Being part of a working team is a requirement for successful implementation. It is impossible to include students with special needs "on your own"; team collaboration is a fundamental component of the process (Crawford & Porter, 1992; Scruggs & Mastropieri, 1994; Thousand, Villa & Nevin, 1994).

Willard (1994) notes that collaborative relationships among six groups are essential for inclusive schooling: a) parents, teachers, and school, b) school personnel, c) administrators, d) policy makers, e) community agencies, and f) colleges and universities. Elliot and Sheridan (1992) indicate that working with a team that includes teacher, parent, and consultant can be especially beneficial in resolving problems for children having difficulties. They offer seven characteristics of effective teams: a) group leadership, b) planning activities, c) agenda setting, d) clarifying communication, e) participation of group members, f) conflict management, and g) review of group processes.

For teachers, working with a team to solve specific issues as they arise is very advantageous. One effective method for school problem solving is the Teacher Assistance Team (TAT) developed by Chalfant, Pysh, and Moultrie (1979), revised by Porter (1994) as Teachers Helping Teachers. This is a concise, structured process in which teachers present a problem and work with an in-school team to solve it. It lasts only a half-hour, and is used by many schools at lunch time to discuss issues and create concrete, practical answers to problems.

With a team behind them, teachers are ready to implement the instructional program with their students.

Activities with students: Teachers may benefit from the following suggestions for addressing students' individual needs:

1. *Gather information on academic levels.* You may want to give informal, teacher-made assessments to get information about the students' knowledge and skills in your content area, and perhaps in basic reading and mathematics, in order to develop appropriate learning objectives and curricular modifications.

2. *Develop student priorities.* Participate in a process in which the priorities and overall objectives for the student with a disability are identified. MAPS (McGill Action Planning System) is one process for planning the student's academic and social priorities (Forest & Lusthaus, 1989, 1990). A team of teachers, family, student, peers, and others participate in a group process in which the student's strengths, needs, and learning objectives are established. This process creates consensus among all participants about the priorities, providing a foundation for the development of a more specific IEP (individual educational plan).

3. *Establish an individual educational plan (IEP).* Collaborate with special education support staff, parents, and students to develop a specific plan of action for your students with special needs.

Historically, IEP meetings have not usually included general education teachers, but increasingly they are called upon to participate. This is very important; how can a student's program be designed without the general educator present? Your presence guarantees you can comment on at least three critical issues: a) is the IEP appropriate to the student's needs, b) are you able to implement the IEP, and c) do you need additional support to do it? A good resource for learning more is Schultz and Carpenter's (1995) text on mainstreaming; they present a set of questions for general education teachers to ask before and during IEP meetings, to ensure their successful participation.

Another important participant, often forgotten, is the student. We sometimes talk *about* students instead of talking *with* them; yet they frequently have excellent insight into their learning strengths and weaknesses, and their needs.

4. *Make classroom modifications.* Learn to adapt your curriculum (what is taught) and instruction (how it is taught) to the needs and level of the students with special needs in your class.

Most modifications are based on common sense; the fundamental question is: what are the students' learning difficulties, and how can I make a change to fit their needs?

A detailed discussion of modifications is not possible in this chapter, but excellent resource materials are available. Hallahan and Kauffman (1994) present a very fine review of practical adaptations for students with each type of disability; Schultz and Carpenter (1995) provide a thorough overview of modifications of curriculum and instruction for students with exceptionalities in general education classes; Heron and Jorgensen (1995) explain the importance of "front loading" these adaptations for each lesson; Giangreco and Putnam (1991) review methods for modification that do not require new materials or new curricula.

Multilevel instruction (Collicott, 1991) is one such method that is used extensively in New Brunswick and throughout Canada. It is especially promising because it is a way to modify instruction—using the same class curriculum and materials—for students who have learning problems as well as for students who are "gifted." A concise explanation of multilevel instruction is presented by Squires (1994) in the Canadian CEC newsletter *Keeping in Touch.*

5. *Design instructional strategies for student success.* The instructional approaches you use play a significant role in the success of your students. Three approaches that can facilitate learning in a heterogeneous class are multiple intelligences, cooperative learning, and learning styles.

Multiple intelligences. Howard Gardner's theory of multiple intelligences (Gardner, 1987, 1993) provides a foundation for reaching students whose strengths vary. The seven intelligences are: a) linguistic: intelligence of words, b) logical-mathematical: intelligence of numbers and reasoning, c) spatial: intelligence of pictures, d) musical: intelligence of tone and rhythm, e) bodily-kinaesthetic: intelligence of the whole body and the hands, f) interpersonal: intelligence of social understanding, and g) intrapersonal: intelligence of self-knowledge.

Schools are typically organized around only two intelligences: linguistic and logical-mathematical. If a student is strong in these, success comes easily; the goal of using multiple intelligences is to enable students to achieve by using strengths in their own intelligences.

Armstrong (1994) and Hoerr (1994) describe how the theory of multiple intelligence can be applied to curriculum, instruction, and evaluation. Armstrong provides a challenge to secondary teachers: He suggests teachers ask the following question: How can I...

- Use the spoken or written word (**linguistic**)?
- Use numbers, calculations, logic classifications, or critical thinking (**logical/mathematical**)?
- Use visual aids, visualization, colour, art, metaphor, or visual organizers (**visual**)?
- Bring in music or environmental sounds, or set key points in a rhythm or melody (**musical**)?
- Involve the whole body, or provide hands-on experiences (**bodily/kinaesthetic**)?
- Engage students in peer or cross-age sharing, cooperative learning, or large-group simulation (**interpersonal**)?
- Evoke personal feelings or memories, or give students choices (**intrapersonal**)?

Cooperative learning. Cooperative learning is another instructional method that can facilitate success in heterogeneous classrooms (Johnson, Johnson & Holubec, 1992, 1993, 1994). In cooperative learning, the teacher structures working groups, teaches social skills needed to work cooperatively, and assigns academic tasks that meet performance criteria.

Like any new approach, cooperative learning takes time to master. Begin in small doses, teaching your students the interpersonal skills they need to work capably in cooperative groups. There are excellent resources for teachers on cooperative learning: Johnson, Johnson & Holubec's *New Circles of Learning: Cooperation in the Classroom and School* (1994) and Putnam's *Cooperative Learning and Strategies for Inclusion: Celebrating Diversity in the Classroom (1993)* are just two of the many available books.

Learning styles. Paying attention to students' learning styles is another way of enhancing successful learning in diverse classrooms. All students differ in their approaches to learning, and understanding their own styles is productive for students and teachers. Students vary in the sensory modality in which they are most comfortable (e.g., visual, oral, kinaesthetic). They also differ in the way they go about learning: there are innovative, analytic, common sense, and dynamic learners. They vary in their response to different kinds of content: some are comfortable with personalized, social learning; others relate more easily to impersonal, abstract learning.

Researchers have found that when the teacher's instructional style matches the students' learning styles, student achievement is enhanced (Dunn & Dunn, 1987; McCarthy, 1987). Teachers cannot be expected to match their teaching to any one student's style, but they can increase student success by using a variety of teaching methods so that all learners have the opportunity to use their own learning style preferences.

6. *Build skills in classroom management.* A heterogeneous classroom with modified instruction works best in a classroom in which there is a foundation of respect and self-discipline. One excellent approach for secondary students is "Discipline with Dignity," developed by Curwin and Mendler (1988). Their underlying theme is that teachers should preserve and respect their students' dignity and their own dignity. They believe that teachers should teach students responsibility, not obedience. They present three dimensions of their approach, which are prevention, action, and resolution. Within each dimension, they provide practical, concrete strategies for classroom situations. Their strategies include practical ways of reducing uncooperative behaviour and resolving conflicts between students and teachers.

Another superb resource on classroom management, very relevant for secondary schools, is a text written by Jones and Jones (1995) entitled *Comprehensive Classroom Management: Creating Positive Learning Environments for All Students.*

Activities with parents: Throughout the implementation phase, there are many ways in which parents and teachers can cooperate:

1. *Invite parents to participate in developing individual plans.* Each student should have a MAPS and an IEP planning session to identify priorities and develop specific goals and objectives. Parents are integral to these processes, for they bring an overall picture of the student that is essential for developing relevant goals and objectives.

2. *Seek to make planning meetings welcoming and meaningful to parents.* When parents are invited to attend meetings, use common sense to make them welcome, just as you would to make someone comfortable in your own home.

3. *Invite parents to school activities that match their interests and availability.* In addition to attending meetings, parents may wish to be involved in school in other ways; outline the possibilities your school offers.

Phase 3: Evaluating and Reporting Student Progress

Few topics in the education of all students, not just those with special needs, generate as much controversy as the assessment, evaluation, and reporting of student progress. As research has grown regarding the need to reform education and develop high-level thinking skills in students, dissatisfaction with normative, traditional, multiple-choice assessment has also grown (Neill & Medina, 1989).

As a result, there has been an explosion of "alternative" forms of assessment: authentic assessment, portfolio assessment, exhibits, hands-on experiments, writing across the curriculum, and curriculum-based assessment (Herman, Aschbacher & Winters, 1992; Herman & Winters, 1994; Marzano, Pickering & McTighe, 1993). Reforms in assessment and evaluation have led to reforms in the reporting of results, with more emphasis now on the students' process and growth in learning, and less emphasis on grades alone (Guskey, 1994).

Activities with students: Many educators teaching high school students with special needs in their classes are grappling with a basic, perplexing question: How do I appropriately evaluate my students' progress?

1. *Select appropriate assessments.* Educators recommend that teachers use criterion-referenced, rather than norm-referenced, assessments for students with special needs in heterogeneous classrooms (Shriner, Ysseldyke & Christenson, 1989; Deno, 1985). Norm-referenced tests compare students to their peers. Criterion-referenced tests, on the other hand, make judgments about students' performance vis-à-vis the curriculum: they identify the skills that students have (and have not) mastered.

2. *Link evaluation to instruction.* The most common form of criterion-based assessment is **curriculum-based assessment** (CBA), which looks at student performance in relation to the curriculum that is taught. "Evaluation and interpretation of what a student has learned should not be an activity conducted outside and apart from instruction, but an integral part of it" (Cullen & Pratt, 1992, p. 178).

3. *Modify teacher-made tests.* Teachers can modify tests to make them appropriate for learners with special needs. Many test adaptations are easy to design; for those that are more difficult, consult with your teaching team or special education resource staff to help you make sensible adaptations.

4. *Use a variety of assessment and evaluation methods.* Explore some of the new concepts in assessment, such as assessment grounded in a collection of students' work (portfolio assessment), or assessment based upon the multiple intelligences (Hoerr, 1994).

Cullen and Pratt (1992) outline the variety of ways that practitioners evaluate students in their inclusive system in Waterloo, Ontario; this provides an example of the many methods available for gathering student information.

- Cumulative record review
- Student-teacher interview
- Observation
- Informal testing
- Teacher-made tests
- Group projects
- Student contracts
- Peer evaluation
- Self-evaluation

Activities with parents: High schools generally organize four to six conferences a year for reporting students' progress to parents, and an additional meeting time for students with special needs to review progress on the IEP.

Some parents who are interested in their child's education cannot attend these organized conferences; yet their absence can be misunderstood as lack of interest or lack of cooperation (Fine, 1990; Finders & Lewis, 1994; Lipsky, 1989). How can teachers work to overcome this problem?

1. *Overcome barriers to attendance.* Turnbull and Turnbull (1990) describe common barriers faced by parents in attending conferences:

- Logistical problems, such as lack of transportation and child care, inability to attend at the set time, and difficulty in making arrangements for both parents to be present
- Communication problems, arising from insensitivity shown by the school personnel to language and culture, and difficulties arising when parents and professionals disagree
- Lack of understanding of the school system, such as information regarding the IEP process and the overall organization of the school and school system
- Feelings of inferiority, which can come from some parents feeling they are not respected in the decision-making process, that they are outnumbered by the professionals, or that they are being blamed for their child's difficulties
- Uncertainty about the child's exceptionality

2. *Prepare for parent conferences.* Review the student's progress carefully before the conference, putting together information on academic and social dimensions. Presenting specific data to parents, rather than generalized comments, serves several purposes: it shows parents that you care enough to have invested time and effort in preparing for the conference; it enhances your role as a competent professional; "it diminishes the likelihood of a debate over whether a student's grade is fair, or whether a student's behaviour really warrants concern" (Jones & Jones, 1995, p. 114).

3. *Communicate effectively and respectfully.* Suggestions here include: don't blame the parent for a student's difficulties; focus on positive characteristics and progress of the student; when speaking about problems, be specific and descriptive; use a practical problem-solving approach to discussing the problem. Strive for concrete ideas about what to do, rather than dwelling on what is wrong, and show faith in the parents' capacity to work on problems, with assistance.

In spite of all your good work, you will usually face some situations in which parents arrive angry, critical, and confrontational. Jones and Jones (1995) suggest 10 pointers to cope in an effective, professional manner:

- Greet the parent in a pleasant manner.
- Use active listening to defuse the parent's emotions.

- Look genuinely interested and listen carefully.
- Present a calm, professional manner.
- Ask the parent what he or she wishes to accomplish.
- Set a time limit if necessary.
- Ask the parent how the student feels about the problem.
- Be honest.
- Emphasize specific data.
- Tell the parent what will be done to deal with the problem.

4. *Seek suggestions from parents.* Finders and Lewis (1994) reported on suggestions parents made (to teachers and administrators) to improve conferences and bring parents to school: a) clarify how parents can help, b) encourage parents to be assertive, c) develop trust, d) build on home experiences, and e) use parent expertise.

5. *Consider using alternate methods to report students' progress.* Arranging formal face-to-face conferences is only one way for teachers and parents to communicate, and for some parents, this may not be a feasible method. Take the extra time to find another way. One possibility is the telephone; another is written communication—letters, notes, agenda books, daily progress reports.

Phase 4: Transition Planning for the Next Grade

What can teachers do with one another, with students, and with parents to plan a smooth transition from one grade to the next?

Activities with students:

1. *Establish a transition process.* Participate in developing a process for students to move to the next grade. Teachers can share information about the students and their requirements *before* and *after* the transfer occurs.

2. *Include the student in planning the transition.* Students need to become knowledgeable about the options they have for the next year, especially in relation to courses and experiences (e.g., work study); they should have the opportunity to express their views and be involved in the final decisions that are made.

Activities with parents:

1. *Seek parent views about the next year.* In addition to speaking with the students and future teachers, teachers planning transition need to contact parents about their views and preferences.

2. *Provide parents with information.* Be sure to provide information and support to families *before*, *during*, and *after* transitions take place.

Macrolevel Cycle: Transition from High School to the Community

The next steps after high school are filled with both hope and uncertainty for all students. For those with disabilities, the process for planning "life after high school" often begins years before high school ends. Although there are differences of opinion about exactly when post-high school planning should begin, there is consensus that the "place and pray" technique, too frequently used in the past, be replaced with responsible transitional planning (Sobsey & McDonald, 1988).

Exiting High School: A New Life Cycle Transition

The passage of a student with disabilities from high school to the community has a distinguishing feature: it is not just the student who is in transition, but really the student's whole family (Sailor, 1989). Parents often have difficulty imagining what their son's or daughter's future will hold when high school is over, and they have grave concerns about what will happen after they die. These concerns usually surface during this time of change.

Thus, the goals for transitional planning address both the needs of students and their families. Sobsey and McDonald (1988) suggest that these goals are a) to ensure a smooth transition from one environment to the next for individuals and their families, and b) to help individuals with disabilities achieve successful adult functioning.

Transition Models for Students with Disabilities

Interest in the movement from school to adult life for students with disabilities has increased dramatically in the past decade. This has arisen from several concerns: the large numbers of special-needs students who drop out of high school (Lichtenstein, 1993), the high rates of unemployment of special-needs students who succeeded in graduating, and the poor financial status of most adults with disabilities (Roeher Institute, 1992). Educators are recognizing that "one of education's most important goals is to prepare students to be fully participating members of their communities" (Dragan, 1994, p. 1).

Although transitional models differ in some respects, most have the same underlying themes and concepts. Blalock (1988) notes that features essential to success include:

- Consumer and parent input and involvement
- Adequate preparation of young adults, including a) early vocational assessment, b) prevocational skills education, c) strong, relevant vocational skills training, d) social and interpersonal skill development, and e) independent living skills training

- Individualized transition plans
- Interagency collaboration and cooperation
- Training of local agency representatives to serve on transition teams
- Provision of employer incentives

When does transition planning begin? Specialists agree that planning should begin no later than age 16 and as early as age 14 (Wehman, 1992). This guideline is based on one important rationale: when teachers know students' and families' aspirations, they can build the learning experiences, skills, and behaviours that students will need to achieve their goals.

Parent and Student Roles in Planning Transitions

Perhaps in no other area is parental planning so important. Before facing "life after high school," parents can rely, if they wish, on the good judgment of educators to plan for their sons and daughters. Services after high school, however, are inadequate and poorly organized. The service system is fragmented; there are many gaps, no clear eligibility criteria, long waiting lists, and simply an unavailability of what is needed. Without a strong, cohesive, comprehensive service system, parents are left to act as the main coordinators and advocates for their (young adult) children.

Students, even those with significant disabilities, should be a part of the transition planning process. "It is difficult, if not unrealistic, for a 16 or 17 year-old adolescent to accurately plan what he or she would like to achieve as an adult, but it is even more unrealistic for a team of professionals to plan...without the active participation of the student in question" (Wehman et al., 1988, p. 210).

Researchers indicate that many families fail to plan adequately for the future of their son or daughter with a disability (Campbell & Essex, 1994; Turnbull et al., 1989). Sometimes the difficulty of developing a design for the future lies in the uncertainty of what will be available for their (young adult) children. Campbell and Essex (1994) found that families were inhibited from creating future plans because they lacked information about community services.

It is for this reason that Patton and Browder (1988, p. 298) stress that transitional planning should be conducted *with* parents, not *for* them. "Without the active and informed involvement of parents, the potential of individuals with disabilities to gain greater independence and to participate in the opportunities and responsibilities of adult life is not likely to come to fruition."

Although researchers are consistent in calling for strong parent involvement in transitional planning, Sobsey and McDonald (1988) lend an important reminder: pressure on parents to become engaged in program planning may increase stress on the family (which may be already at its maximum), and it is important for professionals to know when it is in the best interests of the family to play less of a role. The important thing is that the family feels welcome to participate, but it is up to them to decide to what extent they will be active.

The Classroom Teacher's Role

As a general education teacher, you probably will not have a major role in planning your students' transition to adult life; this responsibility falls into the role of the special or vocational education staff. It is important, however, to show students your sincere interest and enthusiasm for their work placements, to be aware of the demands related to their vocational training, and to be open, if it is relevant, to linking their work in your class with the vocational objectives they are trying to meet.

If there is no transitional or vocational planning process in your high school, you may wish to become involved in getting one started. Inclusive education is still in its infancy, and there is a large gap between what *should* exist and what *does* exist. It takes time, and many committed teachers and administrators, to develop the necessary systems for students to graduate high school, well-prepared for their next stage of life.

Summary

Classroom teachers in secondary schools across Canada have an important challenge before them: to effectively teach the unprecedented number of students in their classrooms who have diverse needs and abilities.

We recognize that classroom teachers at the high school level may have little previous experience or training in working with students who have disabilities and their families. We encourage you to take on this responsibility with sincerity and energy, and we hope the chapter has provided you with some helpful ideas and insights to carry out your role.

Students and families have a lifetime of challenges and issues; we hope you will see your involvement as an opportunity to make a contribution. As parents ourselves of four children, we have two adolescents with disabilities, and we know the remarkable joy of working with teachers who "care," who are doing their best for our children! As parents, we welcome your involvement in our lives and the lives of our children, as they grow through adolescence into adulthood. You can make a difference in creating a bright future!

SUGGESTED RESOURCES

Inclusive Education, Family, and Disability

Organizations: The following organizations engage in training, research, publication, and/or advocacy regarding inclusion in families, schools, and community.

Beach Center on Families and Disability, Bureau of Child Research, 4138 Haworth Hall, Lawrence, KS, 60045. Phone 913-864-7600.

Canadian Association for Community Living, 4700 Keele Street, Downsview, ON, M3J 1P3. Phone: 416-661-9611.

Canadian Council for Exceptional Children, 1010 Polytek Court, Unit 36, Gloucester, Ottawa, ON, K1L 9J2. Phone: 613-747-9226.

Center for Developmental Disabilities, 499 C Waterman Building, University of Vermont, Burlington, VT, 05405. Phone: 802-656-4031.

Center on Human Policy, Syracuse University, 200 Huntington Hall, Syracuse, NY, 13244-2340. Phone: 315-443-3851.

Centre for Educational Leadership, Faculty of Education, McGill University, 3700 McTavish Street, Montreal, PQ, H3A 1Y2. Phone: 514-398-4770.

Centre for Integrated Education and Community, 24 Thome Crescent, Toronto, ON, M6H 2S5. Phone: 416-658-5363.

G. Allan Roeher Institute, 4700 Keele St., Downsview, ON, M3J 1P3. Phone: 416-661-9611.

Inclusion Press, 24 Thome Crescent, Toronto, ON, M6H 2S5. Phone: 416-658-5363.

Institute on Community Integration (UAP), College of Education, University of Minnesota, 111 Pattee Hall, 150 Pillsbury Drive SE, Minneapolis, MN, 55455. Phone: 612-624-1349.

Institute on Disability: A University Affiliated Program, 10 Ferry Street, #14, University of New Hampshire, Concord, NH, 03301. Phone: 603-228-2084.

Learning Disabilities Association of Canada, 323 Chapel, Suite 200, Ottawa, ON, K1N 7Z2. Phone: 613-238-5721.

PEAK (Parent Education and Assistance Program) Parent Center, Inc., 6055 Lehman Drive, Suite 101, Colorado Springs, CO, 80918. Phone: 719-531-9400.

Schools Are For Everyone (SAFE), P.O. Box 583, Syracuse, NY, 12310. Phone: 518-455-2096.

Publications: The following manuals, newsletters, and journals focus especially on inclusive schooling and parent/family issues.

ARCHtype (newsletter). Advocacy Resource Centre for the Handicapped, 40 Orchard View Boul., Suite 255, Toronto, ON, M4R 1B9. Phone: 416-482-1254.

Entourage. Roeher Institute, 4700 Keele Street, Toronto, ON, M3J 1P3. Phone: 416-661-9611.

Goodman, G. (1994). *Inclusive classrooms from A to Z: A handbook for educators.* Columbus, OH: Teachers' Publishing Group.

Inclusion News. 24 Thome Crescent, Toronto, ON, M6H 2S5.

Inclusion of troubled children. *Journal of Emotional and Behavioral Problems, 3*(3), Fall, 1994 special issue.

Inclusion Times. National Professional Resources Institute, 25 S. Regent Street, Port Chester, NY, 10573.

Learning Disabilities Association of Canada (1991). *Directory of resources.* Ottawa, ON: Learning Disabilities Association of Canada.

Roeher Institute (1989). *Family support: An annotated bibliography.* Toronto: Roeher Institute.

TASH Newsletter. The Association for Persons with Severe Handicaps, 11201 Greenwood Avenue North, Seattle, WA, 98133. Phone: 206-361-8870.

Teaching Exceptional Children. The Council for Exceptional Children, 1920 Association Drive, Reston, VA, 22091-1589.

The Exceptional Parent. 605 Commonwealth Avenue, Boston, ME, 02215. Phone: 800-247-8080.

The inclusive school. *Educational Leadership, 52*(4), December 1994/January 1995 special issue.

Vandercook, T., Wolff, S., Flower, D., & Doyle, M.B. (1993). *Inclusive education for learners with severe disabilities: Print & media resources.* University of Minnesota: Institute on Community Integration.

REFERENCES

Armstrong, T. (1994). Multiple intelligences: Seven ways to approach curriculum. *Educational Leadership, 52*(3), 26–28.

Aslanian, C.B., & Brickell, H.M. (1980). *Americans in transition: Life changes as reasons for learning.* New York: College Entrance Examination Board.

Baker, E.T., Wang, M., & Walberg, H.J. (1995). The effects of inclusion on learning. *Educational Leadership, 52*(4), 33–35.

Barry, A.L. (1995). Easing into inclusion classrooms. *Educational Leadership, 52*(4), 4–6.

Behr, S. (1990). *Literature review: Positive contributions of persons with disabilities to their families.* University of Kansas: Beach Center on Families and Disability.

Blalock, G. (1988). Transitions across the lifespan. In B.L. Ludlow, A.P. Turnbull & R. Luckasson (Eds.), *Transitions to adult life for people with mental retardation—Principles and practices* (pp. 3–20). Baltimore: Paul H. Brookes.

Bos, C., & Vaughn, S. (1994). *Strategies for teaching students with learning and behavioral problems.* Toronto: Allyn and Bacon.

Brotherson, M.J., Backus, L.H., Summers, J.A., & Turnbull, A.P. (1986). Transition to adulthood. In J.A. Summers (Ed.), *The right to grow up: An introduction to adults with developmental disabilities.* (pp. 17–44). Baltimore: Paul H. Brookes.

Brown, L., Albright, K.Z., Rogan, P., York, J., Solner, A.U., Johnson, F., VanDeventer, P., & Loomis, R. (1988). An integrated curriculum model for transition. In B. Ludlow, A.P. Turnbull & R. Luckasson (Eds.), *Transitions to adult life for people with mental retardation—principles and practices* (pp. 67–81). Baltimore: Paul H. Brookes.

Brown, L., Nietupski, J., & Hamre-Nietupski, S. (1976). The criterion of ultimate functioning and public school services for the severely handicapped student. In A. Thomas (Ed.), *Hey, don't forget about me: Education's investment in the severely, profoundly, and multiply handicapped* (pp. 58–82). Reston, VA: Council for Exceptional Children.

Campbell, J., & Essex, E. (1994). Factors affecting parents in their future planning for a son or daughter with developmental disabilities. *Education and Training in Mental Retardation and Developmental Disabilities, 29*(4), 222–28.

Centre for Educational Research and Innovation. (1986). *Transition to adult and working life for young people who are handicapped: Towards a unified concept of transition.* Paris: Organization for Economic Co-operation and Development.

Chalfant, J.C., Pysh, M., & Moultrie, R. (1979). Teacher Assistance Teams: A model for within building problem-solving. *Learning Disability Quarterly, 2*(3), 85–96.

Choate, J.S., Enright, B.E., Miller, L.J., Poteet, J.A., & Rakes, T.A. (1992). *Curriculum-based assessment and programming* (2nd edition). Toronto: Allyn and Bacon.

Cohn, S., & Latus, T. (1994). A 14-year-old's story of inclusion. *Journal of Emotional and Behavioral Problems, 3*(3), 3–7.

Collicott, J. (1991). Implementing multi-level instruction: Strategies for classroom teachers. In G. Porter & D. Richler (Eds.), *Changing Canadian schools: Perspectives on disability and inclusion* (pp. 191–218). Toronto: Roeher Institute.

Cotton, K. (1990). *Effective schooling practices: A research synthesis.* Portland, OR: Northwest Regional Education Laboratory.

Crawford, C., & Porter, G. (1992). *How it happens: A look at inclusive educational practice in Canada for children and youth with disabilities.* Ottawa, ON: Health and Welfare Canada.

Cullen, B., & Pratt, T. (1992). Measuring and reporting student progress. In S. Stainback and W. Stainback (Eds.), *Curriculum considerations in inclusive classrooms* (pp. 175–96). Baltimore: Paul H. Brookes.

Curwin, R., & Mendler, A. (1988). *Discipline with dignity.* Alexandria, VA: Association for Supervision and Curriculum Development.

Deno, S.L. (1985). Curriculum-based measurement: The emerging alternative. *Exceptional Children, 52,* 219-32.

Dragan, E. (1994). Transition planning: What schools need to know. *CEC Today, 1*(7), 1 & 14.

Dunn, R., & Dunn, K. (1987). *Teaching students through their individual learning styles: A practical approach.* Reston, VA: Reston.

Elliot, S., & Sheridan, S. (1992). Consultation and teaming: Problem solving among educators, parents, and support personnel. *The Elementary School Journal, 92*(3), 315–38.

Emmer, E.T., Evertson, C.M., Clements, B.S., & Worsham, M.E. (1994). *Classroom management for secondary teachers* (3rd edition). Toronto: Allyn and Bacon.

Endicott, O. (1990). How does Canada measure up against international human rights standards? *Entourage, 5*(2&3), 9.

Evans, I.M., Okifuji, A., Engler, L., Bromley, K., & Tishelman, A. (1993). Home-school communication in the treatment of childhood behavior problems. *Child and Family Behavior Therapy, 15*(2), 37–60.

Finders, M., & Lewis, C. (1994). Why some parents don't come to school. *Educational Leadership, 51*(8), 50–54.

Fine, M.J. (1990). Facilitating home-school relationships: A family-oriented approach to collaborative consultation. *Journal of Educational and Psychological Consultation, 1*(2), 169–87.

Forest, M., & Lusthaus, E. (1989). Promoting educational equality for all students: MAPS and Circles of Friends. In S. Stainback, W. Stainback & M. Forest (Eds.), *Educating all students in the mainstream of regular education* (pp. 43–57). Baltimore: Paul H. Brookes.

Forest, M., & Lusthaus, E. (1990). Everyone belongs with the MAPS Action Planning System. *Teaching Exceptional Children, 22*(2), 32–36.

Gajria, M., Salend, S., & Hemrick, M. (1994). Teacher acceptability of testing modifications for mainstreamed students. *Learning Disabilities Research & Practice, 9*(4), 236–43.

Gallivan-Fenlon, A. (1994). "Their senior year": Family and service provider perspectives on the transition from school to adult life for young adults with disabilities. *Journal of the Association for Persons with Severe Disabilities, 19*(1), 11–23.

Gardner, H. (1987). *Frames of mind.* New York: Basic Books.

Gardner, H. (1993). *Multiple intelligence: The theory into practice.* New York: Basic Books.

Gearheart, B.R. (1974). *Organization and administration of educational programs for exceptional children.* Springfield, IL: Thomas.

Giangreco, M., & Putnam, J. (1991). Supporting the education of students with severe disabilities in regular education environments. In L. Meyer, C. Peck & L. Brown (Eds.), *Critical issues in the lives of people with severe disabilities* (pp. 245–70). Baltimore: Paul H. Brookes.

Gross, J. (1994). Pitfalls for parents. *Journal of Emotional and Behavior Problems, 3*(3), 8–10.

Guskey, T. (1994). Making the grade: What benefits students? *Educational Leadership, 52*(2), 14–20.

Hallahan, D.P., & Kauffman, J.M. (1994). *Exceptional children: Introduction to special education* (6th edition). Toronto: Allyn and Bacon.

Halvorsen, A.T., & Sailor, W. (1990). Integration of students with severe and profound disabilities: A review of research. In R. Gaylord Ross (Ed.), Issues and research in special education (pp. 110–72). New York: Teachers College Press.

Heacox, D. (1991). *Up from underachievement.* Minneapolis, MN: Free Spirit Press.

Henderson, A. (1987). *The evidence continues to grow: Parent involvement improves student achievement.* Columbia, MO: National Committee for Citizens in Education.

Herman, J, Aschbacher, P., & Winters, L. (1992). *A practical guide to alternative assessment.* Alexandria, VA: Association for Supervision and Curriculum Development.

Herman, J., & Winters, L. (1994). Portfolio research: A slim collection. *Educational Leadership, 52*(2), 48–55.

Heron, E., & Jorgensen, C.M. (1995). Addressing learning differences right from the start. *Educational Leadership, 52*(4), 56–58.

Hoerr, T. (1994). How the New City School applies the Multiple Intelligences. *Educational Leadership, 52*(3), 29–32.

Johnson, D., Johnson, R., & Holubec, E. (1992). *Advanced cooperative learning* (2nd edition). Edina, MN: Interaction Book Co.

Johnson, D., Johnson, R., & Holubec, E. (1993). *Cooperation in the classroom* (Revised). Edina, MN: Interaction Book Co.

Johnson, D., Johnson, R., & Holubec, E. (Eds.) (1994). *New circles of learning: Cooperation in the classroom and school.* Alexandria, VA: Association for Supervision and Curriculum Development.

Jones, V., & Jones, L. (1995). *Comprehensive classroom management: Creating positive learning environments for all students.* Toronto: Allyn and Bacon.

Jorgensen, C.M. (1995). Essential questions—inclusive answers. *Educational Leadership, 52*(4), 52–55.

Lichtenstein, S. (1993). Transition from school to adulthood: Case studies of adults with learning disabilities who dropped out of school. *Exceptional Children, 59*(4), 336–47.

Lipsky, D.K. (1989). The roles of parents. In D.K. Lipsky & A. Gartner (Eds.), *Beyond separate education: Quality education for all* (pp. 159–80). Baltimore: Paul H. Brookes.

Lipsky, D., & Gartner, A. (1989). *Beyond separate education: Quality education for all.* Baltimore: Paul H. Brookes.

Lobato, D. (1990). *Brothers, sisters, and special needs.* Baltimore: Paul H. Brookes.

Ludlow, B., Turnbull, A.P., & Luckasson, R. (1988). *Transitions to adult life for people with mental retardation—principles and practices.* Baltimore: Paul H. Brookes.

Lusthaus, E. (1986). Persons with mental retardation as contributors: An emerging social role. *Canadian Journal on Mental Retardation, 1*(2), 24–31.

Lusthaus, E. (1987). Persons with disabilities: From isolation to full participation. In D. Ray & R. Ghosh (Eds.), *Social change and education in Canada* (pp. 247–62). Toronto: Harcourt, Brace & Jovanovich.

Lusthaus, E., Gazith, K., & Lusthaus, C. (1992). Each belongs: A rationale for full inclusion. *McGill Journal of Education, 27*(3), 293–310.

Martin, R. (1978). Legal regulations of services to the developmentally disabled. In M. Berkler, B. Bible, S. Boles, D. Deitz & A. Repp (Eds.), *Current trends for the developmentally disabled* (pp. 5–23). Baltimore: University Park Press.

Marzano, R.J., Pickering, D., & McTighe, J. (1993). *Assessing student outcomes: Performance assessment using the Dimensions of Learning Model.* Alexandria, VA: Association for Supervision and Curriculum Development.

Maxwell, C.H., Thomas, J.W., & Pogoloff, S.M. (1993). "The second shock: A qualitative study of parents' perspectives and needs during their child's transition from school to adult life." Unpublished manuscript. University of Wisconsin-Madison.

McCarthy, B. (1987). *The 4-MAT system: Teaching to learning styles with right/left mode techniques.* Barrington, IL: Excel.

Mendler, A. (1994). Behavior management in the inclusive classroom. *Journal of Emotional and Behavioral Problems, 3*(3), 59–60.

Meyer, D.J. (1993). Lessons learned: Cognitive coping strategies of overlooked family members. In A.P. Turnbull, J.M. Patterson, S.K. Behr, D.L. Murphy, J.G. Marquis, M.J. Blue-Banning (Eds.), *Cognitive coping, families, and disability* (pp. 81–93). Baltimore: Paul H. Brookes.

Meyer, L. (1994). Quality inclusive schooling: How to know it when you see it. *The Association for Persons with Severe Disabilities Newsletter, 20*(10), 18–22.

Meyer, L.H., & Eichinger, J. (1994). *Program Quality Indicators (PQI): A checklist of most promising practices in educational programs for students with disabilities* (3rd edition). Syracuse, NY: Syracuse University School of Education.

Moore, D., & Littlejohn, W. (1992). Trends toward increased family-school collaboration. *Contemporary Education, 64*(1), 40–45.

Neill, M., & Medina, N. (1989). Standardized testing: Harmful to educational health. *Phi Delta Kappan, 70,* 688–97.

Nisbet, J., Clark, M., & Covert, S. (1991). Living it up! Analysis of research on community living. In L. Meyer, C. Peck & L. Brown (Eds.), *Critical issues in the lives of people with severe disabilities* (pp. 115–44). Baltimore: Paul H. Brookes.

O'Brien, J., & Forest, M. (1989). *Action for inclusion: How to improve schools by welcoming children with special needs into regular classrooms.* Toronto: Frontier College Press.

Patton, J.R. (1986). The buzzword is "transition." *AAMD Education Division Newsletter,* Spring, 2.

Patton, J.R., & Browder, P.M. (1988). Transitions into the future. In B. Ludlow, A.P. Turnbull & R. Luckasson (Eds.), *Transitions to adult life for people with mental retardation—Principles and practices* (pp. 293–312). Baltimore: Paul H. Brookes.

Paul, J.L., Porter, P.B., & Falk, G.D. (1993). Families of children with disabling conditions. In J.L. Paul & F.J. Simeonsson (Eds.), *Children with special needs: Family, culture, and society* (pp. 3–24). Montreal: Harcourt Brace Jovanovich.

Polloway, E.A., Smith, J.D., & Patton, J.R. (1984). Learning disabilities: An adult development perspective. *Learning Disabilities Quarterly, 7,* 179–86.

Porter, G. (1994). *Teachers Helping Teachers: Problem solving teams that work.* Toronto: Roeher Institute.

Porter, G., & Richler, D. (1991). *Changing special education practice: Law, advocacy, and innovation.* In G. Porter & D. Richler (Eds.), *Changing Canadian schools: Perspectives on disability and inclusion* (pp. 9–33). Toronto: Roeher Institute.

Powell, T.H., & Gallagher, P.A. (1993). *Brothers & sisters: A special part of exceptional families* (2nd edition). Baltimore: Paul H. Brookes.

Putnam, J.W. (1993). *Cooperative learning and strategies for inclusion: Celebrating diversity in the classroom.* Baltimore: Paul H. Brookes.

Reynolds, M., & Birch, J. (1982). *Teaching exceptional children in all America's schools* (2nd edition). Reston, VA: Council for Exceptional Children.

Roeher Institute (1991). *The right to fair and equal treatment.* Toronto: Roeher Institute.

Roeher Institute (1992). *On target? Canada's employment-related programs for persons with disabilities.* Toronto: Roeher Institute.

Roeher Institute (1994). *Keys to understanding: An orientation manual on the history, issues and alternatives for people with intellectual disabilities.* Toronto: Roeher Institute.

Sailor, W. (1989). The educational, social, and vocational integration of students with the most severe disabilities. In D.K. Lipsky & A. Gartner (Eds.), *Beyond separate education: Quality education for all,* (pp. 53–74). Baltimore: Paul H. Brookes.

Sarason, S. (1985). *Psychology and mental retardation: Perspectives in change.* Austin, TX: Pro-Ed.

Schultz, J., & Carpenter, C. (1995). *Mainstreaming exceptional students: A guide for classroom teachers.* Toronto: Allyn and Bacon.

Schumaker, J.B., & Deshler, D.D. (1995). Secondary classes can be inclusive, too. *Educational Leadership, 52*(4), 50–51.

Scruggs, T., & Mastropieri, M. (1994). Successful mainstreaming in elementary science classes: A qualitative study of three reputational cases. *American Educational Research Journal, 31*(4), 785–811.

Shea, T., & Bauer, A. (1991). *Parents and teachers of children with exceptionalities: A handbook for collaboration* (2nd edition). Toronto: Allyn and Bacon.

Sheridan, S.M., & Kratochwill, T.R. (1992). Behavioral parent-teacher consultation: Conceptual and research considerations. *Journal of School Psychology, 30*(2), 117–39.

Shriner, G., Ysseldyke, J., & Christenson, S. (1989). Assessment procedures for use in heterogeneous classrooms. In S. Stainback, W. Stainback & M. Forest (Eds.), *Educating all students in the mainstream of regular education* (pp. 159–81). Baltimore: Paul H. Brookes.

Smith, C. (1993). Cultural sensitivity in working with children and families. In J.L. Paul & F.J. Simeonsson (Eds.), *Children with special needs: Family, culture, and society* (pp. 113–21). Montreal: Harcourt Brace Jovanovich.

Smith, W. (1994). *Equal educational opportunity for students with disabilities: Legislative action in Canada.* McGill University: Office for Research on Educational Policy.

Sobsey, D., & McDonald, L. (1988). Special education: Coming of age. In B. Ludlow, A.P. Turnbull & R. Luckasson (Eds.), *Transitions to adult life for people with mental retardation: Principles and practices* (pp. 21–44). Baltimore: Paul H. Brookes.

Spearling, D. (1994). Assessment and reporting: A natural pair. *Educational Leadership, 52*(2), 10–13.

Squires, D. (1994). Multi-level instruction. *Keeping in Touch* (Newsletter of the Canadian Council for Exceptional Children), October 3–4.

Stainback, S., Stainback, W., & Forest, M. (1989). *Educating all students in the mainstream of regular education.* Baltimore: Paul H. Brookes.

Stainback, W., & Stainback, S. (1990a). Facilitating peer supports and friendships. In W. Stainback & S. Stainback (Eds.), *Support networks for inclusive schooling: Interdependent integrated education* (pp. 51–64). Baltimore: Paul H. Brookes.

Stainback, W., & Stainback, S. (Eds.). (1990b). *Support networks for inclusive schooling: Independent integrated education.* Baltimore: Paul H. Brookes.

Stainback, W., Stainback, S., & Wilkinson, A. (1992). Encouraging peer supports and friendships. *Teaching Exceptional Children, 24,* 6–11.

Steere, D.E., Wood, R., Pancsofar, E.L., & Rucker, R.E. (1993). Vocational training for secondary-level students with severe disabilities. *Teaching Exceptional Children, 25*(4), 7–11.

Strickland, B. (1993). Parents and the educational system. In J.L. Paul & F.J. Simeonsson (Eds.), *Children with special needs: Family, culture, and society* (pp. 231–55). Montreal: Harcourt Brace Jovanovich.

Taylor, S., & Searl, S. (1987). The disabled in America: History, policy, and trends. In P. Knoblock (Ed.), *Understanding exceptional children and youth* (pp. 5–64). Boston: Little, Brown & Co.

Thorin, E., & Irvin, L. (1992). Family stress associated with transitions to adulthood for young people with severe disabilities. *Journal of the Association for Persons with Severe Disabilities, 17,* 31–40.

Thousand, J.S., Villa, R.A., & Nevin, A.I. (Eds.). (1994). *Creativity and collaborative learning: A practical guide to empowering students and teachers.* Baltimore: Paul H. Brookes.

Turnbull, A.P. (1985). "Positive contributions that members with disabilities make to their families." Paper presented at the American Association on Mental Deficiency Annual Meeting, Philadelphia, PA.

Turnbull, A.P., & Summers, J.A. (1985). "From parent involvement to family support: Evolution to revolution." Paper presented at the Down Syndrome State-of-the-Art Conference, Boston, MA (April).

Turnbull, A.P., & Turnbull, H.R. (1990). *Families, professionals, and exceptionality: A special partnership* (2nd edition). Toronto: Merrill.

Turnbull, A.P., Summers, J.A., Backus, L., Bronicki, G.J., Goodfriend, S.J., Roeder-Gordon, C. (1987). *Stress and coping in families having a member with a developmental disability.* Washington, DC: DATA Institute.

Turnbull, H.R., Turnbull, A.P., Bronicki, G.J., Summers, J.A., & Roeder-Gordon, C. (1989). *Disability and the family: A guide to decisions for adulthood.* Baltimore: Paul H. Brookes.

U.S. Department of Education (1987). *What works: Research about teaching and learning* (2nd edition). Washington, DC: U.S. Department of Education.

Van Reusen, A.K., Harrell, J.E., & Lasky, B.A. (1987). *The education planning strategy.* Lawrence, KS: Excellent Enterprises.

Villa, R.A., & Thousand, J.S. (1992). Student collaboration: An essential for curriculum delivery in the 21st century. In S. Stainback & W. Stainback (Eds.), *Curriculum considerations in inclusive classrooms: Facilitating learning for all students* (pp. 117–42). Baltimore: Paul H. Brookes.

Villa, R.A., Thousand, J.S., Stainback, W., & Stainback, S. (Eds.). (1992). *Restructuring for caring and effective education: An administrative guide to creating heterogeneous schools.* Baltimore: Paul H. Brookes.

Vitello, S., & Soskin, R. (1985). *Mental retardation: Its social and legal context.* Englewood Cliffs, NJ: Prentice-Hall.

Wehman, P. (1992). *Life beyond the classroom: Transition strategies for young people with disabilities.* Baltimore: Paul H. Brookes.

Wehman, P., Moon, M.S., Everson, J.M., Wood, W., & Barcus, J.M. (1988). *Transition from school to work.* Baltimore: Paul H. Brookes.

Wikler, L., Wasow, M., & Hatfield, E. (1983). Seeking strengths in families of developmentally disabled children. *Social Work,* 313–15.

Willard, E. (1994). Redesigning schools to make inclusion work. *Journal of Emotional and Behavioral Problems, 3*(3), 24–27.

Wolfensberger, W. (1975). *The origin and nature of our institutional models.* Syracuse, NY: Human Policy Press.

C H A P T E R 11

Computers in Secondary Education: Practices Today, Preparing for Tomorrow

Maurice G. Hollingsworth

Palliser Regional Schools

Introduction

The challenges faced in today's classrooms may largely be attributed to changes in our social structure and advances in technological development. North American schools face greater diversity than ever before. From our pluralistic society, students arrive from different cultures, with vastly differing value structures. As a group, students offer more heterogeneity in terms of ability, aptitude, and values than students from previous generations.

Such diversity brings strength in that it is representative of the pluralistic community where we live. It also brings serious challenges to today's teacher, a teacher who has a mandate to prepare his or her charges for a world beyond high school, a world where change is rapid and ever-evolving technologies increase the pace.

This chapter focuses upon one of the most revolutionary forces that has affected education over the past several hundred years. Computing technologies will influence students, not only within the confines of today's schools, but well beyond such geographical boundaries. These technologies will revise our concepts of education and our methods of educating people. Most fundamentally, computing technologies will modify our lives in terms of communications, culture, and our approaches to learning. Alan Kay (1991, p. 148) aptly observes:

> I have no doubt that as pervasively networked intimate computers become common, many of us will enlarge our points of view. When enough people change, modern culture will once again be transformed, as it was during the Renaissance.

Employment and Education

As a base point for exploring diversity and the role of technology in education, it would be worthwhile to first examine the broad objectives of educating students in secondary educational settings. First and foremost, a general objective may be to educate students so their entrance into the world beyond high school is met with a level of preparedness that gives them both confidence and a set of abilities that will enable them to succeed.

Second, we must prepare learners who have an appreciation for learning and view learning as an ongoing lifelong process. The rate of change in today's world requires ongoing upgrading of skills and knowledge. Many job types require higher levels of education than previously and many other types of jobs are being eliminated or phased out due to changes in technology and the economy. It has been suggested that the average employee will see two or three career changes during their employable years; such change requires an ability and interest in ongoing learning.

Employment Levels of People with Disabilities

According to Statistics Canada, approximately 13% of our population have some form of disability that interferes with daily living activities (*Highlights from the Canadian Health and Disability Survey,* 1985). Although this is a relatively large proportion of our population, it has not been until the past few years that some of the needs of this group have been identified within our legislation. The Canadian Charter of Rights and Freedoms, section 15(1) (Greene,

1989) specifies the requirement for equal rights for minorities in Canada and specifically includes people with a "mental or physical disability." This legislation was later followed with the passage of Bill 62 (1986), which addressed the need for equity employment. This bill requires all federally regulated employers with 100 or more employees to develop an annual plan defining their implementation of an employment equity program. This plan must then be submitted to the Minister of Employment and Immigration and is available for public inspection (Coates, 1986).

However, even given the identification of this group of people and the further legislative milestones toward improving employment equity, people with disabilities generally remain unemployed and are much less likely to be employed than their nondisabled counterparts. Gower (1988) found that 42% of disabled Canadians were employed, whereas 67% of the nondisabled population of the same age bracket—15 to 64 years—were employed. A refined analysis of these figures (Hollingsworth, 1992) suggests that level of education seriously impacts the probability of being employed. The greater the level of education held by the individual, the greater the likelihood that the individual will be employed. This is most pronounced for people with disabilities. People with disabilities with elementary or no education are much less likely to be employed when compared to people with disabilities who have received a post-secondary education. Only 28% of disabled women with elementary or no education are employed, whereas 69% of disabled women with a post-secondary education are employed.

A similar trend is found in the statistics of men with a disability: 33% of men in this group that have an elementary or no education are employed. In contrast, 78% of disabled men who have a post-secondary education are employed. The difference in probability of employment for people with disabilities, given these different education levels, is striking. There seems to be little doubt that higher levels of education do hold a strong benefit for people in general, and particularly for people with a disability in the realm of employment.

These statistics could simply be viewed relative to their effect upon gross national product. However, at a human level it represents much more than this. Employment provides not only a source of income and security for the future but it also forms much of how we define ourselves.

Employment in the Information Age

If employment, per se, is fundamental to our psychological well-being, then access to employment and choice of employment are equally fundamental. Choice can only be accommodated if one's education and experiences effectively meet the requirements of the job market. For example, training, knowledge, and experience in the art of typesetting, using older lead-based plating technologies, will not lend itself directly to employment using today's technologies. Knowledge of automotive technologies is not complete in today's market without some background in using electronics-based diagnostic tools. Secretarial positions generally require some knowledge of word processing versus strictly requiring typing skills. Most analyst positions require advanced analysis tools using a computer.

Business Week (1993) reports that technology is indeed reshaping the labour market. Although the economy grew in 1992, several hundred thousand technical, clerical, and middle-management positions were eliminated. Most of these eliminations were attributed to technologies that provided information and new ways of completing old jobs. However, this is not to conclude that on the grand scale jobs in general are on the decline due to advances in technology. Rather, it is indicative of how employment is changing and how the type of jobs available are changing. While positions in the clerical, technical, and middle-management areas were shrinking, jobs in computer-related areas were growing. Jobs in companies that supply software and data-processing services witnessed growth, as did jobs in technology consulting. The authors cite data from the Bureau of Labor Statistics that indicate growth has occurred in excess of 6% over the previous four years in the following areas: software and computer services, education, cable television, business consulting, movie production, health care, museums, and recreation services.

As a short, nonscientific exercise, the author conducted a case study of a local newspaper. He created three categories of job types. First were those that involve direct computing, such as computer-assisted designers, programmers, systems analysts, and computer graphic designers. Second were those jobs that involve information management at the more general level, typically involving the use of computers. These positions included such job types as data management, risk analysts, and market analysts. Finally, there was the category of positions that made no direct or indirect mention of computing skills. Such jobs may or may not involve the use of computers, but made no mention of such background in the advertisement.

Scanning through a local newspaper, the *Calgary Herald,* yielded a listing of 116 advertised positions. Categorizing these into each of the three job types resulted in the following rough statistics: 32% of the positions required direct, ongoing use of computing skills; 26% of the positions were information management positions; and 42% of the positions made no direct comment regarding the necessity of computing background, although such background may have proven advantageous in competition for these positions. Figure 11.1 summarizes these statistics and highlights the fact that more than 50% of the advertised positions related directly or indirectly to experience in using information-age tools on the job.

FIGURE 11.1
Advertised Job Types from the *Calgary Herald* (November 14, 1992)

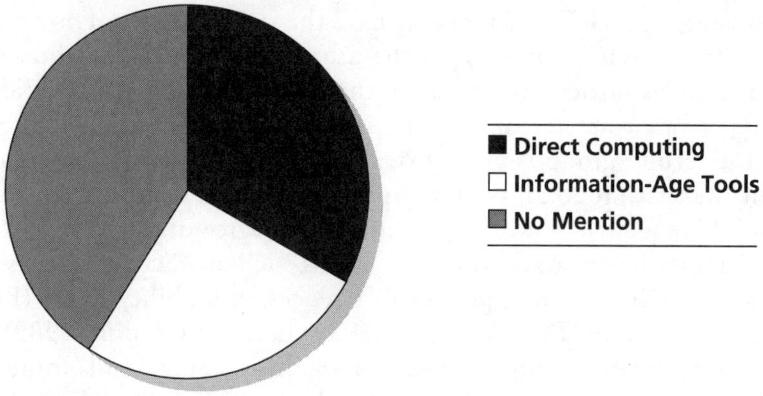

Educational Equity in the Information Age

Given that information-age tools, access to these tools, and opportunity to use these tools across a breadth of problem-solving environments are critical to the preparation of young people for an employment arena quite unlike that of even 10 years ago, we must be conscious of and work fervently toward ensuring equity in the utilization of modern computing technologies. Sharon McCoy Bell, recipient of the 1993 Computerworld Smithsonian Information Technology Leadership Award for Education, summarizes equity concerns by looking at the impact of the "information highway" (Stephenson, 1994, p. 9).

> Highways, whether they are sea lanes or interstates or paths through the wood—highways connect people. Now in America, the highways led to the creation of the suburbs. Now I can live in Connecticut and I can work in New York City, and I can leave the problems behind me. So with the information highways, you leave the have-nots behind the same way the interstate highways left the have-nots somewhere else. Maybe not in a geographical location, but in a conceptual, academic, cognitive place. All the haves will move to this higher plane of thinking and all the have-nots are left here.

Until such time as computers become as ubiquitous as hand calculators we must ask, "How do we ensure equal access to information-age technologies?" In other words, how do we avoid a two-tier education system, where some students hold ready access to technologies and other students simply lack access?

Before exploring research on equity and computers, it is important to have a firm understanding of the meaning of equity. Writers have generally differentiated between the terms **equity** and **equality** (Sutton, 1991). Equality describes sameness in quantity; for example, each group of students is given the same set of software or each individual may have the same number of hours of access to computers in school. Equity on the other hand carries a qualitative property that implies justice; for example, the first group is given additional specialized software to meet some of the specialized needs within that group or maybe the second group is given extra computer time at school because students in the first group all own computers at home. Equity, then, may be a purposeful inequality that brings about some degree of justice.

Researchers have looked at equity across such characteristics as socioeconomic status, ethnic origin, gender differences, and ability levels (Becker & Sterling, 1987; Collis, Kass & Kieren, 1989; Levin & Gordon, 1989). Sutton (1991) in a review of the literature looked at equity and computers in pre-college education during the 1980s. Her review examined gender, social class, and racial inequities with regard to access to computers. This review generally revealed that females, lower socioeconomic status (SES) groups, and racial minorities typically had less access to computers. Additionally, she looked at process variables and outcome variables in the literature. Her research suggests that not only does equity need to be explored within the context of "access," but it also must be explored with regard to type of computer use.

Sutton summarily states, "The evidence indicates that computer use during the 1980s did not bring education closer to equal education opportunity. Rather it maintained and exaggerated existing inequities in education in input, processes of computer learning, and output" (p. 494).

Some current, and more focused, research brings future hope to Sutton's somewhat negative findings. One must be mindful that a tremendous influx, though not yet fully realized influx, of computers into classrooms occurred through the 1980s. Bearing this in mind, one might anticipate shifts in availability, access, and type of utilization.

Nolan, McKinnon, and Soler's (1992) research highlights some aspects of such a shift. Their study of 240 junior high school New Zealand students compares a number of results to an earlier (1988) study. They noted that, although home access to a computer was still less for students of lower SES families compared to higher SES families (1.6:1), the ratio had improved since their 1988 study (2.1:1).

Art Bardige, chairperson of the Software Publishers Association's National Curriculum Standards Committee, draws an interesting analogy when looking at the equity issue. He likens technology equity access to the dilemma faced by education a century ago as schools turned from recitation boards (small easels) to textbooks and books. At that time, people did not know how they would afford the movement to books, yet maintained it as a vision that led to a textbook-driven curriculum. One of the solutions to the potential inequity at that time led to the building of libraries (Mageau & Chion-Kenney, 1994). Solutions to today's inequities likely exist. We simply need the creativity and energy to achieve such solutions.

Computing Applications in Secondary Education

During the past decade, a shift has occurred from using computers as programming tools and instruments for "technology literacy" to using computers as tools for learning. During the initial phases of this shift, business education courses taught students how to use information-age tools. However, the role of computing tools extends beyond the convenience of modifying, adding, or deleting bits of information. As the functionality of computing tools evolved and as access to computers improved, creative teachers found computers fulfilled a critical role as tools to develop critical thinking and problem-solving skills.

Authors such as Salomon, Perkins, and Globerson (1991) have explored how computing technologies can extend human intelligence and can serve as partners in problem-solving environments. These authors distinguish between effects *with* technology, more specifically having an effect on a problem at hand, versus effects *of* technology, more specifically generalized problem-solving abilities resulting from use of the technology. An example is in order. One may display certain arithmetic skill in using an abacus. This represents effects with technology. This is differentiated from the ability the abacus user may develop and adopt even in the absence of the abacus; simply as a result of ongoing practice in using the abacus, certain skills are developed that otherwise may not exist. This is the effect *of* technology. The distinction is important. Technology may serve not only to resolve specific problems at hand, but it may also modify the manner in which we resolve other problems in the absence of the technology.

This following discussion examines critical thinking and problem-solving skills within the context of some of the primary computing software tools that are available in schools today. Independent of computer brand or model, almost all microcomputers are capable of running the following software tools—some with more ease of use than others. The choice of primary applications has been purposeful. None of these software tools require expensive, "high-end" computing hardware that may or may not be accessible in the average school.

This is not to argue against fast and extremely flexible computing hardware. Such hardware also plays an important role in education. It is recognized, however, that, frequently, access to such equipment is limited.

Word Processing

Word processing is one of the most popular and well-utilized software applications currently available on microcomputers. Teachers perceive it as the most useful of all software applications for their own use as well as for their students (Woodrow, 1991). There is little doubt that word processing makes revision and other surface level modifications easier and faster. If, however, this is the only outcome of moving from pen and paper to computer, then this advent, in effect, provides only a surface level improvement.

Hawisher (1989) in a brief summative review of writing research finds that surface-level revision, namely editing mechanical errors, is employed by students in their use of computers. Students generally submit papers that have fewer mechanical errors when using a word processor over using a handwritten approach. Although the findings are relatively conclusive that students using computers generally produce work with less surface-level errors, the research is somewhat less clear regarding improvements in quality of writing when students use computers.

Snyder (1993) presents a well-controlled quasi-experimental study comparing the writing skills of students using a computer to those using pen and paper. Given the longitudinal nature of this study, some of the controls managed within the study, and the fact that active instruction and leadership were provided to guide students toward quality writing, this study is worthy of close consideration. Snyder's study includes 51 year-8 Australian students from two classes. Although it was not possible to randomly assign students to the control and experimental groups, the researcher did measure the difference between the two groups across such variables as English marks, mathematics marks, and performance on the ACER Intermediate Test G. There were no statistically significant differences between the two groups on these variables.

Other significant controls found in this study included having the same teacher instruct both control and experimental groups. The writing program was devised collaboratively by the teacher and researcher and was aimed at creating an environment in which students were actively engaged in writing. The primary writing principles that provided the conceptual framework for instruction were the value of explicit instruction, an understanding of the processes by which texts are written and improved, and the importance to the writer of assessing the quality of the final product.

Students were expected to take an active role in shaping their own writing through the revisionary process. A distinction was drawn for students between revision as simply a mechanics exercise—correcting spelling, grammar and general proofreading—as opposed to revision as a higher-level skill involving rethinking and restructuring their work.

The study covered an eight-month period with four 50-minute classes being held every six school days. One group completed all writing exercises using pen and paper, while the second group used a computer and a word-processing program (Apple IIe with *Bank Street Writer*).

Three focal genres of writing were targeted: narrative form, argument, and report. Throughout the study, students in both groups were expected to submit a completed writing task every two weeks. Time was held constant for students in both groups to complete written assignments. Additionally, students were invited on a weekly basis to make entries into an ongoing journal.

A pre-test on each of the genres was given to students in both groups prior to the study and a post-test on each of the genres was given at the end of the study. In all, this provided a sample of 306 writing samples. Each writing sample was retyped, including errors, to counter any potential bias in marking the pen-based versus word-processor-based assignments.

The following measures were applied to these writing samples: a) text production, which simply looked at the number of words as a measure of productivity and a correlate of quality, b) text complexity based upon a syntactic complexity measure, c) text precision as a measure of spelling, punctuation, grammar, and usage, d) global quality assessment as a holistic measure of overall quality, and e) a pooled global score as a composite score of each of the above.

Results of this study found no difference between groups on either the text production or text complexity measure. Statistically significant differences were found between groups on text precision, namely the students' abilities to find and modify spelling, punctuation, and grammar errors. Students in the computer group demonstrated fewer mean errors across all three genres on both the pre-test and on the post-test when compared to the pen-based group.

Similarly, on global quality ratings students from the computer-based group generally outperformed the pen-based group. Statistical significance was found on the "argument" and the "report" genres. This finding is particularly relevant when one considers that the skills found in argument and report genres are skills that extend into other high school curricular areas and into most post-secondary curricular areas.

Finally, the pooled global scores yielded a statistically significant difference between groups, suggesting that the use of the word processor contributed to improved quality over students using pen and paper.

Integrating Word Processing

Word processing appears to benefit students not only in terms of improving their editing capabilities and practices, but most importantly in terms of improving their overall quality of writing. Students writing with a word processor tend to submit papers that are of higher quality than those submitted using pen and paper.

Word processing may serve as a foundational software tool for students. It can be used as the base tool for importing most other types of application software data. It may be used as a base point to conceptually link parts of a database, a spreadsheet, graphical information, graphs, and thoughts acquired through "on-line" telecommunications.

Databases

A fundamental skill in today's information intensive society is the ability to find specific information amid large bodies of information. Databases serve as organizational bodies that contain large sets of information. The ability to actively search information within these databases, and even the ability to develop small databases, are vital skills in today's work and study environments. In a survey of secondary teacher perceptions of computer needs, Woodrow (1991) found that teachers rated "databank accessing" as the second greatest area of computer need held by their students. Eighty-four percent of the teachers surveyed felt database access was a useful or extremely useful skill.

Databases have the power to directly involve students in the curricula, rather than simply observe hypothesis and relations from the sidelines. As reported by Pea (1987), databases, though originally popular in science and business classes, are now serving a role in social studies, home economics, and health education.

As an example, Jagger, Layton, and Veek (1988) describe a small database and how it can be used to involve students in secondary social studies research. The authors developed a database to teach students about world power. One of their databases consisted of 167 countries each with 28 database categories. These categories included such factors as population, gross national product, political system, alliance membership, literacy level, area, value of imports and exports, number in armed forces, and percentage of population with safe drinking water.

Unlike the traditional textbook, students were able to interact with the information, creating and testing hypotheses, searching for specific pieces of information, and creating new information from existing information (i.e., energy deficiency based upon amount of energy consumed and amount of energy produced). Active comparisons were possible. For example, in one lesson students were asked to compare a highly industrialized democracy, Japan, to a highly industrialized Marxist-Leninist state, USSR, and then to a third-world country, Bangladesh. Questions that sprung from such an interactive learning environment were dynamic in nature: what factors might be important to consider, or where do some of the largest differences appear? Students were able to formulate comparisons and ideas not otherwise attainable and achieve results not otherwise possible within the same time frame.

Databases may reside within a single computer's hard disk drive, on a schoolwide network, or be accessible through a telecommunications network. Naturally, the larger the scope of the database or the more specialized the database, the more likely one may need to use telecommunications as a vehicle to a distant database.

Integrating Databases

Databases serve the curriculum anywhere that quantities of organized information may be found. Therefore, many parts of our high school curriculum could use a database as a basis for concept development. As another additional social studies example, one may maintain a country-by-country "visual database" of a variety of countries. As various current events information is raised in class, graphical pictures, and maybe even animation clips of famous people from that country could be accessed from the database. Additionally, the database may serve as a basis for comparing geographic, political, and social aspects of the country with other countries.

Databases provide a powerful means of viewing, controlling, and organizing information. Naturally, such a tool is central in an era where information has become fundamental.

Spreadsheets

Although spreadsheet instruction originated in the business education lab, applications for spreadsheets are found in math classes, science classes, and other settings that need to explore interdependent quantitative variables. Much attention has been paid over the past several years to the areas of problem solving and critical thinking as skills that are vital to today's graduating students. Computer spreadsheets represent one of the tools that are fundamental to the application of new problem-solving strategies in the Information Age. Lambrecht (1993) refers to such tools as "cognitive enhancers."

Spreadsheets may be used in one of two manners. Students may be expected to develop templates for solving given problems, then use these self-developed templates as a basis for solving problems. Alternatively, students may be provided templates to solve given problems. Lambrecht argues that the latter approach may be most appropriate for addressing the cost-accounting area. Student development of a template was found not to improve accounting achievement and also limited repetitive application of problems to the same template. The objective in Lambrecht's research was to have students learn a hierarchy of concepts of increasing conceptual complexity: concepts ranging from "percentage/rate/base" and simple interest to concepts of present value and future value annuities. Construction of a spreadsheet template for each of the seven concepts in the curricula was seen as a potential distracter away from the primary intent of teaching business concepts concerning time value of money: "...teachers wishing to focus on business concepts recognize that understanding spreadsheet operations does not assure correct solution to business problems: understanding business concepts is fundamental to an accurate spreadsheet solution (McCombs, 1986; Weida, 1991)" (Lambrecht, 1993, p. 512). Lambrecht points out that helping students avoid the mechanics of calculating through the provision of pre-developed spreadsheet templates allows them to focus on concepts at a more advanced level. Students are able to study a given problem, determine the model that best applies to this problem type, and then apply the given model to the problem.

This is not to imply that students should never develop their own spreadsheet templates. Rather it signifies that differing curricular objectives and material suggest different approaches.

Integrating Spreadsheets

If there are calculations or mathematical modelling involved in a curricular area, then spreadsheets may provide a valuable tool for exploring the subject area. Math, physics, chemistry, and business education are all senior high school subjects that benefit from effective instruction that integrates computer spreadsheets.

Additionally, simulations are possible via computer spreadsheets. For example, one may use a spreadsheet to teach probability. In a classic introduction to probability, a coin or dice may be tossed repeatedly to demonstrate the probability of given cases arising. A computer simulation of the same event can provide greater conceptual depth.

Telecommunications

Although computing telecommunications capabilities have been available for well over a decade, it is only in the past short while that such capabilities have come to the general public's attention. The "information highway" has recently received significant media coverage as a result of some of the initiatives put forth by the Clinton administration (Gore, 1991) and similar discussions by the Chrétien government.

The common functions available on most data networks and computer bulletin boards include E-mail, forum discussions, data downloading and uploading, and access to large-scale databases. E-mail is quite simply an electronic post office. Communications are sent privately from one individual to another, except that the message may be picked up by the recipient almost immediately after it is sent. Forum discussions are similar to E-mail in that a message is sent to another individual or group. Unlike E-mail, the message is openly posted for anyone to read. This provides a basis for including others in an ongoing discussion on the given topic.

Data uploading or downloading is the capability to move sets of information (i.e., word-processing documents, pictures, or sounds) or computer programs to and from your computer. Authors can share research findings or collaborate on a writing project, while maintaining a smooth flow of information and communications between participants.

Almost any information on any topic is available on-line. For example, the Internet offers information on weekly activity of earthquakes around the world, daily statistical releases from Statistics Canada, all Supreme Court decisions since 1989, United Nations resolutions, the current national weather (including weather maps), and the Americans with Disabilities Act.

A wide breadth of databases are also available on-line. These include such disparate topics as the NASA Extragalactic Database, ERIC, or the National Library of Medicine database. The largest of all of these networks is the Internet. The Internet was created in 1983 as an offshoot of several military networks combined with a number of university networks. Estimates of upward of 20 million people access the Internet, with approximately 3 to 5 million people using it daily.

Integrating Telecommunications

Suggesting what curricular areas would benefit from telecommunications is somewhat like suggesting which curricular areas might benefit from "communication." Telecommunications is in its infancy. It will likely become a key determinant in the way in which students will learn.

Integrating Computers into the Secondary Curricula

To more clearly depict how computers may be integrated into the curriculum and to provide a detailed understanding of the specifics of integrating computers into the curriculum, two sample lessons are presented. These lessons provide an illustration of how computers and information-age skills may be integrated into common secondary education curricula. Each of these samples has been used by the author with students in junior and senior high school settings. These particular lessons have been chosen because they reflect learning with computers, learning across different types of software tools, and learning that provides a focus on skills that relate directly to employment and life after high school.

Sample Lesson 1 (Word Processing/Page Layout)

This lesson is part of a larger instructional unit in a work experience program that draws on the local community for work experiences. The class forms a company that offers specific services contracted to businesses or individuals

TABLE 11.1
Overview of Computing Activities in a Word Experience Unit

Software Type	Associated Activities
Word Processor	• Guide the class through a brainstorming activity to determine the type of work they will target in your community (i.e., mowing lawns, shovelling snow, newsletter delivery, etc.). Use a word processor and, if possible, large-screen projection as a means of noting the various ideas. • Guide the class through another brainstorming activity to determine a name for the company.
Graphics Software	• Study company logos and discuss how they relate to the company image. • Discuss the overall image you want to project through your company image. • Using computer graphics software (i.e., *DazzleDraw, MacDraw, MacPaint, SuperPaint,* or *Paint*), create a logo that projects your company's image.
Print Shop	• Study magazine full-page advertising for ideas on poster advertising. • Prepare a poster advertising the company and service offerings.
Word Processor or Page Layout	• Look at sample invoices from other businesses in the community, then use a word processor to prepare an invoice that reflects your company's logo and image. • Prepare a generic thank-you letter template that can be used later to create personalized company thank-you letters.
Database	• Track potential and current employers, their addresses, and phone numbers.
Spreadsheet	• Track income and expenses within the company.

in the community. The goal of the instructional unit is to help students gain an understanding of the rudiments of starting and running a small business, including such skills as marketing, advertising, customer relations, scheduling, and bookkeeping. Before undertaking a project similar to the following, be sure to investigate requirements specific to your province, jurisdiction, and school that apply to work experience programs.

An overview of some of the computer-related activities within the unit are presented in Table 11.1. This unit is potentially very large in scope; therefore, in the interest of space, only one lesson from this unit is detailed.

Advertisement Lesson (Class: Work Experience Program)

Lesson Objectives

1. Students will identify poster advertising that provides a simple, yet powerful, message.
2. Students will identify poster advertising that makes good use of white space.
3. Students will prepare a poster using the *Print Shop* software program to advertise their company. This poster will project the image of the company that students have determined, in a previous lesson, as important to the company.

Time Frame

- Two 45-minute class periods

Materials

- Computer(s), *Print Shop* software and printer(s)
- Magazines with one-page advertisements

Procedures

1. Using magazines from the school library, lead students through several examples of one-page advertising that are simple and yet provide a powerful message. Contrast these examples with advertising that is less effective either through poor use of white space or through a weak message.
2. Provide students with several magazines. Have students leaf through the magazines, marking both good examples and weak examples of advertising based upon the criteria of good use of white space and a simple, yet powerful, message.
3. Using the logo and image information that the class has determined in a former lesson, have students share ideas on presenting a simple, powerful message that may be used within their own advertisement.

4. Demonstrate how to use the *Print Shop* program to create a single-page advertisement. Point out that for this software program the main keys on the keyboard are the Space Bar, Arrow keys, and the Return key (or the mouse if the software version provides a windowed environment). Show students how to vary fonts, change graphic sizes, and control placement of text and graphics. If time permits, students may develop their own graphics for use within the advertisement. In this case, demonstrate how to use the graphics editor.
5. Provide time for students to use the computer(s) to complete their advertisement. Provide guidance, as necessary, on using the software and in creating a meaningful advertisement.
6. Upon completion of the advertisements, discuss locations and permissions required for posting the information.

The above lesson could be undertaken by using several different types of software. The *Print Shop* (approximately $70, available from Broderbund Software) is presented in this lesson because of its simplicity to use. Besides being very easy to use, it is generally available in most schools. If students are more sophisticated computer users, they may alternatively use other software tools such as a word processor with graphics capability (i.e., *ClarisWorks, Microsoft Works, Microsoft Word* or *WordPerfect*), or if the students are very adept at using computers they may use a page layout program (i.e., *PageMaker*).

The use of the computer is not the focal direction of this lesson, but it makes the task of creating the advertising poster easier and creates a quality product, and the process used by the students in creating the poster more closely parallels the approach and tools generally used by advertising agencies today.

Sample Lesson 2 (Spreadsheets)

This sample lesson is designed to teach students the cost of borrowing money or receiving credit. Students use the computer to "play" with variables, experimentally learning how adjusting various aspects of the borrowing formula—the interest rate, the amortization period, or the down payment—can keep borrowing costs to a minimum.

A variety of amortization programs are available for different computers. Some run as an independent programs, while others work with a spreadsheet. The following example uses a $20 template and associated exercises (available from Learning Designs). It requires *Excel, Lotus 1-2-3,* or other common spreadsheet packages and will work on any Macintosh, MS-DOS, or Windows computer.

Figure 11.2 illustrates the spreadsheet "loan calculator" used in this exercise. Use of the calculator is easy and allows students to focus on the objectives at hand. It enables students to comprehend the effect of each variable on the cost of borrowing, instead of requiring a focus on the mechanics of getting correct numbers into a hand calculator in an extremely long and unwieldy calculational process.

FIGURE 11.2
***It's Your Money* Amortization Calculator**

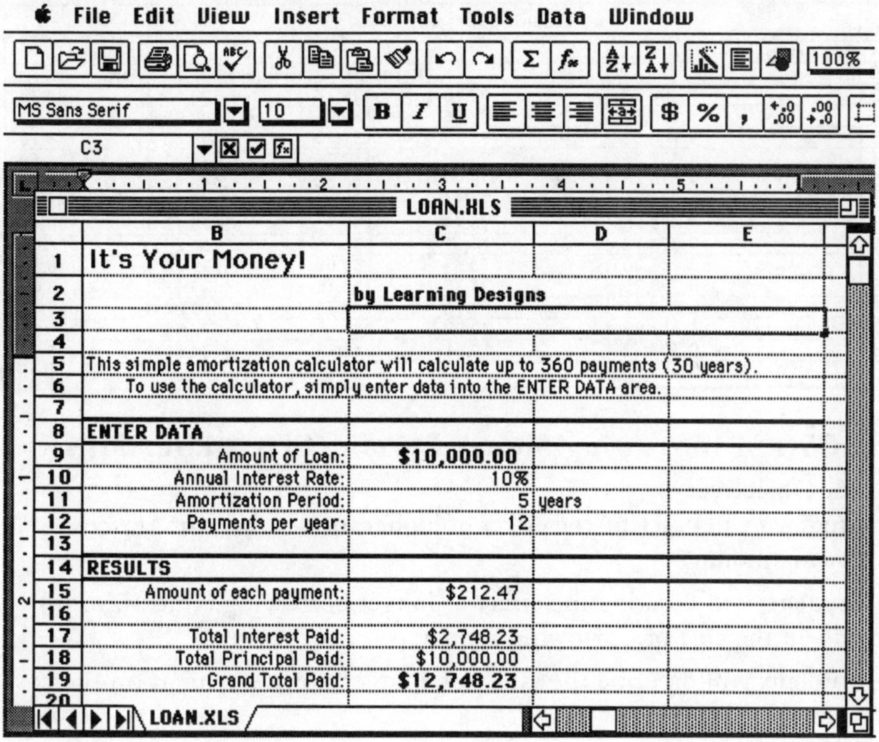

This approach also maintains an advantage over using an amortization book of tables, as it can provide additional background information. Figure 11.3 illustrates how one can see a breakdown of the calculations demonstrating the amounts of interest and principal being applied to each payment.

FIGURE 11.3
It's Your Money Amortization Calculation Details

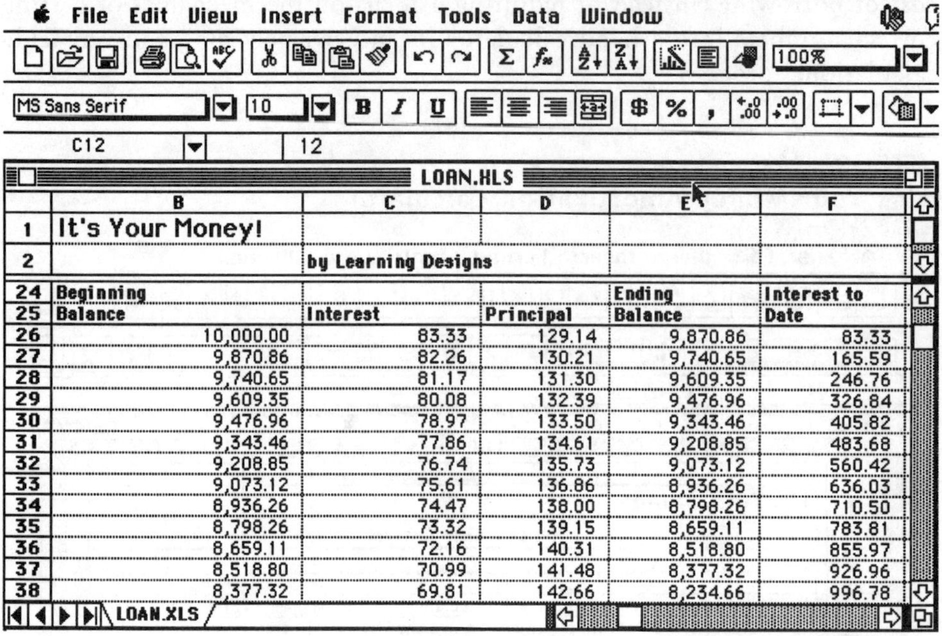

	B	C	D	E	F
1	It's Your Money!				
2		by Learning Designs			
24	Beginning			Ending	Interest to
25	Balance	Interest	Principal	Balance	Date
26	10,000.00	83.33	129.14	9,870.86	83.33
27	9,870.86	82.26	130.21	9,740.65	165.59
28	9,740.65	81.17	131.30	9,609.35	246.76
29	9,609.35	80.08	132.39	9,476.96	326.84
30	9,476.96	78.97	133.50	9,343.46	405.82
31	9,343.46	77.86	134.61	9,208.85	483.68
32	9,208.85	76.74	135.73	9,073.12	560.42
33	9,073.12	75.61	136.86	8,936.26	636.03
34	8,936.26	74.47	138.00	8,798.26	710.50
35	8,798.26	73.32	139.15	8,659.11	783.81
36	8,659.11	72.16	140.31	8,518.80	855.97
37	8,518.80	70.99	141.48	8,377.32	926.96
38	8,377.32	69.81	142.66	8,234.66	996.78

The Cost of Borrowing Money Lesson (Class: Life Skills)

Lesson Objectives

1. Students will describe the effect of higher interest rates on the cost of borrowing money.
2. Students will describe the effect of longer borrowing (amortization) periods on the cost of borrowing money.
3. Students will describe the effect of a larger down payment on the cost of borrowing money.

Time Frame

- Two 45-minute class periods

Materials

- Computers, spreadsheet software and the *It's Your Money* software
- *It's Your Money* handouts (see chapter appendix)
- Classified ads from a newspaper and a listing of current bank rates

Procedures

1. Lead the class toward an understanding of why banks charge interest on loans. Use a simple example of lending a student some money but wanting a given amount of cash in return for forfeiting your money for awhile. Extend this concept to bank loans.
2. Introduce students to the concepts of "principal," "interest," "interest rate," and "amortization period" through the above example.
3. Demonstrate how to use the *It's Your Money* calculator.
4. Give students the *It's Your Money* handouts to be completed using the *It's Your Money* calculator. (See Appendix 11A.)
5. Provide guidance, as necessary, on using the software and in guiding students' comprehension of how each variable impacts the cost of borrowing money.
6. Have students use ads in the newspaper to answer the final questions on the handouts.

Computers and Disability

Not surprisingly, people with disabilities generally require access to the same basic set of software tools as everyone else, but may require "equity tools" to gain access or to gain equitable access to them. As Bromley and Lakatos (1985) point out, there has been high demand to acquire the skills necessary to use basic computing tools.

The world that students enter after high school has changed from the one that most teachers have entered upon their exit of high school or university. Computers have contributed to dramatic change through increased manufacturing using fewer workers, enhanced transportation, distribution and storage systems, and improved communications and telecommunications (Moursund, 1986).

Demands upon the educational system have also changed. The National Education Association of the United States has recommended the placement of a computer on every teacher's desk (Marks, 1989). Educational visionaries such as David Thornburg have explored the finances and logistics of supplying computers for every student and every teacher, as well as providing the necessary staff training and support structures (Betts, 1994). If our educational system encourages students to gain access to computers, integrate computers into curricula and generally gain from the advantages of tools of the 21st century (Alberta Education Technology in Education Committee, 1987), yet fails to ensure equitable access for persons with disabilities (or any other diverse group), we have certainly created a new handicapping condition and compounded the existing handicap.

Part of the solution is to ensure access through "equity tools"—hardware and software tools that are specifically designed to address the needs of a particular disability. These tools may be input devices, output devices, or software with special design features. Equity tools and productivity tools are not necessarily mutually exclusive. For example, a common word processor may be used by the entire class. A student with a visual disability may require a speech synthesis program that works in conjunction with the word processor to provide auditory feedback about what is being typed and what currently exists in the document.

Alternatively, equity tools may serve as independent stand-alone tools that, to some degree, assist the individual in overcoming the disability. The ABLEDATA database, for example, lists several thousand products that may aid individuals with disabilities.

Lazzaro (1993) provides an excellent overview of some of the equity tools and resources that may enhance the lives of people with disabilities. For persons with vision impairments, he details a variety of speech synthesizers that may be used to gain access to a range of other software tools, including the software tools described above. For persons with low vision, he describes numerous magnification systems, some of which are independent hardware components and others that are software based and, hence, able to enlarge the computer screen, again allowing the use of common software tools.

Technologies for persons with hearing impairments incorporate more common technologies such as fax and electronic mail. The visual nature of today's computers lends relatively well to some of the needs of people with hearing impairments. Some specialized software eases use through the provision of visual feedback in place of the typical computer "beep."

Persons with motor impairments or speech impairments sometimes require modifications to ease input into the computer. Adapted keyboards may have enlarged keys, recessed keys, or programmable keys that allow a given key to symbolize more than a single letter. Software is also available to give greater control over the keyboard. For example, simultaneous access to the Shift key and another key can be a barrier for persons with a motor disability, as can the auto-repeat feature built into most keyboards. Software solutions for these and other keyboard problems are presented. For some persons with disabilities, a different system of input is required. For example, this may take the form of a single switch and a scanning keyboard. Alternatively, the user may wear a headset that tracks head movement, then uses a puff and sip switch to simulate the use of a mouse.

From a research perspective, the application of equity tools in combination with support services can assist people with disabilities in an academic environment. Research by Shell, Horn, and Severs (1988) looked at the impact of providing post-secondary disabled students with access to laptop computers, adaptations for computer access (equity tools), instructional support in the use of technology, and academic support services. The primary goal of this project was to enhance academic performance through the combination of traditional academic support services and computing technologies. Shell et al. examined several dependent variables including drop-out rate, semester grade point average (GPA), cumulative GPA, and percentage of students on academic probation or suspension. Results of this research indicated that students who had received the combined support outperformed students who had previously received traditional academic support services in terms of semester and cumulative GPAs. Students who received computer and academic services for their entire time in college had significantly fewer academic suspensions and probationary periods. As well, results suggest that greater use of these services was related to better academic performance.

Similarly, Keddy (1989) found that the use of technology by individuals with disabilities offered improved opportunities. The author indicates that 70% of visually impaired people of working age are unemployed. This contrasts sharply with an American Foundation for the Blind database that indicates only 15% of more than 700 visually handicapped technology users are unemployed.

If the utilization of equity tools improves student progress in post-secondary settings and in employment opportunities, then by simple extension it may be argued that equity tools have an important role to play in secondary settings for students with disabilities. It could easily be argued that disabled students are at further risk of being marginalized by not gaining access to the tools and knowledge base of the Information Age.

Our Role as Teachers

Some of our current approaches to using computers in education may be analogous to a "calculator literacy class." The imaginary "calculator literacy class" is where students are taught how to use calculators. Calculators are not used in any other educational context, but are addressed in this special class. Obviously, this fails to make sense. Why would one not use the calculator as part of the math curriculum or in a physics classroom? Simply decontextualizing the teaching of calculators into a narrow instructional strand via the "calculator literacy class" that has no application within any other context of the educational environs serves little purpose for students studying "calculator literacy." It also leaves students studying math and physics at a disadvantage studying advanced concepts where a calculator may be used to allow focus on the concepts, rather than the mechanics.

Unfortunately, offering decontextualized computer instruction has been our historical approach. If we are to realize effect *with* and effect *of* technologies, students must have ample opportunity to practise using information-age tools as part of an integrated practice—namely within the general context of education, not specifically within decontextualized "computing literacy" segments.

The primary reason that this is failing to occur within classrooms today is simply a lack of teacher knowledge of computers or how to incorporate computers into their instructional area. Sharon McCoy Bell indicates that our challenge is to give teachers the skills necessary to make technology a true learning tool (Stephenson, 1994).

Hasselbring (1991) cites a national survey that indicates less than one-third of education majors perceive themselves to be prepared to teach with computers (American Association of Colleges for Teachers, 1987). Equally problematic, only 30% of teachers have had at least 10 hours of computer training.

Hunt and Bohlin's (1993) research concludes that although students in teacher education programs generally agree that the ability to use computers is a useful skill for living in today's society, many do not see that they need a firm mastery of computers for their future work.

What Steps Can Teachers Take?

1. Learn to use the primary computing tools outlined earlier. In-depth knowledge of these tools is a prerequisite to offering necessary knowledge and skills to your students.
2. Explore methods of integrating computing tools into your teaching as a means of addressing higher-order thinking skills and problem solving.
3. Explore ways of using computing tools to offer greater equity within your classroom.
4. Seek out an Internet account, either through your university or, if you live in a large urban centre, alternatively through a local "freenet."
5. Patiently approach the learning of computers as a "lifelong learning experience."
6. Purchase an affordable computer. High-end computers provide lots of flexibility and speed, but they also include a high-end price tag. If possible, find a computer that has a "windowed" interface. This interface is available on all Macintosh computers and on DOS-based computers with Windows 3.1. The "windowed" user interface provides a more intuitive approach to using the computer.

If you are purchasing a new computer, accept the fact that it will decline rapidly in value as newer machines come onto the market. Also recognize, however, that the older machine, though not as fast, and though may not run some contemporary software, continues to be functional, and will continue to provide you with the ability to run necessary basic computing tools described earlier.

7. Become familiar with a variety of computing resources. This includes software, newsletters, books, magazines, and agencies. See Suggested Resources.

As educators, our ability to provide meaningful information-age tools and learning opportunities that integrate computers into curricular areas is critical to giving our students a worthwhile, valued educational experience. This applies to *all* students in our classrooms and particularly to students with disabilities, students with special needs, or students from other diverse groups.

Summary

This chapter has focused on preparing students, and most particularly students with disabilities, for learning and working in an Information Age by exploring both employment and educational issues. As it is recognized that computing technologies will have an impact on our learning and working lives, we run the risk of introducing serious inequities if we cannot achieve equitable access to computing technologies and instruction using these technologies.

Key computing tools have been discussed (word processors, databases, spreadsheets, and telecommunications) and methods of integrating these into curricular areas have been explored. Specialized "equity tools" were examined that may assist students with disabilities within learning and work environments.

Fundamental computing tools have been the focal topic of the computers in education segment of this chapter. Other areas of computers in education also deserve attention and may be further explored by the reader. These include such topics as multimedia, hypermedia, and software that is designed for the reader's area of specialty or interest (in science: scientific computing tools such as MathCad; in music: software for sound generation and notation; in art: the realm of graphics, animation, and special effects such as morphing; in social studies: access to on-line information, databases, and people; in language arts: e-mail access to communicate with people in distant lands; in early childhood: CD-ROM technologies that are just plain fun; in mathematics: advanced mathematical tools such as Theorist, MathCad, or Mathematica; etc.)

We have computing technologies today that can enhance the way in which we educate our youth. Our youth hold high expectations for contemporary approaches to instruction. The challenge that resides is to prepare ourselves as educators with knowledge and skills that have meaning in an Information Age.

APPENDIX 11A

It's Your Money!

Part I. The Effect of Interest Rate

Question 1: You want to buy a new car that costs $15,000. You have $3000 to use as a down payment. You plan to borrow the rest of the money from your bank. The bank will loan you money at a 8% interest rate. You plan to make monthly payments for the next 4 years on the car.

a. How much money have you borrowed? __________

b. What is the amortization period? __________ years

c. What is the interest rate? __________

d. How much is the monthly payment? __________ per month

e. What are the total interest costs on this loan? __________ **total interest**

ILLUSTRATION 11.1
It's Your Money!

Question 2: This is the same as Question 1 again. However, this time interest rates have risen to 10%.

a. How much money have you borrowed? ___________
b. What is the amortization period? ___________ years
c. What is the interest rate? ___________
d. How much is the monthly payment? ___________ per month
e. What are the total interest costs on this loan? ___________ **total interest**

Question 3: This is the same as Question 1 again. However, interests rates have risen more and are now at 12%.

a. How much money have you borrowed? ___________
b. What is the amortization period? ___________ years
c. What is the interest rate? ___________
d. How much is the monthly payment? ___________ per month
e. What are the total interest costs on this loan? ___________ **total interest**

Write the general rule that applies to Questions 1 to 3.

BORROWING RULE 1. The Interest Rate.
The higher the interest rate that is charged by the bank, the ______ you pay in interest.

Part II. The Effect of the Amortization Period

Question 4: You want to buy new computers to start running your own business. The computers cost $5000. You have $1000 to use as a down payment. You plan to borrow the rest of the money from your bank. It will loan you money at a 10% interest rate. You plan to make monthly payments on the computers for the next 5 years.

a. How much money have you borrowed? ___________
b. What is the amortization period? ___________ years
c. What is the interest rate? ___________
d. How much is the monthly payment? ___________ per month
e. What are the total interest costs on this loan? ___________ **total interest**

Question 5: The same as Question 4, but you decide to make payments across 3 years instead.

a. How much money have you borrowed? ___________
b. What is the amortization period? ___________ years
c. What is the interest rate? ___________
d. How much is the monthly payment? ___________ per month
e. What are the total interest costs on this loan? ___________ **total interest**

ILLUSTRATION 11.2
It's Your Money!

Question 6: The same as Question 4, but you decide to make payments across only 1 year.

a. How much money have you borrowed? __________
b. What is the amortization period? __________ years
c. What is the interest rate? __________
d. How much is the monthly payment? __________ per month
e. What are the total interest costs on this loan? __________ **total interest**

Write the general rule that applies to Questions 4 to 6.

> BORROWING RULE 2. The Amortization Period.
> The less time that you take to pay off your loan, the ________ you pay in interest.

Part III. The Effect of the Down Payment

Question 7: You need to borrow money to buy a house. The house you are buying costs $85,000. The current interest rate is 10%. You have $10,000 to make as a down payment.

a. How much money have you borrowed? __________
b. What is the amortization period? __________ years

c. What is the interest rate? __________
d. How much is the monthly payment? __________ per month
e. What are the total interest costs on this loan? __________ **total interest**

Question 8: The same as Question 7, but you have $15,000 to use for your down payment.

a. How much money have you borrowed? __________
b. What is the amortization period? __________ years
c. What is the interest rate? __________
d. How much is the monthly payment? __________ per month
e. What are the total interest costs on this loan? __________ **total interest**

Question 9: The same as Question 7, but you have $20,000 to use for your down payment.

a. How much money have you borrowed? __________
b. What is the amortization period? __________ years
c. What is the interest rate? __________
d. How much is the monthly payment? __________ per month
e. What are the total interest costs on this loan? __________ **total interest**

ILLUSTRATION 11.3
It's Your Money!

Write the general rule that applies to Questions 7 to 9.

> BORROWING RULE 3. The Down Payment.
> The more you have for a down payment, the ________ you pay in interest.

Part IV. Your Turn

Question 10: You want to buy a car. Use your newspaper to find a car that you would like. You will borrow the money to buy the car. You can pay as much as $200 per month. Also find today's current interest rates in the newspaper and use this as part of your calculation. (*Note:* Usually the bank's interest rate is higher than the prime rate shown in the newspaper.)

What are current interest rates listed in the newspaper? ____________

How much does the car cost? ____________

How much will you place as a down payment? ____________

How much will each monthly payment cost? ____________

What amortization period did you choose? ____________

Why?

____

____

____

How much will you pay in interest costs? ____________

How much will the car cost altogether, counting both interest and principal? ____________

Question 11: Using your understanding of the three rules of borrowing, answer each of the following questions.

Which loan will cost less?
a) A loan at an 8% interest rate.
b) A loan at a 10% interest rate. ____________

Which loan will cost less?
a) A loan amortized over 5 years.
b) A loan amortized over 3 years. ____________

Which loan will cost less?
a) A loan with a large down payment.
b) A loan with a small down payment. ____________

SUGGESTED RESOURCES

Agencies, Advocates, and Organizations

Alliance for Technology Access, Jacquiee Brand, Director, 1307 Soana Ave., Albany, CA, 94706. Information, support, and ideas for implementing equity tools.

Apple Computer Office of Special Education, 202525 Mariani Ave., Cupertino, CA, 95014. Advocate and researcher.

Council for Exceptional Children, Technology and Media Division, TAM, c/o CEC, 1920 Association Dr., Reston, VA. Publication that focuses upon contemporary work in using technologies with people who have disabilities.

IBM Corp., National Support Centre for Persons with Disabilities, PO Box 2150, Atlanta, GA, 30055. Advocate and researcher.

Technical Resource Centre, #200, 1201-5 St. S.W., Calgary, AB. An exemplary model of providing information, offering assessments, and loaning software and equity tools to assist people with disabilities.

Trace Research and Development Centre, S-151 Waisman Centre, 1500 Highland Ave., Madison, WI, 53705. Researches equity tools. Provides information on equity tools for various types of disabilities.

Software Resources

Aldus Corp., 411 First Ave. S., Seattle, WA, 98104. Primary titles: *PageMaker; SuperPaint.*

Broderbund Software, 500 Redwood Blvd., P.O. Box 6121, Novato, CA, 94948. Primary titles: *Print Shop; Living Books Series; DazzleDraw.*

Claris Corp., 5201 Patrick Henry Dr., Santa Clara, CA, 95052. Primary titles: *ClarisWorks; MacDraw; MacPaint.*

Davidson Software, P.O. Box 2961, Torrance, CA, 90509. Primary titles: *Math Blaster; KidWorks.*

Learning Designs, 18 Edgewood Blvd., Lethbridge, AB, T1K 6G7. Primary titles: *It's Your Money; Master Geographer.*

Microsoft Corp., One Microsft Way, Redmond, WA, 98052. Primary titles: *Microsoft Word; Microsoft Excel; Microsoft Windows; Paint Program.*

Sampling of Resources that Address Disabilities and Equity Tools

ABLEDATA Database—Assistive technologies database. *Contact:* 800-227-0216; 301-588-9284.

ABLED-LINK—Bulletin board (Calgary, AB). *Contact:* 403-282-4459.

America Online—Telecommunications service with several information areas. *Contact:* 800-227-5938; 703-448-8700.

Closing the Gap News (newsletter & conference)—Newsletter of adaptive technologies and approaches. *Contact:* P.O. Box 68, Henderson, MN, 56044.

CompuServe—Telecommunications service with several information areas. *Contact:* 800-848-8199; 614-457-0802.

Internet (a complete list of relevant Internet resources is too lengthy to include)—Behavioral and Emotional Disorders in Children, Blindness, Communication Disorders, Deafness, and Research and disability. *Contact:* listserv@suvm.inre.asu.edu; listserv@uafsysb.uark.edu; listserv@rpitsvm.bitnet; listserv@siucvmb.bitnet; listserv@ryevm.ryerson.edu.

Square_Hole_BBS—Bulletin board (Nanaimo, BC). *Contact:* 604-754-0838.

Trace R&D Center—Rehabilitation aides research and development. *Contact:* 608-262-2966; 608-263-5408 (TDD).

Vision BBS—Bulletin board (Ottawa, ON). *Contact:* 613-523-8199.

(i) Table 3. A sampling of resources that address disabilities and "equity tools."

(ii) Note: Bulletin Boards are often volunteer services and can change phone numbers or fall out of existence without warning.

(iii) Note: A complete list of relevant Internet resources is too lengthy to include.

Books, Magazines, Newsletters, and Audiovisuals

Adaptive Technologies for Learning and Work Environments, American Library Assoc., Chicago, IL. Good introduction to the variety of "equity tools." Excellent list of resources in the appendices.

Closing the Gap News, P.O. Box 68, Henderson, MN 56044. Excellent newspaper on current "equity tools."

International Society for Technology in Education (ISTE), 1787 Agate St., Eugene, OR, 97403. Excellent source of written material and some software for pre-college teachers. Also offers Distance Education courses for university credit.

Ready, Set, Go! SET-BC, British Columbia Ministry of Education (1990). VHS 15 min. Information on assistive device.

The Computing Teacher, ISTE Publication. Monthly magazine. Great source of ideas for integrating technology into the classroom.

REFERENCES

Alberta Education Technology in Education Committee. (1987). *Visions 2000: A vision of educational technology in Alberta by the year 2000.* Alberta Education.

Becker, H.J., & Sterling, C. (1987). Equity in school computer use: National data and neglected considerations. *Journal of Educational Computing Research, 33*(3), 289–311.

Betts, F. (1994). On the birth of the communication age: A conversation with David Thornburg. *Educational Leadership, 51*(7), 20–23.

Borow, H. (1979). Shifting postures toward work: A tracing. In S.G. Weinrach (Ed.), *Career counseling: Theoretical and practical perspectives.* New York: McGraw-Hill Book Co.

Bromley, J., & Lakatos, J. (1985). Software tools: A one-semester secondary school computer course. *The Computing Teacher, 13*(1), 4–5.

Carpenter, C.L. (1992). Plugging in to the Information Age. *The Computing Teacher, 19*(7), 38–39.

Coates, M.L.J. (1986). *Employment equity: Issues, approaches and public policy framework.* Kingston, ON: Queen's University Industrial Relations Centre.

Collis, B.A., Kass, H., & Kieren, T.E. (1989). National trends in computer use among Canadian secondary school students: Implications for cross-cultural analyses. *Journal of Research on Computing in Education, 22,* 77–89.

Gleckman, H., Carey, J., Mitchell, R. Smart, T., & Roush, C. (1993). The technology payoff: A sweeping reorganization of work itself is boosting productivity. *Business Week,* June 14, 1993.

Golden, B., & Farmer, C. (1993). *An incomplete guide to the Internet: especially for K-12 teachers and students.* NCSA Education Group, University of Illinois.

Gore, A. (1991). Infrastructure for the Global Village. *Scientific American, 265*(3), 150–53.

Gower, D. (1988). Employment of disabled Canadians. *Canadian Social Trends—Statistics Canada.* Summer issue.

Greene, I. (1989). *The charter of rights.* Toronto: James Lorimer & Co.

Hannafin, R.D., & Savenye, W.C. (1993). Technology in the classroom: The teacher's new role and resistance to it. *Educational Technology, 33*(6), 26–31.

Hasselbring, T.S. (1991). Improving education through technology: Barriers and recommendations. *Preventing School Failure, 35*(3), 33–37.

Hawisher, G.E. (1989). Computers and writing: Where's the research? *English Journal, 78*(1), 89–91.

Highlights from the Canadian health and disability survey: 1983–84. (1985). Statistics Canada, Health Division, Minister of Supply and Services Canada.

Holland, J.L. (1966). *The psychology of vocational choice: A theory of personality types and model environments.* Waltham, MA: Blaisdell Publishing Co.

Hollingsworth, M. (1992). Computing technologies: A cornerstone for educational and employment equity. *The Canadian Journal of Higher Education, 12*(1), 14–26.

Hunt, N.P., & Bohlin, R.M. (1993). Teacher education students' attitudes toward using computers. *Journal of Research on Computing in Education, 25*(4), 487–97.

Jagger, A., Layton, T., & Veek, B. (1988). Making sense of world power. *The Computing Teacher, 15*(9), 16–18.

Kay, A. (1991). Computers, networks and education. *Scientific American, 265*(3), 138–48.

Keddy, B.A.S. (1989). Methods of adapting computers for use by disabled students. *Journal of Postsecondary Education and Disability, 7*(1), 17–16.

Lambrecht, J.L. (1993). Applications software as cognitive enhancers. *Journal of Research on Computing in Education, 25*(4), 506–20.

Lazzaro, J.L. (1993). *Adaptive technologies for learning & work environments.* Chicago, IL: American Library Association.

Levin, T., & Gordon, C. (1989). Effect of gender and computer experience on attitudes towards computers. *Journal of Educational Computing Research, 5,* 69–88.

Mageau, T., & Chion-Kenny, L. (1994). Facing the future. *Electronic Learning, 14*(2), 36–40.

Marks, B. (1989). A computer on every teacher's desk. *Update, 2*(2), 1–2.

Moursund, D. (1986). The information era: What does it mean to education? *The Computing Teacher, 13*(5), 4–5.

Moursund, D. (1989). Why are our colleges of education continuing to graduate computer illiterate teachers? *The Computing Teacher, 16*(9), 4.

Moursund, D. (1990). The Information Age: Evolutionary and revolutionary change. *The Computing Teacher, 17*(7), 4.

Nolan, P.C.J., McKinnon, D.H., & Soler, J. (1992). Computers in Education: Achieving equitable access and use. *Journal of Research on Computing in Education, 24*(3), 299–314.

Pea, R.D. (1987). Integrating human and computer intelligence. In R.D. Pea, & K. Sheingold, (Eds.), *Mirrors of minds: Patterns of experience in educational computing.* Norwood, NJ: Ablex Publishing Corp.

Salomon, G., Perkins, D.N., & Globerson, T. (1991). Partners in cognition: Extending human intelligence with intelligent technologies. *Educational Researcher, 20*(3), 2–9.

Shell, D.F., Horn, C.A., & Severs, M.K. (1988). Effects of a computer based educational center on disabled students' academic performance. *Journal of College Student Development, 29,* 432–40.

Snyder, I. (1993). The impact of computers on students' writing: A comparative study of the effects of pens and word processors on writing context, process and product. *Australian Journal of Education, 37*(1), 5–25.

Stephenson, C. (1994). An interview with Sharon McCoy Bell. *The Computing Teacher, 21*(5), 9–11.

Suerko, B. (1989). Origin of individual difference in importance attached to work: A model and a contribution to its evaluation. *Journal of Vocational Behavior, 34*(1), 28–29.

Super, D.E. (1957). *The psychology of careers: An introduction to vocational development.* New York: Harper & Row Publishers.

Sutton, R. (1991). Equity and computers in the schools: A decade of research. *Review of Educational Research, 61*(4), 475–503.

Weida, N.C. (1991). Teaching students to think of spreadsheets as mathematical models. *Journal of Education for Business, 66*(5), 283–86.

Woodrow, J.E.J. (1991). Teacher's perceptions of computer needs. *Journal of Research on Computing in Education, 23*(4), 475–96.

CHAPTER 12

Promoting Post-School Educational Opportunities for Students with Diverse Needs

Jennifer Leigh Hill

University of Victoria

Introduction

The purpose of this chapter is to discuss the various options available to students with disabilities after completing their secondary education. The chapter will begin with a discussion of the importance of schooling for students, both with and without disabilities, particularly in terms of the changing times that are occurring as Canada enters the 21st century. Statistics on the educational attainment of students with disabilities will be compared to those on students without disabilities, and factors that may contribute to students with unique learning needs leaving school prior to graduation school will be explored. Different approaches to retaining students in school until a graduation certification is awarded will be discussed, as will efforts to ensure students make a successful transition either into the world of work or into the post-secondary educational setting. While it is recognized that not all students with disabilities will be able to complete a post-secondary education for a variety of reasons, one of which being the impact of their disability on their pursuit of further studies, it must also be recognized that there is a gap between those that can complete a high school education and those that do, as well as a gap between those who can complete a post-secondary education and those who actually enrol in such a program. No longer is it acceptable to perpetuate the "culture of low expectations" (Panitch, 1992); teachers, counsellors, and all other interested parties must work collaboratively with students to ensure that students with disabilities are able to meet their true potential.

The Importance of Schooling

Over the past century, the amount of education required by an individual to pursue many vocational opportunities has steadily increased. In the late 1800s, the ability to sign one's name, rather than marking an "X," indicated the individual was literate, and therefore employable; by the early 1900s the possession of the equivalent of a fourth-grade education was necessary for most jobs. After World War II many employment opportunities were beginning to require a minimum of eight years of education; by the 1980s graduation from high school was deemed to be the minimal requirement for 53.3% of all jobs (LaFleur, 1992).

One has only to look at the economic history of Canada to understand the changes in educational standards required for entrance into the labour market. In the early 1900s, Canada was predominantly a rural society and the majority of persons in the workforce were involved in the production of "staples" required to sustain life (e.g., the fur trade, fishing, forestry, and farming). During and after the First World War, rapid commercial and manufacturing development was the hallmark of the emerging Industrial Revolution, which continued until after the Second World War. During this time, as Canada changed from an economy based predominantly on self-sufficiency to an economy based on a free market characterized by a "more sophisticated and complex system of production and exchange" and "an increased number of occupations" (Legendre, 1985), the need for more training was evidenced. Legendre (1985) in examining the relationship between work opportunities, education, and training in this changing world, cited the following factors that lead individuals to seeking additional training: technological progress, office reorganization, the shift toward employment in the tertiary sector (i.e., nonmanual occupational groups), unemployment or the threat of being unemployed, the possibility and the attractions of job mobility, and the search for a higher standard of living.

Now, at the end of the 20th century, another revolution is sweeping across Canada: a technological revolution in which it is expected that there will be a significant reduction in clerical and low-ranking specialized jobs in the tertiary sector, partially balanced by the creation of new specialized jobs in the industries that either produce and/or use the new technologies (Legendre, 1985). As Canada moves from a "low-tech" to a "high-tech" society, the demands for further education are expected to be even greater. While changes in the economic base have led to changes in training needs in order for individuals to enter the highly competitive work source, LeCompte and Dworkin (1991, p. 29) have suggested that there may be three other possible reasons for the current state of "educational inflation." They are as follows: a) the education provided by schools today is so "deficient" that students must remain in school longer in order to achieve the same level of skills that had been mastered in a shorter period of time in the past, b) schools are now functioning as "finishing schools," ensuring that employees will behave in a manner acceptable to their employers, and c) students must acquire more advanced credentials to "distinguish" themselves from others competing for the same job. Regardless of the reasons, the changes have occurred and the importance of schooling has never been greater.

As one would expect, along with a change in educational requirements for job entry, there has been a corresponding decrease in the rate of students leaving school prior to graduation (i.e., drop out rate). [For this chapter, the terms **drop-out, noncompleter,** and **early school leaver** will be used interchangeably, even though the word "drop-out" has developed a "pejorative or stigmatizing connotation associated with individual failure" (Human Resources and Labour Canada, 1993, p. 6). It is not the intent of the author to degrade those who do not complete school prior to graduation.]

The future for students who drop out of school before graduating is bleak. Human Resources and Labour Canada (1993) has reported that early school leavers have fewer jobs, work longer hours in blue-collar primary industries, processing occupations, or service jobs, and receive more public money in unemployment benefits, social assistance/welfare, or family allowances than those who graduate. It was also found that drop-outs were more likely than graduates to be unemployed: 34% of males leavers were unemployed compared to 23% of graduates, and 26% of female leavers were unemployed compared to 18% of graduates. However, it was also reported that 97% of graduates and 96% of drop-outs either planned to pursue further education and/or training or were interested in acquiring new skills.

In a major study undertaken to measure the economic costs of students from the class of 1989 leaving secondary school prematurely, the Conference Board of Canada (LaFleur, 1992) reported that Canada would lose more than

$4 billion over the working lifetimes of the nearly 137,000 youths who had dropped out. It was estimated that each male noncompleter would lose nearly $129,000 in 1992 dollars over his working lifetime compared to the female drop-out who would forfeit $107,000. Aside from examining the market-related factors, such as loss of taxation revenue to the country and lowered lifetime earnings for the individual, the Conference Board also examined the "less easily measured" nonmarket related factors related to dropping out. They included the following: lower nonwage benefits at work (e.g., poorer working conditions, lowered status), lower level of personal health, decreased opportunity for mobility and training, decreased probability of finding a job, lower return on investment portfolio, less highly educated offspring, decreased financial security, and decreased cultural enjoyment (p. 6).

While these findings are disturbing, in the future individuals without a graduation certificate from high school *as well as* some post-secondary education may be seriously disadvantaged in their attempts to find employment. Similar to the changes in the entry level to the job market that have occurred throughout this century, as mentioned previously, new standards for competitive employment are emerging in North America. It has been estimated that 40% of all new jobs created before the year 2000 will require more than 16 years of education and/or training (Employment and Immigration, 1990a) and few will require less than a high school diploma. The following excerpt, from the introduction to a recent report by Employment and Immigration Canada (1990b, p. 1), perhaps best highlights the urgent need for increased training in a changing world:

> Canada's ability to become globally competitive is increasingly dependent upon the capacity of its workforce to acquire new skills and knowledge and upgrade existing ones. The challenges posed by structural changes in the economy, emerging technologies, and pressures to improve productivity mean that the need for adult education and training has never been greater.

Students with Diverse Needs: Statistics Regarding Educational Attainment

While education is considered important for all youth, it has been suggested that schooling may be even more important for persons with diverse learning needs. Marder (1992) posited that "educational credentials attest to skills, knowledge, and a work ethic that can help focus an employer on a person's *abilities* rather than *disabilities* [italics added]" (p. 3-1). While completing a high school program or enrolling in post-secondary studies may not necessarily guarantee future success, if individuals with unique learning needs are going to compete with their nondisabled peers, their teachers, administrators, and parents need to encourage students to remain in school. For not only do the schools provide skill training to students, they also provide the students with important opportunities to access support services, such as counselling and job placement, which may be vital for them to make the transition to the world beyond the high school (Marder, 1992).

The findings of a recently published National Longitudinal Study of Special Educational Students, involving 1930 students with special needs conducted in the United States (Wagner, D'Amico, Marder, Newman & Blackorby, 1992), have shown the drop-out rate for students with disabilities to be higher than that for nondisabled students (37.1 vs. 21% respectively) (Marder, 1992).

While it is unknown how many students with diverse learning, behavioural, linguistic, and/or cultural needs in Canada drop out of school annually, data from Statistics Canada have documented the highest level of schooling obtained by persons who have a disabling condition. The *Health and Activity Limitation Survey* (HALS), a post-censal survey of 3.3 million persons with disabilities (13.2% of the total population) conducted in 1986–87, revealed relatively low levels of education for most persons with a physical or psychological disability (Statistics Canada, 1990). In the group of 1.76 million persons with disabilities in the 15 to 64 year age bracket (10.7% of the total population), 28.9% reported that they had less than eight years of formal schooling (i.e., had dropped out prior to graduation); 39.9% of the respondents indicated that they had finished high school. The combined total of 68.8% is significantly higher than that found for individuals without disabilities in the same age group (i.e., 54.7%) (Statistics Canada, 1989).

Dropouts

Similarities and Differences

While there is disagreement on the meaning of the term **drop-out**, one commonly accepted definition has been proposed by Morrow (1986). In an article entitled "Standardizing Practice in the Analysis of School Dropouts," Morrow defined a **drop-out**, a **noncompleter**, or an **early school leaver** as "any student, previously enrolled in a school, who is no longer actively enrolled as indicated by fifteen days of consecutive unexcused absence, who has not satisfied local standards for graduation, and for whom no formal request has been received signifying enrollment in another state-licensed educational institution" (p. 49). It should be noted, however, that this definition does not attempt to distinguish between those students who leave school voluntarily and those who leave against their own volition.

Reich and Young (1975) in their study of 544 students from inner Toronto schools identified four primary subgroups (and the respective percentages of the total population) within the group of drop-outs who chose to leave school: a) the **work-oriented drop-out**, the student, most often male, who leaves to join the work force because he wants to, (53%); b) the **classic drop-out**, the hostile, aimless, troubled student who leaves school because it represents an unpleasant situation/place (23%); c) the **homemaker**, the female counterpart to the work-oriented drop-out, who may or may not be pregnant at the time of dropping out, and who does not perceive school as necessary to accomplish the goal of setting up a household and raising a family (6%); and d) the **intellectual elite**, the student, most often older than the other drop-outs and closest to completing his or her course of study, who leaves school because it is perceived to be irrelevant, despite the student's ability to succeed in it (3%). Reich and Young also identified two groups of students who leave even though they may wish to remain (or are at least capable of remaining). They included: a) the **family supporter**, the student, most often first-generation immigrant, who is forced by his or her parents to leave due to an obligation to assist the family economically during a period of financial need (7%); and b) the **cultural isolate**, the student, most often a recent immigrant, for whom school is not a pleasant place, due to language problems and social distance from peers, even though the student has had a relative degree of success (i.e., he or she had a satisfactory grade point average at the time of leaving) (2%).

Students who drop out more than once are often referred to as **drop-backs** or **stop-outs**. They are the students who drop out of school temporarily, only to return at a later date, sometimes within the same academic year (i.e., "drop back in"), in order to obtain a high school diploma or its equivalent (i.e., GED). Unfortunately, even though drop-backs return "to school sadder and wiser," many fail in their attempt to obtain a high school diploma (Karp, 1988) and drop out a second time. Those that do remain until graduation are sometimes referred to as **continuers** or **persisters**.

Regardless of why a student opts to drop out, the stigma of dropping out is considered to be devastating by many. Karp (1988, p. 15) perhaps best expressed this notion:

> Drop-outs are the silent third in the system. Although, many might make a lot of noise while they are in class, their leaving generally causes hardly a ripple. They slip from school into a narrowly circumscribed work world, an articulate, sensitive, and adequately intelligent group of young people wearing an academic mark of Cain.

Those who remain in school until graduation, referred to as **graduates** or **school completers**, should be differentiated from those who stay in school until graduation even though they would prefer to leave—a group often referred to as the **tuned out**. These students remain in school physically, but "give up" on school. They are the students who "are entrapped by truancy policies, parental expectations, personal aspirations, and child labor laws" and whose "consequent level of alienation prevents them from being deeply affected by what goes on in school" (LeCompte & Dworkin, 1991, p. 52).

Drop-outs should also be differentiated from those students who leave involuntarily because of being "dropped" by the school. This group includes those who are "aged out" (i.e., students who are required to leave because they have exceeded the age in which the school system provides an education to its residents), those who are forced out or pushed out (i.e., "undesirable" students required to leave due to action taken by the local school administration, such as those who are suspended or expelled for repeated infractions of the school's code of conduct), and those who are excluded from obtaining an education (i.e., students who fall under an exclusionary clause of the local school's act, such as those forced to withdraw as a result of contracting a communicable disease).

Factors Associated with Dropping Out

A considerable body of research has been devoted to examining *why* students drop out of school. According to Gajar et al. (1993, p. 110) two lines of inquiry into the phenomenon have evolved over time. In the past, researchers maintained a student-centred perspective that attempted to identify the personal and family characteristics that are unique to drop-outs; more recently, researchers have begun to examine the organizational and social dimensions of schools that contribute to students leaving school prematurely or to being "at risk" for leaving. These factors have been identified and summarized extensively in the literature and are presented in Tables 12.1, 12.2 and 12.3 (adapted from Barber & McClellan, 1987; Bucci & Reitzammer, 1992; Ekstrom, Goertz, Pollack & Rock, 1986; Gajar, Goodman & McAfee, 1993; Hahn, 1987; Human Resources and Labour Canada, 1993; Karp, 1988; King, Warren, Michalski & Peart, 1988; LeCompte & Dworkin, 1991; Morris, Pawlovich & McCall, 1992; Neufeld & Stevens, 1992; Sullivan, 1988; Wagner, D'Amico, Marden, Newman & Blackorby, 1992; Wehlage & Rutter, 1986; Wolman, Bruininks & Thurlow, 1989). It should be noted that many researchers have concluded that dropping out is not simply the result of the combination of one or two factors, rather those that leave school prematurely leave for a "complex and often interrelated set of academic, social, economic and personal reasons" (Morris et al. 1992, p. 29).

TABLE 12.1
Student-Related Factors Contributing to Students Dropping Out of School

Factors Related to Demographics

- Dropouts are more likely to be male than female (60% vs. 40%, respectively).
- Minority students, excluding students of Asian descent (e.g., Latino and African-American students in the United States, Aboriginal students in Canada) leave school more frequently than nonminority students. In Canada immigrants are less likely to drop out (11%) compared to Canadian-born students (17%).
- The highest drop-out rates occur in grades 9, 10, and 11.
- Ages of dropping out are highest at 15, 16, and 17; those who drop out at 18 or 19 are usually well behind their peers in terms of credit accumulation, making their chance of graduating remote.
- Students tend to drop out in the months of February and March or in the summer following the ninth or tenth grade.
- Drop-outs are more likely than graduates to marry at an earlier age, thus making returning to school to complete their education difficult; many have dependent children.
- Sixty-nine percent of drop-outs (compared to 33% of graduates) come from a "high-risk" background group (e.g., lower SES, single- and no-parent families).

Factors Related to School Performance

- Drop-outs score below average on achievement and aptitude measures; some drop-outs have undiagnosed learning disabilities and/or learning problems; without proper remediation students may blame themselves for their inability to achieve.
- Drop-outs have a poor academic record (i.e., poor grades), lack basic skills (particularly in math and reading), and/or have language difficulties; they are unable to keep up with school work; they do less homework; they also participate less in classes than graduates.
- Drop-outs were previously held back or retained in school (i.e., repeated a grade), resulting in the students being over age. The more a student was retained, the greater the chance the student would drop out before graduation.
- Drop-outs are in general or basic-level courses (i.e., in a lower-ability track).
- Drop-outs dislike one or more courses; many fail one or more classes in the last year of school.
- Drop-outs often do not attend school due to truancy and/or illness, pregnancy, illness in student's family and/or work; school demands and home demands are difficult to reconcile; many students are exhausted from having to go to school, from working part time (particularly those who work more than 15 hours per week), and from having to do their homework.

Factors Related to Personality/Ego

- Drop-outs exhibit low self-esteem and self-confidence and have a poor self-concept; they are often ashamed of the difficulties they are encountering in school; they have fewer friends than students who remain in school; their friends tend to be those not attending any school; they associate with peers who did not consider high school completion important.
- Drop-outs have an externalized locus of control, a low need for self-development, and low feelings of personal efficacy.
- Drop-outs are concrete rather than abstract thinkers, having a tendency to focus on tangible items.
- Drop-outs have inadequate goals and low aspirations; they are short-range goal setters (i.e., they need immediate gratification) and have no plans for post-secondary education.
- Drop-outs are work-driven; work is an "attractive" alternative to school, as is military service (seen as a "safety net" of last resort).
- Drop-outs are forced to make early transition into adulthood. For males, the need to contribute financially to the well-being of the family often is a major factor. For females, the most frequent reasons for dropping out include pregnancy and/or marriage.

Factors Related to Attitude

- Drop-outs feel a general alienation from school; they lack interest in school, as do their friends who also feel alienated; drop-outs often report that they just "don't fit in."
- Drop-outs have a general feeling of boredom; they cannot measure the relevance of their school subjects; to them, education is an abstraction, without proven relevance.
- Students perceive there is little connection between doing well in school and any real rewards out of school; to them school is meaningless and the curriculum is irrelevant; education is neither intrinsically valuable, nor a means to an end.
- Drop-outs have the feeling that no one in school cares and/or is willing to provide help; at-risk students perceive that they are treated differently from high achievers; many report that their teachers are unfair and that they feel neglected and/or misunderstood; many drop-outs leave school without speaking to any staff member.
- Some drop-outs report that the reason they dislike school so much is fear (e.g., fear of gangs, fear of weapons).
- Drop-outs perceive they are too old for school and that they have enough education to go to work; they feel that "real learning" begins when you leave school and get a job; drop-outs have low educational and occupational aspirations.

Factors Related to Attitude (*continued*)

- Drop-outs dislike discipline and rules.
- Drop-outs feel pressured by peers to avoid success in school; they prefer to "hang out" than attend school and succeed; some leave school in an attempt to escape failure.
- Many drop-outs report that "there is nothing" that could persuade them to remain in school. Approximately half of all drop-outs report that at the time they dropped out, they intended to return to school. However, unless they return shortly after dropping out, most fail to complete their high school education, citing "lack of time," "no need for further education," "having a job," or "lacking the money necessary to return," as their most frequent reasons for remaining out.

Factors Related to Deviant Behaviour

- Drop-outs have problems with teachers, school administrators, counsellors, and other students, resulting in disruptive behaviour, discipline problems, and the cutting of classes; this behaviour often leads to detention, suspension, and/or expulsion.
- Drop-outs often have trouble with police, resulting in institutionalization or incarceration.
- Many drop-outs exhibit delinquent behaviour.

TABLE 12.2
Family-Related Factors Contributing to Students Dropping Out of School

Factors Related to Demographics

- Drop-outs come from low socioeconomic status families; poverty, insecurity, poor nutrition, poor hygiene, and homelessness are common; the family moves frequently.
- In a few cases the parents demand that the student leave school to help support the family financially; many families of drop-outs are on welfare.
- Students in urban areas are more likely to drop out than students in rural and suburban areas.

Factors Related to Parents/Siblings

- Drop-outs come from families with single-parent households; the drop-out often has many siblings.
- The father is often employed in blue-collar occupations; the mother often works.

Factors Related to Parents/Siblings (*continued*)

- In comparison to parents of graduates, the parents of drop-outs are not well educated, have lower educational expectations for their offspring, and lack a sense of the value and importance of education; they are less likely to be interested in or to monitor both in-school and out-of-school activities.
- There is a weak educational or motivational support system in the home (e.g., fewer study aids at home, less opportunity for nonschool-related learning).
- The families of drop-outs are often disrupted/chaotic, plagued by conflict and dissension; drop-outs are unable to get along with family members.

TABLE 12.3
School-Related Factors Contributing to Students Dropping Out of School

Factors Related to Demographics

- Neighbourhood schools lack the desired program or course; the students have transportation problems necessitated by going to schools outside the catchment area.
- Schools are overcrowded and there is little individual attention given; students leave because of gangs or racial problems; there is a low degree of order and discipline.
- The student body has lowered academic expectations.

Factors Related to School Administration/Staffing

- Schools are an administrative nightmare; conditions are chaotic, students are without textbooks, desks, equipment/materials; fiscal arrangements of the school encourage early dismissal of students.
- Schools experience low school attendance rates and high failure rates.
- School reform movements and resulting pressure are exacerbating an already difficult situation.
- There is a high level of disempowerment experienced by staff; there is weak leadership from the administration.
- Schools are perceived to be rigid and inflexible.
- There are not enough counsellors to assist students; the counsellors end up practising counselling "triage," only dealing with the most serious problems.

Factors Related to Curricular Issues

- School is perceived to be boring, humiliating, and unappealing; students feel that they are treated as if they have lower IQs; emphasis is placed upon students who are college-bound; schools misuse the results of standardized tests; schools practise "tracking".

Factors Related to Curricular Issues (*continued*)

- Schools do not provide students with the information they need to gain access to appropriate programs, to succeed in their lessons, and to articulate their desired career aspirations.
- Departmentalization and moving from class to class prevent students from bonding with individual teachers; a small amount of time is engaged in actual instruction; a low percentage of time is spent in interactive learning.
- Learning tasks that structure the curriculum have become so divided and subdivided into minute tasks and activities that students have no sense of cognitive goals or overall topics.
- "General education" courses are viewed as being inappropriate alternatives to standard matriculation courses; they are seen as "watered-down" versions of college-preparatory courses; there are not enough vocational/trade courses; courses do not offer sufficient depth.
- Minority students found their ethnic groups to be portrayed stereotypically in texts and in the instruction offered by their teachers.

Factors Related to Staff Competence

- Teachers are seen to care very little about their own teaching; recitation, in which the teacher lectures or the student works as a total class on written assignments, is predominant; going to school is a passive activity; much of the school curriculum is devoted to "busywork"; teachers stress grades too much.
- Teachers are viewed to be incompetent; they need to be more helpful, accepting of individual differences, willing to talk with and listen to students, even-tempered, considerate, caring, personable, humane, encouraging, and freedom-oriented.
- Teachers do not have control of the class; teachers show favouritism to the more academically capable students; there is insufficient time for teacher-student interaction outside of class.

Students with Special Learning Needs: Factors Leading to Dropping Out

Whether or not students who have diverse learning needs drop out of school for the same reason(s) as students without such problems has been of interest to several researchers. Wolman et al. (1989, p. 17) examined the factors and found "apparent similitudes that exist between dropout-prone students and students with a high propensity to be in special education, particularly those with mild handicaps." They found that students in special education programs left school for the following reasons or combination of reasons:

a) negative attitudes and feelings toward school, b) low participation in school-related activities, c) low achievement and aptitude measures, d) grade repetition, e) poor attendance and disruptive behaviour, and f) socioeconomic factors. The overlap was so evident that the authors concluded that "it can be assumed that a substantial number of children with mild handicaps could belong to both high-risk populations [i.e., at risk for dropping out and at risk for being classified as handicapped]" (p. 17).

While many studies have investigated the impact that the type of disability or the functional level of the student has upon the decision of students with special needs to drop out of school, few studies have examined the effect of **class placement** (i.e., special class or regular class) on the decision to withdraw from school. Those who have examined the impact of integration in the past have not shown consistent findings (Wolman et al., 1989). However, more recently, Wagner (1992, pp. 8–12), in reporting the findings of the National Longitudinal Study of Special Educational Students (NTLS), made the following statement regarding the likelihood of youth with disabilities in various class placements staying in school:

> Students with similar disability, individual, and household characteristics were less likely to fail courses if relatively more of their time was spent in special education rather than regular education classes. Students who participated in occupationally specific vocational education were significantly less likely to be absent from school, fail their courses, or drop out of school than were students with the same disability and demographic characteristics but who were not vocational students. Students who received help from a tutor, reader, or interpreter were significantly less likely to drop out, controlling for other differences between youth.

For some students, regardless of the presence or absence of a disability, specialized programs (i.e., alternative programs, special education classes) may encourage students to stay in school; however, the findings of the NTLS also strongly support the inclusion of academically strong students who have the potential to pursue a post-secondary education in regular classrooms. These researchers found that youth with special needs in academic post-secondary programs (i.e., in universities and community colleges) had spent approximately 80% of their time in regular education classes in high school, compared to those students who did not pursue post-secondary education who spent only 63% of their time in integrated settings (Newman & Cameto, 1993).

Retaining Students: Different Approaches to Prevent Early School Leaving

Leaving school prematurely is the culmination of many factors that have contributed to a situation being perceived to be intolerable by the student. Dropping out does not occur as an isolated event, rather an accumulation of events over time. Barrington and Hendricks (1989, p. 316) have traced the academic history of the typical drop-out:

> The future dropout shows a clear indication of academic problems by the third grade...The poor attendance and underachievement increases as the student goes into middle school, and by seventh grade failing grades are present. By ninth grade a pattern of high absences, failing grades, and a low overall GPA [grade point average] is well established, and it continues until the student drops out of high school.

Three approaches have been taken to decrease soaring drop-out rates (Neufeld & Stevens, 1992). The first has been referred to as the "**fix the child**" approach. Here, the child is seen as the "problem." By identifying the child who does not fit into the system as it is, the premise is that the school can either provide "treatment" for the child at risk of dropping out or "force" the child out of the system. In the "**fix the components of the system**" approach, where it is viewed that the system is principally responsible to the "normal" students who fit in (i.e., the majority of the student population), the approach is to identify the students at risk and then create alternative programs to "rehabilitate" them, or in some cases to move them through the school on "parallel tracks." Neufeld and Stevens have referred to this as "tinkering" with parts of the system, for the established system remains virtually unchanged. In the final approach, "**restructuring the system**," the premise is that the whole system needs to be examined with a view of extensive restructuring, thereby helping not only those at risk for dropping out but the entire school population. This approach views dropping out as a complex problem with no single or simple answers and involves an integrated effort by many (e.g., students, parents, teachers, administrators, business community, social service providers). According to Neufeld and Stevens, restructuring calls for the incorporation of successful elements identified in the literature on "special education, school effects, school climate, effective schools, effective teaching, and cooperative education" (p. 13).

Characteristics of Successful Drop-Out Prevention Programs

Several researchers have identified and summarized the characteristics of successful programs in the literature on drop-out prevention. They are presented in Table 12.4 (adapted from: Hamby, 1989; Karp, 1988; LeCompte & Dworkin, 1991; Mann, 1986; Morris et al., 1992; Neufeld & Stevens, 1992). Characteristics related to administration and staffing (e.g., strong school leadership, mentoring environment), curricular issues (e.g., curricular efforts that encourage the healthy development of self-esteem and self-confidence), staff training and level of competence (e.g., ability to meet the needs of a diverse student population), and to the family and the community in which the student and family is a stakeholder (e.g., need for counselling) are outlined in this table. Interestingly, in one study 13% of drop-outs felt that the system should not change, rather the students themselves had to change (Karp, 1988).

TABLE 12.4
Characteristics of Successful Drop-Out Prevention Programs

Characteristics Related to Administration/Staffing

- Ensure strong and consistent school leadership and effective school-based management; encourage a team approach to learning; encourage administrative staff to be flexible; have clearly stated and widely disseminated classroom and school goals; enhance teacher morale; create a professional teacher workforce.
- Provide a caring, secure, and mentoring environment for all students; establish a school climate where achievement is respected and rewarded; eliminate tracking.
- Promote daily school attendance; establish truancy/attendance monitoring programs; review school/class discipline policies and school suspension policies.
- Request input from students and involve them in the decision making; encourage students to take initiative and to show responsibility; institute flexible scheduling.
- Establish linkages between different levels of schooling to facilitate student transition; establish a mentoring/caseworker program to monitor potential drop-outs.
- Ensure that students stay at a grade level appropriate to age; use individualized student assessments; provide students with regular feedback about progress.
- Offer flexible alternatives that will allow students to take control of their lives and allow them to "juggle" their various commitments and still remain in school; build economic incentive policies for staying in school.

Characteristics Related to Administration/Staffing (*continued*)

- Provide year-round schooling; have flexible graduation criteria.
- Decrease class size; provide individual and individualized instruction for at-risk students; focus prevention efforts on younger students who are potential drop-outs; keep drop-out prevention programs small in size; incorporate sustained adult contact; provide a homework hot-line and a problems hot-line.
- Ensure that teachers have time to talk to students regularly; provide counsellors to assist students with personal/educational/career issues, starting at the elementary grades.
- Provide staff development/awareness programs emphasizing early identification; allow opportunities for teachers to keep up with new developments in their field.

Characteristics Related to Curricular Issues

- Introduce quality kindergarten programs; place high priority on school resources for the early elementary grades and improve the quality of teaching throughout the grades.
- Help each student to establish and progress toward meaningful career goals; provide more opportunities for career exploration in secondary schools; link what is learned in school to what is needed on the job; make learning "meaningful" to the students.
- Have more emphasis on building self-esteem and self-confidence, on life skills and decision making; recognize and act upon the interrelatedness of student self-esteem and successful school performance.
- Focus programs on basic skills; assist students to develop effective learning and study skills; emphasize problem-solving skills; provide comprehensive support in reading and mathematics.
- Provide instruction in such areas as interpersonal skills, money management, family living and parenting, leisure time management, personal hygiene and self-care; emphasize lifelong learning and citizenship responsibilities.
- Provide specific prevention programs on drugs, alcohol, pregnancy.
- Provide health care, family planning education, child-care services for young adolescents.

Characteristics Related to Staff Competence

- Ensure the use of a wide range of instructional techniques.
- Provide more emphasis on nonuniversity-bound students; make the courses more relevant and functional; offer work readiness programs; interface school and community resources; link job training to long-term employment.
- Meet the broad range of disadvantaged students' needs; provide home/community/school liaison or support programs for First Nation and ethnocultural families; increase articulation and coordination among all the social services that are responsible for providing assistance to children.

Characteristics Related to Family/Community

- Ensure all stakeholders (students, parents, other interested persons) are aware of the magnitude of the problem and the actions being taken to address the problem (e.g., provide written reports for the school/local newspaper; interview students, administrators, and parents as part of a TV documentary).
- Encourage parental participation in school learning activities; support parent advisory committees; provide specific information sessions for parents.
- Provide counselling for parents of at-risk students; ensure parents attend parent-teacher meetings, if necessary by moving the meeting to the home of the student or the workplace of the parent.
- Establish school-community partnerships and effective school/business collaboration.

An often unrecognized resource in drop-out prevention is the classroom teacher, for "regardless of the quality of the plan or the theoretical soundness of the [drop-out prevention] program design, the implementation by practitioners, especially teachers, ultimately determines the success of the effort" (Bucci & Reitzammer, 1992, p. 63). Teachers cannot change the socioeconomic status of the family or alter the fact that a student has been previously retained in school; however, they can change the instructional environment of the student. In a truly inclusive school, all students must feel that they belong, that they are valued, and that they can succeed. In order to enhance students' self-esteem, Nave (1991, cited in Bucci & Reitzammer, 1992, p. 65) has suggested that teachers must do the following:

- Take time to reinforce the importance of a student's need by actively listening to each student.
- Acknowledge the student's needs, dreams, and problems.
- Place high expectations on each student.
- Believe that every student can learn.
- Believe that every student will learn.
- Believe in the student's own ability to find the key to unlock the his or her intrinsic motivation.

Two Strategies to Reduce Alienation: Promoting Meaningful Contact

To prevent youth at risk from dropping out, two specific approaches have been found to be particularly effective. Both strategies involve adults playing an instrumental role in monitoring the progress of the student, thereby attempting to lessen the feelings of alienation often expressed by students who have dropped out. While there are similarities between the techniques, one accrues little or no costs, whereas the other necessitates the direct or indirect expenditure of funds (i.e., salaries and/or release time for staff).

The first approach involves the use of **mentors**—adults willing to volunteer their time to support students. Mentors serve as role models, guiding the student into new experiences and providing attention and support that will influence students to complete school and plan for the future (Bucci & Reitzammer, 1992; Morris et al., 1992). Possible mentors include young adults from local colleges or universities, senior citizens, business persons, and community leaders; particularly effective are individuals who were former drop-outs themselves. Ideally, mentorships are implemented long before the student considers dropping out, as such relationships take time to develop and will have little effect after the student has already decided to leave.

The second involves the employment of **caseworkers**, individuals hired specifically to follow the at-risk students through their high school years. Caseworkers can also provide extended outreach services, matching students to available programs and services in the community as they make the transition from school to work or from secondary to post-secondary educational settings. It has been suggested that the caseworker, who identifies and assists potential drop-outs, be paid by a "formula" that assures tracking until the students have "achieved self-sufficiency" (Hahn, 1987). It should be noted that a casework system will have little, if any, effect if the caseloads of the workers are excessively high and the students are spread over multiple sites.

Teachers or counsellors, although not paid directly to provide a monitoring role, as in the case of designated caseworkers, can function as both mentor and caseworker. Once matched to a particular student, not necessarily in the teacher's homeroom or on the counsellor's caseload, time would have to be allocated for regular meetings with the student, ideally on a weekly basis. Karp (1988) has suggested that a teacher's timetable should include at least one period a day for mentoring; a similar arrangement could be made for counsellors. To be effective, the teachers or counsellors would have to follow the student on a long-term basis to provide the continuity so necessary for students who are considering leaving school.

These two strategies reflect the suggestions made by students who have dropped out, their teachers and their parents. Karp (1988) in a study of 843 drop-outs in the province of Ontario asked former students if "any one thing might have kept them in school." Twenty-four percent indicated that teachers' encouragement and involvement would have been instrumental; 14% reported encouragement from family, and 9% reported encouragement from friends. When teachers were asked to suggest ways in which the drop-out problem might be alleviated, 27% indicated more guidance/counselling and 24% recommended lower class size and more individual attention; only 5% indicated better teaching. Nineteen percent of parents indicated that teachers should be more caring and should have a better relationship with students; 15% indicated that teachers should be more available to give extra help; and 11% indicated more counselling and/or more guidance facilities. Interestingly, in the same study 37% of the students reported that they had not discussed leaving school with anyone. Forty-five percent of drop-outs had discussed leaving school with their parents, 11% with guidance counsellors, 6% with principal or administrator, and 4% with their teacher(s). When asked whether or not their teachers were opposed to their decision to leave school, 28% voluntarily stated that the teachers "didn't care."

While it is hoped that all students will remain in school until graduation, the role of the school does not necessarily end when the student is given his or her diploma. Many students, especially those with diverse learning needs, require assistance in making the transition from school to work or from school to post-secondary education settings.

Transition: Preparation to "Move On or Move Out"

> The outcomes experienced by youths with disabilities for employment, residential status, and social and interpersonal relationships are disappointing. Although rates vary from state to state, most youths with disabilities are either not employed or underemployed. Few youths live independently, many are not well integrated into their communities, and some appear to be lonely. Overall, youths with disabilities face a very uncertain future that holds little promise of improving as they age. (Chadsey-Rusch, Rusch & O'Reilly, 1991, p. 26)

Reading these words one would hope that the authors were referring to far distant times, but such is not the case. Research has consistently shown that adolescents with diverse learning needs struggle to achieve independence and self-sufficiency. The importance of providing services that will assist students in making the transition from school into the world of work or further study is now being recognized as being paramount.

Recent legislation in the United States (Public Law 101-476), passed in 1990, has mandated that transition services be included in the Individual Education Plans (IEPs) of *all* students with special needs, 16 years of age or older. According to Martin, Marshall, and Maxson (1993, p. 53), the law has defined transition services as a "coordinated set of activities that promote movement from school to post-school environments" and must contain activities "that match student needs, preferences, and interests." While such legislation is not contained in most provincial school acts in Canada, interest in supporting transitional plans and activities is evident. Lawton et al. (1988, p. 77), in their study on how high schools in Ontario might increase student retention, made the following statement:

> The transition from school to work represents a critical period in the life of an individual. Regardless of educational credentials, finding suitable employment is a milestone and an achievement most people remember... The transition process begins during the school years and ends some time after an individual becomes established in an occupation; it is a process through which every young person must go, regardless of educational level.

Transition from Secondary School to Work

While the literature on transitions is noted for its discussions of the practices considered crucial, Johnson and Rusch (1993) have suggested that there is limited research on the types, quality, and degree of transition planning services available and that more evidence is needed to determine the relationship between "what is accepted as 'best practice' in transition and post-school outcomes" (p. 9). One study, by Karge, Patton, and de la Garza (1992), that attempted to examine whether or not a disparity exists between the percentage of students with mild disabilities (i.e., students with learning disabilities, behaviour disorders, and mild mental retardation) currently receiving transition services and the percentage of students who wanted and needed such services is worth noting even though the sample size was limited (i.e., 36 students and 37 professional educators). Karge and her colleagues investigated 12 specific variables and found a significantly *low level of existing instruction* and services as compared to a *high level of need* for such services, as indicated by the responses of both students and professional educators.

1. *Job maintenance skills:* Ninety-six percent of the respondents felt that instruction in job maintenance skills was vital. However, it was believed that only 34.7% of students were receiving this type of training. The authors recommended that at least one semester-long course be provided with instruction in how to dress appropriately, to fill out time cards, to get along with co-workers and supervisors, to interact with the public, and to accept and give praise.

2. *Parent training and self-advocacy:* For educators, the area of greatest need was for parents to receive training and support regarding their child's vocational development and transition planning (98.7%). Students did not feel quite so strongly (91.0%), giving a combined need of 94.9%. The two groups believed that only 26.2% of parents were receiving such training. It was suggested by the authors that parent training activities be included in the transition programs for students so that the parents would be as well informed

as their children on how to access services, thereby enabling them to eventually "take over" the role of the transition team.

3. *Individual transition plans (ITPs):* Students and teachers believed that 25.2% of students had ITPs developed at least two years prior to the students leaving school; however, they reported that 94.6% of students should have them in place by that time. This area was recognized by students as the area of greatest need (95.3%). Karge et al. recommended that the transition team should include the student, family members, school personnel, adult agency personnel, community liaisons, and other support personnel, and that the plans include detailed goals and objects for each of the areas of need (e.g., job maintenance skills, job search skills).

4. *Job search skills:* Overwhelmingly, it was found that students were not currently receiving enough needed and beneficial instruction in this area. Students and educators combined reported that only 35.9% of students were receiving this type of instruction, compared to 94.5% of the students who they perceived as needing it. The researchers recommended that the following areas of instruction be included in the student's secondary level program: a) how to search for job opportunities, b) how to develop a résumé that outlines not only prior work experience but transferable life experiences, c) how to fill out job applications neatly, accurately, and completely, d) how to interview for a job, and e) how to obtain the necessary documents for getting a job.

5. *Job-related functional academics:* Students and teachers together reported that only 35.2% of students were currently receiving instruction in the area of functional academics, compared to 93.7% who needed such instruction. The authors recommended that functional academics (e.g., reading and writing on the job, figuring computations, estimating and making change) should be incorporated into "traditional" academic areas, such as English and mathematics.

6. *Student participation in ITP planning and meetings:* Both groups recognized that students need to be part of the decision-making process. Currently only 20.8% of students were believed to be involved, compared to 93.2% who should. In order to become more involved, Karge et al. suggested the following: a) students should write a "draft "of their own ITP as part of a class assignment, including a list of their own specific goals, b) students should be encouraged to be the prime decision makers in terms of when and where the ITP meeting be held, and c) students should be in attendance.

7. *Self-advocacy skills for job and community:* Both students and professionals indicated that there was a significant need for self-advocacy training (92.6%) as compared to what exists (23.2%). While the authors acknowledge that this is an area of training formerly provided by parents, they recommend that advocacy training be incorporated into the high school curriculum, perhaps in the language arts area.

8. *Counselling for post-secondary options:* While it was recognized that counselling was the most available service to students at that time (37.6% of the students were believed to be receiving counselling), the students and educators also acknowledged that there were many more students who needed this service (92.4% of the respondents indicated a need for counselling). Karge et al. suggested that this finding may reflect the need for more career counselling, rather than the currently available traditional academic counselling for college-bound students.

9. *Paid jobs in the community before graduation:* Students and teachers both agreed that there was a need for work experience (89.3%). It was estimated that only 26.2% had such opportunities. It was recommended by the researchers that high schools offer support to students in finding jobs, as part of job search and job maintenance skills training.

10. *Referral to adult agencies before graduation:* Both groups were of the perception that there was a significant discrepancy between the level of current referrals (28.5%) and the need for early referrals (88.7%). The authors suggested that since it can take anywhere from 12 to 24 months to access most adult agencies, the process should be started when the student is in grade 10, with the goal that the student achieve "active status" with the agency before graduation.

11. *Mobility and transportation skills:* Students and educators reported that they believed few students (20.8%) were receiving the necessary training in this area, compared to those that needed it (86.9%). Even though professionals perceived this as the lowest priority need (only 83.1% of educators stated that students needed training in this area), the authors recommended that students receive at least four weeks of structured, systematic instruction that covered how to apply for bus passes, call for and/or read and interpret bus route information, use public transit safely, and travel independently from home to school to work site.

12. *Plan and access recreation activities:* Not only did both students and professionals indicate that few students were instructed how to plan and access recreation activities (24.7%), there was a significant difference in the perception of the need for such services (85.2%). It should be noted that this was the area of least need according to both groups. The authors indicated that students need to be taught alternatives to just "hanging out" or being in gangs.

It is obvious in examining the results of this study that there is a perception held by both students and staff that in order for students to successfully make the transition into the world of work the following must occur: a) an emphasis must be placed at the high school level on curricular content that is functional/work-oriented in nature, rather than the remedial academics that have been stressed in the past, b) planning must begin early, well in advance of graduation, so that the linkages can be made, resulting in a smooth transition out of school and into the next phase of the student's life, and c) that while some students may need only minimal support or instruction, others may need either follow-up or follow-along support to ensure continued success. No comparable study to that of Karge and her colleagues has been undertaken in Canada. Since ITPs are not mandated by law in most provinces, it is likely that if such a examination was conducted, the findings would be similar.

As in the case of appropriate programming for the prevention of dropping out, the implementation of transition planning requires a major restructuring of the school system. In the inclusive school the challenges are great, and many questions are yet to be answered. Will inclusive schools be truly able to respond to the needs of all students, particularly those at the secondary level? If teachers continue to be bound to the traditional classroom and teaching methods, how will students with unique learning needs survive in an environment in which failure is inevitable? And finally, during times of fiscal restraint, will there be sufficient resources available to ensure the funding required to support transitional programs that link students to either the workforce or to the various post-secondary educational settings that may provide them with the training that they need to achieve their occupational goals? Students with special needs, it is hoped, will no longer be forced into the traditional, stereotypical jobs common in the past, such as piano tuning for the blind and basket weaving for those who are auditorily impaired. Similarly, it is hoped that students graduating from today's changing schools will not leave without the skills needed to be competitive in their search for employment. As students with challenging learning needs gain their rightful place alongside their nondisabled peers, it is hoped that the unique needs of the students will not be forgotten.

Transition from Secondary to Post-Secondary Settings

As mentioned in the introduction to this chapter, the need for *some* post-secondary education appears to becoming increasingly important for obtaining a job for *all* persons entering the workforce. Even though the educational system has been criticized for being preoccupied with college-bound youth (William T. Grant Foundation, 1988, cited in Chadsey-Rusch et al., 1991), the completion rates for post-secondary education remain relatively low, particularly for those with disabilities. In Canada, information obtained by means of the 1986 census and the 1986–87 post-censal survey (Statistics Canada, 1989, 1990) has shown that only 31.2% of those with disabilities, between the ages of 15 and 64, had some post-secondary education compared to 42.6% of the nondisabled population in the same age group. While these percentages may be low, it has been reported that the enrolment of students with disabilities in post-secondary programs has shown steady growth in Canada (see Hill, 1992) and in the United States (see Gajar et al., 1993; HEATH Resource

Center, 1991). Wilchesky (1986), a Canadian, offered four plausible reasons for the rise in numbers: a) increased pressure from self-help and advocacy groups to accept and accommodate students with special needs, b) projected decreased enrolment due to declining birth rate, resulting in universities and colleges actively recruiting "nontraditional" students (e.g., students who are middle-aged and elderly, students with physical and psychological difficulties, veterans), c) awareness of the broadening "social mission" of post-secondary institutions to provide more opportunities for students with disabilities, and d) the passage of legislation that mandates integration and the provision of services to ensure that students are able to access educational programs.

While it has been predicted that the enrolment rates will continue to increase, particularly since "more disabled persons are exercising their rights to receiving higher education" (Sergent, Sedlacek, Carter & Scales, 1987, p. 3), it should not be forgotten that many students will need specific assistance to successfully make the transition. Traditionally, students without disabilities planning to enter post-secondary programs have been able to obtain information from high school counsellors, teachers, parents, and/or other students regarding such issues as the types of programs available, the reputation of specific institutions, and the availability of financial support. Nondisabled students are often encouraged by those around them to pursue a post-secondary education, and in many cases students know others who have attended, are attending, or are planning to enter institutions of higher education in the future. Such is not always the case for students with unique learning needs. In some cases, students may be actively discouraged from pursuing a post-secondary degree/diploma by individuals, such as counsellors and advisers, who have preconceived notions that they will not be able to succeed (Nagler, 1993); in other cases, students may be encouraged but may run into difficulty in trying to access the necessary information to make informed choices (Hill, 1994), or may encounter resistance from institutions (e.g., inaccessible buildings, lack of services) that portray the "message that students with a disability are not welcome on campus" (Fitchen, 1988).

Students with disabilities face a particularly unique dilemma when considering the move from high school to university or college. At the elementary and secondary school level, school staff are required to identify the students' needs and provide the necessary services (e.g., materials, equipment, curricular modifications) needed for success; however, at the post-secondary level, the students move into an environment where the onus is on the student to make the necessary arrangements for assistance (Brinckerhoff, Shaw & McGuire, 1992; Fairweather & Shaver, 1990; Scott, 1991). This "change in legal status" (Scott, 1991) often results in delays in obtaining services, which in turn may impact on the ability of students to pursue a program of studies.

Similar to the assistance that can be offered to students to ensure successful transition from school to work, educators and parents can help students move from one educational program to another. In order to help those students who have the potential to access post-secondary education, teachers, administrators, therapists, and parents need to make a concerted effort throughout the student's high school year to assist the student to meet his or her academic goals. Though much of the work occurs in the final years of school, there is much that can be done to prepare the student to move on in the earlier grades of high school, in terms of identifying student vocational and academic goals, ensuring an appropriate individualized transition plan is developed, and finally in assisting the student to apply and prepare to move to the new setting (e.g., trade school, community college, or university). These major events are depicted in Tables 12.5 and 12.6.

TABLE 12.5
Transition Time Line

TRANSITION TIME LINE

Initial Transition Planning	Ongoing Transition Planning	Exit Transition Planning
Grades 7 & 8	**Grades 9 & 10**	**Grades 11 & 12**
1. Identify student vocational/academic goals. • In IEP meetings, counselling sessions, and/or informal conferences have students discuss what s/he would like to pursue in terms of possible future career path(s). • Ensure students have an understanding of their strengths and weaknesses and have students compare interests with strengths/weaknesses. • Communicate with parents and teachers to determine whether choice(s) are realistic (given the student's academic ability, physical ability, etc.). • Have students explore future career choices (through print and non-print media, visits by guest speakers/potential role models, worksite visits, etc.).	1. Review and update vocational/academic goals. → • Set up appointment with school guidance/vocational counsellor to help students define future goals through further discussion of potential career paths and formal/informal assessment. • Conduct further in-depth research regarding potential career paths, specifically in terms of academic requirements (e.g., examine occupational and labour market information, read publications such as the *Occupational Outlook Handbook* and the *Dictionary of Occupational Titles*).	1. Review and update vocational/academic goals. → → • Specify potential post-secondary educational settings that offer training in area of chosen career path (e.g., technical schools, vocational schools, community colleges, universities). • Encourage students to attend "college nights" or "college fairs" to obtain further information regarding potential post-secondary educational setting and services that may be required (e.g., specialized housing). • Encourage students to visit post-secondary institutions and meet with special services staff from the Office of Students with Disabilities.

TRANSITION TIME LINE (*continued*)

Initial Transition Planning

Grades 7 & 8

2. Write individual transition plan (ITP) and initiate individual educational plan (IEP) to support ITP.

- Identify appropriate content/ subject and elective academic courses for graduation and entrance to appropriate post-secondary educational setting and plan/offer accordingly.
- Identify appropriate specialized "independence" instruction (e.g., instruction in the area of daily living skills, behaviour control, social skills, self-advocacy skills) & plan/offer accordingly.
- Ensure student has instruction in specific "survival" skills required for success in post-secondary settings (e.g., note-taking skills, test-taking skills, learning strategy skills, study skills) and plan/offer accordingly.
- Identify appropriate placement (e.g., regular academic program, vocational program).

Ongoing Transition Planning

Grades 9 & 10

2. Review ITP and IEP to ensure appropriateness.

- Identify order and spacing of required and elective academic courses (to ensure reasonable workload through senior high school) and ensure completion as required by "schedule."
- Identify order and spacing of specialized instruction and ensure completion as required by "schedule."
- Identify need for remedial instruction (e.g., strategy instruction) and plan/offer accordingly.

Exit Transition Planning

Grades 9 & 10

2. Review ITP and IEP to ensure appropriateness.

- Arrange for student to complete required entrance tests (e.g., college entrance tests, Scholastic Aptitude Tests) under "nonstandard conditions" (e.g., large-print testing materials, untimed testing period, using a scribe), if appropriate.
- Ensure student is linked with adult services agency/worker (e.g., CNIB) to ensure student is formally added to adult caseload.

3. Apply to various institutions. (See Table 12.6).

TABLE 12.6
Exit Transition Planning

EXIT TRANSITION PLANNING

Grades 11 & 12

Application Phase

- Develop a personal transition/exit file containing:
  - — latest IEP/ITP
  - — documentation of disability
  - — recent test scores/assessment summary (including college entrance test scores)
  - — list of required accommodations
  - — summary of learning style (i.e., strengths and areas of need)
  - — letters of recommendations
  - — names of contact persons at student's secondary school (e.g., counsellor, teachers)
- Assist student to apply for post-secondary program (e.g., obtain and complete application forms, apply for housing, financial aid).
- Discuss the importance of self-identification of disability and ensure student has made contact with appropriate service providers and discussed needed services (e.g., interpreters, books on tape).
- Ensure student has made contact with appropriate service providers and clearly delineated the necessary services that will be required (e.g., interpreters, books on tape).
- Ensure student has made contact with government agencies providing financial assistance/adaptive equipment (e.g., VRS, SET BC).

Acceptance Phase

→

- Ensure student has made contact with appropriate service providers in the community (e.g., Handidart, CNIB, ACLD).
- Assist student to access other community services (e.g., setting up a chequing account, locating doctors/therapists, etc.).
- Encourage student to participate in "student-helping-student" mentorship program (i.e., student matched on interests/disability with current student at post-secondary setting).

Entrance Phase

→

→

- Ensure student has made contact with staff from Office for Students with Disabilities to finalize required services (e.g., taped texts, notetakers, modified exams, interpreters) and to plan a long-term individualized post-secondary educational plan (IPEP).
- Encourage student to attend summer orientation program for students with disabilities (if available) at post-secondary institution.
- Assist student to select appropriate first-year courses (consider workload, difficulty level, learning styles) in conjunction with academic adviser.
- Encourage student to contact instructors to obtain syllabus and to discuss possible modifications in instruction, examinations, and assignments; encourage students to begin reviewing texts, reading assignments, and planning for assignments.
- Assist student to arrange for assisted or priority registration (if required).
- Encourage student to join support group for students with disabilities.

By examining the transition time line shown in Table 12.5, it can be seen that planning begins no later than grade 7 and continues until the young adult has graduated from high school. In the initial transition planning stage (i.e., grades 7 and 8), the primary focus is on identifying the student's vocational and/or academic goals; the goals are further refined in grades 9 and 10, the ongoing transition planning phase. No later than grade 11 or 12 (i.e., the exit transition planning phase), the student's goals are considered in relationship to the various potential post-secondary educational settings that may be able to offer training in the area of the chosen career path. In Table 12.6, the final exit transition planning phase is further broken down into the application phase, the acceptance phase, and the entrance phase. The focus at this point is to ensure that the student makes the proper linkages between the high school setting and to the educational setting in which he or she hopes to enrol. While it is recognized that many of the tasks during the high school exit transition planning phase are, and should be, the responsibility of the student, it is important that school staff (e.g., teachers, counsellors) monitor each period to ensure that the various steps are completed in the right sequence and at the right time.

Summary

In the past, students with diverse educational needs were isolated from their nondisabled peers by being placed in segregated special schools or special classes. In these settings, the special education teacher traditionally took on the role of planning and implementing educational programs for the students—programs that often focused on the vocational preparation of students when they reached the secondary school level. As students with special needs moved into regular education classrooms, some students continued to be provided with the services of specialist staff and were offered appropriate programming geared to meet their unique needs; unfortunately, in a few cases, others have received little assistance, particularly in schools where fiscal restraint has resulted in the laying off of staff (e.g., special education teachers, vocational teachers) and the cutting back of appropriate courses of study (e.g., work study programs) in an attempt to balance decreased budgets.

With the merger of special education and general education there has been a call for a collaborative or team approach to decision making. Nowhere is this more critical than in assisting students with special needs to meet their potential as adults. There is an urgent need for the development of "transition teams" that will assist students to move on to new settings and transition "facilitators" or "specialists"—professionals who are hired specifically to provide and coordinate transitional services (Gajar et al., 1993). Transition planning begins with the development of an individual transition plan, long before the student leaves the high school environment (either as a drop-out or as a graduate) and the teams should include a variety of "constituencies that have a stake in the student's success" (Gajar et al., 1993, p. 120), such as special education teachers, regular teachers, vocational instructors, rehabilitation counsellors, employment counsellors, parents, and students. By providing assistance to students, it is hoped that the "youths of tomorrow will experience better outcomes than the youths of the past" (Chadsey-Rusch et al., 1991, p. 30).

SUGGESTED RESOURCES

Association on Higher Education and Disability (AHEAD), P.O. Box 21192, Columbus, OH 43221. Publishes a monthly newsletter entitled *ALERT* and the *Journal of Post-Secondary Education and Disability.* Sponsors special interest group on Canadian programs.

Council for Exceptional Children, 1920 Association Drive, Reston, VA 11091-1589. Professional organization dedicated to improving educational outcomes for individuals with exceptionalities. The Division on Career Development and Transition publishes a journal entitled *Career Development for Exceptional Individuals.*

HEATH Resource Center, 1 Dupont Circle, NW, Suite 800, Washington, DC 20036. A national clearinghouse on post-secondary education for individuals with disabilities. Recent publications, available at no charge, include *Making the most of your opportunities: A guide for postsecondary education for adults with handicaps* (1989), *Getting ready for college: Advising high school students with learning disabilities* (1990), and the *Resource Directory* (printed annually).

National Association of Vocational, Education Special Needs Personnel, c/o Athens Technical Institute, U.S. Highway 29 North, Athens, GA 30610. A membership organization of secondary and post-vocational education professionals. Publishes the *NAVES-NP Journal.*

REFERENCES

Barber, L.W., & McClellan, M.C. (1987). Looking at America's dropouts: Who are they? *Phi Delta Kappan, 69,* 264–67.

Barrington, B.L., & Hendricks, B. (1989). Differentiating characteristics of high school graduates, dropouts, and nongraduates. *Journal of Educational Research, 82,* 309–19.

Brinckerhoff, L.C., Shaw, S.F., & McGuire, J.M. (1992). Promoting access, accommodation and independence for college students with learning disabilities. *Journal of Learning Disabilities, 25,* 417–29.

Bucci, J.A., & Reitzammer, A.F. (1992). Teachers make the critical difference in dropout prevention. *The Educational Forum, 57,* 63–70.

Chadsey-Rusch, J., Rusch, F.R., & O'Reilly, M.F. (1991). Transition from school to integrated communities. *Remedial and Special Education, 12*(6), 23–33.

Ekstrom, R.B., Goertz, M.E., Pollack, J.M., & Rock, D.A. (1986). Who drops out of high school and why? Findings from a national study. In G. Natriello (Ed.), *School dropouts: Patterns and policies* (pp. 52–69). New York: Teachers College Press.

Employment and Immigration (1990a). *Good jobs, bad jobs: Employment in the service economy. A statement by the Economic Council of Canada.* Ottawa: Minister of Supply and Services Canada.

Employment and Immigration (1990b). *The 1990 adult education and training survey.* Ottawa: Statistics Canada.

Fairweather, J.S., & Shaver, D.M. (1990). A troubled future? Participation in postsecondary education by youths with disabilities. *Journal of Higher Education, 61,* 332–48.

Fairweather, J.S., & Shaver, D.M. (1991). Making the transition to postsecondary education and training. *Exceptional Children, 57,* 264–70.

Fitchen, C.S. (1988). Students with physical disabilities in higher education: Attitudes and beliefs that affect integration. In H.E. Yuker (Ed.), *Attitudes toward persons with disabilities.* New York: Springer.

Gajar, A., Goodman, L., & McAfee, J. (1993). *Secondary schools and beyond: Transition of individuals with mild disabilities.* New York: Merrill.

Hahn, A. (1987). Reaching out to America's dropouts: What to do? *Phi Delta Kappan, 69,* 256–63.

Hamby, J.V. (1989). How to get an "A" on your dropout prevention report card. *Educational Leadership, 46*(5), 21–28.

HEATH Resource Center (1991). Facts you can use. *Information from HEATH, 10*(2), 1–3.

Hill, J.L. (1992). Accessibility: Students with disabilities in universities in Canada. *Canadian Journal of Higher Education, 22,* 48–83.

Hill, J.L. (1994). Speaking out: Perceptions of students regarding adequacy of services and willingness of faculty to make accommodations. Manuscript submitted for publication.

Human Resources and Labour Canada. (1993). *Leaving school: Results from a national survey comparing school leavers and high school graduates 18 to 20 years of age.* Ottawa, ON: Minister of Supply and Services Canada.

Johnson, D.R., Bruininks, R.H., & Thurlow, M.A. (1987). Meeting the challenge of transition service planning through improved interagency cooperation. *Exceptional Children, 53,* 522–30.

Johnson, J.R., & Rusch, F.R. (1993). Secondary special education and transition services: Identification and recommendations for future research and demonstration. *Career Development for Exceptional Individuals, 16,* 1–18.

Karge, B.D., Patton, P.L., & de la Garza, B. (1992). Transition services for youth with mild disabilities: Do they exist, are they needed? *Career Development for Exceptional Individuals, 15,* 47–68.

Karp, E. (1988). *The drop-out phenomenon in Ontario secondary schools: A report to the Ontario study of the relevance of education and the issue of dropouts.* Toronto: Queen's Printer.

King, A.J.D., Warren, W.K., Michalski, C., & Peart, M.J. (1988). *Improving student retention in Ontario secondary schools.* Toronto: Queen's Printer.

LaFleur, B. (1992). *Dropping out: The costs to Canadians.* (Report No. 83-92-E). Ottawa: Conference Board of Canada.

Lawton, S.B., Leithwood, K.A., Batcher, E., Donaldson, E.L., & Stewart, R. (1988). *Student retention and transition in Ontario high schools: Policies, practices, and prospects.* Toronto: Queen's Printer.

LeCompte, M.D., & Dworkin, A.G. (1991). *Giving up on school: Student dropouts and teacher burnouts.* Newbury Park, CA: Corwin Press.

Legendre, C. (1985). Work. In J.H. Marsh (Ed.), *The Canadian encyclopedia: Volume III* (pp. 1965–68). Edmonton, AB: Hurtig.

Mann, D. (1986). Can we help dropouts? Thinking about the undoable. In G. Natriello (Ed.), *School dropouts: Patterns and policies* (pp. 3–19). New York: Teachers College Press.

Marder, C. (1992). Education after secondary school. In M. Wagner, R. D'Amico, C. Marder, L. Newman & J. Blackorby (Eds.), *What happens next? Trends in Postschool outcomes of youth with disabilities* (pp. 3-1–3-40). Menlo Park, CA: SRI International.

Marder, C., & D'Amico, R. (1992). *How well are youth with disabilities really doing? A comparison of youth with disabilities and youth in general.* Menlo Park, CA: SRI International.

Martin, J.E., Marshall, L.H., & Maxson, L.L. (1993). Transition policy: Infusing self-determination and self-advocacy into transition programs. *Career Development for Exceptional Individuals, 16,* 53–61.

Morris, S., Pawlovich, W., & McCall, D. (1992). *Evaluating the effectiveness of school drop-out prevention strategies: Some suggestions for future research. Final Report.* Ottawa: Canadian Education Association.

Morrow, G. (1986). Standardizing practice in the analysis of school dropouts. In G. Natriello (Ed.), *School dropouts: Patterns and policies* (pp. 38–51). New York: Teachers College Press.

Nagler, M. (1993). The disabled: The acquisition of power. In M. Nagler (Ed.), *Perspectives on disability* (2nd edition). Palo Alto, CA: Health Markets Research.

Neufeld, G.R., & Stevens, A. (1992). *Stay in school initiates: Book 1: A summary of school dropouts and implications for special education.* Kingston, ON: Canadian Council for Exceptional Children.

Newman, L., & Cameto, R. (1993). *What makes a difference? Factors related to postsecondary school attendance for young people with disabilities.* Menlo Park, CA: SRI International.

Panitch, M. (1992). Transition to post-secondary education: From the margins to the core. In R. Warick (Ed.), *Access to post-secondary education for persons with disabilities: Research forum proceedings* (pp. 40–51). Vancouver, BC: Disability Resource Centre, University of British Columbia.

Reich, C., & Young, V. (1975). Patterns of dropping out. *Interchange, 6*(4), 6–15.

Roessler, R.T., Brolin, D.E., & Johnson, J.M. (1990). Factors affecting employment success and quality of life: A one year follow-up of students in special education. *Career Development for Exceptional Individuals, 13,* 95–107.

Ryan, A.G., & Price, L. (1992). Adults with LD in the 1990s. *Intervention in School and Clinic, 28*(1), 6–20.

Sergent, M.T., Sedlacek, W.E., Carter, R.T., & Scales, W.R. (1987). *A national survey of services provided for disabled students in higher education.* (Research Report No. 19–87). College Park, MD: University of Maryland. (ERIC Document Reproduction Service No. ED 297 668).

Scott, S.S. (1992). A change in legal status: An overlooked dimension in the transition of higher education. *Journal of Learning Disabilities, 24,* 459–66.

Statistics Canada. (1989). *The nation: School and major field of study.* (Catalogue 92–110). Ottawa, ON: Minister of Regional Industrial Expansion.

Statistics Canada. (1990). *The Health and Activity Limitation Survey. Highlights: Disabled persons in Canada.* (Catalogue 82–602). Ottawa, ON: Minister of Regional Industrial Expansion.

Sullivan, M. (1988). *A comparative analysis of drop-outs and non drop-outs in Ontario secondary schools: A report to the Ontario Study of Relevance of Education and the Issue of Dropouts.* Toronto: Queen's Printer.

Wagner, M. (1992). Transition: Changes, challenges, cautions. In M. Wagner, R. D'Amico, C. Marder, L. Newman & J. Blackorby (Eds.), *What happens next? Trends in postschool outcomes of youth with disabilities* (pp. 8-1–8-14). Menlo Park, CA: SRI International.

Wagner, M., D'Amico, R., Marder, C., Newman, L., & Blackorby, J. (Eds.). (1992). *What happens next? Trends in postschool outcomes of youth with disabilities.* Menlo Park, CA: SRI International.

Wehlage, G.G., & Rutter, R.A. (1986). Dropping out: How much do schools contribute to the problem? In G. Natriello (Ed.), *School dropouts: Patterns and policies* (pp. 70–88). New York: Teachers College Press.

Wilchesky, M. (1986). "Post-secondary programmes and services for exceptional persons: North American trends." Paper presented at the Canadian Symposium on Special Education Issues, Toronto, Ontario (March). (ERIC Document Reproduction Service No. ED 294 389).

Wolman, C., Bruininks, R., & Thurlow, M.L. (1989). Dropouts and dropout programs: Implications for special education. *Remedial and Special Education, 10*(5), 6–20, 50.

CHAPTER 13

A Thematic Review and Some Further Considerations

Jac J.W. Andrews

University of Calgary

Introduction

The authors in this book have presented their views regarding the best ways to accommodate student diversity in today's schools. As one reviews the authors' practical suggestions, common themes emerge. First, many of the authors indicate that *group effort* is often more beneficial than individual effort in the teaching and learning transaction. Second, many of the authors suggest that teachers need to be *proactive and adaptive* in addressing the unique learning needs of their students. Third, many of the authors appear to advocate for an *educational climate* that maximizes student opportunity and potential, and develops acceptance and appreciation of individual differences.

This chapter has two parts. In the first part, major themes from the text are presented and expanded. The second part of the chapter provides an overview of three conditions that can enable teachers to better accommodate student diversity in their classrooms. These very important conditions are: administrative leadership and support, professional training and development, and educational research.

Themes

Group Effort

One of the major underlying themes in this book is that people should work together. Many of the authors have recommended that teachers collaborate with one another, form partnerships with other professionals and parents, and promote cooperative learning experiences among their students. As noted by Costa (1991, p. 12) "together, individuals surface ideas, then bounce and batter them about, thereby eliciting thinking that surpasses individual effort. As individuals engage in problem solving, conversation, and consensus seeking, multiple perspectives are expressed, dissonance created and reduced, discrepancies perceived and resolved, and alternatives weighed."

Teachers Working Together

Teaming approaches provide an opportunity for teachers to collaborate with their colleagues in order to address the complexities of student management and instruction. Teachers, administrators, and specialists inside the school need to learn how to collaborate with each other in order to effectively plan and implement successful instructional adaptations and accommodations. Concomitantly, teachers, administrators, and specialists within the school need to learn to collaborate with parents and professionals outside the school to take advantage of the available resources from the community that can be used to better meet the needs of students.

For many people, it is not easy to work with others. Some people feel uneasy because they lack experience working in groups and some people are generally uncomfortable in sharing their ideas with others. Hence, team members might need to learn how to interact and problem-solve with others within a group. As noted in this book, important skills to master include ways to deal with one's own feelings, how to be supportive of others, handle resistance, resolve conflict, set goals, and listen to others. These collaborative skills can lead to effective decision making and empower teachers and other group members to take responsibility for student outcomes and make significant educational changes.

Successful development, implementation, and maintenance of collaborative and cooperative groups requires a collaborative work ethic and environment within the school. According to Phillips and Mccullough (1990), when a collaborative work ethic is assimilated throughout the entire school, it empowers teachers to support each other and help one another solve problems. In working towards a collaborative work environment, teachers should have opportunities to meet with one another to discuss the problems they are facing, and pool their expertise and resource materials (Idol & West, 1991).

Collaborative efforts must be highly regarded and promoted by school administration. Principals can facilitate collaboration among teachers by encouraging them to collectively find ways for dealing with student diversity, providing time for them to interact with one another during the school day, and reinforcing their collaborative efforts (Johnson, Pugach & Devlin, 1990). Principals can provide leadership in the process of collaboration by showing commitment to ongoing professional development opportunities that can better prepare teachers with the essential skills for collaboration and by modelling collaboration with teachers and others in appropriate situations (Idol & West, 1991).

Teachers Working with Parents

Currently, there is a greater emphasis on the role of parents in educational problem solving and decision making. As noted in this book, teachers are becoming increasingly aware of the importance of knowing more about their students' families for addressing their needs and for working in partnership with parents.

Both teachers and parents can benefit from school-home partnerships. Teachers can find out from parents more information about how students approach their learning and gain assistance with respect to program planning and instruction. Parents can find out more about their child's strengths and weaknesses and get help from teachers in enhancing their child's functioning at home and in school. However, in order for parent-teacher partnerships to be successful, schools must provide a school climate that is perceived by parents as open, friendly, and helpful. Moreover, schools must promote a philosophy of partnership and make sure that parents are treated the same ways as teachers during collaborative activities (Henderson, Marburger & Ooms, 1986).

School-home partnerships can also be aided when teachers are cognizant of the diversity of families. Families differ in terms of employment, cultural background, values and beliefs, parenting skills, challenges and hardships, attitudes towards education, and family functioning and subsequent adaptation. When teachers know more about family attitudes and feelings regarding education and the school environment, they can form more mutually beneficial relationships with parents.

Students Working Together

Many authors in this book have pointed out that students' academic and social development can be enhanced when they are given opportunities to successfully interact with their peers in a variety of cooperative and collaborative activities. However, it is important to note, that just like teachers, many students will not find it easy to work with their peers. They will also need to learn how to collaborate with one another in order for them to realize the mutually beneficial consequences of group effort.

To develop and sustain successful group activities, students need to be given sufficient opportunities to work with others in the classroom and be supported by their teacher for their collaborative efforts. Collaborative and cooperative learning approaches can foster appreciation and acceptance of student diversity within the classroom. However, collaborative and cooperative methods have to be carefully planned and appropriately orchestrated.

Teaching approaches that promote student collaboration can also develop important social skills. Many students have social interaction problems and experience interpersonal difficulties. Collaborative learning methods can be used as a way to provide continuity between the teaching of academic and social skills.

Proactive and Adaptive Teaching

Another underlying theme throughout this book is that teaching students with diverse needs in regular classrooms requires teachers to be instructionally proactive and adaptive. However, remember that adaptive instruction "is **not** isolated individualized instruction (a child sitting alone completing a worksheet); it may involve ordinary or even greater amounts of direct group instruction [highlight added]" (Reynolds & Birch, 1988, p. 72). According to Wang (1993), teachers who take a proactive and adaptive approach to teaching: 1) identify and monitor students' learning characteristics, 2) prepare educational plans based on students' abilities, needs, and interests, 3) modify school environments to correspond to student differences, and 4) use direct and indirect interventions in a variety of settings and grouping arrangements to build students' basic skills and develop their higher-order thinking skills so that they can be adaptive to changes in their environment.

Identifying and Monitoring Students' Learning Characteristics

In the past, assessment practices were used most often to make predictions about students' learning and to place students in programs according to their ability levels and the expectations that teachers had about their potential for success (Reynolds & Birch, 1988). Currently, assessment practices are considered to be a much more integral part of instruction.

Informal assessment practices are becoming increasingly relied upon as a primary source of information for teachers. Although teachers use test data routinely to make educational decisions about their students, testing is only part of the process that enables teachers to gain more insight about their students and design and deliver appropriate instruction.

When teachers are identifying their students' learning characteristics, they should consider the following principles of assessment. First, tests typically estimate students' performance from isolated samples of behaviour at one point in time. To better appreciate a students' functioning in a particular area, it might be better to use a multiple assessment approach (e.g., the combined use of observation techniques, work sample analysis, and checklists) that can be used under different circumstances and at different times and offer a more robust indication of students' performance in a particular subject area. Second, teachers should know the purpose of their assessment. Is the information obtained from the assessment going to be used to develop an intervention program, evaluate students' progress, compare students' performance with their peers, or be used to assist students in their understanding of their own functioning? Essentially, different assessment practices are more appropriately applied when the intentions of the assessment are realized. Third, as noted in this book's chapter on assessment, teachers should consider the extent to which the assessment technique measures what it is supposed to measure, and the degree to which the information gained from the assessment technique is accurate and reliable.

As assessment practices have become more concurrent with instruction, teachers have become more interested in how students' learning can be better addressed. The aim has become to observe students' performance with respect to a variety of tasks and conditions and determine the type and degree of instructional procedures necessary to successfully develop students' learning and better their ability to deal with the task demands.

Preparing Educational Plans

Results from assessment practices form the basis of educational plans for students. Flexible planning is required for accommodating student diversity. Moreover, the focus of the plans should be more on the learner than on the curriculum. Hence, along with covering important content it is also important that students learn how to better direct their own learning, work cooperatively with others, and become independent decision makers and problem solvers.

According to Clark and Peterson (1986, p. 267), "teacher planning does influence opportunity to learn, content coverage, grouping for instruction, and the general focus of classroom processes." Some factors that influence planning include teacher-related factors (e.g., teachers' knowledge, skills, competence, and motivation to plan), environment-related factors (e.g., demands for content coverage and accountability), and student-related factors such as interest in subject matter, background knowledge, and use of learning strategies (Schumm, Vaughn, Haager, McDowell, Rothlein & Saumell, 1995).

Modifying School Environments to Correspond to Student Differences

Increasing diversity within classrooms demands teachers to be more responsive to the individual needs of students. Teaching approaches and procedures need to be aligned to particular goals and objectives. However, teachers do not need to construct lesson plans for each student. Rather, teachers can develop lesson plans for the entire class that incorporate individualized learning objectives.

Students benefit from teachers who provide structure and clarity in their lessons and who facilitate student thinking, problem-solving and decision making. Students also benefit from teachers who summarize and reinforce the content of lessons when necessary, pace their lessons appropriately, and maximize student engagement.

According to Rosenshine and Stevens (1986) teachers should review the previous day's work, present new content and skills, provide opportunity for student practice of skills, check for student understanding, and reteach concepts if necessary.

Using Direct and Indirect Interventions

According to Meyen (1990), Vergason and Anderegg (1991), and Bos and Vaughn (1991), direct instruction, learning strategies instruction, and guided instruction (sometimes referred to as mediated or scaffolded instruction) have stood the test of time, research, and application as effective practices for students with diverse needs.

Direct instruction is an adaptive group-based approach to teaching that focuses on the development of students' basic skills. The critical instructional features of direct instruction include an explicit step-by-step teaching strategy; student mastery for each step; fast pacing, error-free learning; teacher directed activities towards independent work; use of adequate, systematic practices with a range of examples; and cumulative review (see Gersten & Carnine, 1986; Gersten, Woodward & Darch, 1986). Students involved in direct instruction have demonstrated substantial gains in achievement (Becker & Carnine, 1981; Bourbeau, 1984; Darch, Carnine & Gersten 1984; Doyle, 1983).

Strategy-based instruction is premised on the view that learning is an active and constructive process (Shuell, 1986; Wittrock, 1986) involving the learner's control and regulation of cognitive processes used to acquire, store, retrieve, and apply knowledge. Teaching students to assume control over the learning process by showing them and having them practise learning strategies has been shown to have value for all students.

Among the better known strategy programs are The Learning Strategies Curriculum (Deshler, Warner, Schumaker & Alley, 1983) for learning disabled adolescents, Informed Strategies for Learning (Paris, Cross & Lipson, 1984), which focuses on reading comprehension; and The Strategies Program for Effective Learning and Thinking (SPELT) (Mulcahy, Marfo, Peat & Andrews, 1986), which is an inclusive learning and thinking curriculum that can be implemented across all subject areas from the elementary to high school curriculum.

Guided instruction is a way that teachers can help their students bridge the gap between their present capabilities and learning goals. In guided instruction, teachers work with students on academic tasks that are too difficult for the student to accomplish independently but can be carried out successfully through the teacher's guidance, modelling, and demonstration. Gradually, there is a shift from teacher-regulated activity to student-regulated learning and an increased willingness to participate in the learning process (Brown & Ferrara, 1985).

Guided instruction is sometimes referred to as scaffolded instruction (Tharp and Gallimore, 1988) or mediated instruction (Haywood, 1987), and comes from the sociocultural theory of learning where the teacher focuses on the process of learning and encourages the student by providing support as he or she develops new knowledge and skills. Instruction should involve socially embedded activities in which teachers help their students bridge the gap between their present capabilities and their intended learning goals. Gradually, teacher support is reduced and the responsibility for learning is placed in the hands of the students.

The most important underlying factor in successfully teaching and managing students with diverse needs is the establishment and maintenance of classroom climate. Teachers need to develop positive personal relations with their students in order to engage them in collaborative and cooperative learning activities.

Classroom Climate

Classroom environments need to be safe and secure places for the students where they can feel comfortable expressing their views and where diversity is clearly accepted. Environments should be conducive to peer interaction and be perceived as positive and accommodating.

Presenting a Positive Attitude

Attitudes are learned and influenced by the degree of knowledge and amount of experience an individual has with particular people and situations (Smith, Price & Marsh, 1986). If teachers value diversity and believe that all students can benefit from instruction, they will behave in ways that reflect these values and beliefs.

Some school activities that reflect a positive attitude towards teaching students with diverse needs include: 1) experienced teachers mentoring new teachers; 2) parents working as volunteers within the classrooms; 3) teachers being honoured for their collaborative efforts and instructional innovations; 4) teachers making adaptations and modifications in their teaching; 5) teachers using programs and activities that match students' abilities and interests; and 6) teachers using peer teaching or tutoring approaches in their classrooms.

Showing Acceptance and Appreciation

The importance of valuing diversity is recognized by Barth (1990), who says, "I would prefer my children to be in a school in which differences are looked for, attended to, celebrated as good news, as opportunities for learning...Differences offer a free, abundant, and renewable resource. I would like to see our compulsion for eliminating differences replaced by an equally compelling focus on making use of these differences to improve schools. What is important about people—and about schools—is what is different, not what is the same" (pp. 514–15).

It would be very difficult for successful teaching and learning to take place in the absence of strong and respectful teacher-student relationships. Teachers can build bonds with students and between students by creating a classroom community that recognizes the importance of interpersonal relationships and that reinforces the idea of sharing and working together.

Some ways that teachers can facilitate acceptance and appreciation for student diversity include: 1) talking to students about their life experiences, 2) reinforcing the worth of people who make up diverse populations, and 3) providing activities that highlight students' important contributions to the class.

Promoting Self-Identity

Schools should be a place where individuality is valued and validated. As pointed out by Branthwaite (1985), a person's self-confidence and feelings of self-worth influence the way he or she interacts with others. Students must be able to view themselves positively in order to have satisfactory interpersonal relationships. Moreover, a positive self-concept is the foundation for developing acceptance and respect for others who are different from ourselves.

Teachers can promote students' positive self-perceptions by providing opportunities for students to experience harmonious and beneficial social interactions. Additionally, teachers can be good listeners, respect the views of their students, and communicate their belief in them as competent learners.

Conveying a Sense of Belonging

Students need to feel safe and secure, experience a sense of belonging and affection (Maslow, 1968), and believe that they are legitimate members of the classroom. Teachers should strive to create classroom communities where students' needs and interests are accommodated and their contributions are valued. For students to feel they belong in the classroom, they need to be able to fully participate in the general routines and rituals of the classroom. In some cases, students will need supports to be part of the rituals of the classroom.

Maintaining High Expectations

Teachers should have high expectations for all their students. Students need teachers who can inspire them, build their confidence, and challenge them to reach their potential. Students need to be supported in their risk taking and they need to know that their teachers have confidence in their ability to achieve their goals. Students should be praised for their efforts towards meeting learning expectations and for the successful steps made in meeting performance standards (Scruggs & Mastropieri, 1992).

Showing Sensitivity and Empathy

For teachers to be sensitive and empathic towards their students they need to be able to view the world from their students' perspective. When students feel that their teachers respect them and understand their thoughts and feelings, they are much more likely to relate positively with their teacher and feel comfortable within the classroom. As noted by David Aspy and Flora Roebuck, "students learn more and behave better when they receive high levels of understanding, caring and genuineness, than when they are given low levels of them" (cited in Rogers, 1983, p.199).

It is becoming increasingly necessary for teachers to be aware of the different cultural and ethnic backgrounds of their students and be sensitive and empathic to their diverse social experiences. Teachers should also be aware that through their actions and words they convey their attitude for multicultural and second language learners. Teachers can show their sensitivity and empathy by 1) giving students a chance to share some of their cultural experiences with one another, 2) encouraging students to discuss their feelings regarding their immigration to Canada, 3) structuring student groups in ways that allow everyone in the class to learn about each other differences, 4) creating learning centres that highlight cultural diversity, 5) reminding students of multicultural events in the community, and 6) taking students on field trips that expose students to various forms of diversity.

Enhancing Motivation

Students' interest in learning can be enhanced by showing them ways to be successful in their learning. Successful learners are not passive recipients of information. Rather, they set goals for themselves, implement strategies to achieve their goals, monitor their work, and evaluate their efforts. Many ineffective learners are not motivated to learn because they lack the ability to reflect upon and regulate their learning. Students' desire to learn can be increased by helping them be more purposeful, organized, and strategic in their approach to learning.

Some students attribute their successes to luck rather than to their own efforts and attribute their failures to factors beyond their control. Students who attribute success and failure to factors beyond their control are very often less willing to engage in academic tasks compared to those students who attribute their performance to controllable factors such as effort (Weiner, 1984). Teachers can help their students make more appropriate attributions by training students to relate their failures to insufficient effort and their successes to perseverance and appropriate strategy use. Effort feedback related to successful achievement enhances students' motivation and skills (Schunk, 1982), and improves their sense of control (Fulk & Mastropieri, 1990).

Scruggs and Mastropieri (1992) point out that some students have poor motivation because they view school as an endless series of assignments. They suggest that teachers can improve their students' attitudes toward school work by helping them set goals and monitor their progress toward meeting those goals. Moreover, they can increase students' effort by rewarding their quick and efficient task completions with either "free time" or some desired activity.

Modelling

Modelling is the acquisition of behaviours as the result of observing other people (Bowd, McDougall & Yewchuk, 1994). An effective model is someone who clearly demonstrates a skill or process that informs the learner about what she or he needs to do to achieve the desired goal (Wood, 1993).

As noted throughout this book, an important goal for students is to learn how to cooperate and collaborate with others. Teachers can promote student cooperation and collaboration by encouraging student discussion and interaction, and structuring learning experiences that allow students to build positive and beneficial relationships with one another.

Enabling Conditions

Administrative Leadership and Support

Teachers need support from their principals to deal with the problems and issues related to teaching students with diverse needs in the classroom. Supportive leadership from school district superintendents and school principals can positively impact program development and teachers' instructional efforts with respect to student diversity (Good & Brophy, 1989; Reynolds, Martin-Reynolds & Mark, 1982; Thousand & Villa, 1991).

In a study conducted by Miles and Simpson (1989), teachers reported that they were willing to teach students with diverse needs in their regular classrooms on the condition that they be part of the planning process and provided that certain modifications recommended by them were adopted (e.g., reduced class size, provision of support services, and paraprofessional assistance in the classroom). One implication from this study is that if school administration helps teachers help themselves deal with student diversity, then programs and practices might be strengthened.

When teachers believe that their principals have a positive attitude with respect to student diversity, they have more confidence that they will get more administrative support relative to the initiation, development, and implementation of innovative approaches for teaching students with diverse needs. Vivian Correa (1990) points out that "teachers who are entrusted with responsibility for school-based changes and school-based management arrive at solutions to problems that more accurately meet the needs of students, parents, and communities" (p. 8). Although school principals are becoming more positive toward the integration of students with special needs into regular classrooms (Centre, Ward, Parmenter & Nash, 1985), all administrators need to provide their teachers with more assistance and support to deal with diversity in their classrooms. According to Wood (1993), principals should assist them by:

- Arranging for in-service training activities for teachers and participating in these activities

- Consulting with other principals and administrators who have successfully implemented programs for meeting the diverse needs of students
- Supporting within school teaming approaches for instructional planning and classroom teaching
- Developing a collaborative network with administrators and teachers from other schools, and with parents and professionals in the community
- Designing procedures to evaluate school-based programs

Professional Training and Development

Many teachers believe that they are underprepared to teach students with diverse needs (Post & Roy, 1985). Moreover, teacher federations acknowledge that teachers are not provided with sufficient professional training and development (Csapo, 1981). According to a survey of provincial Deputy Ministers of Education in Canada, regular classroom teachers across Canada are not being adequately prepared to teach students with diverse needs in regular classrooms (Hill, 1988).

Pre-Service Training

Present and future teacher education programs will need to place more emphasis on training teachers to effectively educate students with diverse needs in regular education classrooms (Brophy & Good, 1986; Simpson, Whelan & Zabel, 1993). However, beyond enhancing future general educators with diversity-related teaching skills, teacher preparation programs should provide courses and experiences that reflect an overall vision that pervades the entire curriculum (Galuzzo & Pankratz, 1990). Teachers are facing the enormous challenge of educating an increasing population of students with diverse needs while being in the midst of extensive educational reform (Gable, McLaughlin, Sindelar & Kilgore, 1993). Therefore, they need to have the knowledge base and skill competencies that will help them assume new roles and responsibilities and address the increasing diversity in their classrooms.

It seems clear that university faculties of education and public schools should develop a partnership and jointly prepare teachers to renew schools and educate a broad range of students who have different backgrounds and abilities. Teachers in training should share a common core of professional content and experience and understand the mission and circumstances of schools (Goodlad & Field, 1993) that will allow them to successfully apply programs and approaches to reach the desired educational goals.

Based on the directions recommended by the authors of this book, students in faculties of education should be provided with educational experiences that develop their competencies in areas such as 1) collaboration and consultation skills that will help them work with others to solve problems and design programs related to teaching heterogeneous groups of students, 2) teaching methods that will enable them to provide adaptive instruction to students with diverse needs, 3) assessment techniques that allow them to better understand the developmental potential of their students and inform them of ways to better accommodate their learning and behavioural capabilities, 4) management techniques for dealing with students who have behavioural difficulties, 5) multicultural activities that help students appreciate diversity, and 6) microcomputer applications that can assist teachers with some of their responsibilities and prepare students for a world that will involve higher technologies.

In line with the above suggestions, Lovitt (1993); Pugach (1992); Simpson, Whelan, & Zabel (1993); and Gable (1993) offer the following recommendations for pre-service teacher training:

- Prospective teachers should have field experiences with excellent teachers in a variety of locations and across different levels of schooling (e.g., elementary schools, junior high schools, high schools).

- Prospective teachers should have opportunities to work in schools that have a wide range of ethnic diversity in order to learn about other cultures.

- Prospective teachers should have the chance to work collaboratively with specialists (e.g., psychologists, counsellors, occupational therapists, special educators).

- Prospective teachers should be given a number of experiences with parents (e.g., informal meetings, volunteer assistance programs, parent-teacher conferences) to learn how to interact with parents and become aware of the roles they can play in students' education.

- Prospective teachers need to be taught various ways to instruct, manage, and assess students in classrooms and be given opportunities to practise these procedures.

- Prospective teachers should be given opportunities for reflection to clarify what they have learned from practice and consider how their teaching affects each student.

- Prospective teachers should be given opportunities to learn to balance group needs with those of individuals, to accommodate social differences, and to facilitate self-esteem among students who are neglected or rejected by their peers.

- Prospective teachers should be extensively trained in current technological advances in education.
- Prospective teachers should have training that emphasizes both the attitudes and skills required for successful collaboration.
- Prospective teachers should become knowledgeable about the services that can be provided by nonschool systems such as medicine, mental health, welfare, corrections, and day-care, and learn how to access and coordinate these services to best serve their students.

In-service Training

In-service training programs can help teachers who are working in schools acquire the knowledge and skills that can address their identified needs. In-service training programs provide schools with a mechanism for ongoing staff development. Staff development efforts provide opportunities for all of the teachers in the school to renew their commitment to teaching, set educational goals, design instructional strategies, and practise learned skills in their classrooms. According to Murray (1993) effective staff development programs require:

- An educational climate that supports collegiality and collaboration and encourages experimentation and risk taking
- The use of research paradigms, effective teaching models, and principles of learning and change
- The participation and leadership of teachers and administrators who share responsibility for decision making
- Resources and sufficient time to have comprehensive staff development and appropriate incentives and rewards for the participants
- The congruence of visions for change with goals, processes, and support structures

Educational Research

One of the most effective ways of improving the education of students in Canada is through research studies involving Canadian teachers and students. Researching what works within educational contexts is a time-consuming and often prosaic task that "requires dogged pursuit of reliable answers to research questions and protracted public scrutiny of one's data and their interpretation" (Kauffman, 1993). Nevertheless, within the last couple of decades, school-based research has contributed to more effective practice in classrooms (e.g., Becker & Gersten, 1982; Brophy, 1983; Deshler, Schumaker, Alley, Warner & Clark, 1982; Emmer, Everston & Anderson, 1980; Greenwood, Carta & Hall, 1988; Wong, 1986) and, therefore, has proven to be a worthwhile endeavour.

Advances in educational knowledge and practice through applied research programs require substantial funding. Unfortunately, funding for educational studies in Canada is very limited. While acknowledging the reality of limited resources throughout Canada to carry out research and development, it is important to strengthen the empirical base of education and ensure that accountable strategies and approaches are being used.

According to a variety of educational researchers (Fuchs & Fuchs, 1990; Hollowood, Salisbury, Rainforth & Palombaro, 1995; Lovitt, 1993; Scruggs & Mastropieri, 1994) some future directions in research might include:

- To investigate more effective instructional procedures to promote knowledge that transfers across situations
- To investigate better routines for teachers that can reduce their paperwork and stress
- To investigate how intensive the instructional context needs to be to create effective and efficient learning in integrated and inclusive settings
- To investigate the relationship among curriculum methods, instructional methods, and learner outcomes in inclusive educational settings
- To investigate alternative assessment approaches that can better inform teachers about what to do with their students and how much improvement their students are making on the skills and behaviours that are being taught to them
- To investigate collaborations among parents and teachers with respect to such things as the types of information that should be shared, the frequency with which that information should be shared, and the formats that can be used to share information
- To investigate the nature of collaborations among and between school personnel and outside professionals regarding student diversity
- To investigate the validity and degree to which peer collaborations, effective teaching skills, positive classroom atmosphere, administrative support, and professional development can be implemented in schools that are less successful in accommodating learner diversity

Conclusion

This chapter has brought together the major themes in this book for teaching students with diverse needs and has presented some salient enabling conditions for ensuring quality education for all students. The challenge that resides within us is to prepare ourselves with the knowledge and skills that can help us deal with the multifaceted and complex nature of today's classrooms. Change efforts are pivotal to the future success of all schools facing increasing student diversity. With this point in mind, I end this book by paraphrasing Skrtic (1991).

> *Change efforts are successful in schools if people want change and if people act to change.*

SUGGESTED RESOURCES

Buzzell, J.B., & Piazza, R. (1994). *Case studies for teaching special needs and at-risk students.* Albany, NY: Delmar Publishers Inc.

Morsink, C.V., Thomas, C.C., & Correa, V.I. (1991). *Interactive teaming: Consultation and collaboration in special programs.* New York: Merrill.

Porter, G.L., & Richter, D. (Eds.). (1991). *Changing Canadian schools: Perspectives on disability and inclusion.* North York, ON: The Roeher Institute.

Samuels, M., Burrows, I., Scholten, T., & Theunissen, D. (1992). *Asking the right questions: Assessment and programme planning for adults with learning difficulties.* The Learning Centre, Calgary, AB.

Villa, R.A., Thousand, J.S., Stainback, W., & Stainback, S. (Eds.). (1992). *Restructuring for caring and effective education: An administrative guide to creating heterogeneous schools.* Baltimore, MD: Paul H. Brookes.

Wang, M.C. (1992). *Adaptive education strategies: Building on diversity.* Baltimore, MD: Paul H. Brookes.

REFERENCES

Alberta Education (1992). *Integrated services review.* Yellowhead school division, No. 12, Edmonton, AB: Alberta Education.

Barth, R. (1990). A personal vision of a good school. *Phi Delta Kappan, 71,* 512–71.

Becker, W., & Carnine, D. (1981). Direct instruction: A behaviour therapy model for comprehensive educational intervention with the disadvantaged. In J. Bijou & R. Ruiz (Eds.), *Behaviour modification.* Hillsdale, NJ: Lawrence Erlbaum.

Becker, W.C., & Gersten, R. (1982). A follow-up of Follow Through: The later effects of the direct instruction model on children in fifth and sixth grades. *American Educational Research Journal, 19,* 75–92.

Bos, C.S., & Vaughn, S. (1991). *Strategies for teaching students with learning and behavioural problems* (2nd edition). Toronto: Allyn and Bacon.

Bourbeau, P. (1984). *An experimental analysis of the generalization of teaching skills from the classroom to trained and untrained bank settings in the community.* Unpublished doctoral dissertation. University of Oregon, Eugene.

Bowd, A., McDougall, D., & Yewchuk, D. (1994). *Educational psychology for Canadian teachers.* Toronto: Harcourt, Brace & Co.

Branthwaite, A. (1985). The development of social identity and self-concept. In A. Branthwaite & D. Rogers (Eds.), *Children growing up* (pp. 34–42). Philadelphia: Open University Press.

Brophy, J.E. (1983). Classroom organization and management. *The Elementary School Journal, 83*(4), 265–86.

Brophy, J., & Good, T. (1986). Teacher behaviour and student achievement. In M.C. Wittrock (Ed.), *Handbook of research on teaching,* (3rd edition, pp. 328–75). New York: Macmillan.

Brown, A., & Ferarra, R. (1985). Diagnosing zones of proximal development. In J.V. Wertsch (Ed.), *Culture, communication, and cognition* (pp. 273–305). Cambridge: Cambridge University Press.

Centre, Y., Ward, J., Parmenter, T., & Nash, R. (1985). Principals' attitudes toward the integration of disabled children into regular schools. *The Exceptional Child, 32,* 149–61.

Chomicki, S., & Kysela, G. (1993). Teacher attitudes towards mainstreaming: What do they think and what do they need? A literature review. *Exceptionality Education Canada, 3*(4), 61–79.

Clark, C.M., & Peterson, P.L. (1986). Teachers' thought processes. In M. Wittrock (Ed.), *Handbook of research on teaching* (pp. 255–96). New York: Macmillan.

Correa, V.I. (1990). Advocacy for teachers. *Teaching Exceptional Children.* (Winter), 7–9.

Costa, A.L. (1991). The school as a home for the mind: A climate for thinking. In. R. Mulcahy, R. Short, & J. Andrews (Eds.), *Enhancing learning and thinking* (pp. 11–20). New York: Praeger.

Csapo, M. (1981). Teachers' federations in the mainstream. *B.C. Journal of Special Education, 5*(3), 197–218.

Darch, C., Carnine, D., & Gersten, R. (1984). Explicit instruction in mathematical problem solving. *Journal of Educational Research, 4,* 155–65.

Deshler, D.D., & Schumaker, J.B. (1984). An instructional model for teaching students how to learn. In J.L. Graden, J.E. Zins, & M.J. Curtis (Eds.), *Alternative educational delivery systems: Enhancing instructional options for all students* (pp. 391–411). Washington, DC: NASSP.

Deshler, D.D., Schumaker, J.B., Alley, G.R., Warner, M.M., & Clark, F.L. (1982). Learning disabilities in adolescent and young adult populations. Research implications. *Focus on Exceptional Children, 15*, 1–12.

Deshler, D.D., Warner, M.M., Schumaker, J.B., & Alley, G.R. (1983). Learning strategies intervention model: Key components and current status. In J. McKinney & L. Feagans (Eds.), *Current topics in learning disabilities*, Vol.1. Norwood, NJ: Ablex.

Doyle, W. (1983). Academic work. *Review of Educational Research, 53*(2), 159–99.

Eisner, E.W. (1991). What really counts in schools. *Educational Leadership, 48*, 10–17.

Emmer, E.T., Evertson, C.M., & Anderson, L.M. (1980). Effective classroom management at the beginning of the school year. *The Elementary School Journal, 80*(5), 219–31.

Fuchs, D., & Fuchs, L.S. (1990). Making educational research more important. *Exceptional Children, 57*(2), 102–07.

Fulk, B., & Mastropieri, M.A. (1990). Training positive attitudes: "I tried hard and did well." *Intervention in School and Clinic, 26*, 79–83.

Gable, R.A., McLaughlin, V.R., Sindelar, P., Kilgore, K. (1993). Unifying general and special education teacher preparation: Some cautions along the road to educational reform. *Preventing School Failure, 37*(2), 5–10.

Galuzo, G.R., & Pankratz, R.S. (1990). Five attributes of a teacher education program knowledge base. *Journal of Teacher Education, 41*, 7–14.

Gersten, R., & Carnine, D. (1986). Direct instruction in reading comprehension. *Educational Leadership, 43*(7), 70–78.

Gersten, R., Woodward, J., & Darch, C. (1986). Direct instruction: A research based approach to curriculum design and teaching. *Exceptional Children, 53*, 17–31.

Good, T.L., & Brophy, J.E. (1989). School effects. In M.C. Wittrock (Ed.), *Handbook of research in teaching* (pp. 570–602). American Educational Research Association.

Goodlad, J.I. (1990). *Teachers for our nation's schools.* San Francisco: Jossey-Bass.

Goodlad, J.I., & Field, S. (1993). Teachers for renewing schools. In J.I. Goodlad & T.C. Lovitt (Eds.), *Integrating general and special education* (pp. 229–52). Toronto: Maxwell Macmillan Canada.

Greenwood, C.R., Carta, J.J., & Hall, V.R. (1988). The use of peer tutoring strategies in classroom management and educational instruction. *School Psychology Review, 17*, 258–75.

Haywood, H.C. (1987). A mediational teaching style. *The Thinking Teacher, 4*(1), 1–6.

Henderson, A.T., Marburger, C.L., & Ooms, T. (1986). *Beyond the bake sale: An educator's guide to working with parents.* Washington DC: National Committee for Citizens in Education.

Hill, J.L. (1988). Integration in Canada: Implications for the certification of regular education teachers (RETS). *Canadian Journal of Special Education, 4*(2), 123–31.

Hollowood, T.M., Salisbury, C.L., Rainforth, B., & Palombaro, M.M. (1995). Use of instructional time in classrooms serving students with and without severe disabilities. *Exceptional Children, 61*(3), 242–53.

Idol, L., & West, J.F. (1991). Educational collaboration: A catalyst for effective schooling. *Intervention in School and Clinic 27*(2), 70–78.

Johnson, L.J., Pugach, M.C., & Devlin, S. (1990). Professional collaboration. *Teaching Exceptional Children.* (Winter), 9–11.

Kauffman, J.M. (1993). How we might achieve the radical reform of special education. *Exceptional Children, 60*(1), 6–16.

Lovitt, T.C. (1993). Retrospect and Prospect. In J.L. Goodlad and T.C. Lovitt (Eds.), *Integrating general and special education* (pp. 253–74). Toronto: Maxwell Macmillan Canada.

Mallory, B.L., & New, R.S. (1994). Social constructivist theory and principles of inclusion: Challenges for early childhood special education. *The Journal of Special Education, 28*(3), 322–37.

Maslow, A. (1968). *Toward a psychology of being.* New York: D. Van Nostrand.

Meyen, E. (1990). Quality instruction for students with disabilities. *Teaching Exceptional Children, 22*(2), 12–13.

Miles, B.S., & Simpson, R.L. (1989). Regular educators' modification preferences for mainstreaming mildly handicapped children. *The Journal of Special Education, 22*(4), 479–91.

Mulcahy, R.F., Marfo, K., Peat, D., & Andrews, J. (1986). *A strategies program for effective learning and thinking (SPELT): Teachers' Manual.* Edmonton: Cognitive Education Project, University of Alberta.

Murray, L.B. (1993). Putting it all together at the school level: A principal's perspective. In J.L. Goodlad and T.C. Lovitt (Eds.). *Integrating general and special education.* Toronto: Maxwell Macmillan Canada.

Odell, S.J. (1989). Developing support programs for beginning teachers. In *Assisting the beginning teacher* (pp. 19–38). Reston: VA: Association of Teacher Educators.

Paris, S.G., Cross, D.R., & Lipson, M.Y. (1984). Informed strategies for learning: A program to improve children's reading awareness and comprehension. *Journal of Educational Psychology, 76*, 1239–52.

Paris, S.G., & Oka, E.R. (1986). Self-regulated learning among exceptional children. *Exceptional Children, 53*(2), 103–08.

———. (1986). Children's reading strategies, metacognition, and motivation. *Developmental Review, 6*, 25–56.

Phillips, V., & Mccullough, L. (1990). Consultation-based programming: Instituting the collaborative ethic in schools. *Exceptional Children, 56*(4), 291–304.

Post, L., & Roy, W. (1985). Mainstreaming in secondary schools: How successful are plans to implement the concept? *NASSP Bulletin, 69*, 71–179.

Pugach, M.C. (1992). Unifying the preservice preparation of teachers. In W. Stainback and S. Stainback (Eds.), *Controversial issues confronting special education: Divergent perspectives* (pp. 255–69). Toronto: Allyn and Bacon.

Reynolds, B.J., Martin-Reynolds, J., & Mark, F. (1982). Elementary teachers' attitudes towards mainstreaming educable mentally retarded students. *Education and Training of the Mentally Retarded, 17*, 171–76.

Reynolds, M.C., & Birch, J.W. (1988). *Adaptive mainstreaming: A primer for teachers and principals* (3rd edition). New York: Longman.

Rogers, C. (1983). *Freedom to learn for the 80's*. Columbus, OH: Bell and Howell.

Rosenshine, B., & Stevens, R. (1986). Teaching functions. In M.C. Wittrock (Ed.), *Handbook of research on teaching* (3rd edition) (pp. 376–91). New York: Macmillan.

Schumaker, J.B., & Sheldon, J. (1985). *Learning strategies curriculum: The sentence writing strategy.* Lawrence, KS: University of Kansas.

Schumm, J.S., Vaughn, S., Haager, D., Mcdowell, J., Rothlein, L., & Saumell, L. (1995). General education teacher planning: What can students with learning disabilities expect? *Exceptional Children, 61*(4), 335–52.

Schunk, D.H. (1982). Effects of effort attributional feedback in children's perceived self-efficacy and achievement. *Journal of Educational Psychology, 7*, 548–56.

Scruggs, T.E., & Mastropieri, M.A. (1992). Effective mainstreaming strategies for mildly handicapped students. *The Elementary School Journal, 92*(3), 389–409.

Skrtic, T.M. (1991). The special education paradox: Equity as the way to excellence. *Harvard Educational Review, 61*(2), 148–206.

———. (1991). *Behind special education: A critical analysis of professional culture and school organization.* Denver: Love Publishing Co.

———. (1994). Successful mainstreaming in elementary science classes: A qualitative study of three reputational cases. *American Educational Research Journal, 31*(4), 785–811.

Shuell, T.J. (1986). Cognitive conceptions of learning. *Review of Educational Research, 56*, 411–36.

Simpson, R.I., Whelan, R.J., & Zabel, R.H. (1993). Special education personnel preparation in the 21st century: Issues and strategies. *Remedial and Special Education, 14*(2), 7–22.

Slavin, R.E., Madden, N.A., & Leavey, M. (1984). Effects of team assisted individuation on the mathematics achievement of academically handicapped and nonhandicapped students. *Journal of Educational Psychology, 76*, 814–19.

Smith, T.E.C., Price, B.J., & Marsh, G.E. (1986). *Mildly handicapped children and adults.* St. Paul, MN: West Publishing.

Stainback, W., & Stainback, S. (1989). Common concerns regarding merger. In S. Stainback, W. Stainback, & M. Forest (Eds.), *Educating all students in the mainstream of regular education* (pp. 255–74). Baltimore, MD: Paul H. Brookes.

Swicegood, P., & Parsons, J. (1989). Better questions and answers equal success. *Teaching Exceptional Children, 21*, 4–8.

Tharp, R.G., & Gallimore, R. (1988). *Rousing minds to life: Teaching, learning and schooling in social context.* New York: Cambridge University Press.

Thousand, J.S., & Villa, R.A. (1991). A futuristic view of the REI: A response to Jenkins, Pious, & Jewell. *Exceptional Children, 57*, 556–62.

Veenman, S. (1984). Perceived problems of beginning teachers. *Review of Educational Research, 54*, 143–78.

Vergason, G.A., & Anderegg, M.L. (1991). Beyond the regular education initiative and the resource room controversy. *Focus on Exceptional Children, 23*(7), 1–7.

Wang, M.C. (1993). The theory and practice of adaptive education. In M. Wang (Ed.), *Adaptive education strategies: Building on diversity* (pp. 1–37). Baltimore, MD: Paul H. Brookes.

Weiner, B. (1984). Principles for a theory of student motivation and their application within an attributional framework. In R. Ames & C. Ames (Eds.), *Research on motivation in education: Student motivation* (Vol. 1, pp. 15–38). New York: Academic Press.

Wittrock, M.C. (1986). Students' thought processes. In M.C. Wittrock (Ed.), *Handbook of research on teaching.* New York: Macmillan.

Wong, B.Y.L. (1986). A cognitive approach to teaching. *Exceptional Children, 53*(2), 169–73.

Wood, J.W. (1993). *Mainstreaming: A practical approach for teachers* (2nd edition). Toronto: Maxwell Macmillan Canada.

To the owner of this book

We hope that you have enjoyed *Teaching Students with Diverse Needs: Secondary Classrooms,* first edition, and we would like to know as much about your experiences with this text as you would care to offer. Only through your comments and those of others can we learn how to make this a better text for future readers.

School ________________ Your instructor's name ________________________

Course ___________ Was the text required? _______ Recommended? _____

1. What did you like the most about *Teaching Students with Diverse Needs: Secondary Classrooms?*

____

____

____

2. How useful was this text for your course?

____

____

____

3. Do you have any recommendations for ways to improve the next edition of this text?

____

____

____

4. In the space below or in a separate letter, please write any other comments you have about the book. (For example, please feel free to comment on reading level, writing style, terminology, design features, and learning aids.)

____

____

____

____

Optional

Your name ______________________________ Date __________________

May Nelson Canada quote you, either in promotion for *Teaching Students with Diverse Needs: Secondary Classrooms* or in future publishing ventures?

Yes _______ No _______

FOLD HERE

MAIL POSTE

Canada Post Corporation / Société canadienne des postes

Postage paid
if mailed in Canada

Port payé
si posté au Canada

Business Reply

Réponse d'affaires

0107077099 01

Nelson

TAPE SHUT

0107077099-M1K5G4-BR01

TAPE SHUT

Nelson Canada
Market and Product Development
1120 Birchmount Rd.
Scarborough, ON M1K 9Z9

PLEASE TAPE SHUT. DO NOT STAPLE.